Y0-BYB-210

ARCHBISHOP ALEMANY LIBRARY
DOMINICAN UNIVERSITY
SAN RAFAEL, CALIFORNIA 94901

JAPANESE FIRMS IN TRANSITION: RESPONDING TO THE GLOBALIZATION CHALLENGE

ADVANCES IN INTERNATIONAL MANAGEMENT

Series Editors: Joseph L. C. Cheng and Michael A. Hitt

Previously Published Volumes:

Volume 12: Edited by J. L. C. Cheng and R. B. Peterson

Volume 13: Edited by J. L. C. Cheng and R. B. Peterson

Volume 14: Edited by M. A. Hitt and J. L. C. Cheng

Volume 15: Edited by J. L. C. Cheng and M. A. Hitt

Volume 16: Edited by M. A. Hitt and J. L. C. Cheng

ADVANCES IN INTERNATIONAL MANAGEMENT   VOLUME 17

JAPANESE FIRMS IN TRANSITION: RESPONDING TO THE GLOBALIZATION CHALLENGE

EDITED BY

THOMAS ROEHL

Western Washington University, USA

ALLAN BIRD

University of Missouri-St. Louis, USA

ARCHBISHOP ALEMANY LIBRARY
DOMINICAN UNIVERSITY
SAN RAFAEL, CALIFORNIA 94901

2005

ELSEVIER
JAI

Amsterdam – Boston – Heidelberg – London – New York – Oxford
Paris – San Diego – San Francisco – Singapore – Sydney – Tokyo

ELSEVIER B.V.	ELSEVIER Inc.	**ELSEVIER Ltd**	ELSEVIER Ltd
Radarweg 29	525 B Street, Suite 1900	**The Boulevard, Langford**	84 Theobalds Road
P.O. Box 211	San Diego	**Lane, Kidlington**	London
1000 AE Amsterdam	CA 92101-4495	**Oxford OX5 1GB**	WC1X 8RR
The Netherlands	USA	**UK**	UK

© 2005 Elsevier Ltd. All rights reserved.

This work is protected under copyright by Elsevier Ltd, and the following terms and conditions apply to its use:

Photocopying
Single photocopies of single chapters may be made for personal use as allowed by national copyright laws. Permission of the Publisher and payment of a fee is required for all other photocopying, including multiple or systematic copying, copying for advertising or promotional purposes, resale, and all forms of document delivery. Special rates are available for educational institutions that wish to make photocopies for non-profit educational classroom use.

Permissions may be sought directly from Elsevier's Rights Department in Oxford, UK; phone: (+44) 1865 843830, fax: (+44) 1865 853333, e-mail: permissions@elsevier.com. Requests may also be completed on-line via the Elsevier homepage (http://www.elsevier.com/locate/permissions).

In the USA, users may clear permissions and make payments through the Copyright Clearance Center, Inc., 222 Rosewood Drive, Danvers, MA 01923, USA; phone: (+1) (978) 7508400, fax: (+1) (978) 7504744, and in the UK through the Copyright Licensing Agency Rapid Clearance Service (CLARCS), 90 Tottenham Court Road, London W1P 0LP, UK; phone: (+44) 20 7631 5555; fax: (+44) 20 7631 5500. Other countries may have a local reprographic rights agency for payments.

Derivative Works
Tables of contents may be reproduced for internal circulation, but permission of the Publisher is required for external resale or distribution of such material. Permission of the Publisher is required for all other derivative works, including compilations and translations.

Electronic Storage or Usage
Permission of the Publisher is required to store or use electronically any material contained in this work, including any chapter or part of a chapter.

Except as outlined above, no part of this work may be reproduced, stored in a retrieval system or transmitted in any form or by any means, electronic, mechanical, photocopying, recording or otherwise, without prior written permission of the Publisher. Address permissions requests to: Elsevier's Rights Department, at the fax and e-mail addresses noted above.

Notice
No responsibility is assumed by the Publisher for any injury and/or damage to persons or property as a matter of products liability, negligence or otherwise, or from any use or operation of any methods, products, instructions or ideas contained in the material herein. Because of rapid advances in the medical sciences, in particular, independent verification of diagnoses and drug dosages should be made.

First edition 2005

British Library Cataloguing in Publication Data
A catalogue record is available from the British Library.

ISBN: 0-7623-1157-6
ISSN: 0747-7929 (Series)

⊗ The paper used in this publication meets the requirements of ANSI/NISO Z39.48-1992 (Permanence of Paper). Printed in The Netherlands.

Working together to grow
libraries in developing countries

www.elsevier.com | www.bookaid.org | www.sabre.org

ELSEVIER   BOOK AID International   Sabre Foundation

CONTENTS

LIST OF CONTRIBUTORS   *ix*

PREFACE
     Thomas Roehl and Allan Bird   *xi*

PART I: ADAPTING TO A CHANGING ENVIRONMENT

ADAPTABILITY AND CHANGE IN JAPANESE
MANAGEMENT PRACTICE: A LONGITUDINAL INQUIRY
INTO THE BANKING INDUSTRY – THROUGH THE BUBBLE
ECONOMY AND BEYOND
     Lane Kelley, Brent MacNab, Reginald Worthley,
     Ian Pagano and Lenard Huff   *3*

LEARNING PROCESS AND THE DYNAMICS OF
CORPORATE GOVERNANCE SYTEMS: THE CASE OF
JAPAN
     Christine Pochet   *31*

THE CHANGING TREND IN LINKS BETWEEN
BUREAUCRACY AND THE PRIVATE SECTOR IN JAPAN
     Andreas Moerke   *61*

THE WINDS OF CHANGE IN JAPANESE TRADE POLICY:
TEXTILE MULTINATIONALS AND INTRA-INDUSTY
CLASHES OVER MARKET PROTECTION
     Saadia Pekkanen and Mireya Solis   *89*

PART II: INTER-ORGANIZATIONAL RELATIONSHIPS

KEIRETSU ORGANIZATION IN A CHANGING ECONOMIC
CONTEXT: THE EVOLUTION OF DEBT AND EQUITY TIES
AMONG KEIRETSU FIRMS
Jean McGuire and Sandra Dow   *115*

M&As IN THE JAPANESE BANKING INDUSTRY: THE MORE
THINGS CHANGE?
Elizabeth L. Rose and Kiyohiko Ito   *139*

DYAD AND NETWORK: MODELS OF
MANUFACTURER–SUPPLIER COLLABORATION IN THE
JAPANESE TV MANUFACTURING INDUSTRY
Didier Guillot and James R. Lincoln   *159*

SAME RULES, DIFFERENT GAMES: VARIATION IN THE
OUTCOMES OF "JAPANESE-STYLE" SUPPLY
RELATIONSHIPS
Glenn Hoetker   *187*

PART III: MNCs ON FOREIGN SOIL

THE TRANSNATIONAL CHALLENGE: PERFORMANCE
AND EXPATRIATE PRESENCE IN THE OVERSEAS
AFFILIATES OF JAPANESE MNCs
*Schon Beechler, Vladimir Pucik, John Stephan
and Nigel Campbell*   *215*

DECLINE OF JAPAN'S PREDOMINANCE IN ASIA
Hideki Yoshihara   *243*

DOES IT REALLY MATTER IF JAPANESE MNCs THINK
GLOBALLY?
*Schon Beechler, Orly Levy, Sully Taylor
and Nakiye Boyaçigiller*   *261*

CHANGES IN THE DETERMINANTS OF PROFIT: A STUDY
OF FOREIGN SUBSIDIARIES IN THE JAPANESE
MANUFACTURING INDUSTRIES IN THE 1980s AND 1990s
Shigeru Asaba and Hideki Yamawaki   289

LIST OF CONTRIBUTORS

Shigeru Asaba	Gakushuin University, Japan
Schon Beechler	Columbia University, USA
Allan Bird	University of Missouri-St. Louis, USA
Nakiye Boyaçigller	Sabanci University, Turkey and San Jose State University, USA
Nigel Campbell	University of Manchester, UK
Sandra Dow	University of Quebec at Montreal, Canada
Didier Guillot	INSEAD Singapore
Glenn Hoetker	University of Illinois at Urbana-Champaign, USA
Lenard Huff	Brigham Young University-Hawaii, USA
Kiyohiko Ito	University of Hawaii at Manoa, USA
Lane Kelley	University of Hawaii at Manoa, USA
Orly Levy	Tel Aviv University, Israel
James R. Lincoln	University of California-Berkeley, USA
Jean McGuire	Concordia University, Canada
Brent MacNab	University of Hawaii at Manoa, USA
Andreas Moerke	German Institute for Japanese Studies (DIJ), Japan
Ian Pagano	University of Hawaii at Manoa, USA
Saadia Pekkanen	University of Washington, USA
Christine Pochet	Université des Sciences Sociales, France

Vladimir Pucik	IMD – International Institute for Management Development, Switzerland
Tom Roehl	Western Washington University, USA
Elizabeth L. Rose	Victoria University of Wellington, New Zealand and University of Hawaii at Manoa, USA
Mireya Solis	American University, USA
John Stephan	University at Buffalo, State University of New York, USA
Sully Taylor	Portland State University, USA
Reginald Worthley	University of Hawaii at Manoa, USA
Hideki Yamawaki	Claremont Graduate University, USA
Hideki Yoshihara	Kobe University, Japan

PREFACE

Struggling economies provide an interesting venue for international management researchers to build and test theory. Struggling economies are characterized by conflict and confrontation between established forces trying to impose conformity and emerging forces seeking variety. Economies once healthy, but in sustained recession, are also fertile sites for exploring the conflict between problem-solving based on traditionally, but no longer, successful strategies and new solutions brought in from outside. Struggling economies also present opportunities for examining the interaction between people and structures, where established relationships are open to question. This volume explores change in one struggling economy – Japan. In doing so, it seeks to draw from the experience of Japanese companies in extending international management theory beyond the boundaries of that one country.

Though the precise date and time remain in question, in retrospect economists are in general agreement that sometime in July 1991, the Japanese postwar "economic miracle" came to a close. The official declaration of a recession would not be made until March of the following year. Even then, it was not clear if Japan was going through yet another short-term down cycle before gearing up to move on, or if it was entering into what has now become known as the "lost decade." Observers intimate with the intricacies of corporate Japan's byzantine and precarious system of financial arrangements were quick to remind that they all along had viewed Japanese economic success as a bicycle trick – done at speed or the whole thing would topple over (Clark, 1979). However, other Japan hands saw in the Japanese business and economic system a set of building blocks arranged in complementary fashion such that there was a "winner's competitive cycle" that rewarded well-managed companies and punished those that were not (Abegglen & Stalk, 1985). Under this view, any external disruption to the system could be weathered because the arrangement of building blocks was sufficiently sturdy to withstand it.

In any event, for international management scholars – and for management and organizational scholars more generally – in the early 1990s, the bloom was off the Japanese rose. The consensus seemed to be that whatever lessons might have been learned by studying Japanese corporations, there was little to be learned from them now. In reality, students of management had not been paying that much attention to Japanese corporate behavior all along. Reviewing major scholarly management journals from 1980 through 1994, Bird and Beechler (1999) found a paucity of scholarly work drawing upon the Japanese experience. Beyond the usual management fads and attendant publication of several trade books in the early 1980s – books such as *Theory Z* (Ouchi, 1980) and *The Art of Japanese Management* (Pascale & Athos, 1981), to name the two most popular – interest in Japanese management was limited largely to the study of lean production systems and quality management programs (cf. Lillrank & Kano, 1989; Womack, Jones & Roos, 1990). These two areas, of course, have great significance and represent major contributions to our understanding of production and manufacturing management. Nevertheless, few management scholars in North America and Europe appeared interested in exploring the theoretical implications of managerial practices that unquestionably differed significantly from those found in the West.

Those scholars who did venture into the Japanese management thicket tended to separate into two camps. The first camp saw bicycle tricks – practices that worked, but only in environments that were believed to be unique and of relatively short duration. This camp held that eventually, as the economy matured and economic growth slowed, significant changes in business strategy and management practices would be required. Though not always explicitly stated, the underlying presumption was that increasing degrees of internationalization of Japanese firms would propel them toward a Western model of strategy and management. The position was essentially one of convergence, i.e. the impact of rising commitment to, and involvement in, international markets combined with the globalization of competition would force Japanese to throw off what were viewed as vestiges of an earlier, more feudal era.

The second camp saw building blocks, the rearrangement of which might be necessary as business conditions evolved, but which, nevertheless, were robust enough as a set to accommodate a variety of environmental shifts. An aging workforce, maturing markets and evolving global conditions might require short-term accommodation, but the underlying foundation was solid, and possibly even more stable and resilient than the Western model.

Though the argument between the two camps carried on through the 1990s, it was not unusual to find non-partisan scholars opting to take a wait-and-see approach. Kenney, Romero, Contreras and Bustos (1999) provided an example of this neutral approach, when they wrote, "There is a significant debate regarding the changes the Japanese industrial relations system is undergoing due to the recent economic crisis. [We] continue to believe that it is too early to draw any firm conclusions regarding fundamental changes in the Japanese system" (p. 166).

One result of the long period of slow growth in Japan – the lost decade – and the attendant uncertainty as to the future direction of Japanese managerial practices is that it has led many international business scholars to adopt a measured aloofness. From the standpoint of theory development in international business, however, this attitude is unfortunate. It has led to a neglect of rare opportunities to observe and analyze how international business organizations react and respond to evolving business conditions at home that are both swift and sizeable. The sudden and then sustained slowdown in the Japanese economy has led to *change* in Japanese institutions and firm strategy. Changes in both overall strategy and in the increased *variety* in individual firm responses to the slower growth have provided rich opportunities for new lines of research.

Internal changes in the Japanese domestic business environment, in combination with external changes in the international environment, have generated strong incentives for Japanese firms to seek new ways to structure and compete. The change has required adjustments in the management of Japanese firms domestically and in overseas markets. For example, reforms in the Japanese commercial code, accompanied by increased foreign investment in Japanese corporations, have led to changes in the corporate governance behaviors of numerous Japanese firms. Just as important, dynamic fluctuations in the international competitive environment mingled with the pressures of an extended domestic recession have pushed Japanese MNCs to shift their approach to overseas manufacturing, forcing many firms to confront and work through the challenge of adapting Japanese production strategies and methods to non-Japanese settings. That same competitive pressure has required substantial changes in the way firms are managed in the domestic market as well, to include internal product development, supplier relations and product development.

Using Japan and its decade-long recession as a backdrop, the articles in this volume explore the ways in which firms and environments interact. Changes in both overall strategy and in the increased *variety* in individual firm responses to the slower growth have provided rich opportunities for new lines of research. The combination of internal changes in the Japanese domestic business environment and external changes in the international environment has generated strong incentives for Japanese firms to seek new ways to structure and compete. The change has required adjustments in the management of Japanese firms domestically and in overseas markets. We believe the articles in this volume demonstrate that the experiences of Japanese MNCs during this period, both at home and abroad, have generated insights for theory development in the broader study of international management.

The volume is divided into three sections. In the first section, four articles address ways in which Japanese firms have adapted to environmental changes in the domestic environment. The second section presents four views of shifts and adjustments in diverse inter-organizational relationships – traditional *keiretsu*, manufacturer-supplier relationships, and mergers and acquisitions. The concluding section addresses the experience of "MNCs on foreign soil." Specifically, three

xiv

articles explore the behavior and consequences of Japanese firms abroad, and one examines the experience of foreign MNCs in Japan during the "lost decade."

A volume such as this does not spring to life fully formed from nothing. The genesis was a special session at the 2001 Academy of International Business Meetings in Sydney, Australia at which a number of presenters and audience members discussed the impact of internal and external forces on the changing nature of Japanese MNCs. The dialogue begun in Sydney was expanded the following June in St. Louis when, in conjunction with the 2002 Association of Japanese Business Studies Annual Meeting, the University of Missouri-St. Louis hosted a one-day colloquium. Invitees to the AIM Special Issue Colloquium had submitted manuscripts in response to a Call for Papers for this volume. Manuscripts presented at the symposium first passed through a rigorous, double-blind review process carried out by a panel of leading Japanese management scholars. The colloquium itself also served as a forum in which authors could both present research and receive comments and critiques through dialogue and informal conversation. Following the colloquium, authors carried out an additional round of revisions, which were again read by reviewers and both editors.

We would be remiss if we did not publicly acknowledge the significant contributions to this volume made by the Association of Japanese Business Studies, the Center for International Studies, and the Eiichi Shibusawa-Seigo Arai Professorship at the University of Missouri-St. Louis, as well as the following group of dedicated reviewers:

Christine Ahmadjian, Hitotsubashi University
Schon Beechler, Columbia University
Mary Yoko Brannen, San Jose State University
Mark Fruin, San Jose State University
Kiyohiko Ito, University of Hawaii
James R. Lincoln, University of California-Berkeley
Shige Makino, City University of Hong Kong
Masao Nakamura, University of British Columbia
Ulrike Schaede, University of California-San Diego
Sully Taylor, Portland State University
Chikako Usui, University of Missouri-St. Louis
Hideki Yoshihara, Kobe University

Lastly, we would like to give special recognition to the series editors, Joseph Cheng and Michael Hitt. Their continued support for this issue, and timely and insightful counsel helped to improve the final product.

Thomas Roehl and Allan Bird
Volume Co-editors

REFERENCES

Abegglen, J. C., & Stalk, G., Jr. (1985). *Kaisha.* New York: Basic Books.

Bird, A., & Beechler, S. (1999). The end of innocence. In: S. Beechler & A. Bird (Eds), *Japanese Multinationals Abroad: Individual and Organizational Learning* (pp. 3–10). New York: Oxford University Press.

Kenney, M., Romero, J., Contreras, O., & Bustos, M. (1999). Labor-management relations in the Japanese Consumer Electronics Maquiladora. In: S. Beechler & A. Bird (Eds), *Japanese Multinationals Abroad: Individual and Organizational Learning* (pp. 151–168). New York: Oxford University Press.

Lillrank, P., & Kano, N. (1989). *Continuous improvement: Quality control circles in Japanese industry.* Ann Arbor: University of Michigan Press

Ouchi, W. (1980). *Theory Z.* New York: Addison-Wesley.

Pascale, R. T., & Athos, A. (1981). *The art of Japanese management.* New York: Basic Books.

Womack, J. P., Jones, D. T., & Roos, D. (1990). *The machine that changed the world.* New York: Macmillan.

PART I: ADAPTING TO A CHANGING ENVIRONMENT

The four papers in this section speak directly to the issue of change and adaptation among Japanese firms in response to environmental shifts. Kelley, McNab, Worthley, Pagano, and Huff's examination of the banking industry leads them to reject the thesis of convergence toward a North American model. They find changes in Japanese institutions to be crossvergent, i.e. commingled national culture and economic influences generating a unique, hybrid culture.

Pochet explores learning dynamics in Japanese corporations. Organizational choices are made under constraints imposed by institutions that are influenced, in turn, by organizational action. Individual and organizational learning is a consequence of this process as competition compels organizations to acquire skills and knowledge to remain viable. Transformation has come through a response to internal rule changes and external pressures, setting off a chain reaction. Pochet's analysis dovetails neatly with Kelly and colleagues and, more importantly, delineates the mechanisms through which crossvergence unfolds.

A distinctive feature of the Japanese business system has been *amakudari* (literally "descent from heaven"), the practice by which bureaucrats retire into senior corporate positions. This phenomenon has been explained in terms of the "developmental state" thesis: amakudari provides a mechanism through which government can align firm behaviors to foster national economic development, at the same time favoring industries and firms that support the government. Examining more than 10,000 amakudari events, Moerke concludes that this thesis has been supplanted by a resource-dependence view. Over time, the power of government agencies to dictate amakudari placements has waned and the balance of power shifted. Corporations now use these events to enhance *their* leverage over the government.

Pekkanen and Solis examine transformations in business-government interactions in the textile industry. Historically, the government provided declining industries with trade protection as it simultaneously sought to open foreign markets to exports. Currently, intra-sectoral differences complicate policymaking due to a breakdown of solidarity among industry members. Fault lines in the collectivist mindset and behavior are a reflection of differing domestic strategies and differing degrees of multinationality. Japanese trade policy is increasingly less a product of external pressure, but rather a consequence of fragmenting industry interests.

ADAPTABILITY AND CHANGE IN JAPANESE MANAGEMENT PRACTICE: A LONGITUDINAL INQUIRY INTO THE BANKING INDUSTRY – THROUGH THE BUBBLE ECONOMY AND BEYOND

Lane Kelley, Brent MacNab, Reginald Worthley, Ian Pagano and Lenard Huff

ABSTRACT

Japanese organizations have been forced to re-evaluate their management systems in light of recent economic and competitive pressures. Much can be learned about the adjustments of the Japanese management mindset, and a more competitive Japan may emerge as a result of successful adaptation. This study makes a longitudinal examination of the dynamic nature of management practices and thinking in the Japanese banking industry. Pressures on key industries in Japan during this time, e.g. the financial sector, provide insight into how adaptable Japanese institutions might be. The study finds important areas of meaningful change, supporting a crossvergence approach.

Japanese Firms in Transition: Responding to the Globalization Challenge
Advances in International Management, Volume 17, 3–30
© 2005 Published by Elsevier Ltd.
ISSN: 0747-7929/doi:10.1016/S0747-7929(04)17001-7

JAPAN – PRECEDENCE OF INDUSTRIAL AND FINANCIAL CHANGE

Historically, Japan is no stranger to navigating challenging and sweeping economic change processes in order to address external environmental conditions. In fact, researchers have identified Japan's ability to effectively adapt, change and evolve – the capability of responding to the external environment – as one of the country's greatest advantages through the 20th century (Abegglen & Stalk, 1985). Additionally, for those who may view the recent economic crisis in Japan as a unique national experience for the country, Rose and Ito (2004) astutely point out that the post-World War I series of recessions/depressions (*c.* 1920–1931) share several identical parameters generally assumed to have been endogenously related to the current crisis (e.g. unsound lending decisions, over-investment with over-capacity to satisfy growing demand). Generally during this period, banks consolidated, increasing the power of the *zaibatsu* related banks.

As the post-World War I difficulties with economic conditions mounted, the influence and rise of the military began to have an ever-increasing significance in Japan's political and commerce landscape. Expansionism and growth aspirations, correlated with the acquisition of more natural resources, led Japan to engage in a Pacific campaign that, in turn, led to World War II. Large budget deficits were realized to support military expenditure, and the military was given the authority to draw funds more directly from private banks. This burden and government intervention created an environment of forced mergers; greatly streamlining the financial industry in a way that the Bank of Japan (associated with the Ministry of Finance) could not have accomplished without the militarist influences (Rose & Ito, 2004).

Post-World War II Japan, greatly taxed by the effects of the war, set out to re-establish its industries. The occupation forces endeavored to abolish the *zaibatsu* organizational structure in an attempt to undermine the strong conglomerate networks that controlled the Japanese industrial enterprises (Bhappu, 2000). The concept of "harmonious" work environments was not a reality during this period, as worker dissatisfaction and massive strikes surfaced in a reaction to what some have described as oppressive conditions – indicating that some of what have been called "pillars" of the Japanese work environment have not always been tacit. However, the successful adaptation of Western practices (e.g. practices such as statistical quality control) and improvements in working conditions would later be perfected and used effectively to compete with the west – providing Japan with an eventual competitive edge (Crosby, 1980; Gabor, 1990) and paving the way for a post-World War II "economic miracle" and period of growth. Despite the abolition of the strong *zaibatsu* system, post-World War II industrial cooperation continued, linking the government, companies, and banks by means of the more modern *keiretsu* version of industrial group collaboration. It is this system that is currently the subject of reform in the wake of the more recent Asian Financial Crisis of 1997. It appears that recent economic crises have compelled Japan to change by restructuring industry and financial practices while simultaneously reconsidering lessons from the past. This interaction between organizational practices and the economic environment provides a meaningful context in which to consider crossvergence.

Convergence, Divergence, and Crossvergence

Convergence is normally viewed as a type of cultural homogenization that results from industrialization and the increased circulation of cross-cultural ideas, thinking, and exchanges (Ogbor, 2000) while Ralston, Holt, Terpstra and Kai-Cheng (1997) place divergence on the other end of the theoretical spectrum as a movement away from sameness, even in light of adaptation of similar economic systems such as free-market capitalism. Some argue that with the development of improved technology and communication, the pace of potential convergence is only quickened (Czinkota & Ronkainen, 1998; Mitchell, Hastings & Tanyel, 2001). Explanations of industry-level cultural shifts within a given national context may not be served well by adhering to over-simplified or strict convergence theories (Ferraro, 1993; George, 1992; Holt, Ralston & Terpstra, 1994; Ohmae, 1990). Immediately following World War II, a type of institutional "forced convergence" between the U.S. and Japan was apparent, but these surface changes should not automatically be taken as deeper cultural convergence (Peterson & Shimada, 1978). Studies conducted during periods of unprecedented economic growth for Japan revealed that the differences between U.S. and Japanese workers' attitudes became more distant during the 1960s and 1970s (Takezawa & Whitehill, 1981; Whitehill & Takezawa, 1968). Nevertheless, with the drive to become multinational, entailing seamless boundaries, some have raised the question as to whether this process drives toward universal corporate cultures in general (Chatman & Jehn, 1994) while others maintain that home-country characteristics remain dominant (Dicken, 1998, pp. 196–197) and that national differences persist (Pauley & Reich, 1997). Child and Yan (2001) suggest that these two extremes on the continuum (divergence versus convergence) can also be labeled respectively as "national" and "transnational" effects on corporate strategies and practices.

Our analysis focuses on a longitudinal path of a different period and economic context for Japan than these earlier studies – one of challenge and decline with increasing unemployment. The financial challenges confronting Japanese institutions continue to raise questions regarding the effectiveness of reform, as corporate borrowers struggle to pay off debt while continuing to receive financing from closely tied banking institutions. It is estimated that Japanese banks will have to write off more than $450 billion in bad loans over the past decade (Zielenziger, 2002). Pressure from major trading partners and other international organizations has placed Japan in the position of having to address some inefficiencies that traditionally have been tied to practices within the *kaisha* (e.g. quasi-nepotistic lending and financial practices). Other astute observers have examined the crippling power that more recent, overly cautious market strategies have had on the *kaisha* during the time period covered by our study (Christensen, Craig & Hart, 2001).

Economic challenges and increased globalization and competition during the time frame of our study provide a good context from which to contrast these earlier studies. DiMaggio and Powell (1983) noted that businesses tend to imitate more successful organizations, and at this particular juncture, as the power of the Japanese economy wanes and struggles with rebound, we may find that certain practices and cultural patterns change in order to stay competitive. However, a key question is whether the change is driven by convergence or driven more by a complex interplay of simultaneous converging and diverging reactions to external pressures in a drive to gain efficiency and remain competitive.

Ralston et al. (1997), in an empirical study examining cultural differences between socialistic and capitalistic nations, examined the *convergence-divergence-crossvergence* (CDC) phenomena. Specifically relevant to our study, Ralston (1993) defined *crossvergence* as a value set "in between" those values found in national culture and economic influences (ideology, policy, trends). Later, Ralston (1997) proposed another perspective whereby individuals and subgroups synergistically integrate both national culture influences and economic influences to form a different, unique value system. Clearly economic influences can encourage cross-national influences to "migrate" to new national boundaries in the form of foreign direct investment, partnerships/international joint ventures, new competition, and a host of other formats. In direct support of this argument, Child and Yan (2001) found evidence that the importation of foreign management practices might be prone particularly to cross-border migration through joint ventures with transnational organizations. In this respect, crossvergence involves a unique result when increased global competition and the migration of ideas and management practices mix with cultural parameters to form and shape new practices and emerging norms.

In addition to the idea that, on an industry level (banking), cultural change and attitudes may be driven by external influences (economic conditions), there is also interesting work that examines subcultural resistance to convergence also called resistance to assimilation (McLeod, 1999), up to the point of intentional separation.

Currently, there are reports of continued non-market-driven lending practices in the Japanese relation between banks and certain keiretsu members, which may be a resistance to the assimilation of new practices (established by the M.O.F. and other regulatory bodies) within this industry subculture.

Why Banking?

The banking industry provides a prime arena to examine change within Japan because of the critical role this particular industry has played (and is playing) in recent economic phenomena (Asian Financial Crisis of 1997) and the importance of change within this industry. Helweg (2000) suggests that the financial sector in Japan is going to have to undergo nothing short of a revolution and that the economy will need to digest the largest financial transformation in its history. Already, institutional changes have been implemented to move this sector toward more market-driven decision-making criteria. Others (Porter, Takeuchi & Sakakibara 2000) echo the importance of extensive financial reform that must take place in Japan as a component of long-term recovery. The examination of management change within this context, and as a platform for examining the potential for change in Japanese organizations in general, provides an environment that seems primed for adjustment in order to address external pressures (e.g. economic reform and competitive pressure).

Supporting the industry-level framework for meaningful cultural and management research, Brislin (1981) suggests that culture can be understood on historical, individual, group, situational/task-specific and industry/organization-specific levels. In this regard, the current research seeks to examine a specific subarea of Japanese culture at the industry level. Porter (1986) suggests that the industry level is of considerable importance because patterns of international competition might vary widely from one industry to another. Also, Kelley, Whatley and Worthley (1987) suggest industry-level studies can effectively help isolate variables that can otherwise become problematic in cultural and cross-cultural studies.

The examination of the potential for change in certain, specific management contexts may be more dynamic than traditional approaches seem to suggest in that:

(1) external environmental pressures, e.g. increased global competition and the use of disruptive technologies by competitors (Christensen et al., 2001), economic conditions and market shifts, might have the potential to endogenously act on aspects of management which is, in turn, pressured to respond in order to maintain competitiveness;

(2) historical events might also provide examples of management shifts for Japan in relation to major external environmental pressures, demonstrating a more dynamic reality for the eco-cultural niche we are examining,

(3) simple examinations of such change using a pure convergence or a pure divergence type of approach might be too limited;

(4) culture on an industry level may respond and change more readily.

Other researchers have argued that there is value in using this type of *disaggregate* approach in developing cultural studies (Casson & Lundan, 1999) and that meaningful, practical insight can be gleaned from industry-level studies.

Theoretical Foundation

Because our research examines cultural parameters using Hofstede dimensions, it is important to review these foundations briefly. A cultural system may be defined as people sharing similar beliefs, customs, norms and "mental programming" (Brislin, Loaner & Thorndike, 1973; Hofstede, 1980a, b). Triandis (1977) emphasizes the subjective context of culture, by which he means people's response to the "man-made part of the environment, or to a group's characteristic way of perceiving its social environment" (Brislin, 1981, p. 423). Most definitions of culture share the following elements: (1) human made elements that are shared through communication; (2) which increase the probability for survival; and (3) result in greater satisfaction for those in the community.

Hofstede's (1980a, b, 1997) seminal work provides a good foundation from which to benchmark the traditional perspectives of a country's culture. Although this work has received some valid critique and suggested improvements (Bond, 1987; Dorfman & Howell, 1988; Hampden-Turner & Trompenaars, 1993; Schwartz, 1990; Triandis, 1995) it holds value as a general framework from which one can view culture (Oyserman et al., 2002). The Hofstede study sampled 116,000 employees of IBM, representing 40 different countries over a two-year period, and constructed four basic cultural dimensions. These dimensions are used in this review as a framework with the realization that there are other frameworks, with highly valuable components, that could also be used (Fiske, 1990; Hampden-Turner & Trompenaars, 1993; Schwartz, 1994; Triandis, 1989, 1972). Often, research that uses the Hofstede dimensions does not actually use the Hofstede measurement tool – as the strength in his work has often been identified for its descriptive richness and not in the actual psychometric tool (Kelley et al., 1987; Oyserman, Kemmelmeier & Coon, 2002).

Hofstede (2002, p. 2) suggests that, "in national culture, all spheres of life and society are interrelated: family, school, job, religious practice, economic behavior, health, crime, punishment, art science, literature, *management* and leadership – there is not such a thing as a separate management or leadership culture." If the theoretical position of this basic framework is correct, examination of change within a specific component of cultural identity (such as a nation's banking industry) might have important implications for the possibility of change on a larger scale – what we call a "spillover effect." Other researchers suggest that meaningful insight can and should be extracted from these more detailed components of national identity. Interestingly, Hofstede also seems to agree that a more detailed level of analysis can create meaningful insight beyond the traditional national cultural identification level – "not only will cultural diversity among countries remain with us, it even looks as though differences within countries are increasing" (Hofstede, 1997, p. 238). We support this particular perspective in our research by specifically examining a segment of national culture (the banking industry) and by clearly defining the scope of our research in management and culture, as suggested by other investigators as well (Boyacigiller & Adler, 1991).

A Typical Culture Map of Japan

Ultimately, our research effort is to clearly develop a subcultural, industry-level research and analysis of culture and change in Japan. Our research findings do not necessarily translate directly to the larger national context for Japan. As Porter (1986) indicates, there is great value in industry level research. Additionally, it is dangerous to develop research that automatically substitutes national identity for cultural identity or to take limited samples and present these as national effects (Adler, 1997; McDonald, 2000). There is also a growing body of research that suggests the importance of regional or subcultural examinations within culturally complex areas (Brislin, 1981; Cheung & Chow, 1999; Cohen, 1998; Oyserman et al., 2002; Porter, 1986; Slotterback & Saarnio, 1996). The following provides: (1) a brief overview of three of the traditional Hofstede dimensions for Japan; along with (2) a brief example of each dimension's historical links to add perspective; and (3) a few examples of how each dimension is related to certain aspects of the banking industry in Japan. As a comparative anchoring point, the general U.S. position of each dimension is also explained.

Japan is often portrayed as a *collectivist* society with a high *power distance*, high *uncertainty avoidance*, and propensity for *quantity of life* aspects.[1] A collectivist stereotype is actually held by many Japanese people, which might act as a social-psychological, self-fulfilling prophesy, further cementing this image (Mouer & Sugimoto, 1986). Early on, researchers often viewed Japan as being at a philosophically/culturally polar opposite position from that of the U.S. (Peterson & Shimada, 1978). Some have suggested that culturally polarizing the "us" and "them" aspects of Western and Japanese cultural comparisons has served as a tool to promote exaggerated differences in building ethnographies (Yoneyama, 1999). In other words, the West may have a propensity to understand the other (e.g. Japan) by seeking to polarize rather than synthesize. The cultural dimensions of a region or nation are sometimes conceptualized as semistatic elements of the group under consideration. Although one cannot automatically assume that national identity equates to cultural identity, research in this area often constructs and examines cultural dimensions under the umbrella of nationality because people are prone to think of the world in terms of the shared, well-known, and convenient parameters of national boundaries. We have developed our review specifically on an industry-level platform to help move away from such an over-generalized approach.

In the following sections, we develop a research position for each of the identified cultural dimensions while also providing potential historical links and banking-industry examples. Our linking of historical elements to the common cultural pattern normally used for Japan is meant to serve as an example and foundation, and is not meant to be either exhaustive or comprehensive, as other valid historical examples and positions could also be developed.

INDIVIDUALISM/COLLECTIVISM

Hofstede cites Japan as being a high collectivist culture where social relations are described as highly important and "tight" (Hofstede, 1997, 2002). Members of social networks and groups feel a strong obligation to maintain social harmony and reciprocity within the group. The collectivism dimension of cultural comparison has received much attention (Oyserman et al., 2002; Triandis, 1995) and arguably can be viewed as the most influential of the Hofstede dimensions. For example, some authors suggest that individualistic cultures may place a higher level of overall importance on certain issues such as ethical self-regulation, (Armstrong, 1996), while others view this perspective as typical Western ethical elitism (Khera, 2001). Nevertheless, individualism, exemplified by the U.S. culture, is characterized by loose-knit social frameworks in which people are expected to watch out for themselves and where in-group/out-group distinctions are less of a focus. In contrast, collectivist societies, such as Japan, are organized via tight social frameworks with high degrees of loyalty and sharp in-group/out-group distinction.

Collectivist cultures may also develop specific and complicated systems for making decisions, establishing loyalty and exchanging favors between in-group members.

Collectivism in Historic Perspective

Collectivism is often directly linked to the Confucian philosophy that proliferated in early Japan. Confucianism's emphasis on social harmony (Dawson, 1993), reciprocity and obligation are clearly supportive and conducive to the core characteristics that have helped to shape the in-group, relationship-driven ties that are evident in the zaibatsu/keiretsu structures and the supportive role related banks have played in this dynamic. This is the *distal* level of culture (Oyserman et al., 2002), which establishes deep foundations through historic teachings, philosophy, language, and religion. Historians have claimed that, early on, too great an emphasis on these aspects of Japanese culture created an ultraconservative, collectivist merchant class in Japan that was overly cautious, semiparalyzed, and lacking in entrepreneurial initiative (Hirschmeier & Yui, 1981). Japan's *Tokugawa era* (1603–1867) was characterized by isolationist tendencies, whereby Japan had limited contact with the West. This period is viewed as the first modern era of Japan (Jansen, 2000) and the beginning of industrial development including shipbuilding, shipping, and electronics. Overtime isolationist tendencies, which can arguably be linked to aspects of collectivism and in-group emphasis, began to soften. Today, one can see signs of the in-group emphasis continuing to soften as Japan becomes more open to foreign ownership, international joint ventures, and Foreign Direct Investment (Helweg, 2000), and as modern technology increases the opportunity for these interactions (Czinkota & Ronkainen, 1998; Mitchell et al., 2001). In fact, Mitchell et al. (2001) specifically cite telecommunications, new broadcast means, and long-distance travel as catalysts for an increased propensity for "cultural borrowing." During the 1920s economic problems that surfaced in Japan were linked, in part, to the highly collectivistic, in-group relations within the *zaibatsu*, whereby financial institutions extended non-market credit decisions.

In the mid-1980s, during and following the phenomenal post-World War II economic growth in Japan, Western scholars touted these same principles, e.g. *Confucian Dynamism* as endogenous in developing the Japanese economic miracle (Bond, 1987). Later (Porter et al., 2000), in light of the Asian financial crisis, scholars began to examine these same distal aspects of Japanese culture as once again problematic. Current reforms in Japan's banking industry are clearly setting out to re-focus away from what many would view as the collectivist tendencies that led to special in-group consideration for affiliated keiretsu organizations beyond what sound market decisions would have dictated.

Collectivism and Banking in Japan

Collectivism is one cultural dimension that traditional treatments of Japanese culture have argued has had a strong impact on the way banking functions in Japan. Close, in-group relationships that developed between banking houses and family-run companies (pre-war zaibatsu and post-war keiretsu) allowed companies from major industrial sectors to link under a main bank. Industrial in-group equity sharing allowed supporting banks to hold some keiretsu group member equity – thus cementing the relations. Also, cross-shareholding has been viewed as an effective defense against hostile takeover; thus maintaining the intricately developed in-group relations. The keiretsu system allowed groups to lock suppliers and distributors into exclusive relationships to ensure a dependable distribution chain and supply of capital from banks (Helweg, 2000; Porter et al., 2000). Over time, these relationships overshadowed market-driven factors such as efficiency, competitive bidding and sound lending practices. In short, collectivistic, in-group affiliations driven by government support outweighed more pure market logic.

In 1998, Big Bang policies were intended to address the Asian Financial Crisis in Japan by organizing financial industry reforms and encouraging more market-driven lending policies. Big Bang policies are driving Japan toward more market-driven criteria for lending which could, as a residual effect, create a climate for departure from what can be described as strong in-group, keiretsu, collectivist tendencies. This drive for more efficient, market-driven parameters has affected other industries, extending beyond the banking sector. For example, Japanese companies, in a quest to reduce duplication and make themselves attractive for consolidation, no longer want to hold high percentages of ownership in related companies (Helweg, 2000). Additionally, there is an increased trend of foreign direct investment and partnerships, as exemplified by Nissan/Renault, Ford/Mazda, DaimlerChrysler/Mitsubishi and GM/Isuzu, Suzuki, Toyota (Schreffler, 2001). These two trends demonstrate a movement away from strong, traditional in-group ties and an opening of the system to out-group members, thus leading to our first hypothesis.

Proposition 1. Aspects of the Japanese banking industry have moved toward a more individualistic cultural perspective.

POWER DISTANCE

Power distance refers to the degree that a culture recognizes the importance of position and other inherent dimensions that might separate one socially from another member of society. Power distance has to do with the extent to which inequality between people is accepted (Hofstede, 2002). For example, the U.S. is viewed as a low-power-distance society where it is often acceptable to address a boss by their first name. In contrast, in a high-power-distance society, it would be more unusual to address elders or senior-level managers in a casual manner (Hofstede, 1980a, b, 1997). A low power distance reflects the egalitarian structure common in many parts of the U.S. and demonstrates a general suspicion of hierarchy (Hofstede, 1980a, b, 2002). Japan is characterized as a high-power-distance society (Hofstede, 1997) where hierarchy plays an important role. Researchers have often linked aspects of high power distance to aspects of Confucian philosophy that dictate order in relations – people in these countries are comfortable with inequality and with fairly specific social roles.

Power Distance in Historic Perspective

On a *distal* level, Japan, through the influence Confucianism, has been strongly influenced by maintaining social harmony through order in relationships. The feudal system of Japan was based on a social order whereby the shogunate and samurai families held significant power over the common people. Radical departure from traditional norms of high power distance began to shift during the end of the Tokugawa era when samurai families replaced the established Tokugawa shogunate with the Emperor Meiji, thus crafting the first movement toward a modern economy. This shift continued through the Meiji Restoration (1868), which established reforms that allowed for more opportunity of the common class, marking a clear shift in the extent of power inequality. This shift allowed citizens to pursue their own interests more freely and reflected an attempt to purposefully increase the potential for social mobility. These reforms also initiated a shift away from the commercial power of the old merchant houses and allowed a freer pursuit of commerce, leaving room for more modern entrepreneurial developments.

Elements of high power distance still exist today in the status accorded toward age (Morrison, Conaway & Borden, 1994) and gender in Japan (Renshaw, 1999; Taylor, 2000). However, shifts in both of these areas are also evident as Japan faces another reality of the external environment – a rapidly declining birth rate required to maintain the current population. This dynamic alone creates a situation where one can observe an increasing number of women entering the ranks of management in Japan. Interestingly, on the domestic front, women in Japan are said to control the household finances, with a husband's salary going directly to his wife (Renshaw, 1999). Although domestic Japanese banks are still reluctant to hire females, foreign banks and financial institutions are driving to bring more female managers to executive positions. For instance, as of 1999, Citibank Japan had nine female vice presidents, with foreign banks hiring and promoting more females; there has been a trend for Japanese banks to follow suit, and the above-average representation of women in banking seems somewhat counterintuitive to the norm (Renshaw, 1999).

Power Distance and Banking in Japan

Although not exclusive to the financial sector, rank as indicated by age has important implications. The tradition of seniority-based pay has held a strong position in the industry (Helweg, 2000) but has also been viewed as a trend that is deteriorating given current reforms. Incentives for early retirement, reduction in the size of corporate boards, and a movement from seniority-based pay systems to merit-based pay systems seem to indicate that the reverence for age and related perspectives of power distance may be shifting. Indeed, some researchers suggest that this traditional level of inequality is being eroded, not only from economic external environment factors which force companies to focus on retaining the best, brightest and most productive employees as opposed to simply the most senior, but also by a younger generation which is questioning traditional practices, thereby (Morrison et al., 1994) guiding us to our second hypothesis.

Proposition 2. Elements of the Japanese banking industry have moved to a lower power distance position.

UNCERTAINTY AVOIDANCE

Uncertainty avoidance refers to the degree to which a culture has acclimated to the acceptance of risk, or the degree to which it is comfortable with the unfamiliar (Hofstede, 2002, 1997). For instance, some societies prefer to operate with formalized rules and regulations, and prefer that activities be clearly regulated with little left to interpretation. Uncertainty avoidance relates to how threatened a society is by ambiguous contexts and the degree to which it will attempt to avoid these situations, i.e. not tolerating deviant ideas or behaviors, and believing in absolute truths. High uncertainty avoidance creates greater overall anxiety and a heightened work ethic (Hofstede, 1980a, b), and Japan is well known for both (Morrison et al., 1994). The essence of uncertainty is that the future is largely unknown, and individuals and societies must find ways of coping with that reality. Cultures characterized by low uncertainty avoidance might breed more entrepreneurs and more creative risk-takers than high-uncertainty-avoiding cultures because the associated ambiguity of such ventures may create too much stress for the latter. Moreover, although uncertainty avoidance should not be associated automatically with risk avoidance, uncertainty-avoiding behaviors tend to reduce ambiguity, which some might view as inherently risky (Hofstede, 1997). While the United States is traditionally, and very generally, viewed as a low-uncertainty-avoidance culture (Hofstede, 1997, p. 123), Japan is traditionally viewed as a high-uncertainty-avoidance culture (Hofstede, 2002). There are indications (Child & McGrath, 2001; Christensen et al., 2001) that aspects of this dimension can be linked to certain elements undergoing dynamic shifts in Japan's overall competitiveness.

Uncertainty Avoidance in Historic Perspective

Japan seems to have had a cautious attitude toward how to cope with uncertainty. Prior to the Tokugawa regime and the 1800s, Japan had relatively less contact with the outside world, and such contact, when established, was carefully controlled (Jansen, 2000). Interaction with the outside world carried with it high levels of uncertainty, which was to be avoided, if possible, and later carefully restricted and controlled. During the Tokugawa era, an overly cautious merchant class seems inclined to stifle entrepreneurial initiative, and specific reforms had to be enacted to help overcome these tendencies during the period of Meiji Restoration (Jansen, 2000; Makoto & Imanari, 1999). Many of today's reforms flirt with forcing organizations to more realistically face the realities of increased uncertainty that come as a concomitant effect of focusing on decisions that are more market-driven. Movement away from established and predictable inter-organizational dependencies, in favor of more discerning, market-driven practices, potentially creates an increase in uncertainty.

Uncertainty Avoidance and Banking in Japan

The traditional relationships between banks and corporations within the keirestsu structure had the effect of reducing the risks of more purely market-driven processes, decisions, and litmus tests. Corporations within the traditional system could rely on in-group members to maintain keiretsu relations, secure business, maintain pricing structure, manage competition, and ensure access to capital resources, thereby greatly controlling ambiguity. Today, the "big bang" restructuring is aimed at making businesses and their relationships with banks more a function of less predictable market forces. Companies intent on enhancing their profitability are compelled to alter their preference from relationship-based business to more market-driven practices. There is a push to support smaller, more innovative, non-keiretsu enterprises. Additionally, changes within the financial sector have begun to spill over into other sectors of the economy (Helweg, 2000). Less government regulation of newer, up-and-coming industries such as communications and technology are also a potential sign of movement toward a greater acceptance of uncertainty, but on a more macro-level.

On a micro-level, individuals within the banking industry may be reacting quite differently. Although long-term goals of macro-level policies may residually compel more acceptance of uncertainty through market-driven decision-making, bank managers operating in the wake of one of the worst financial crises in recent history might react with apprehension to more uncertainty. Government policies enacted to induce more market-driven criteria for lending may serve as a constant reminder of the recent financial crisis to executives responsible for decision-making and lending processes. We hypothesize that although macro-level policies attempt to drive Japanese industry to operate with greater market risk (i.e. more market-driven decision and lending criteria), the organizational response to these changes, coupled with the aftermath of the recent crisis, will create greater uncertainty avoidance in the short term, leading to our final hypothesis:

Proposition 3. Aspects of the Japanese banking industry have moved to a higher position of uncertainty avoidance.

Several caveats are warranted. As Van Wolferen (1989) pointed out, "Japan perplexes the world." Ascribing purely cultural explanation for why shifts have occurred over the last 15 years is not our intent. Rather, our interest in aspects of *crossvergence* reflects an acceptance and understanding of the influence of non-cultural effects as well. We are interested in whether our findings indicate a move away from typical cultural stereotypes of Japan. Prior research has suggested that particular aspects of culture in Japan are more epistemologic of other external environmental phenomena such as political structure than from deeper, distal influences like religion or philosophy (Van Wolferen, 1989; Yoneyama, 1999). Such a perspective supports Minear's (1980) position, which argues for the importance of examining politics as endogenous to culture. It is important to refer to prior research when describing changes in culture that are formed in a relatively short time period. Both Yoneyama and Van Wolferen are skeptical of typical cultural descriptions of Japan that, for example, describe the mindset of the populace as collective to the core. Van Wolferen (1989, p. 3) suggests that many Japanese are individualists but have little choice but to accept the striking communalistic aspects of society that has been controlled by the political elite.

RESULTS/METHODOLOGY

Survey data were collected from mid-level managers from large banks in Japan and the United States as part of a large-scale study that involved seven countries. The sample size for Japan was 259 and 271 for the United States. Part of this recent study replicated questions that were asked in prior management study conducted 15 years earlier. That study had sample sizes of 223 for Japan and 133 for the United States, and also was collected from mid-level managers from large banks in Japan and the United States. Nine Likert-scale items, which were each measured on a 7-point scale, representing constructs of collectivism, uncertainty avoidance, and power distance, were common to both studies. These are listed below.

Collectivism:

C1. Individuals in work groups in this organization work together more than strive for individual recognition.
C2. Managers in this organization take an interest in the personal problems of their subordinates.
C3. This organization rewards cooperative behavior.

Uncertainty avoidance:

UA1. Managers in this organization spend time preparing formal plans such as budgets.
UA2. In this organization, policies and procedures are strictly followed.
UA3. In this organization, job duties are described in detail by written procedures.

Power distance:

PD1. Employees in this organization are afraid to disagree with their boss.
PD2. In this organization, respect is given, based on one's position in the organization.
PD3. Managers in this organization make most decisions without consulting subordinates.

Prior to running a confirmatory factor analysis, missing data were replaced by item mean values for the respective subsamples. For example, if an individual from Japan, who filled out the survey in 1985, left a question blank, the value was replaced by the mean of the given item for the 1985 Japan group. Missing values were handled in this way to ensure that the correlation matrix of the data was positive definite. When this condition is not satisfied, statistical analyses may be suspect. Although listwise deletion of cases would also have ensured positive definiteness, this was rejected because it would have resulted in the removal of all of a participant's data, even if only one item were left blank. A total of 18 missing values were imputed in this way. To examine the assumption that data were missing randomly, dummy variables were constructed that divided the cases into two groups: those with missing values for a given measure and those without. Mean differences on other variables were then compared, and no significant differences were found.

Variables were checked for multivariate outliers by calculating the Mahalanobis distances (the distances from the multivariate centroid). With an $\alpha = 0.001$ cutoff level, only one of the 886 participants produced scores that identified them as outliers. Analyses with the full data and analyses with this outlier excluded were run, and results were virtually identical. The outlier was therefore left in for the final analysis. Randomly selected pairwise scatter plots of the variables were visually examined to conduct an assessment of non-linearity, and no evidence of non-linearly was found.

Because the items were measured on a Likert-type scale, which is clearly not continuous, the covariance matrix was not used as the basis for any of the analyses. Using the PRELIS package that accompanies LISREL, polychoric correlations (between two ordinal variables) were calculated and used for all analyses. Maximum likelihood estimation was employed to estimate all models. The overall chi-square test, the RMSEA (root mean square error of approximation), the CFI (comparative fit index), and the chi-square to degrees of freedom ratio (χ^2/df) were examined to assess model fit.

The overall chi-square test, which tests the null hypothesis of perfect model fit, was provided because of its ubiquitous reporting in the confirmatory factor analytic literature and because of its usefulness in comparing nested models (models with identical structure but an unequal number of free parameters). However, because of its sensitivity to sample size, the chi-square test is generally considered to be an appropriate measure only when the total sample size is less than 200 (Bollen & Long, 1993). Further, this test is affected by the correlations within the model, with higher correlations suggesting poorer fit. The present analyses have a sample size greater than 200 and the correlations within the model were expected to be fairly high (because all variables were hypothesized to reflect management style). Therefore, the chi-square test was not viewed as an appropriate fit index for the present study, except when comparing nested models.

Because of the problems involved with the chi-square test, alternative fit indices have been provided. These include the RMSEA, defined as $\sqrt{[(\chi^2/\mathrm{df}) - 1]/N}$, with values below 0.05 considered to reflect a good model fit; the CFI, defined as $1 - (\chi^2/\mathrm{df})/(\chi^2_{\mathrm{Ind}} - \mathrm{df}_{\mathrm{Ind}})$, where Ind is the independence model (no free parameters), with values greater than 0.90 considered to reflect a good fit; and the χ^2/df, with values less than 2.0 considered to reflect a good model fit (Bollen, 1989).

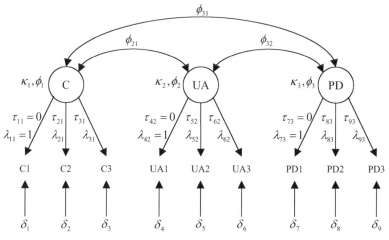

Fig. 1. Measurement Model.

The first step in testing the hypotheses was to assess the overall fit of the full model (the test of form invariance). Form invariance would show that the structure imposed by the hypothesized model is equally viable for all groups. The hypothesized model is shown in Fig. 1, where circles represent the latent constructs, and squares represent the measured indicators. The Greek letters reflect the LISREL model, with τ and λ the intercepts and slopes of the paths from the latent variables to the indicator variables, κ and ϕ the means and covariances of the latent variables, and δ the error variances of the indicators. Absence of a line in the model indicates no hypothesized direct effect, and the parameter has been constrained to zero.

A multiple group confirmatory factor analysis was performed through Jöreskog and Sörbom's LISREL package. The four groups under comparison were Japan 1985 ($n = 259$), Japan 2000 ($n = 259$), U.S. 1985 ($n = 133$), and U.S. 2000 ($n = 271$). The overall test of model fit for the hypothesized full model was statistically significant (Table 1, Model 1.0), rejecting the null hypothesis of perfect model fit. But, the RMSEA, CFI, and χ^2/df all reflected a good model fit. These results provided evidence for the viability of the hypothesized structure across groups and allowed for further testing of the equality of parameters across groups.

Next, to test factorial invariance (equivalence of the λ values across groups), the initial hypothesized model (the full model) was compared to a model in which all of the λ parameters between the four groups were constrained. This constrained model was nested within the full one, so a comparison between the two could be made using the chi-square difference test. The constrained model was significantly

Table 1. Tests of Factorial Invariance and Latent Mean Differences.

	Model	χ^2	df	$\Delta\chi^2$	Δdf	RMSEA	CFI
1.0	Full model (Form invariance)	176.1	96	–	–	0.040	0.91
2.0	Factor loadings (Invariant: All)	262.9	114	86.8[*]	18	0.050	0.83
2.1	Invariant: C	187.7	102	11.6[**]	6	0.040	0.90
2.2	Invariant: UA	180.4	102	4.3[**]	6	0.038	0.91
2.3	Invariant: PD	247.9	102	71.8[*]	6	0.052	0.84
2.4	Invariant: C and UA	192.2	108	16.1[**]	12	0.038	0.91
3.1	Latent means (Invariant: C)	219.1	111	26.9[*]	3	0.043	0.88
3.2	Latent means (Invariant: UA)	252.5	111	60.3[*]	3	0.049	0.88
3.3	Latent means (Invariant: PD)	253.5	111	61.3[*]	3	0.049	0.84

Note: C: Collectivism; UA: Uncertainty Avoidance; PD: Power Distance. Models 2.*x* are compared against Model 1.0, and Models 3.*x* are compared against Model 2.4.
[*]$p < 0.001$.
[**]$p > 0.05$.

degraded, suggesting that factorial invariance was not present (Table 1, Model 2.0).

However, it was not clear if all three constructs lacked factorial invariance, or if only a subset did. To test which specific constructs lacked factorial invariance, three separate models were created, each constraining only a single construct. These three models were then compared with the full model (Table 1, Models 2.1,

Table 2. Maximum Likelihood Estimates and Standard Errors of Factor Loadings and Means.

Parameter	Across-Group Equivalences		U.S. 1985		U.S. 2000		Japan 1985		Japan 2000	
	Estimate	SE	Estimate	SE	Estimate	SE	Estimate	SE	Estimate	SE
λ_{11}	1.00	–								
λ_{21}	1.25	0.13								
λ_{31}	1.15	0.12								
λ_{42}	1.00	–								
λ_{52}	1.20	0.14								
λ_{62}	1.30	0.15								
λ_{73}	1.00	–								
λ_{83}			0.60	0.20	0.41	0.20	−2.80	1.31	0.99	0.12
λ_{93}			1.60	0.60	0.50	0.24	1.55	0.83	0.66	0.12
κ_1			4.23	0.09	4.18	0.09	4.76	0.09	4.42	0.09
κ_2			4.56	0.09	5.01	0.09	4.71	0.09	5.48	0.08
κ_3			4.01	0.09	4.99	0.09	4.35	0.09	4.62	0.09

Note: Values are obtained from Model 2.4.

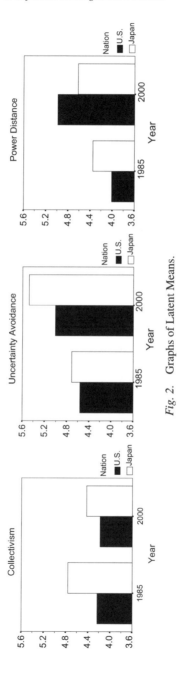

Fig. 2. Graphs of Latent Means.

2.2, and 2.3). Results showed that only Power Distance lacked factorial invariance, and that Collectivism and Uncertainty Avoidance were factorially invariant across all groups. A model was therefore created in which Collectivism and Uncertainty Avoidance were factorially invariant across groups, but Power Distance was not. This model did not show a significantly degraded fit from the full model (Table 1, Model 2.4).

Next, each latent construct was examined for differences in means across groups. Three new models were created that were identical to Model 2.4, except that in each, one latent construct mean was constrained to equality across groups. Each of these constrained models showed a significantly degraded fit from Model 2.4 (Table 1, Models 3.1, 3.2, and 3.3), suggesting that the means were not equivalent. Table 2 provides a list of estimates and standard errors for the λ (slope) and κ (latent mean) parameters. Figure 2 gives a visual representation of the latent means.

To specifically address the three change hypotheses proposed earlier in the paper, we turn to a discussion of how the latent means have changed over this time period. Using the latent means and standard errors provided in Table 2, we first examine Change Hypothesis 1: The Japanese banking industry has moved towards a more individualistic cultural perspective. This hypothesis is supported by the data with a p-value of approximately 0.01 using a Z test for a difference between means adjusted for making multiple comparisons by using a Bonferroni procedure. As a frame of reference, the U.S. banking industry moved only slightly towards a more individualistic cultural perspective. Change Hypothesis 2: The Japanese banking industry has moved to a lower power distance position is not supported by the data. The corresponding p-value for this test is not significant at the 0.05 significance level, and in fact, the latent mean is higher for the most recent data period. In contrast, the U.S. data reveal a very large increase over this time period, so much so that the relative positions of the latent means are reversed. We find support for the last Change Hypothesis: The Japanese banking industry has moved to a higher position of uncertainty avoidance. There was a substantial increase in the latent mean for uncertainty avoidance over this time period ($P < 0.001$). To a lesser degree, the U.S. latent mean also significantly ($P < 0.01$) increased over this same time period.

CONCLUSION

Collectivism/Individualism

Japanese management's position on the Individualism/Collectivism dimensions greatly decreased, indicating that the Japanese have become more individualistic.

Explanation of this tendency may come from external environmental factors such as the current economic challenges previously discussed. The forces may be compelling segments of Japanese industry to adopt more non-collective practices (e.g. shying away from life-long employment, revising quasi-nepotistic financial practices among the *kaisha*). Nevertheless, the data, in part, clearly support earlier work by Child (1981), which indicates that some aspects of organizational design are subject to potential change regardless of cultural identity.

Japan actually moved closer to a U.S. position on this cultural dimension. Whether this is actually convergence or a natural and legitimate strategic option for organizations actively engaged in the competitive global arena is open to debate. Adjusting culturally influenced practices and attitudes within an organization (or even industry) to create greater efficiencies and competitiveness does not automatically support the idea of convergence. Convergence supports the idea that cultures are becoming more homogenized. What our research observes can just as easily be argued as a strategic shift over time to remain competitive in the arena of global competition and markets. Additionally, our remaining hypothesis generally does not support the idea of convergence.

Uncertainty Avoidance

In relation to uncertainty avoidance, we observed the following: (1) an increase in uncertainty avoidance for the Japanese industry time; (2) an increase in both the Japanese and U.S. samples propensity toward uncertainty avoidance; and (3) a larger increase in uncertainty avoidance for the Japanese sample over time. One might point to the economic challenges faced by Japan as a potential explanation for such a marked increase in their propensity toward uncertainty avoidance.

The changes we observe seem to indicate macro-level policy pushing the industry to embrace market based decisions and processes – which could be argued to reflect a push for the industry to abandon familiar practices in favor of more risk. However, as hypothesized, our evidence shows hesitation in the industry-specific sample – showing a marked increase in uncertainty avoidance. Given that the economy is mired in the greatest recession since World War II, banking-industry executives in Japan may be particularly sensitive to issues of uncertainty avoidance. The reality of these pressures becomes even more clear when considering that unemployment rates are at a 50-year high, and corporate bankruptcies have risen to a 17-year high. Perhaps most relevant for this study, bankruptcies at financial and insurance firms rose 26.7% over a year ago (Takato, 2002), and political/economic pressure for financial-industry reform has compelled a series of financial industry mergers (Rose & Ito, 2004). Considering these facts, it would not be unrealistic to argue that the current level of uncertainty and the desire to avoid its effects are felt most profoundly in the traditional financial institutions of Japan.

This position is not out of line with recent work on Japan's movement away from *disruptive technology*[2]-type innovation during our research period (Christensen et al., 2001). The argument is that as companies progress into increasing levels of global success, exploitation of new markets via incremental entry with risky, new, and innovative products or product variations becomes increasingly more difficult to justify to shareholders who want predictable, stable growth – avoiding any uncertainty of equity appreciation. Christensen argues that particularly because of this success, Japan has lost its competitive edge in developing the risky products that it was once adept at introducing and managing. Although our study focuses on banking and not, for example, consumer electronics where the disruptive technology argument might be even more relevant, the increase in uncertainty avoidance observed in our study during the same period seems to go hand in hand. Additionally, Child and McGrath (2001) support this position in arguing the idea that *paradox* and *disembodiment* are likely to be important "core themes of the postmodern organization." The question is whether new policies and developments will be able to jumpstart the important drive to foster appropriate risk-taking and innovation in the face of apprehension.

Power Distance

In our examination of power distance, the research indicated a "cross over" effect – whereby the following was observed: (a) The Japanese and United States samples increased in power distance during the period; (b) Japan was at a higher position relative to the United States for this dimension in 1985 and was in a lower relative position for this dimension in 2000. This is an interesting phenomenon, indicating the possibility that at some point during the period, Japan and the United States directly converged on this parameter, then crossed and switched relative positions, with the United States holding a higher position. This could be the result of increased stratification between rank and file and high-level managers in the United States as mid-level management begins to feel the effects of factors such as downsizing.

This suggests the possibility that middle layers of hierarchy might facilitate interactions or perceptions of contact that ease the propensity for increased power distance. Furthermore, this possibility implies that the elimination of such middle layers might actually increase power distance, which is not out of line with social capital theory, as conceptualized by Coleman (1990), defined as aspects of organizational structure that facilitate interaction/relations among people leading to a desired outcome. Adler and Kwon (2002) recognize a variety of benefits from the development of social capital including improved exchange in information and enhanced communication. For example, mentoring studies have found that less experienced employees can benefit from interaction with senior-level people (Dreher & Ash, 1990) and that the related contacts made within the organization's social network can have a meaningful impact on the protégé's success (Seibert, Kraimer & Liden, 2001). The elimination of middle layers of management may also lead to the elimination of mentoring opportunities and a decrease in meaningful contact opportunities between low-level or new employees and senior-level managers, resulting in a power-distance increase. Furthermore, research is called for to investigate the specific causal mechanisms and endogenous influences behind the observed shift for this dimension.

Crossvergence

Although not explicitly a central aspect of our research, the nature of our findings provides an interesting format from which to consider the convergence hypothesis. The debate between the convergence and divergence perspective is nearly 50 years old and continues today (England & Lee, 1974; England, Negandhi & Wilpert, 1979; Harbison & Myers, 1959; Kelley & Worthley, 1981; Pascale, 1978; Webber, 1969). Multinational companies seek to better understand whether the values of their diverse organizations are becoming more similar (Ricks, Toyne & Martinez 1990). Yip (1992) calls upon organizations to understand diverse value systems and integrate them into a universal corporate culture, whereby value systems of different cultures converge within the specific organization. However, our industry-level findings provide some caution for multinational policies that strive to force convergence. Our findings indicate that it is possible as each subsidiary might have effective, crossvergent modes of reacting to the combination of both cultural foundations and dynamic economic conditions.

Our research found not only converging tendencies between the United States and Japan within the confines of the research context and industry-specific sample but also also divergence. Meaningful insights can be derived from those elements of cultural identity that demonstrated convergence and also from those that did not. This position directly supports Ralston's research (Ralston, Gustafson, Cheung & Terpstra 1993; Ralston et al., 1997), which advocates that convergence and divergence can occur simultaneously. In an important review of the convergence/divergence debate, Child (1981) also found evidence for both convergence and divergence.

Our study found that convergence was specifically not evident in two areas of cultural identification – uncertainty avoidance and power distance. This finding supports earlier work suggesting that some aspects of organizational structure and culture are more subject to change and external environmental pressure than others. For example, Negandhi (1973) found that there is evidence to support the idea that management practices are as much, if not more so, functions of contextual variables such as market conditions as they are sociocultural variables. Our samples demonstrate that, for uncertainty avoidance, divergence actually occurred. We find a mixture of converging and diverging reality depending on which cultural value is being evaluated. A richer understanding of change for industry-level management contexts is in order, supporting Ralston's (1993, 1997) crossvergence position whereby national culture and economic influences mingle to develop a new hybrid culture which is unique. Ralston poses the question as to whether crossvergence is a temporary, transitional state on the path to either convergence or divergence. With the benefit of longitudinal data, we would suggest framing the crossvergence phenomena not so much as a temporary state that eventually leads to either convergence or divergence for the cultural dimension under examination, but rather as a constantly dynamic state, not necessarily on a linear path toward one extreme or the other. Crossvergence suggests that organizations and industries will modify culturally established foundations in response to the external environment in order to remain competitive.

Explicit in the discussion of crossvergence is the recognition that external environmental factors can and do intervene to impact certain aspects of culture. As suggested by Mouer and Sugimoto (1979), skepticism is in order when considering traditional models of Japanese cultural studies that neglect non-cultural possibilities. Although our research spans a 15-year time frame, it is also recognized that non-cultural phenomena could be affecting our findings. These include, for example, membership in various interest groups and the activities such groups pursue (e.g. workplace socialization). However, Mouer and Sugimoto (1979, pp. 32–33) suggest that "careful studies of interest groups at the grass-roots level using cross-sectional and longitudinal data" are in order. In this regard, we believe our research has made a contribution.

Finally, although intuitively suggestive in our research framework, more direct empirical links could be developed to show how specific external environmental pressures, e.g. increased global competition within home-country markets, industry bankruptcy rates, and unemployment, might specifically affect different elements of culture at the organizational level. Moreover, research should examine how the effects of cultural change within institutions may or may not permeate from organizations into other, larger cultural contexts – i.e. the *spillover effects*. In that respect, our study could be expanded to include more countries and other industries, providing a broader base from which to draw conclusions. Additionally, future studies from the same dataset could provide an interesting insight into how propensity to change might be related to such issues as gender and age.

NOTES

1. For a complete review of these cultural identifiers, see Brislin (1993) and Hofstede (1980a, b, 1997).

2. Development of new, innovative, and risky products or services that allows entry into a future market, which has not been fully developed and realized.

REFERENCES

Abegglen, J., & Stalk, G., Jr. (1985). *Kaisha – The Japanese corporation*. New York: Basic Books.

Adler, N. (1997). *International dimensions of organizational behavior* (3rd ed.). Cincinnati, OH: South-Western College Publishing.

Adler, P., & Kwon, S. (2002). Social capital: Prospects for a new concept. *Academy of Management Review, 27*, 17–40.

Armstrong, R. (1996). The relationship between culture and perception of ethical problems in international marketing. *Journal of Business Ethics, 15*, 1199–1208.

Bhappu, A. (2000). The Japanese family: An institutional logic for Japanese corporate networks and Japanese management. *The Academy of Management Review, 25*, 409–415.

Bollen, K. A. (1989). *Structural equations with latent variables*. New York: Wiley.

Bollen, K., & Long, J. (1993). *Testing structural equation models*. Newbury Park, CA: Sage.

Bond, M. (1987). Chinese values and the search for cultural-free dimensions of culture. *Journal of Cross-Cultural Psychology, 18*, 143–164.

Boyacigiller, N., & Adler, N. (1991). The parochial dinosaur: Organizational science in a global context. *Academy of Management Review, 16*, 261–262.

Brislin, R. (1981). *Cross-cultural encounters: Face-to-face interaction*. New York: Pergamon.

Brislin, R. (1993). *Understanding culture's influence on behavior*. Orlando, FL: Harcourt Brace & Co.

Brislin, R., Loaner, W., & Thorndike, R. (1973). *Cross-cultural methods*. New York: Wiley.

Casson, M., & Lundan, S. (1999). Explaining international differences in economic institutions. *International Studies of Management & Organization, 29*, 25–42.

Chatman, J., & Jehn, K. (1994). Assessing the relationship between industry characteristics and organizational culture: How different can you be? *Academy of Management Journal, 37*, 522–553.

Cheung, G., & Chow, H. (1999). Subcultures in Greater China: A comparison of managerial values in the PRC, Hong Kong and Taiwan. *Asia Pacific Journal of Management, 16*, 369–387.

Child, J. (1981). Culture, contingency and capitalism in the cross-national study of organizations. In: L. L. Cummings & B. M. Shaw (Eds), *Research in Organizational Behavior* (pp. 303–356). Greenwich, CT: JAI Press.

Child, J., & McGrath, R. (2001). Organizations unfettered: Organizational form in an information intensive economy. *Academy of Management Journal, 44*, 1135–1148.

Child, J., & Yan, Y. (2001). National and transnational effects in international business: Indications from sino-foreign JVs. *Management International Review, 41*, 53–75.

Christensen, C., Craig, T., & Hart, S. (2001). The great disruption. *Foreign Affairs, 80*, 80–95.

Cohen, D. (1998). Culture, social organization and patterns of violence. *Journal of Personality & Social Psychology, 75*, 408–419.

Coleman, J. (1990). *Foundations of social theory*. Cambridge, MA: Harvard University Press.

Crosby, P. B. (1980). *Quality is free*. New York: Mentor.

Czinkota, M. A., & Ronkainen, I. A. (1998). *International marketing*. Fort Worth, TX: Dryden Press.

Dawson, R. (translation) (1993). *Analects* (Originally 6th-5th century BC). Oxford: Oxford University Press.

Dicken, P. (1998). *Global shift: Transforming the world economy* (3rd ed.). London: Paul Chapman.

DiMaggio, P. J., & Powell, W. W. (1983). The iron cage revisited: Institutional isomorphism and collective rationality in organizational fields. *American Sociological Review, 48*, 147–160.

Dorfman, P., & Howell, J. (1988). Dimensions of national culture and effective leadership patterns. *Advances in International Comparative Management, 3*, 127–150.

Dreher, G., & Ash, R. (1990). A comparative study of mentoring among men and women in managerial, professional and technical positions. *Journal of Applied Psychology, 75*, 539–546.

England, G., & Lee, R. (1974). The relationship between managerial values and managerial success in the United States, Japan, India and Australia. *Journal of Applied Psychology, 59*, 411–419.

England, G., Negandhi, A. R., & Wilpert, B. (1979). *Organizational functioning in a cross-cultural perspective*. Kent, OH: Comparative Administrative Research Institute.

Ferraro, G. (1993). *The cultural dimension of international business*. Englewood Cliffs, NJ: Prentice-Hall.

Fiske, A. P. (1990), *Structures of social life: The four elementary forms of human relations*. New York: Free Press.

Gabor, A. (1990). *The man who discovered quality*. New York: Penguin.

George, R. (1992). *The East-West pendulum*. Englewood Cliffs, NJ: Prentice-Hall.

Hampden-Turner, C., & Trompenaars, F. (1993). *The seven cultures of capitalism*. New York: Bantam Doubleday Dell Publishing.

Harbison, F., & Myers, C. A. (1959). *Management in the industrial world*. New York: McGraw-Hill.

Helweg, D. (2000). Japan: A rising sun? *Foreign Affairs, 79*, 26–52.

Hirschmeier, J., & Yui, T. (1981). *The development of Japanese business, 1600–1980* (2nd ed.). London: Allen & Unwin.

Hofstede, G. (1980a). *Culture's consequence*. Beverly Hills, CA: Sage.

Hofstede, G. (1980b). Motivation, leadership, and organization – Do American theories apply abroad? *Organizational Dynamics* (Summer Issue), 42–63.

Hofstede, G. (1997). *Cultures and organizations – Software of the mind*. New York: McGraw-Hill.

Hofstede, G. (2002). *Cultures recent consequences*. Presentation provided to the University of Hawaii College of Business. Spring, 2002–January 31. Honolulu, HI.

Holt, D., Ralston, D., & Terpstra, R. (1994). Constraints on capitalism in Russia: The managerial psyche, social infrastructure and ideology. *California Management Review, 36*, 124–141.

Jansen, M. (2000). *The making of modern Japan*. Cambridge: Harvard University Press.

Kelley, L., Whatley, A., & Worthley, R. (1987). Assessing the effects of culture on managerial attitudes: A three culture test. *Journal of International Business Studies, 18*, 17–31.

Kelley, L., & Worthley, R. (1981). The role of culture in comparative management: A cross-cultural perspective. *The Academy of Management Journal, 24*, 164–173.

Khera, I. (2001). Business ethics East v. West: Myths and realities. *Journal of Business Ethics, 30*, 29–39.

Makoto, O., & Imanari, T. (1999). Japanese national values and Confucianism. *The Japanese Economy, 27*(March–April).

McDonald, G. (2000). Cross-cultural methodological issues in ethical research. *Journal of Business Ethics, 27*, 89–104.

McLeod, K. (1999). Authenticity within hip-hop cultures threatened with assimilation. *Journal of Communication, 49*, 134–150.

Mitchell, M., Hastings, B., & Tanyel, F. (2001). Generational comparison: Xers in the U.S. and Korea. *International Journal of Commerce & Management, 11*, 35–53.

Morrison, T., Conaway, W., & Borden, G. (1994). *Kiss, bow or shake hands*. Holbrook, MA: Adams Media.

Mouer, R., & Sugimoto, Y. (1979). *Some questions concerning commonly accepted stereotypes of Japanese society*. Australia-Japan Economic Relations Research Project. No. 64. December.

Mouer, R., & Sugimoto, Y. (1986). *Images of Japanese society*. London: KPI.

Negandhi, A. R. (1973). Cross-cultural studies: too many conclusions, not enough conceptualization. In: A. Neghandi (Ed.), *Modern Organizational Theory*. Kent, OH: Kent State University.

Ogbor, J. (2000). Organizational leadership and authority relations across cultures: Beyond divergence and convergence. *International Journal of Commerce and Management, 10*, 48–73.

Ohmae, K. (1990). *The borderless world: Power and strategy in the interlinked economy*. New York: Harper Business.

Oyserman, D., Kemmelmeier, M., & Coon, H. (2002). Cultural psychology – A new look: Reply to Bond (2002), Fiske (2002), Kitayama (2002), and Miller (2002). *Psychological Bulletin, 128*, 110–117.

Pascale, R. T. (1978). Communication and decision-making across cultures: Japanese and American comparisons. *Administrative Science Quarterly, 23*, 91–110.

Pauley, L., & Reich, S. (1997). National structures and multinational corporate behavior: enduring differences in the age of globalization. *International Organization, 51*, 1–30.

Peterson, R. B., & Shimada, J. Y. (1978). Sources of management problems in Japanese-American joint ventures. *Academy of Management Review, 3*, 796–804.

Porter, M. E. (1986). Changing patterns of international competition. *California Management Review, 28*, 9–40.

Porter, M. E., Takeuchi, H., & Sakakibara, M. (2000). *Can Japan compete?* Cambridge, MA: Perseus.

Ralston, D., Gustafson, D., Cheung, F., & Terpstsra, R. (1993). Differences in managerial values: A study of US, Hong Kong and PRC managers. *Journal of International Business Studies, 24*, 249–275.

Ralston, D., Holt, D., Terpstra, R., & Kai-Cheng, Y. (1997). The impact of national culture and economic ideology on managerial work values: A study of the U.S., Russia, Japan and China. *Journal of International Business Studies, 28*, 177–207.

Renshaw, J. (1999). *Kimono in the board room*. Oxford: Oxford University Press.

Ricks, D., Toyne, B., & Martinez, Z. (1990). Recent developments in international management research. *Journal of Management, 16*, 219–253.

Rose, E., & Ito, K. (2004). M & A's in the Japanese banking industry: Past and future. In: T. Roehl & A. Bird (Eds), *Advances in International Management, Japanese Firms in Transition: Responding to the Global Challenge, 17*.

Schreffler, R. (2001). Foreign fit, domestic finish in auto industry partnerships. *Japan Quarterly, 48,* 42–49.

Schwartz, S. H. (1990). Individualism-collectivism: Critique and proposed refinements. *Journal of Cross-Cultural Psychology, 21,* 139–157.

Seibert, S., Kraimer, M., & Liden, R. (2001). A social capital theory of career success. *Academy of Management Journal, 44,* 219–237.

Slotterback, C., & Saarnio, D. (1996). Attitudes toward older adults reported by young adults: Variation based on attitudinal task and attribute categories. *Psychology & Aging, 11,* 563–571.

Takato, D. (2002). Corporate failures soar to 17-year high in Japan. *The Honolulu Advertiser.* Tuesday, January 22.

Takezawa, S., & Whitehill, A. M. (1981). *Workway: Japan and America.* Tokyo: Japan Institute of Labor.

Taylor, S. (2000). Review – Kimono in the boardroom: The invisible evolution of Japanese women managers. *The Academy of Management Review, 25,* 670–672.

Triandis, H. (1972). *The analysis of subjective culture.* New York: Wiley.

Triandis, H. (1977). Subjective culture and interpersonal relations across cultures. In: L. Loeb-Adler (Ed.), *Issues in Cross-Cultural Research. Annals of the New York Academy of Sciences, 285,* 418–434.

Triandis, H. (1989). The self and social behavior in differing cultural contexts. *Psychological Reivew, 96,* 506–520.

Triandis, H. (1995). *Individualism and collectivism.* Boulder, CO: Westview Press.

Van Wolferen, (1989). *The enigma of Japanese power.* London: Macmillan.

Webber, R. A. (1969). Convergence or divergence? *Columbia Journal of World Business, 4,* 75–83.

Whitehill, A., & Takezawa, S. (1968). *The other worker.* Honolulu, HI: East-West Center.

Yip, G. (1992). *Total global strategy: Managing for worldwide competitive advantage.* Englewood Cliffs, NJ: Prentice-Hall.

Yoneyama, L. (1999). Habits of knowing cultural differences: Chrysanthemum and the sword in the U.S. liberal multiculturalism. *Topoi, 18,* 71–80.

Zielenziger, M. (2002). Japan addresses bad-loan problem. *The Mercury News.* October 31.

LEARNING PROCESS AND THE DYNAMICS OF CORPORATE GOVERNANCE SYSTEMS: THE CASE OF JAPAN

Christine Pochet

ABSTRACT

This paper questions the issue of the dynamics of corporate governance in Japan using a conceptual framework adapted from North's theory of institutional change. National systems of corporate governance can indeed be considered a particular case of institutions. We thus suggest transposing North's propositions about institutional change to national systems of corporate governance. As an illustration for our propositions, we choose to use a case study: the so-called Sogo crisis. The Sogo group is a Japanese chain of department stores, which has encountered financial problems in the late 1990s. The handling of those difficulties by the firm's main stakeholders highlights both the recent changes in the Japanese system of corporate governance and the resistance opposed to them.

INTRODUCTION

Globalization of capital markets coupled with the remarkable performance of the Japanese economy throughout the 1980s have brought about an increase in

Japanese Firms in Transition: Responding to the Globalization Challenge
Advances in International Management, Volume 17, 31–60
Copyright © 2005 by Elsevier Ltd.
All rights of reproduction in any form reserved
ISSN: 0747-7929/doi:10.1016/S0747-7929(04)17002-9

the number of comparative studies of national systems of corporate governance. Corporate governance, defined as "the set of organizational mechanisms which constrain managerial discretion and influence decision making" (Charreaux, 1997), can be approached from a microeconomic point of view (i.e. the governance structures of an individual firm), or on a macroeconomic level. In the latter case, macroeconomic approaches deal with national governance systems, and aim at understanding how the institutional framework in a given country (or group of countries) influences managerial discretion in decision-making. Macroeconomic studies generally proceed by stylizing governance structures of large, listed firms, implicitly taken to be representative of the "national model."

Comparative research on corporate governance takes place within a contractual theoretical framework. It has generally followed two distinct paths. First, comparison of corporate governance systems has given rise to proposals of classification (Berglöf, 1990; Franks & Mayer, 1998; Moerland, 1995), all based on the dominant type of control mechanism. In contrast to Anglo-Saxon systems, which belong to a market-oriented type of control mechanism, the Japanese system of governance is grounded in a network-oriented control mechanism. In a dynamic perspective, the issue of the convergence of corporate governance systems as a result of market globalization is also frequently addressed. Second, assuming that there is a link between corporate governance and firm efficiency, some scholars (Rajan & Zingales, 1998) have tried to identify the characteristics of efficient national governance systems and apply these criteria in comparing existing systems. In particular, considering the tendency to mimic the Anglo-Saxon model in developed economies, the superiority of this system compared to others and its transportability to other contexts, especially other cultural contexts, is brought into question.

The aim of this paper is to examine how the Japanese system of governance has been transformed over the last decade (1990–2001) and to offer an interpretation based on North's theory of institutional change (North, 1990, 1993, 1994). Because of its general nature North's explanatory model logically provides a framework that can be used to analyze the dynamics of governance systems. Using this framework, it is possible to go beyond the analyses made on this theme by the two main perspectives: law (La Porta, Lopez-de-Silanes, Shleifer & Vishny, 1997, 1998, 1999a, b) and politics (Roe, 1990, 1994, 2000). It also offers the advantage of bringing together in one analytical framework – built around the concept of learning – individual behavior and institutional evolution. This is useful because, when studying corporate governance, it is also possible to link individual decisions made by the stakeholders of a given firm to the way governance mechanisms operate at the macroeconomic level (Pochet, 2002). For that reason, in order to test the likelihood of the propositions we had made, we felt it was useful to complement our study of the recent changes in the Japanese governance system with a case study which highlights the link between system and structures. We chose Sogo department stores because of their exemplary nature. The handling of the financial distress the group had to face by the different stakeholders, and in particular the turnaround by the Japanese government, brings out both the ongoing evolutions and the factors which oppose them.

The paper is organized as follows. The first section describes the main changes which the Japanese system of governance has undergone over the last ten years. The second section presents North's conceptual framework and his main proposals concerning the mechanism of institutional change. A series of propositions about the process by which a system of governance evolves is derived from them. Lastly, the case study of the Sogo group is related to the points developed in the first part and serves to illustrate the previously forged explanatory framework. The paper sheds light on the role of learning in the dynamics of the Japanese governance system, showing the way it influences decision-making by both individuals and organizations. The result is a mix of deliberate breaking with former rules of governance and permanence of certain behavior models.

RECENT EVOLUTION OF THE JAPANESE SYSTEM OF GOVERNANCE: THE END OF THE J-MODEL?

The J-model is a term coined by Aoki (1990) to depict the Japanese firm, using a stylized, fact-based methodology. According to this model, Japanese firms possess some specific features such as horizontal coordination among operating units, contingent monitoring[1] of management by the main bank, and dual influence of shareholders and employees' interests upon managerial decisions. Together with a view of the Japanese firm, this description provides a model of Japanese corporate governance as it was working at the end of the 1980s. Since then, however, pressure from the United States combined with the long-lasting decline in the performance of Japanese companies throughout the 1990s has caused the Japanese government and major business organizations to reflect on corporate governance. This resulted first in the publication of reports on the subject, notably one made by Keidanren (Federation of Japanese Business Organizations) whose aim was to set forth guidelines for efficient governance based on the Anglo-Saxon model. It also eventually led to a series of reforms aimed at modifying the legal framework for corporate governance. The reform movement begun in the financial sphere in the early 1980s has thus continued throughout the 1990s in spite of the banking crisis. It has even spread further, bringing within its circle corporate law, bankruptcy law and accounting principles. The first subsection sets out these legislative changes. During the same period, notable changes in the behavior of some stakeholders in

Japanese companies (e.g. stockholders, the main bank) have been observed. These changes are described in the second and third subsections.

Legal Changes and their Impact on Governance

The term "insider system," when applied to the Japanese model of corporate governance, alludes to the ownership structure, and in a related way, to the composition of the board of directors of Japanese firms. Their members indeed typically include a large number of the firm's employees, mainly drawn from the ranks of middle executives. There are advantages to this system: for the employees of Japanese firms, the possibility of becoming an administrator one day is powerful motivation. However, the almost total absence of external administrators raises the question of the independence of the board of directors with regard to management. The very fact that internal promotion is seen as a means of obtaining a seat on the board means that there is a subordinate relationship between a majority of the administrators and the management they are supposed to monitor. It is consequently not surprising that the working of Japanese boards of directors has come under vigorous criticism (Kanie, 1998; Yoshimori, 1998), nor that enforced protection of minority shareholders has been demanded by many people.

Dore (2000) places the start of reforms explicitly designed to strengthen stockholders' rights in 1993, when an amendment to the Code of Commerce was voted for that made it easier to bring a civil suit for mismanagement against company directors. Table 1 exhibits the main reforms of the Japanese Commercial Code and the law on stock exchange transactions (*Securities and Exchange Law*) during the 1990s. Their explicit aim is to bring the national system of governance closer to the Anglo-Saxon standards. It is noteworthy that while certain changes incorporated by these reforms are in response to demands from the business community, in particular Keidanren, other changes met with that same community's determined opposition. Thus, the Commercial Code amendments to lift the restrictions on stock options and share buy-backs or the introduction of a holding company structure corresponded to the wishes of Japanese management. However, the reform of accounting principles and the easing of restraints on taking legal action against directors in cases of mismanagement met with strong resistance on the part of Japanese business organizations. On this last point, Keidanren has not abandoned all hope of making the government backtrack, and in its year 2000 report, it proposes substantial modifications of the 1993 law, which aim at limiting the financial consequences for managers when they are sued for mismanagement.

More generally, some scholars such as Kawamoto (1999) have pointed out that the reform process in Japan, especially regarding deregulation, is arduous due to the existence of a so-called "iron triangle" determined to resist fundamental change

Table 1. Legal Reforms Over the 1990s Decade and Intended Impact on Governance.

Area of Reform	Application Date	Implemented Modifications	Objectives in Terms of Governance
Supervising committee (Kansayakkai)	1993	Increase in number of members from two to three, of whom one outsider	Increase in degree of independence of supervising committee and of its ability to work towards improving monitoring of management
Prosecution of directors in civil courts by shareholders for mismanagement	1993	Cut in the cost of legal proceedings	Increase in the number of civil actions taken by minority shareholders: about 200 per year on average according to Dore (2000); the financial risk hanging over the directors is an incentive to perform their duties towards minority shareholders loyally
Stock options	1997	Lift of ban on stock options	A growing number of listed firms are introducing stock option schemes; this kind of mechanism aims at aligning the objectives of shareholders and managers
Share buy-backs	1995	Lift of ban on share buy-backs	By 1998, 45% of listed firms had announced plans for share buy-backs, but only 20% of them implemented it (Yasui, 1999)
	1998	Increase in proportion of capital made open to repurchase	Repurchase of stock can be interpreted as a re-injection of the free cash flow into the market to be used more effectively
Creation of holding companies	1997	Lift of ban on creation of holding companies	Several listed firms have adopted this structure; the multiplication of holding companies creates favorable conditions for the development of mergers and brings into being a new form of control over Japanese management through the risk of takeover bids

Table 1. (*Continued*)

Area of Reform	Application Date	Implemented Modifications	Objectives in Terms of Governance
Accounting principles	1997	Introduction of consolidated financial statements	The reform of accounting principles aims at bringing them into closer harmony with the international standards as defined by the IASC (International Accounting Standard Committee)
	1999	Obligation to show consolidated accounts for those firms whose securities are traded on a market	The reform's objective is to improve the quality of the information made available to investors by abandoning certain rules (the lower-of-cost-or- market method) and by limiting risks of dressing up of financial statements
	2000/2001	Introduction of market-based valuation of financial products	
Bankruptcies	2000	Abolition of the composition law and introduction of a new rehabilitation proceeding	The new procedure is directly based on chapter 11 of the American law and aims at facilitating the reorganization of a distressed firm; its adoption has meant the transfer of power from creditors to management

in government practices. Borrowed from political sciences, the concept of an iron triangle refers to an integrated leadership triangle composed of local politicians from the Liberal Democratic Party (LDP), major corporations, and bureaucrats. Although not confined to Japan, such a phenomenon plays a particularly strong role in a country where the links between the administration and large firms have traditionally been strong.

If the legal reforms described in Table 1 appear to open up the way to a significant evolution of the Japanese system of governance, one should not overestimate their immediate impact. First, they mostly concern only the largest corporations. Second, although these changes may basically be seen as conforming to world standards, one cannot assume that they will go beyond formal resemblance and achieve functional similarity. For example, Dore argues that since the 1993 amendment was passed, the number of civil actions taken by minority shareholders against directors of large firms increased only modestly. This suggests that some cases may have been settled out of court or even brought by blackmailing *sokaiya*. In the same way, while it was intended to increase the independence of the supervising committee, the reform of 1993 did not achieve this goal as firms have bypassed the new regulation by enlisting their auditors among former executives or among the parent company's auditors (Yoshimori, 1995). Finally, the introduction of a new bankruptcy procedure modeled on the United States's Chap. 11, although it implies a legal convergence with the United States model, may result in an impediment for corporate restructuring in Japan in so far as it widens managerial discretion over the troubled firm's future. Designed to replace the Composition Law (*wagihô*), the Civil Rehabilitation Law (*minjisaiseihô*) has been especially aimed at small and medium-size companies. As for larger firms, they come under the Corporate Reorganization Law enacted in 1952. Significantly, since its enforcement in April 2000, large companies have been making extensive use of the new rehabilitation procedure. The success met by the new procedure is such that between April 2000 (when it was brought into force) and December of the same year, the number of procedures opened increased fourfold compared to that of compositions for the same period of the year before (Nihon Keizai Shimbun, January 24, 2001). The reason for this may be not only that the new bankruptcy regime eases filing for court protection and enables much speedier action on restructuring plans, but also that it provides an attractive alternative to harsher procedures.

Weakening of Control by Banks

At the end of the 1970s and throughout the 1980s, the deregulation of financial institutions carried out by the Japanese government manifested itself in profound reforms in banking and securities exchange laws. Although the explicit object of these reforms was not to transform governance practices in Japanese firms, they have nonetheless produced profound upheavals in this field.

First, the protection that the banks had enjoyed due to the regulation of financial markets after the war has gradually been eroded as the financial liberalization process proceeded. From the middle of the 1980s onward, competition from foreign and domestic financial markets increased because of the more favorable financial conditions they offered borrowers. Thus, large firms significantly reduced the share of intermediate funding in their total external resources. Consequently, competition between banks has intensified, thus allowing firms to negotiate more favorable credit terms. At the same time, the decompartmentalization of financial activities allowed banks to broaden the range of services they offer to firms. As a result, the anchor point of the customer relationship between large Japanese firms and their main bank has moved from loans to a diversified range of financial services. Finally, the conditions for intermediate financing have been profoundly modified by the deregulation of the banking sector and particularly by the progressive liberalization of deposit rates. As Guichard (1996) points out, this has led to pressure to raise remuneration of deposits by the large banks which the latter have not been able or willing to carry over to credit rates in order to keep their market share. All these factors have played their part in eroding bank margins and have brought about a transformation of the relationship between firms and banks in Japan.

Nevertheless, it is the economic slowdown of the 1990s and the collapse of the financial "bubble" that, by materializing the risks accumulated by the banking sector, have precipitated the evolution of the relationship between Japanese firms and their main bank. Anxious to offset the dwindling of their funding to large firms, banks have increased the proportion of their loans made to riskier market segments: medium-sized firms, households and real estate. Thus, far from decreasing during the 1980s, bank funding has strongly increased (8–9% on annual average during the second half of the 1980s), and this progression was fostered by the euphoria prevailing in the real-estate market which contributed to the revaluation of collaterals. In these circumstances, the turnabout of the assets markets has caused an accumulation of bad debts on banks' balance sheets. Consequently, banks, which had progressively lost their incentive to exercise control over large firms as a result of the decrease in loans made to this customer segment, now found they lacked the means to help firm in financial difficulties. This had been one of the important functions they carried out in accordance with the prevalent logic in bank-oriented systems (Hoshi, Kashyap & Scharfstein, 1990). Since the late 1990s, there has been an increase in bankruptcies of firms in which the main banks refused any additional aid or any help in reorganizing the debt which would have resulted in disproportionate sacrifice on their part. In governance terms, this loosening of control by banks over large firms raises the question of the protection of the other shareholders, who can no longer hope to free-ride on the monitoring effort the main banks had formerly been willing to make.

Increased Pressure from Shareholders

This phenomenon is linked to modifications in the ownership structure of Japanese firms resulting from a major trend – the dilution of cross-shareholding between large corporations and their main bank. This phenomenon appears to be an indirect consequence of the banking crisis. Major Japanese banks hold stock portfolios whose value in 2001 amounted to as much as 1.6 times the total of their capital account. This stock was the source of important unrealized profits, which represented the difference between the net book value of securities and their market value. However, these unrealized profits grew progressively smaller partly because of a fall in market prices and partly due to the obligation the banks faced to realize part of these profits in order to finance the write-off of bad loans. Moreover, from fiscal 2001 on, mark-to-market accounting was introduced in all banks. As a result, because of the size of their stock portfolios, Japanese banks were very much exposed to share price volatility. To mitigate this price fluctuation risk, they had to cut their shareholding to lower levels, which resulted in the unwinding of cross-shareholding of stocks between banks and firms (Bank of Japan, 2001). In order to speed up this process, in 2001 the Japanese government established restrictions concerning the value of stock that a bank could hold. In concrete terms, they must restrict the amount of their stockholding within the limit of their own capital and must part with excess stock within a given period of time. Thus, the general reduction in cross-shareholding which began around 1992 (Fukao, 1999) will in all likelihood increase in the near future. Opening up Japanese companies' capital to outsiders contributed to the substitution of partners who were anxious to maintain a long-term business relationship with others who were more inclined to demand satisfactory profitability on the part of management. With the coming of foreign investors, the Japanese market has indeed seen the introduction of active control as practiced by American institutional investors, in particular CalPERS, which has invested more than 4 billion yen in Japanese firms and published in 1998 a code of best practices concerning corporate governance. The market has also seen diffusion among Japanese investors who are, in turn, making themselves heard. Yasui (1999) notes that foreign investors' influence is greater than their relative importance in terms of capitalization (about 10% at the end of 1998) due to the lack of liquidity in the financial market resulting from the large proportion of stable investors. In terms of market turnover, foreign investors represented a third in 1998.

In light of this brief review of the main changes in the Japanese system of corporate governance over the last ten years, we now propose a framework in which to analyze the dynamics of corporate governance systems.

THE DYNAMICS OF CORPORATE GOVERNANCE SYSTEMS: A CONCEPTUAL FRAMEWORK

The evolution of national systems of corporate governance is still a very recent area of scholarship. As noted in the Introduction, more research has been devoted to comparing systems in different countries. In other respects, some historical studies concerning the American system of governance (Calomiris & Rammirez, 1996; Kroszner & Rajan, 1994; Simon, 1998), or the Japanese one (Okazaki, 2000; Takeda, 1999), provide interesting insights in terms of static comparison. Nonetheless, we still have a very fragmentary understanding of the way in which one system evolves into another, as we lack a real theory of the evolution of corporate governance institutions.

Some studies on comparative corporate governance do, however, cast light on the origins of present day systems and thus on the dynamics that led to their emergence, with the aim of explaining the existence of differences between these systems. These studies share a common characteristic: they tend to spotlight one particular explanatory factor and, for this reason, will be termed monocausal approaches. After briefly presenting their arguments, we will consider North's theory of institutional change. As Charreaux (1997) points out, by removing the hypothesis of an exogenous institutional framework implicitly stated by the contractual theories of the firm, North's approach can provide an explanatory framework for the evolution of corporate governance systems.

Monocausal Approaches

Two perspectives can be distinguished among the monocausal approaches towards the evolution of corporate governance systems. One series of studies made by La Porta et al. (1997, 1998, 1999a, b) emphasizes the influence of the legal system and especially the amount of protection it provides to investors, to explain the characteristics of a governance system. The political approach, however, considers that the set of institutions of corporate governance is directly influenced by the prevailing ideology in a given national sphere, in which ideology is embodied in the political institutions. This thesis has been expounded by Roe (1994, 2000). Such a distinction between a legal and a political approach actually takes place within a current debate confronting Coffee (1999) and Roe (2000) as to which explanation better suits the evidence of a sharp disparity among national systems, especially when comparing the importance of equity markets.

The Legal Approach
The main results of La Porta et al. may be summarized as follows. When the ownership of large companies in developed economies is observed, firms controlled by families or the State seem to be the norm and managerial firms the exception. Consequently, the agency problem in these firms occurs less between professional managers and shareholders than between controlling and minority shareholders (La Porta et al., 1999a). Similarly, there exist significant cross-national differences in the size of financial markets and also in commercial law (La Porta et al., 1997). A common classification of commercial legal systems contrasts common law systems with those based on Roman law. The analysis of their contents in terms of mechanisms designed to protect outside investors (i.e. both shareholders and creditors) highlights the fact that common law systems afford these stakeholders far better protection than do those based on Roman law (La Porta et al., 1998).

The legal tradition suggests that there is a causal link between these diverse empirical findings and considers that the degree of protection provided to investors by corporate law will strongly influence the way a given national system of governance is structured. In particular, highly protective systems can be associated with flourishing financial markets, a lower degree of ownership concentration, and an efficient allocation of funding between firms. Providing outside investors a better protection therefore becomes the set goal for countries that do not yet fulfill the necessary condition for a satisfactory development of financial markets (La Porta et al., 1999b). The legal approach thus makes legal reforms, and more specifically those reforms that strengthen the rights of outside investors, the driving force behind the evolution of national systems of corporate governance.[2]

The Political Approach
Roe's (1994) research concerned initially the USA, and he first stated his political thesis under the following terms: the rise of the public firm in the United States results at least as much from favorable political conditions as from a process of natural selection which would be the sign of the high degree to which this organizational form is adapted to the needs of the American economy. Roe demonstrates how American-style populism fragmented financial intermediaries, making dispersed ownership inevitable in the United States. In order to fill out his analysis, he then goes on (Roe, 2000) to study European countries and gives

evidence of a close correlation between the place those countries occupy on a left-right political continuum on the one hand, and on a close-to-diffuse ownership continuum, on the other hand. Thus, social democracies show public firms with a concentrated ownership structure, which remains the best way for shareholders to control higher managerial agency costs. It is possible to draw an implication in terms of dynamics from this political explanation of the differences between national systems of corporate governance: in a given country, the evolution of corporate governance institutions is linked to political change. Consistent with this view, Roe and Bebchuk (1999) have stressed the importance of path dependency in predicting the future evolution of corporate governance systems. They argue that both "sunk adaptive costs, complementarities, network externalities, endowment effects, and multiple optima" and persistence of a rent-seeking behavior by those who benefit from existing corporate structures may constrain and probably overcome the competitive forces pushing for convergence of corporate governance systems.

To sum up, the current debate as to which way governance systems evolve over time seems to take place within the usual disagreement between neoclassical economists emphasizing efficiency considerations and other scholars who see political forces and path dependency as principally shaping and constraining this evolution. However, the political explanation of the change in systems of governance does not appear to be incompatible with an analysis made in terms of the evolution of legal rules. On the contrary, in so far as the latter can be considered to reflect a political line, both explanations offered by monocausal approaches appear to be largely complementary, provided that the legal domain under consideration is not restricted to those laws that protect investors but is extended to include the whole legal system. For this reason, it seems fruitful to go beyond monocausal approaches and attempt to develop a more global conceptual framework. In this respect, the one forged by North to analyze institutional change appears to be relevant in so far as it can be applied to systems of governance.

Going Beyond Monocausal Approaches: The Theory of Institutional Change Applied to Systems of Corporate Governance

North's contribution to economic analysis is the result of a continuous improvement, in process for the last 30 years, of a fundamental idea: that of institution. *Institutional Change and American Economic Growth*, written in collaboration with Lance Davis in 1971, introduces for the first time the idea of institution, thus providing a new interpretation of economic growth in the United States. Continuing the work of Coase (1937) on transaction costs, North brings back into economic analysis the notions of formal rules, political decisions and collective action which had for a long time been excluded and confined to the spheres of law, political science, and sociology (Myhram & Weingast, 1994). Having also directed his attention to institutional dynamics, he has related economic analysis to history. Finally, with the aim of enhancing the explanatory power of his conceptual framework, North refined it by including the latest results of a scientific discipline whose contribution he deems to be essential for the understanding of institutional change: cognitive sciences.

After giving a synthesis of the conceptual framework developed by North for institutional change analysis, we will examine the way in which it can be adapted to systems of corporate governance which are seen as a particular type of institution settings.

North's Contribution to the Theory of Institutional Change

We present North's principal propositions about institutional change in two parts: first, we show how the institutional framework influences decision-making at a moment in time; then, we describe factors that drive institutional change and the process by which institutions evolve over time.

Static analysis: Decision-making in a given institutional framework. The analytical framework is fundamentally that of neoclassical theory. North (1994) retains the assumption of scarcity and hence competition, as well as the analytical tools of microeconomic theory. This framework is, however, modified through re-examination of the rationality assumption, and by adding the dimension of time to the analysis. The two are moreover partly linked as, in a dynamic context, decision-making is made more difficult because of the uncertainty surrounding the future. Making explicit reference to Simon (1986), North considers that under conditions of uncertainty, substantive rationality does not hold in explaining individual choices. Rather, modeling the latter will require the use of procedural rationality. This means, in particular, that these choices depend on the way each individual perceives the surrounding reality, and this perception in turn depends on the way the mind interprets the information it receives. North uses the term mental models to describe the interpretative schemes through which each individual models their perception of the environment and of the opportunities that it provides. These perceptions aggregate to form belief systems and ideologies. Ideologies are made up of a framework of mental models shared by a plurality of individuals, which provides both an interpretation of the environment and a prescription as to how that environment should be structured. The concepts of belief system and of ideology form the link between individual mental models and institutions, the latter being defined as "the humanly devised constraints that structure human interaction." At any moment in time, the institutional framework that is in force in a given society is the embodiment of the prevailing ideology. The idea of bargaining power is explicit in North (1993, p. 3; 1994, p. 361), who clearly indicates that the rules in force, or at least the formal rules, have been created to serve the interests of those who had the power to make them. While there is a logical relation from mental models to institutions, the converse is also true. Indeed, the institutional framework, inasmuch as it forms an incentive structure to individual action, is one of the essential ingredients in the formation of mental models. In particular, it models the perceived benefits by individuals and organizations of acquiring different kinds of skills and knowledge.

Dynamic analysis: The process of institutional change. Using a sports metaphor, North (1990) considers that institutions are the rules of the game, and organizations are the players. Building a theory of institutions that includes an explanation of their evolution requires conceptually differentiating the rules, be they formal or informal, with their own enforcement characteristics, from the players, e.g. the organizations that bring together individuals bound by a common purpose to achieve objectives. With this separation, it becomes possible to base a theory of institutional change on the dynamics of individual choices.

Choices are made, as we have just seen, under the constraints imposed by institutions. However, the institutional framework will evolve and be altered, precisely because it is the outcome of decisions taken by individuals who, like the organizations that coordinate their actions, have a perception of their environment that changes over time. Institutional change thus arises out of the continual interaction between institutions and organizations in a context of scarcity and hence competition. Competition forces organizations to continually invest in skills and knowledge to survive. The learning process that results, both individual and organizational, is the driving force behind institutional change. Through this learning process, and also because of exogenous changes in the external environment, mental models evolve to allow individuals to perceive new opportunities, with higher pay-offs, in a modified institutional context.

As we have already shown, it is the bargaining power between the opposing interests that determine the new rules, which finally emerge. Institutional change thus bears two characteristics. It is incremental and path-dependent: It is incremental in that the learning process presupposes a progressive accumulation of knowledge, either the result of experience[3] or acquired in a formal manner, and it is path-dependent because of the cultural heritage passed on from one generation to another. The integration of the cultural dimension into the theory of institutional change is one of the characteristics of this analytical framework that makes its application to national systems of corporate governance particularly attractive.

From Institutional Change to the Dynamics of Corporate Governance Systems
According to the definition given in the Introduction, a national system of corporate governance can be seen as a subset of a country's global institutional framework, i.e. that part of it comprising the institutions whose aim is to limit managerial discretion. It seems possible therefore to derive from the theoretical framework proposed by North some specific propositions concerning the evolution of corporate governance systems over time. This task has already been performed by Wirtz (2000), who applied it to the French system of governance. The set of propositions we set out here derive from a somewhat different reading of North's work as we give less importance to the individual entrepreneur's role in the process of change in governance system and also to the link between managerial discretion and a firm's sources of finance.

Our starting point in attempting to adapt North's propositions to corporate governance systems is to specify, in the case of corporate governance, which part of the environment mental models represent. If, as North suggests, the institutional framework embodies the prevailing ideology in a given society, it is necessary to specify the nature of the object these shared mental representations are applied to and the prescriptions they convey in connection with it.

In this respect, a survey of the academic literature and of the public debate on corporate governance shows that the latter relates to the source, the use, and the limits of power in the firm. To specify the first of these, i.e. to address the question of the legitimacy of power, and then to depict the way this power should be exercised, implies reference, at least implicitly, to a representation of what a firm is. This means, in turn, raising the question of its constituents and of whose interests its managers should serve.

From a theoretical point of view, there is a plurality of competing models of the firm. According to their implications, they can be classified in two categories in terms of governance: those for which the owners' interests constitute the ultimate objective of management may be referred to as shareholder theories of the firm; those that adopt a pluralistic conception of the firm and of the interests its managers should take into account belong to stakeholder theories. Regarding the reality of control rights allocation in the firm, comparative corporate governance scholarship sheds light on cross-national differences in this matter. For example, according to Yoshimori (1995), the Japanese concept of the corporation is a pluralistic one, which means "the firm belongs to all the stakeholders, with the employees' interests taking precedence." Conversely, in the U.K. and the U.S., the prevalent concept is a shareholder-oriented one, where the firm is the private property of its owners. Hence, our first proposition:

Proposition 1. Where corporate governance is concerned, ideologies provide a representation of what a firm is and a prescription as to whose interests it should be run for. A national system of corporate governance is the embodiment at a moment of time of the prevailing ideology concerning corporate governance.

The shared mental models, in which ideologies consist, will evolve through time, in matters of corporate governance as elsewhere. Consequently, national systems of governance will also evolve. The mainspring of this evolution is the learning process. This dimension, essential to institutional dynamics, is the focus of North's more recent work (Denzau & North, 1994). Learning is described there as developing a structure to interpret the varied data provided by the world. Built upon the experiences of the individual, this structure consists of categories that serve as a basis for forming mental constructs. Some experiences will confirm and reinforce previous categories and models, while others will lead to modifications.

However, the feedback derived from new experiences may lead to two forms of learning. North distinguishes between the simple parameter updating (similar to that of a computer) and the change in the structure of concepts and mental models termed representational redescription. Taken from Clark and Karmiloff-Smith (1993), this concept denotes the reorganization of categories and concepts leading to the forging of an increasing number of abstract mental constructs. Typically, the reconceptualization associated with representational redescription occurs when prior beliefs fail to solve problems that individuals have not previously experienced.

While the first type of evolution is by nature slow and gradual, representational redescription is associated with more radical changes. The evolution of mental models in the long term can thus be described using a punctuated equilibrium model (Denzau & Grossman, 1993), i.e. as a series of long periods of slow, gradual change punctuated by relatively short periods during which a break occurs. Those periods are likely to coincide with representational redescription.

However, in order to understand how ideologies evolve we need to move from the individual to the social level. This raises the problem – which has not yet been solved – of the aggregation of changes in individual mental models. In this matter, North considers that the work of Bikhchandani, Hirshleifer, and Welch (1992) on information cascades opens up promising perspectives.[4] To sum up:

Proposition 2. National systems of corporate governance evolve under the influence of the dynamics of mental models through the learning process. The pace of this process is not constant; it accelerates for relatively brief periods.

Proposition 2 may relate to Japan in so far as the economic and financial crisis placed most economic agents in a situation they had not faced before. In such a case, customary behaviors may not be effective any more. The issue is then to understand how individuals will change their way to react to the new problems they have to solve and how they come to redesign their representation of the outside world. The relative stability of the Japanese governance system that emerged at the end of World War II compared to the change that occurred throughout the 1990s also exemplifies a sudden acceleration in the pace of evolution of the corporate governance system.

The following proposition concerns the orientation taken by the evolution of national systems of corporate governance. Proposition 1 underlined the fact that a national system of governance reflects the allocation of power made at a moment in time, in both formal and informal ways, between the various stakeholders of the firm. In this respect, the legal system in particular performs a crucial function by codifying the respective duties of the firm and its stakeholders. Nevertheless, in so far as this allocation reflects the bargaining power of these different stakeholders, it is liable to evolve over time, either because the balance of power is modified or because the most powerful among the stakeholders sees a new opportunity to reinforce interests.

Because it is impossible to directly influence informal rules, legal reform is the preferred means of intentionally modifying systems of corporate governance. North (1993, p. 1) underlines the fact that these reforms are induced by economic or social organizations (through the person of their leaders who are called entrepreneurs) pressuring political bodies. As regards corporate governance, business organizations, trade unions, and associations of minority shareholders are likely to play this role in the evolution of legislation. As noted previously, in the Japanese case, Keidanren has played a significant role in either pushing some legal changes (as was the case with stock-options, share buybacks and holding companies) or lobbying to reduce their impact (as in the case of the amendment on directors' responsibility).

Each bargaining group will try to get the rules modified in a way that most favors its interests given the new for opportunities gain that it perceives. The way these opportunities are perceived depends on the evolution of mental models through the learning process. In this respect, the process of representational redescription may lead to shared mental models that are so modified that the prevailing ideology is replaced by another.

In the case of corporate governance, it means that the underlying vision of the firm will have evolved, thereby causing a redefinition of the hierarchy of the interests involved, according to the new way their relative legitimacy is perceived. The balance of power between the different stakeholders will thus be drastically changed, as will be the action-outcome mappings included in the individual mental models. Therefore, a recasting of the corporate governance system is likely to occur, at least in its formal part. Consequently:

Proposition 3. The direction of change in a national system of corporate governance will depend on the perception by some categories of stakeholders of new gain opportunities, should the rules be altered, and on their ability to impose new rules. The latter may be due to a change in the ideology concerning corporate governance.

We must keep in mind, however, that corporate governance system forms a set of control mechanisms, each linked to the others to form a coherent whole. As others (La Porta et al., 1997) have pointed out, these mechanisms are often interdependent, whether in a complementary or substitutable way. This reciprocally dependent nature of governance institutions confers a high degree of complexity on national systems and makes it very difficult to introduce legal reforms aimed at achieving a particular objective. The modification of any particular governance mechanism may lead to changes in the behavior of the firm's stakeholders that are difficult to foresee, and the result of which may be to hinder or even to thwart the intended effects of the reform. Here again, the foregoing comments provided illustrate this issue. The will to increase the independence of the supervising committee has come up against large firms' reactions, which succeeded in thwarting the new rule. We have here in the sphere of corporate governance an illustration of the difficulties of learning due to the complexity of the real world and to the inadequacy of the information feedback coming from individual experience.

Unlike what would result from instrumental rationality, the action-outcome mappings in individual mental models have no chance of naturally converging, no more than erroneous models have of being corrected. The lack of a clear understanding of the way formal and informal rules interweave and of the relative strictness with which each type of rule is enforced makes it difficult to modify corporate governance systems through legal reforms. It also implies that the transfer to other countries of formal rules, having proved their efficiency in a particular national context, will lead to results very different from those expected (North, 1994, p. 366). Thus:

Proposition 4. The modification of one or more governance mechanisms through the channel of legal reform without taking into consideration the links that exist with the rest of the system can induce unexpected, potentially perverse, side effects.

In the case of Japan, it may be possible to consider that the deregulation of the financial sector throughout the 1980s led to banks that were deprived of incentives to monitor large firms, while at the same time, no substitute disciplinary mechanism had emerged. This "control vacuum," in turn, may explain the increasing pressure by shareholders upon management, as they can no longer free-ride on the main bank's efforts to monitor large firms. In that case, typically, the change in bank governance provoked unforeseen, perverse effects.

The purpose of our last proposition is to make use of North's work to take up the debate on the convergence of national systems of governance. The issue is to argue whether, as an outcome of financial globalization, the Anglo-Saxon norm in corporate governance according to which corporations should be run in the exclusive interests of their shareholders is likely to be adopted by an ever greater number of countries, thus achieving convergence of national systems which noticeably differ today. The question is particularly relevant as regards Japan, whose economy has, since the beginning of the last decade, been exposed to an increased global competition in both the capital and product markets.

Denzau and North (1994) make a contribution in answering this question in that they explicitly raise the question of the convergence of individual mental models through the learning process. As no two individuals have exactly the same experiences, their perceptions of the outside world and accordingly their mental models should tend to diverge. However, the opposite is observed because the common cultural heritage bequeathed by previous generations provides a means of reducing divergence in the mental models of people belonging to a particular cultural group. At the same time, this heritage also constitutes a means of unifying mental models over time. The existence of a wide variety of cultural heritages encapsulating the experiences of past generations in different environments explains both the coexistence, at any moment in time, of different patterns of corporate governance systems and the persistence of differences over time.

For all that, can we conclude that these differences will remain unchanged? This does not seem to be the case. North mentions exposure to others' ideas as one mode of learning. Now, in matters of governance, financial globalization contributes to such a phenomenon. Coming up against mental models stemming from a different culture may, if this confrontation echoes problems encountered by a majority of individuals at the same time, give rise to a transformation of prior beliefs, i.e. a representational redescription. Of course those who support the established ideology will try to resist but, according to Denzau and North (1994, p. 13), the climate of opinion may evolve progressively as new meanings in terms and concepts are brought from related mental models by analogy or metaphor. As this process develops, the gap between those mental models formerly used and those emerging become widens such that inconsistencies may appear at the institutional level. This will result in a crisis in the corporate governance system.

This crisis may be resolved by changes which will reduce the divergence between national systems without making them identical, however, as acculturation always implies a reinterpretation of the imported elements so that they can fuse into the original cultural context. In short, it does not seem possible to settle the debate on convergence in a conclusive manner.

Proposition 5. The evolution of national systems of corporate governance is path-dependent. However, learning through the confrontation with mental models stemming from other cultures leads to a reduction in differences between national systems.

The propositions we have delineated aim at building a coherent conceptual framework that enables us to apprehend the dynamics of national systems of corporate governance. They attempt to provide explanations of both the process and the product of change in governance institutions. Although they are susceptible to application to any country, as suggested throughout this section, recent changes in the Japanese system of governance raise the opportunity of putting them to the test there.

THE CASE OF SOGO DEPARTMENT STORES: MOVING TOWARDS A MARKET-ORIENTED SYSTEM?

Our purpose in this section is to evaluate the propositions stated in our theoretical framework against results drawn from the study of a recent case, that of the financial crisis that the Japanese chain of department stores Sogo went through. Information concerning the evolution of the crisis and the way it was handled by the group's stakeholders was obtained from Japanese and international publications that covered the various stages of the negotiations between Sogo and its creditors, at first in an informal way and afterwards in connection with civil rehabilitation proceedings. After summarizing the main events that led to Sogo's profound restructuring, the case will be analyzed in terms of bringing out the changes in governance structures within the group and their relationship with the evolution of the Japanese system as a whole.

From Financial Crisis to the Sogo Bankruptcy

A brief of the main stages in the crisis that the Sogo department stores went through and its conclusion are presented in Table 2. A few further facts are necessary to put these events into perspective with respect to the Japanese system of governance.

Table 2. Chronology of the Sogo Crisis.

- 27 April 2000: Sogo's vice-president Abe commits suicide.
- 28 April 2000: Sogo's management reports a loss of $1.4 billion for FY 1999. A restructuring plan is forged with its main bank, the Industrial Bank of Japan (IBJ), which itself agrees to forgive debts of $2 billion.
- 3 July 2000: The Deposit Insurance Corporation (DIC) announces that it will purchase Sogo's debt worth $2 billion from Shinsei Bank and abandon half of it. Opposition parties, public opinion and some members of the ruling Liberal Democratic Party (LDP) protest against the use of public funds to save a poorly managed firm.
- 12 July 2000: The LDP asks Sogo to withdraw its rescue plan and to file for bankruptcy.
- 16 July 2000: Start of the civil rehabilitation proceedings (*Minjisaisei*). Sogo, whose debt amounts to $17 billion, is given 6 months to present a new rehabilitation plan or to find a buyer before its final liquidation.
- 26 July 2000: Sogo's former chairman (who resigned as chairman in April 2000), Hiroo Mizushima, and eight other Sogo executives resign. Shigeaki Wada, former president of the Seibu Chain, is appointed as special adviser of Sogo.
- 12 September 2000: Mizushima and 16 other executives are ordered to pay 6 billion yen to the Sogo group in damages for losses incurred through past business deals.
- 27 October 2000: The 10-year rehabilitation plan is submitted is presented by Sogo's new management to creditors.
- 29 January 2001: Mizuho Financial Group announces that it will forgive nearly $1 billion of Sogo's debt.
- 31 January 2001: Approval of Sogo's rehabilitation plan by 90% of the 3300 creditors present. The plan is ratified by the Tokyo District Court.
- February 2001: Business tie-up with Seibu department stores, including information system and product distribution.
- 20 November 2001: Sogo announces that it will merge its merchandise department with that of Seibu the following spring.

Sogo is a trading company established in 1830 in Osaka. It was incorporated in 1913, and until the early 1960s, it remained small. Its growth really began in 1962 when Hiroo Mizushima, who was a former executive of the Industrial Bank of Japan (IBJ), became chief executive officer. Sogo then progressed from having three stores in 1962 to 41 in 2000, of which 14 were situated outside Japan. Mizushima's strategy was based on savvy real-estate transactions, which proved to be very profitable, especially during the 1980s. This policy gave him practically unlimited funds with which to finance his expansion, which spiraled upwards and was fueled by the continual revaluation of real-estate assets that served as security for loans.

The start of Sogo's troubles was the economic downturn of 1991 and the bursting of the financial and real-estate bubble. Several factors combined to precipitate the group's decline. First of all, having made real-estate strategy paramount, Sogo neglected the retail business, which resulted in an impaired brand image. Sogo, like other department stores around the world, is also victim to the unfavorable consequences of a shift in customer preferences. In times of economic crisis, price has become an important factor in the decision to buy and *depâtos*[5] traditionally have high prices due to the huge mark-up they place on products they sell. Lastly, the deregulation of the retail sector which began in 1992 has progressively abolished the protection which department stores had enjoyed since 1973 and hastened the arrival of new competitors: supermarkets, convenience stores, and discount shops.

However, the chain retained the banks' confidence and, up to 1999, was considered to be a reliable debtor. This blindness on the part of Sogo's bank creditors, especially its main bank IBJ, appears to be due to two factors. There was the existence of long-standing personal relationships between several Sogo executives, including the chairman, and IBJ for whom they had worked formerly. Additionally, the opaqueness that surrounded the group's financial health resulted from its myriad operations, i.e. 127 subsidiaries, each of which presented separate financial statements. It was not by chance that the truth about Sogo's financial health was revealed in April 2000. It was in that year that new accounting standards were introduced, thus forcing the group to present consolidated accounts.

Sogo's main bank, according to the prevailing logic in bank-oriented systems, immediately began working on a restructuring plan. According to this plan, debt forgiveness amounting to $5.9 billion, out of a total of $17 billion, would be requested from its creditor banks. When submitted to the 73-bank consortium, in line with the so-called convoy system, it gained the approval of a majority. Shinsei Bank, however, the second largest lender to Sogo following IBJ, and which was asked to write off loans with a face value of almost a billion dollars, refused. This lack of solidarity on the part of Shinsei Bank, unusual in Japanese practice, can be explained by the fact that, since March 2000, this firm[6] had been the property of Ripplewood Holdings, a group of American investors. The purchase contract contained a latent defect warranty clause. The latter stipulated that, as a secondary loss countermeasure, the government would buy from Shinsei Bank (at nominal value) any loans made by LTCB if the collateral backing them fell in value by more than 20% from the time the loans were assumed by the relaunched institution. As Sogo's borrowings met these conditions, Shinsei Bank's behavior was thus consistent with its shareholders' interests.

The purchase of Shinsei Bank's loans to Sogo by the state-run Deposit Insurance Corporation (DIC) put the onus of deciding whether to participate in Sogo's recovery plan on the Financial Reconstruction Commission (FRC), an independent financial regulator. DIC's President, Noboru Matsuda, justified the decision to accept debt forgiveness by putting forward the need to prevent failures among the group's 10,000 suppliers, to avoid forcing Sogo into bankruptcy proceedings and to increase the reorganization plan's chances of succeeding. This decision, however, ignited a firestorm of debate about the legitimacy of using public funds to rescue a non-financial company from the consequences of its own poor business decisions. Although the involvement of the DIC indicates that Sogo was politically well connected, this connection did not prove effective enough to rescue Sogo. Actually, the Japanese public opinion seems to have concluded that corruption, added to mismanagement, did not justify a public bailout. At the end of a severe outcry, the Japanese government was forced to second-guess its decision and, through the intermediary of Shizuka Kamei, chairman of the LDP's Policy Research Council, warned Sogo officials that their restructuring plan "will fail unless it can generate public support and understanding." The very same day, Sogo's management drew their own conclusions from this about-face and formally filed for protection from creditors in the Tokyo District Court. The government's signal is clear: henceforth, large troubled firms cannot count on the generosity of either the banks or the government, which up to now had tended to prop up weak companies.

Comparison Between the Sogo Case and the Theoretical Framework

The Sogo case illustrates the conflict between two implicit conceptions of the firm that imply different ways of arbitrating between the interests of the diverse stakeholders, particularly when it comes to dealing with the firm's financial distress. The first conception emphasizes the idea of a cooperative game between shareholders and employees (Aoki, 1984, 1988), while the second stresses the property rights of those entities who hold a firm's capital (Grossman & Hart, 1986; Hart & Moore, 1990). The ideology on which the Japanese system of governance is based, as described by Aoki (1988), rests on the idea that a company is a coalition between two categories of stakeholders: shareholders and employees. Strategic decisions taken by management must maintain the balance negotiated through mediation between the interests of these two constituents. Embedded in Aoki's view of the Japanese firm is also the recognition that banks play a crucial although contingent monitoring role. Only in bad situations are they inclined to interfere with a firm's management, assuming the responsibility for various rescue operations (Sheard, 1989), and thus providing the firm with a virtual insurance against bankruptcy (Berglöf, 1989). The contrast between this conception of the firm and that on which corporate governance is based in the Anglo-Saxon system is obvious. In the latter case, the sole interests deemed to be legitimate are those of the shareholders. Because of their status as residual claimants of the firm, shareholders have the strongest incentive to make the right decisions, and their interests coincide with collective interests. Consequently, when a client firm becomes financially troubled, the bank's decision as to whether to provide new funding to the distressed firm or "pull the plug" should be made with respect to the interests of the bank's shareholders.

It is clear that the management of Shinsei bank were guided by this logic in their reaction to Sogo's difficulties. Joining the bailout of Sogo would indeed have meant depriving their shareholders of the opportunity to dispose of bad loans at their face value. The behavior of the other banks and especially that of the main bank was on the contrary in accordance with Japanese corporate governance norms. The firm's survival was sought to preserve jobs and the reputation of IBJ as a competent supervisor. IBJ agreed to important financial sacrifices to achieve this double aim. The difference between these two attitudes, each of which is in line with the logic of a particular ideology regarding corporate governance, is consistent with Proposition 1, regarding the link between corporate governance and firm representations.

Let us now consider the volte-face of the Japanese government in the face of Sogo's financial distress. It is symptomatic of a sudden change in the preferences manifested by the political bodies. The system aimed at saving firms at all costs in order to preserve jobs was rejected in favor of strict market logic: firms which are poorly managed must be eliminated. The ultimate decision was the result of pressure from various stakeholders upon the government: taxpayers, Shinsei bank, opposition members, but also members of the LDP ruling party. But this decision ran contrary to the logic behind the Japanese system of corporate governance. Shared mental models about the legitimacy of the different interests at stake in a troubled firm therefore seem to have changed. Two modes of learning can apparently be cited to explain this evolution: feedback from past experience and confrontation with foreign mental models. Regarding the first point, it seems likely that the handling of the banking crisis by the Japanese government, which involved rescuing several financial firms by injecting huge amounts of public funds, provoked growing exasperation on the part of taxpayers. Furthermore, even though the economic and social issues that were at stake in the survival of these firms were plausible arguments in the eyes of Japanese public opinion, the extension of this generosity to non-financial firms that were notoriously poorly managed did not have the same legitimacy. The second point invokes the influence of the Anglo-American model of corporate governance on both political and business circles. The evolution described in our first section concerning legal reforms and the reactions of minority shareholders and banks illustrates this influence. The legal framework was partly revised in April 2000 in order to replace the former composition procedure, which was used very little, with a reorganization procedure largely modeled on Chap. 11 of the U.S. Bankruptcy Code. Opposition to the free play of market forces comes in the recurrence of informal support on the part of the Japanese government. The government's decision to break with such a practice appears to be the result of a change in several stakeholders' mental models, in accordance with Proposition 2, stating that learning is the mainspring of institutional change.

The precedent created by the refusal of the Japanese authorities to support the Sogo group indubitably confirms the change in the balance of power between a company's stakeholders. It is primarily a clear signal to Japanese banks to strengthen their competencies in assessing firms' viability as well as the risks involved, and an incentive to break with the common practice of propping up large corporations and other banks. In this respect, it implicitly approved the example of Shinsei bank whose behavior is thus. For the management of Japanese large firms, it is also an indication that there has been a radical change in the way a company's troubles will be handled. In place of discreet negotiations with creditors conducted by the main bank, firms more often will be forced to file for bankruptcy, which may well end in the firm's liquidation and the taking of legal action against its management in the case of mismanagement.[7] Finally, for the employees of these firms, it confirms the increasing insecurity that arises from the greater risk of economic lay-offs if a firm is restructured and also from the possible loss of their job if their employer is liquidated.[8] As Lechevalier (2001) points out, in a paper on the recent evolution of employment relations in Japan, the calling into question of lifetime employment in large corporations entails the severance of the implicit contracts that they had formed with their employees during periods of growth. The environmental change to which these firms must adapt has brought their management to perceive the advantages that would result from a modification of the institutions concerning lay-offs in order to favor job flexibility, thus illustrating Proposition 3 about the orientation of institutional change. Two business organizations, Keidanren and Keizai Doyukai, have noted the difficulty for Japanese firms finding within their own internal labor market the requisite skills. They point to the necessity of firms favoring the reallocation of labor-force external labor market mechanisms. In so far as Japanese labor law imposes few constraints on employers in this respect, it is the informal rules that have to be modified. However, it is difficult to initiate the evolution of cultural norms. In this respect, alliances with foreign firms, such as that concluded between Renault and Nissan, help a firm to become acculturated to new labor management practices.

The successive modifications undergone by Japanese economic institutions, especially those that result from American pressure, appear to have initiated a series of chain reactions that political and economic leaders are unable to control. The financial deregulation of the 1980s, which modified the competitive position of banks and opened up Japanese firms' capital to foreign investors, has hastened the evolution of the Japanese corporate governance system as a whole. On the one hand, by increasing the proportion of direct funding of Japanese firms, it undermined the long-term logic that prevailed in their relationship with banks. On the other hand, by allowing foreign investors to take control of bankrupt Japanese banks (as in the case of the Shinsei Bank), it helped to generalize behavior that broke with the traditional practice of supporting financially distressed firms. While weakening the banks' incentive to monitor firms and at the same time inciting them to take greater risks (as in the case of IBJ with Sogo), the development of financial markets did not immediately bring in its wake the creation of control mechanisms capable of substituting for that performed by banks. The slow growth period of the 1990s plainly revealed the consequences of a general lack of control by materializing the bulk of the risks taken both by the banks and by the borrowing firms. In accordance with Proposition 4, regarding institutional complementarities, the efficiency of the governance system was jeopardized by the change in part of the rules (in this case the informal ones) that regulated it, while the impact of the legal reforms that brought about these changes had not been foreseen. Seen in this light, the reforms of the 1990s may be considered an attempt to repair this flaw in the control system. It was indeed the new accounting standards that revealed the extent of Sogo's losses. Similarly, the recent modernization of Japanese bankruptcy law can be seen as a response to the need to replace banks in performing the function of reorganizing large Japanese troubled firms. Lastly, the increased pressure that shareholders put on management – the increasing number of legal proceedings taken against them as well as a greater demand for transparence and profitability – can be seen as an attempt on the part of outsiders to substitute direct control of Japanese firms for the control that, for a long time, was left to their principal banks and has now been weakened.

The Sogo case can be seen as a decisive turning point in corporate governance in Japan because of its symbolic importance. It illustrates the weakening of network-based control mechanisms and the beginnings of the transformation of Japanese economy towards market capitalism. In this sense, we can observe, as Proposition 5 about convergence suggests, a convergence of the United States and Japanese systems of governance. This convergence can be explained, in part, by the fact that the stakeholders in Japanese firms, as a whole, have been exposed to a shareholder-oriented type of governance ideology, which differs from that which has determined the nature of their relationship since the end of the World War II. In so far as the actions of some institutions, inspired by this ideology, appeared to be beneficial to stakeholders having the power to alter the rules of corporate governance, the system has entered into an evolutionary phase that follows a long period of stability. Must we conclude, therefore, that the Japanese system of corporate governance will pursue this evolution until it finally becomes identical to the American model? We have several reasons to doubt that. First, the capacity of some stakeholders to resist change should not be underestimated. Although the government did finally choose to reject the rescue plan initially proposed by Sogo, the primary reaction of Japan's financial regulators, who are theoretically independent, had been to plead social order and employment consequences to justify the forgiveness of part of Sogo's debt to Shinsei Bank. Furthermore, the discretionary power of the courts to influence the progress and the outcome of the civil rehabilitation proceedings, which were started in April 2000, is important. In this context, it is possible that the new legal framework will function simply as a formal window dressing to cover actual practices that are little different from those that prevailed in the case of private workouts. This symptom of the influence of cultural heritage would tend to perpetuate the former system. In so far as the plan voted by creditors results in the forgiveness of loans amounting to what was initially proposed in April 2000, the Sogo case seems to exemplify this point. Such a view is consistent with Ramseyer and Nakazato's (1999) work on Japanese law. The laws, in their view, are there to provide the guidance for non-formal resolution systems, which typically is the case with Sogo.

CONCLUSION

The aim of this paper was to examine the changes that the Japanese system of corporate governance underwent over the period 1990–2001 and to propose an interpretation derived from North's theory of institutional change. On the first point, the evolution of the governance system appears to have been influenced both by changes in the legal rules governing the organization of power within companies and by changes in informal norms of behavior of some stakeholders (especially banks and minority shareholders), which were part of Japanese business culture. These changes, which are of a general nature, were illustrated by a case study of the Sogo chain of department stores. On the second point, a series of propositions were put forward based on North's work on institutional change. Our analysis demonstrated how the very general conceptual framework offered by this theory could be applied in order to understand of the dynamics of corporate governance institutions. Although the propositions were meant to apply to any national system, it seemed appropriate to confront them with the Japanese case in so far as the latter has undergone a noticeable acceleration of its evolution during the last 10 years, appearing to put into practice mechanisms of a similar type to those mentioned by North. This attempt did, however, entail the risk of being placed on an analytical level that is too general. Thus, we called the Sogo case into play. Alternating thus between the evolution of Sogo's governance structures and that of the Japanese system taken as a whole, and thereby combining two different focus points, helped to test the explanatory power of our conceptual framework. The role of the learning process, in its diverse modes, is thereby made clear through the way it influences individual and collective decision-making: deliberate breaking with former rules of governance, but also permanence of certain behavior models. The limits to a study of the dynamics of corporate governance systems stem from the complexity of the phenomenon under study. In this respect, the theory of institutional change opens up fruitful perspectives for research in so far as its global analytical framework enables us to integrate and to go beyond the viewpoints provided by unidimensional approaches.

NOTES

1. Contingent monitoring refers to the fact that the main bank acts as a silent partner as long as the firm remains profitable and becomes active only in case of financial troubles.
2. Coffee (1999) points out that convergence in corporate governance will occur not at the level of corporate laws but at the level of securities regulation, which plays a critical role in reducing agency costs and may trivialize path-dependent variations in national corporate law.
3. North (1990) explicitly refers to Nelson and Winter (1982) and to their concept of routines embodying the knowledge acquired through the repetition of similar experiences.
4. These authors suggest that only a small number of individuals make choices based on their own mental models, the majority simply following the leaders and adopting the same choices. When the leaders' mental models evolve, others will first of all mimic them, and subsequently their own mental models will evolve to re-establish certain coherence between their behavior and their mental representation of reality.
5. An apocope for English *department store*.
6. Formerly Long Term Credit Bank of Japan (LTCB), this private banking firm was nationalized by the Japanese government in 1998, having virtually declared bankruptcy, and subsequently sold to a consortium led by Ripplewood Holdings LLC. Shinsei Bank also played an important role in forcing the bankruptcy of Life Co. and Dai-Ichi Hotel Ltd.
7. However, this new procedure breaks with Japanese bankruptcy law in force until 2000, which was a fairly incoherent collection of procedures taken either from German law (very protective of creditors) during the Meiji era, or from the former American Chap. 10 (which was also very constraining for management) after the World War II (Pochet, 2001).
8. Sogo's restructuring plan as approved by its creditors and ratified by the Tokyo district court entails the suppression of over 3000 jobs out of a total of 10,000 for the group.

REFERENCES

Aoki, M. (1984). *The cooperative game theory of the firm.* Oxford: Oxford University Press.
Aoki, M. (1988). *Information, incentive and bargaining structure in the Japanese economy.* Cambridge: Cambridge University Press.

Aoki, M. (1990). Towards an economic theory of the Japanese firm. *Journal of Economic Literature*, *28*, 1–27.

Bank of Japan (2001). Developments in profits and balance sheets of Japanese banks in fiscal 2000 and banks' management tasks. *Bank of Japan Quarterly Bulletin* (November), 73–130.

Berglöf, E. (1990). Capital structure as a mechanism of control, a comparison of financial systems. In: M. Aoki, B. Gustafsson & O. E. Williamson (Eds), *The Firm as a Nexus of Treaties* (pp. 237–262). London: Sage.

Bikhchandani, S., Hirshleifer, D., & Welch, I. (1992). A theory of fads, fashion, custom, and cultural change as informational cascades. *Journal of Political Economy*, *100*, 992–1026.

Calomiris, C., & Rammirez, C. (1996). The role of financial relationships in the history of American corporate finance. *Journal of Applied Corporate Finance*, *9*, 52–74.

Charreaux, G. (1997). Vers une théorie du gouvernement des entreprises. In: G. Charreaux (Ed.), *Le Gouvernement des Entreprises: Corporate Governance, Théorie et Faits* (pp. 421–469). Paris: Economica.

Clark, A., & Karmiloff-Smith, A. (1993). The cognizer's innards: A psychological and philosophical perspective on the development of thought. *Mind and Language*, *8*, 487–519.

Coase, R. H. (1937). The nature of the firm. *Econometrica*, *4*, 386–405.

Coffee, J. C. (1999). The future as history: The prospects for global convergence in corporate governance and its implications. Working Paper No. 144, Columbia Law School.

Denzau, A. T., & Grossman, P. (1993). *Punctuated equilibria: A model and application of evolutionary economic change*. Unpublished manuscript, Economics Department, Washington University.

Denzau, A. T., & North, D. C. (1994). Shared mental models: Ideologies and institutions. *Kyklos*, *47*, 3–30.

Dore, R. (2000). *Stock market capitalism: Welfare capitalism, Japan and Germany versus the Anglo-Saxons*. New York: Oxford University Press.

Franks, J., & Mayer, C. (1998). Ownership and control in Europe. In: P. Newman (Ed.), *New Palgrave Dictionary of Economics and The Law* (pp. 722–730). New York: Palgrave Macmillan.

Fukao, M. (1999). *Japanese financial instability and weaknesses in the corporate governance structure*. Paris: OECD.

Grossman, S., & Hart, O. (1986). The costs and the benefits of ownership: A theory of vertical and lateral integration. *Journal of Political Economy*, *94*, 691–719.

Guichard, S. (1996). La crise du système bancaire japonais. *Economie Internationale*, *67*, 5–29.

Hart, O., & Moore, J. (1990). Property rights and the nature of the firm. *Journal of Political Economy*, *98*, 1119–1158.

Hoshi, T., Kashyap, A., & Scharfstein, D. (1990). The role of banks in reducing the costs of financial distress in Japan. *Journal of Financial Economics*, *27*, 67–88.

Kanie, A. (1998). Les défaillances du système de contrôle des sociétés au Japon. Working Paper, University of Poitiers.

Kawamoto, A. (1999). Unblocking Japanese reform. *OECD Observer*, April 2002 issue.

Kroszner, R., & Rajan, R. G. (1994). Is the Glass-Steagall Act justified? Evidence from the U.S. experience with universal banking 1921–1933. *American Economic Review*, *84*, 810–832.

La Porta, R., Lopez-de-Silanes, F., Shleifer, A., & Vishny, R. (1997). The legal determinants of external finance. *Journal of Finance*, *52*, 1131–1150.

La Porta, R., Lopez-de-Silanes, F., Shleifer, A., & Vishny, R. (1998). Law and finance. *Journal of Political Economy*, *106*, 1113–1155.

La Porta, R., Lopez-de-Silanes, F., Shleifer, A., & Vishny, R. (1999a). Corporate ownership around the world. *Journal of Finance*, *54*, 471–517.

La Porta, R., Lopez-de-Silanes, F., Shleifer, A., & Vishny, R. (1999b). Investor protection: Origins, consequences, reform. NBER, Working Paper No. 7428.

Lechevalier, S. (2001). Japon: La sécurité de l'emploi au cœur du compromis salarial émergent. *Chronique internationale de l'IRES, 68*, 9–20.

Moerland, P. W. (1995). Alternative disciplinary mechanisms in different corporate systems. *Journal of Economic Behavior and Organization, 26*, 17–34.

Myhram, J., & Weingast, B. R. (1994). Douglass C. North's contributions to economics and economic history. *Scandinavian Journal of Economics, 96*, 185–193.

Nelson, R., & Winter, S. G. (1982). *An evolutionary theory of economic change*. Cambridge, MA: Harvard University Press.

North, D. (1990). *Institutions, institutional change and economic performance*. Cambridge, MA: Harvard University Press.

North, D. (1993). Five propositions about institutional change. Working Paper, Center for the study of Political Economy, Washington University, St. Louis, MO.

North, D. (1994). Economic performance through time. *American Economic Review, 84*, 359–368.

Okazaki, T. (2000). Corporate governance. In: M. Okuno-Fujiwara & T. Okazaki (Eds), *The Japanese Economic System and its Historical Origins* (pp. 97–144). New York: Oxford University Press.

Pochet, C. (2001). Traitement légal de la défaillance et gouvernance: Une comparaison internationale. *Revue internationale de droit économique, 4*, 465–488.

Pochet, C. (2002). Institutional complementarities within corporate governance systems: A comparative study of bankruptcy rules. *Journal of Management and Governance, 6*, 343–381.

Ramseyer, J. M., & Nakazato, M. (1999). *Japanese law: An economic approach*. Chicago: University of Chicago Press.

Roe, M. J. (1994). *Strong managers, weak owners: The political roots of American corporate finance*. Princeton, NJ: Princeton University Press.

Roe, M. J. (2000). Political preconditions for separating ownership from corporate control. *Stanford Law Review, 53*, 539–606.

Roe, M. J., & Bebchuk, L. A. (1999). A theory of path dependence in corporate governance and ownership. *Stanford Law Review, 52*, 127–170.

Sheard, P. (1989). The main bank system and corporate monitoring and control in Japan. *Journal of Economic Behavior and Organization, 11*, 399–422.

Simon, H. (1986). Rationality in psychology and economics. In: R. M. Hogarth & M. W. Reder (Eds), *Rational Choice: The Contrast between Economics and Psychology* (pp. 25–40). Chicago: University of Chicago Press.

Simon, M. C. (1998). The rise and fall of bank control in the United States: 1890–1939. *American Economic Review, 88*, 1077–1093.

Takeda, H. (1999). Corporate governance of Zaibatsu during the interwar period. *Entreprises et Histoire, 21*, 90–99.

Wirtz, P. (2000). Mental patterns, corporate finance and institutional evolution: The case of the French corporate governance system. Working Paper, University of Burgundy, Dijon.

Yasui, T. (1999). *Corporate governance in Japan*. Paris: OECD.

Yoshimori, M. (1995). Whose company is it? The concept of the corporation in Japan and the West. *Long Range Planning, 28*, 33–44.

Yoshimori, M. (1998). La gouvernance des entreprises au Japon: Les causes de son dysfonctionnement. *Finance Contrôle Stratégie, 1*, 173–199.

THE CHANGING TREND IN LINKS BETWEEN BUREAUCRACY AND THE PRIVATE SECTOR IN JAPAN

Andreas Moerke

ABSTRACT

Japan has been conceived of as being a "developmental state." However, given that Japan has, since 1992, been contending with a post-bubble "crisis period," it is important to examine whether or not the resultant deregulation has altered the government-industry nexus. This paper focuses on amakudari, a core administrative guidance medium, within four core industries to measure the extent and direction of regulatory change. The findings show that amakudari networks have weakened, with corporations only employing bureaucrats deemed as being useful, supporting the hypothesis that there has been a "paradigm shift" from a "developmental state" to a "resource dependence" view.

INTRODUCTION

Over the past few years, the "need to change" has been frequently addressed by Japanese policymakers and executives. Indeed, evidence of change can be clearly seen. One need only think of the deregulation of the financial industry, the new electoral system, or, to name one recent example, the 2002 changes in the commercial law which had far-reaching consequences for stock options.

Japanese Firms in Transition: Responding to the Globalization Challenge
Advances in International Management, Volume 17, 61–88
Copyright © 2005 by Elsevier Ltd.
All rights of reproduction in any form reserved
ISSN: 0747-7929/doi:10.1016/S0747-7929(04)17003-0

However, focusing only on the permanence of such changes is insufficient to enable us to substantiate what may be occurring in Japan. It is necessary to examine the institutions undergoing change (or remaining the same), and the extent to which this change is occurring. It is equally important to analyze the direction of change. By doing so, we can determine whether the Japanese economy and society are undergoing the fundamental, deep and structural transformation that would allow us to refer to a "regime shift" (Pempel, 1997).[1]

The relations between the state and the private sector are without doubt one of the critical dimensions that constitute a "regime." As numerous publications show, these relations as well as the debates about them have undergone considerable change.

Although some researchers trace the beginning of industrial policy back to the industrialization of Japan (Pauer, 1995, p. 31), it is a matter of common understanding that the state bureaucracy has continued to play a crucial role in the development of Japan following World War II. The "developmental state" theory claims that the Japanese state adopts a promotional and protective industrial policy in order to achieve economic growth and close the gap on Western industrialized countries (Johnson, 1982; Schaede, 2000; Yamamura, 1997). As part of this initiative, high-ranking bureaucrats drafted proposals for politicians, who more often than not were sensible enough to follow them. However, a close relationship between the regulators (i.e. the bureaucracy) and the regulated parties (the private sector) also evolved. The so-called "iron triangle" was used to symbolize these relationships (Fig. 1).

To comprehend the government-industry relationship, one must take into account the fact that these relations are multidimensional. Because government authorities adopt a regulatory function (and indeed continue to influence the environment in which companies operate), corporations found it prudent to connect with ministries for counseling and lobbying. The bureaucracy-industry relationship is characterized by administrative guidance (*gyosei shido*)[2] and the appointment of ex-bureaucrats to private industry (*amakudari*).[3] The two are interconnected and reliant on each other.

This relationship structure contributed to the enormous growth rates of the Japanese post-war economy.[4] However, in Japan as elsewhere, a system can never be better than the people involved and the surroundings they create. Two main factors point to the necessity for structural changes:

(1) The ongoing support provided to Japanese companies made them stronger, internationally successful, and thus less dependent on domestic support and less willing to follow advice.[5] Financial independence, and deregulation of

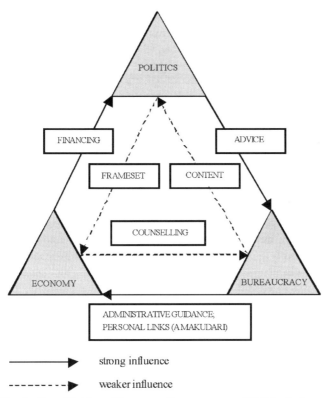

Fig. 1.   Inter-Linking of Economy, Bureaucracy and Politics in Japan.

the industries in which companies operated, were the inevitable preconditions, both more or less realized from the 1980s onwards.

(2) A number of failed policy measures and scandals had a major impact. Failed policy initiatives are most evident. With the well-known "Plan for Remodeling the Japanese Archipelago," Tanaka Kakuei delivered something similar to a blueprint to seal the surface of the country with concrete wherever possible – for the sake of the construction industry and jobs (and consequently the benevolence of voters).[6] "Failed policy" is also the only possible assessment of the increase in the consumption tax in 1997. This measure resulted in a dramatic reduction in spending – and thus failed to provide the additional tax revenue intended. Yet, it is not only inaccurate predictions of future developments that are responsible for the current bad standing of the bureaucracy in Japan. In the 1990s, after the bubble burst, the suspicions

of certain people were confirmed: The ties between corporations and the bureaucracy were sometimes too intimate. Sasakawa Ryōichi's "Shipbuilding Industry Foundation" is one example, where well-paid posts for numerous ex-bureaucrats were provided in reward for their favors (Samuels, 2001, p. 16). A second example is the arrest of Okamitsu Nobuharu, during his tenure as administrative vice-minister in the Ministry of Health and Welfare, for allegations that he accepted a golf-club membership worth 16 million yen, together with other "gifts" (Pempel, 1997, p. 349). Nearly every financial institution had a "MoF tan" and had – in smoothing the relations to the ministry – given dinners in lavish restaurants, and, in many cases, even offered bribes (Blechinger, 2000).

As with almost everything, the relationship between the bureaucracy and industry in Japan can be viewed in different ways. The first interpretation fits nicely into the framework of the "developmental state":[7] The state bureaucracy exerts influence in accordance with its subjective industrial policy. A strong state is also able to control and influence corporations on an informal basis, and certain authorities have the power to second retired personnel to companies. In a highly regulated environment, where state institutions have the power to reward benevolence and punish non-cooperative behavior, companies are well advised to accept these ex-bureaucrats and follow their advice.

There are also benefits for corporations in accepting retiring government personnel. These bureaucrats embody certain knowledge acquired during their time working for the authorities. This in-depth knowledge of regulation, together with a dense personal network, can make these people invaluable for companies. Framed in this way, the industry-bureaucracy relationship can also be understood in terms of the "resource-dependence view": A corporation does not consider itself as self-sufficient, but rather as dependent on outside resources. These resources include not only material goods, but also knowledge and the opportunity to influence the environment favorably. Forming alliances, or employing people with access to certain resources, is one way to secure those resources.[8]

There is a well-established body of research on different aspects of the government-business relationship in Japan, particularly in the area of "amakudari." For instance, the question as to who initiates the process can be answered differently: It is either government institutions (Calder, 1989; Usui & Colignon, 1997, 1999) or corporations (Schaede, 1995, 1998). Research on the motives of both corporations in appointing ex-bureaucrats (for example, to obtain access to information and personal resources; van Rixtel, 1995; van Rixtel & Hassink, 1998) and conversely institutions (to reinforce industrial policy by supporting certain industries; cf. Nakano, 1998; Schaede, 1994) is also extensive.

The problems with most of these findings are twofold. First, only a few of them really address change in the relationship or in the amakudari process.[9] Second, they investigate a process in a regulated environment, mostly using data from the early or mid-1990s. However, as has already been shown, deregulation has changed the environment in which Japanese corporations operate:

(1) On the administrative level, the reform initiated under Prime Minister Hashimoto (and claimed to be continued under Prime Minister Koizumi) is intended to scale down bureaucratic influence and provide a greater level of flexibility. An increased level of transparency should be achieved by removing supervisory functions and everyday executive responsibilities from the ministries and transferring these to independent agencies (Blechinger, 1998, p. 17).
(2) The revision of the Anti-Monopoly Law in 1997, and of the Commercial Law in 2002, provides corporations with completely new opportunities (as a single example, the opportunity to create a holding company).[10]
(3) In the case of the financial markets, commencing with the revision of the Foreign Exchange and Control Law in 1980, and continuing with growing intensity during the "Japanese Big Bang," deregulation cannot be denied (cf. Schaede, Hoshi & McMillan, 1997).

Yet, the question as to how administrative guidance is supposed to work in a deregulated environment, and if corporations would still be willing to accept this kind of guidance, or if regulation changes to self-regulation, as was demonstrated in the case of trade associations (Schaede, 2000), remains unanswered.

These are the points this paper attempts to clarify. In the theoretical framework of the developmental-state theory and the resource-dependence view, it deals with the question as to whether the initiative for amakudari is changing, whether the interaction between regulation, industry and industrial organization has changed, and in what direction this change is going. Based on extensive empirical research and a broad and very recent database, a new scale has been developed to measure the connections between corporations and the state bureaucracy. To do so, the range of an ex-bureaucrat's personal network was examined – thus providing a broader approach for the analysis than was the case for other researchers. The time span is sufficiently long and the data sufficiently recent to allow clear statements about the development and current status of these relationships. It can be shown that:

(1) Differences between industries become less important (although they cannot be completely ignored).
(2) Features of industrial organizations, such as embeddedness in corporate groups, still play an important role, although differences in the network with the bureaucracy are lessening.

(3) Large corporations are no longer the favored place of descent.

Combined with the results from the regression analysis (which shows that personal networks established by boards of directors in the latter half of the investigation period have a stronger impact on sales than those in the first), this research leads to the conclusion that a paradigm shift has indeed taken place: In a deregulated environment, corporations can more easily choose whether or not to appoint ex-bureaucrats to their boards of directors – thus securing necessary resources for favorable development.

Two caveats should be added. This chapter identifies trends in amakudari relations in four industries. Therefore, care should be taken in generalizing the findings to other industries. Perhaps more importantly, change in Japan is gradual. None of the institutions and mechanisms shown here vanished completely during the period of investigation. Change is, to borrow T. J. Pempel's words, ". . . less a matter of 'yes' or 'no' and more a matter of 'how much?' and 'along which dimensions?' " (1997, p. 336).

This chapter adopts the following structure. The next section develops hypotheses drawn from the literature. The third section explains the research methodology and dataset, whereas the fourth section describes the empirical analysis, extensively using econometric methods. The concluding section of the chapter discusses the implications of the findings.

MANIFESTATION OF LINKS BETWEEN BUREAUCRACY AND THE PRIVATE SECTOR

General Assumption: Deregulation Leads to Decreasing Amakudari

Developmental state theory suggests that a state will adopt a promotional and/or protectionist industrial policy in order to emulate other nations. As far as the four industries investigated in this paper are concerned, this objective was previously achieved. Corporations in these industries compete internationally, and some of them are among the most successful companies worldwide. Furthermore, the Japanese markets for these products are largely open.[11] It is reasonable to conclude that the objective of developmental state policy has been attained, and that companies may act independently. Furthermore – as shown above – scandals and erroneous policy measures have undermined the trust in the bureaucracy. This leads to the overall supposition that:

> **H1.** Amakudari networks (i.e. the number of ex-bureaucrats in the boards as well as their internal status) are weakening.

Amakudari as a Way of Enforcing Industrial Policy

If Japan is viewed as a developmental state that has adopted a promotional and protective industrial policy (Schaede, 2000), it is appropriate to look at the numerous plans developed by Japanese ministries and government institutions to develop the country.[12] The identification of "target industries" should ensure that resources are used efficiently. Japanese industrial policy includes acceptance of cartels within certain industries, administrative guidance measures, and the use of personal networks. Article 103 of the Government Employee Act (*kokka komuin ho*) specifies that bureaucrats during the first two years after retirement may have no links to those sectors in which they have held a regulatory function in the last five years of their term of office. In certain cases, however, exceptions are made (Tsutsuumi & Yamaguchi, 1997, p. 8). As pointed out quite frequently in various literature (cf. Usui & Colignon, 1997) and confirmed by the author's interviews, there is often a clear link between the regulating institution and the industry into which an ex-bureaucrat is descending. Citing the example of the telecommunications sector, Nakano (1998, p. 109) notes, "these *amakudari* officials owe their positions in the directorships of telecommunications companies to the fact that they are members of an elite group with regulatory power rather than for any other reasons."

Given that industrial promotion and deregulation measures are not applied equally to all industry sectors, this leads to the hypothesis that:

H2. Amakudari networks differ across industries.

Attempts to develop the Japanese post-war economy concentrated on isolation of internal markets and on export promotion. The latter effort was represented by the creation of a "Supreme Export Council"[13] and the creation and activities of JETRO.[14] Therefore, it is not surprising that companies in export-intense sectors have a particularly high number of *amakudari* appointments to their boards (Schaede, 1995, p. 314). The reason for this is access to first-hand information and support from state representatives involved in the external market development.

The continuing economic recession in Japan, and the reluctance of the U.S. government to put excessive pressure on the Japanese government, appears to have resulted in a decrease in the number and intensity of trade negotiations between the U.S. and Japan in the 1990s. Of the three major trade initiatives between 1985 and 1998, the Structural Impediments Initiatives commenced in 1989, the Semiconductor Trade Agreement was concluded in 1991, and the Framework Talks collapsed in 1994 (Pempel, 1997, p. 344).

From the above, one can conclude that the need for corporations to maintain good amakudari networks in order to promote their exports is decreasing. This leads to the following hypothesis:

H3. The interdependence between export orientation and amakudari networks is decreasing.

Amakudari, Industrial Policy and Keiretsu

It has already been mentioned that the Japanese state supported the formation of cartels as one element of industrial policy. In order to achieve economic growth, the state also actively supported the re-formation of industrial groups (*keiretsu*) from parts of the former *zaibatsu*, as well as their diversification into several new areas of the economy. Kikkawa (1996, 188ff) points out that the authorities provided considerable support and guidance when the "Big Six" *keiretsu* groups invested in new technologies or developed new industries. The keyword for this is "one-set-ism" (*wansettoshugi*), meaning the strategy that – when developing a new industry – each "Big Six" group defined (or founded) at least one enterprise per target industry to be part of the still-regulated game. Co-ordination and guidance were achieved through the "old boys" networks.

Previous investigation with this data set has shown that *keiretsu* firms tend to be larger than non-*keiretsu* firms (Moerke, Görtzen & Zobel, 2000, p. 22). Furthermore, within the "Big Six" horizontal *keiretsu* groups, an "insurance" function exists, which is equivalent to profit margins, thus making sure that in the long term, *keiretsu* firms have had more stable results (Lincoln, Gerlach & Ahmadjian, 1996; Moerke, 1999) and, consequently, attract more ex-bureaucrats. This is matched in the findings made by other researchers. Usui and Colignon (1997) point out that the horizontal *keiretsu* firms have long been a favored place of employment for *amakudari* bureaucrats. As a result, this study sought to verify if the links that existed in high growth periods between industrial groups and the bureaucracy are still in use, and how these are related to the companies' results:

H4. Amakudari networks continue in horizontal *keiretsu* firms.

Since economic success is not monocausal, proving a direct link between amakudari networks and corporate performance is unlikely. This does not mean, however, that methods developed under the framework of critical success factor analysis cannot also be applied to this field. One widely used methodology is to compare a group of successful companies with a group performing less well in order to identify differences with regard to certain characteristics, for instance investment behavior, board structures, and so forth.

We examined the difference between successful and badly performing firms with regard to their amakudari network based on previous research on success factors in Japanese companies (Moerke et al., 2000). The conclusion drawn from a survey carried out in support of this study,[15] is that ex-bureaucrats prefer to descend to corporations achieving good results:

H5a. There is a positive correlation between amakudari network and economic success.

H5b. However, following the overall pattern of development, the close links between successful corporations and bureaucracy are weakening.

The Paradigm Shift: From State Regulation to Self-Regulation

The question as to which parties initiate the *amakudari network* is not easily answered. A consideration of the motives of the parties involved, however, might be helpful. The motives of the bureaucracy as a whole can be explained by its role in the Japanese State and its impact on Japanese (industrial) policy (Aoki, 1988; Göseke, 1997; Johnson, 1989). The bureaucracy plays an important part in policymaking in Japan (Miyamoto, 1996) as well as in policy implementation. Up until the 1980s at least, the bureaucracy was viewed as the group leading the country. *Amakudari* networks were used as one means of policy implementation.

The theoretical approach used to explain this phenomenon is called the "*push perspective*" (Nakano, 1998). Aoki (1988, p. 267), for example, holds the view that, "... there is a strong push effect from the ministry ..." Johnson (1989), Schaede (1994) and Tsutsuumi and Yamaguchi (1997) also argue in support of the push perspective.

For the individual civil servant, an obvious advantage of *amakudari* is the compensation. By obtaining a well-paid position in the private sector, the ex-bureaucrat is compensated for years of lower pay. According to Kim (1996), a 30-year old civil servant receives a salary of approximately 30% less than that of a managerial employee in a private company. This view was shared by some interviewees, who pointed out that among bureaucrats, one finds "excellent personnel" (*yushuna jinzai*). Assets of resource thus bring us back to the resource-dependence view mentioned above. Furthermore, amakudari is not necessarily limited to one appointment. Successful ex-bureaucrats may look for additional appointments after the elapse of a certain time (for instance, the period specified to acquire pension entitlement). This ongoing *amakudari* is called "wataridori" (migratory bird) (Usui & Colignon, 1999, p. 51).

Conversely, there is a view that corporations are those who take the initiative in *amakudari* appointments. This perspective is referred to as the "pull perspective." Koyama (1996), for instance, states that numerous companies seek to obtain capable personnel assets through the employment of amakudari (Koyama, 1996, pp. 182, 184). The definition of those assets may vary, since the needs of the corporations are different. For some, it may be the dense personal network that ex-bureaucrats have been able to build up during their time in the ministries. For other companies, it is the regulatory knowledge possessed by the respective bureaucrat that is the most valuable resource. In times of global competition, information represents an important advantage. Knowledge of what is going on in the industry can be crucial for success.

Clearly, the period from 1985 to 1998 was characterized by major changes in the Japanese economy. The economic success and Japan's trade imbalance caused Western countries, especially the United States, to criticize Japanese policy and demand deregulation in a number of sectors. Demands for deregulation were successful in several areas, including manufacturing, agriculture, and financial markets to name but a few. Yet, to believe that deregulation meant the total opening of the markets is misleading. As Schaede (2000) clearly points out, there has been a shift from government regulation to self-regulation through industry associations.

In the case of *amakudari* networks, it should again be pointed out that the bursting of the economic bubble revealed severe shortfalls in Japanese industrial policy, and the reputation of the bureaucracy as a knowledgeable elite to be trusted was shaken considerably by a number of scandals, including bribery and misuse of funds, amongst other things. This has reduced the incentive to appoint members of the former elite purely on the basis of their status or experience. State institutions are facing increasing difficulties in seconding their personnel to other institutions.

Linking those two points – increasing self-regulation and decreasing power of the regulators – it may be assumed that the characteristics of amakudari networks are also undergoing change. To investigate this, two different time spans were defined: The first is from 1985 to 1991 and is referred to as the "bubble period"; the second is the "crisis period" from 1992 to 1998. Those two time spans were compared in order to investigate the differences, summed up in the following hypothesis regarding a paradigm shift:

H6. Resource-dependent corporations have increasing discretion in the selection and placement of ex-bureaucrats.

METHODS

Data

This paper is based on data in the "Kaisha database" of the Science Center for Social Research in Berlin, using Japanese business reports in accordance with the Commercial Law (= *yuka shoken hokokusho*), and is now maintained at the Center for Japanese Studies of the Beisheim Graduate School of Management, WHU. It contains data from the unconsolidated accounts of 111 companies since 1970 in the following five industrial sectors: chemicals, machine tools, electrical engineering, pharmaceuticals, and transportation/automotive. Reports from companies in the automotive sector cover the years 1985–1998. This database was created to enable a German-Japanese comparison, its structure is therefore based on the "German Database" at the Science Center.

The "Kaisha Database" was compiled from a sample of the largest companies listed on the first section of the Tokyo Stock Exchange in 1992, due to the enormous significance larger companies assign to real net output in Japan. In order to remain open for wider research approaches, as much information as possible was compiled from the annual accounts with the highest possible level of detail. To date, data from 1970 to 1998 have been recorded. As a result, over 3600 records with 720 variables and more than 135 workfiles each are available. For a detailed description, see Albach et al. (1997).

For this chapter, data from the automotive, electronics and electrical engineering as well as the machine tool industries were selected based on their high export orientation. The pharmaceutical sector, only minimally successful in export and still highly regulated, provided a control sample. Seventy-seven firms were used in the analysis. The time span investigated covered the period between 1985 and 1998.

Both financial data and biographical information were used in the analysis. Additionally, about 50 persons from the four industries, as well as mass media and research institutions, were interviewed to provide further background and insight. Discussions regarding individual issues were held with Japanese managers in person wherever possible. Financial information for the analysis was drawn from the "Kaisha Database" and from Japanese company reports (*yuka shoken hokokusho*). These reports contain a section with biographical profiles of the directors, in which information is provided on their university degrees, career to date, including employment in other companies or government institutions, areas of responsibility and hierarchical level achieved. This degree of disclosure – which would be unthinkable in German companies – facilitates the detailed analysis necessary to ascertain links to other entities. Thus, the analysis is based on publicly available material. It is not intended, and indeed would be difficult, to discern all possible ties between directors, including those based on personal friendships, memberships in golf clubs, unreported payments, etc.

With the focus on personal ties to institutions of the state bureaucracy, the object of investigation in this chapter was the question of how the relationship (the "amakudari network") has changed over time.

To do so, the biographical profiles of the directors found in the annual reports were examined for evidence of previous engagement in a government institution or other public entity. Apart from the ministries, government entities included the Bank of Japan, the Fair Trade Commission, JETRO (Japan External Trade Organization), the Patent Office and technical inspection agencies, JR (Japan Railways), NTT (Nippon Telecom & Telegraph) and the radio and TV organization, NHK (Nihon Hoso Kyokai). Although JR and NTT have since been privatized, they are still clearly subject to government influence. As a result, NTT continues to be closely linked to the Ministry of Post and Telecommunications and other government institutions (cf. Takahashi, 1995, p. 191).

A BUREAUCRAT index was developed to establish the significance of such links. The most important feature of the index is that it takes all appointments with government entities of a certain person into account. The reason for this is that bureaucrats are embedded in a network, and this network, as well as the knowledge gained during their employment in several institutions, is valuable for the company. This process of determining links and their influence was carried out in several stages, as outlined below.

Determining the Influence of the Institution
Biographical data for each individual were reviewed to determine if the person had worked in the public sector. If so, a value between 1 and 3 was assigned to each position held, depending on the institution. A high score (=3) indicated a high value of the network for the company, since contact to, and direct information from, the regulating institution can be maintained. An example of this is the Ministry of Post and Telecommunications with respect to companies in the electrical/electronics industry, and MITI with regard to the mechanical engineering/machine tools sector. Conversely, the Ministry of Health was adjudged to have little influence in the mechanical engineering sector, etc.

The classification of institutions is outlined in Table 1. The primary determinant of institutional influence was the extent to which authorities could affect operation of the company. Beyond that, the classification can be explained as follows: based on interviews, the maximum number of points was allocated to members of parliament based on their distinctive personal networks, the utilization of

Table 1. Classification of Network Potential Per Institution and
Industrial Sector.[a]

Institution	Pharmaceuticals	Mechanical Engineering	Electrical/ Electronic Industry	Automobile
Bank of Japan	2	2	2	2
Environment Office	2	2	2	2
Fair Trade Commission	3	3	3	3
Foreign Trade Organizations (bôeki kaigi senmon iinkai etc.)	2	2	2	2
Japan Export-Import Bank	1	1	1	1
Japan Railways	1	1	1	1
JETRO	1	1	1	1
Members of Parliament	3	3	3	3
Ministry for Health and Welfare	3	1	1	1
Ministry for International Trade and Industry	1	3	3	3
Ministry for Land and Forestry	1	1	1	1
Ministry for Post and Telecommunications	1	2	3	2
Ministry of Construction	1	3	2	2
Ministry of Finance (MoF)	2	2	2	2
Ministry of Foreign Affairs	1	1	1	1
Ministry of Internal Affairs	1	1	1	1
Ministry of Justice	1	1	1	1
Ministry of Labor	1	1	1	1
Ministry of Transport	1	2	2	2
NHK	1	1	2	1
NTT	1	1	3	1
Patent Office	3	2	3	2
Regional Autonomy Organs	1	1	1	1
Self-Defense Forces	1	1	2	1
Technical Test Authorities	1	1	3	1

Source: Author's classification.
[a] Relative 3: high in influence; 1: relatively low influence.

which can be of immense benefit to the companies. The Fair Trade Commission, *Kōsei torihiki iinkai*, received the highest number of points based on its potential to impose sanctions perceived as critical to private sector companies (Ueki, 1996) and on the opportunity to negotiate with former colleagues against those sanctions. JETRO was rated at just above zero points (i.e. slightly exceeding unimportance), because the industries studied have a strong export orientation or are endeavoring to establish one. NHK, as the state broadcasting and television network, is important to the electrical/electronics industry due to its close links with the Ministry for Post and Telecommunications. The latter has itself employed a large number of former ministry bureaucrats and is responsible for setting the standards for the technical equipment used in the video and audio industry.

One has to take into consideration that personal networks developing during time in an institution are maintained. Well-known examples are the alumni organizations of universities (*Josuikai* for *Hitotsubashi*, *Mitakai* for *Keio*, and so on), where meetings are regularly held, and membership information is widely available. Therefore, in the case of employment in several agencies, each was given a rating, and then ratings were summed.

Determining the Role in the Board of Directors
The next step in determining influence involved determining the position of an amakudari executive in relation to the hierarchical structure of the entire board. Japanese corporations are hierarchical in structure, and there are radically varying degrees to which each rank may participate in the decision-making process (cf. Hirata, 1996). The board of directors, which is (de jure) elected at the shareholders' meeting, consists of directors at several levels, beginning with the Chairman (*kaicho*), the President (*shacho*), Senior Managing Directors (*senmu torishimariyaku*), Managing Directors (*jomu torishimariyaku*) and the Directors (*torishimariyaku*). Each position is not necessarily found in every company. Representative Directors (*daihyo torishimariyaku*) are chosen from among the top-level directors. They fulfill the task of representing the company and often make decisions regarding its strategy and business objectives relatively independently (Hirata, 1996; Otto, 1997, p. 55, referring to an investigation of Keizai Doyukai in 1996). *Sodanyaku* are often ex-company presidents who are theoretically no longer in service, but nevertheless maintain their personal network and supply their knowledge. The higher the person's rank, the more likely their opinion will be heard and followed by the decision-making group or person. For this reason, different scores were assigned to the individual positions. Their scores were then multiplied by the index of links with bureaucratic institutions mentioned above:

Table 2. Calculation of the Amakudari Network Intensity.

Director A	Director B
Value of each amakudari director's network for the firm	
Ministry of Telecomm. = 3 points	MITI = 3 points
NTT = 3 points	JETRO = 1 points
NHK = 3 points	
Total = 9 points	Total = 4 points
Including the rank of the respective person	
Representative Director = 3 p	Ordinary Director = 1 point
Value × Rank = 9 × 3 = 27 points	Value × Rank = 4 × 1 = 4 points
Addition	
27 + 4 = 31 points	
Integration	
Step (a) The board consists of	
1 representative director (3 points)	
+ 1 senior managing director (2 points)	
+ 5 directors (1 point each, 5 points in total)	
Therefore, the total sum of all ranks is 10 points.	
Step (b) Calculating the relative weight of the amakudari network: 31/10 = 3.1	

- 3 points for representative directors (*daihyo torishimariyaku*), as the highest ranking board members, and for "consultants" (*sodanyaku*)
- 2 points for senior managing directors (*senmu torishimariyaku*) and managing directors (*jomu torishimariyaku*)
- 1 point, and thus no additional weighting, for directors (*torishimariyaku*) and auditors (*kansayaku*).

Summing Network Influence

If more than one director with a background in the state bureaucracy is on board, the values of the several directors were summed up.

Calculating Amakudari Network Intensity

In the final step, it is calculated in relation to the total of all ranks on the board. Table 2 illustrates the overall calculation.

ANALYSIS

Analysis of amakudari network intensity proceeded from companions of innovative statistics to examination of correlation results and finally to multivariate regression analysis. The amakudari network has visibly weakened. In 1986, the average amakudari network ratio over the entire sample was 11.8. In 1998, the ratio had fallen to 7.4. A t-test found a significant difference at a = 0.05. This can be explained partly by the reduced work force observed in the electronics and automotive companies from the mid-1990s. The drop in amakudari networks, however, is greater than the reduction in the overall work force. In summary, Hypothesis 1, a decreasing *amakudari* network, is confirmed. The following, more sophisticated analysis of industry and *keiretsu* effects further prove this argument.

Industry-Bureaucracy Networks and Industrial Policy

In view of the industrial policy in Japan and the previously described relationship mechanisms, differences between the industries were expected. Figure 2 confirms and illustrates this expectation. Over the entire period, the differences between the mean values for all industry types are statistically significant at a level of 0.05 or less. It should be noted that dividing in the subperiods of 1985–1991 and 1992–1998, the values for the pharmaceutical and mechanical engineering industries are so close that the difference between these two industries is no longer significant.

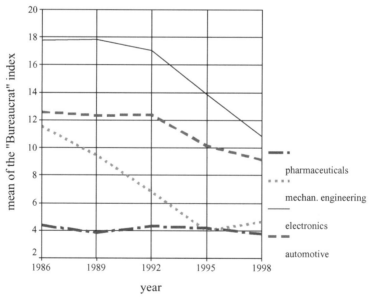

Fig. 2. Links with the Bureaucracy Based on Industry Type. *Source:* Author's estimations.

Table 3. Comparison of the Average Amakudari Network in the Industries.

Industry	1985–1991	1992–1998
Pharmaceuticals	4.13	4.09
Machine tools	9.33	4.96[**]
Electronics/electrical	15.64	12.90[*]
Automotive	12.30	10.51

Source: Author's calculation.
[*]Correlation significant at the level of 0.05 (bilaterally).
[**]Correlation significant at the level of 0.10 (bilaterally).

The higher incidence of links for companies in the electrical/electronic and automobile industries, as well as their steady decline, is obvious. It is, however, puzzling that pharmaceuticals – one of the most heavily regulated industries in Japan – shows the lowest level of *amakudari*. It may be that other ways of exerting influence and information flow are used in this industry. Anecdotal evidence from interviews with professionals points to the existence and use of "study groups" (*benkyokai* or *kenkyukai*) as one possible means of influence.

Since our aim is to investigate changes, the mean value of amakudari network density for each industry in the "bubble period" (1985–1991) was compared with that in the "crisis period" (1992–1998). Table 3 provides an overview and information regarding the statistical significance of this comparison.

The average network value clearly differs significantly in the machine tool and electronics/electrical industries, whereas the changes in the automotive and pharmaceutical industry did not occur at a comparably high level. In summary, we can conclude that H2, amakudari networks differ by industry type, is confirmed.

Also noteworthy is the surprisingly low level of amakudari networks in the pharmaceutical industry, compared to the other industries, which concurs with Schaede's (1995) argument that export-oriented companies in particular frequently employ ex-bureaucrats. In the current study, the correlation of export ratio and ties with the bureaucracy is positive and statistically significant in both the automobile and machine tool sectors. Pearson's correlation coefficient is positive over the entire study period, but becomes weaker post-1989 onwards (Table 4). This may be interpreted as a sign that at least until the mid-1990s, good relations with the bureaucracies paid off in terms of a higher export share. However, the question as to whether this is a consequence of the exertion of industrial policy by the government and ministries, or of corporations proactively appointing ex-bureaucrats to benefit exports, remains unanswered.

Table 4. Correlation of Export Share and Amakudari Network.

Year	Pearson's Coefficient of Correlation
1986	0.208[*]
1989	0.250[**]
1992	0.205[*]
1995	0.194[*]
1998	0.139

Source: Author's calculation.
[*]Correlation significant at the level of 0.05 (bilaterally).
[**]Correlation significant at the level of 0.10 (bilaterally).

According to the results in Table 4, one can conclude that the interdependence of export orientation and amakudari for the investigated industries is weakening, thus confirming Hypothesis 3.

Amakudari, Industrial Policy, and Keiretsu

It was assumed that the Japanese state would also influence industrial organization so as to enable the implementation of particular industrial policies. The next phase of investigation comprised analysis of differences in the intensity of amakudari network with respect to the group structure of each company. A set of definitions developed during the establishment of and work with the "Kaisha Database" at the Science Center in Berlin was also used here (cf. Albach, 2000; Görtzen, 2001; Moerke et al., 2000; Zobel, 2000). The following subgroups were defined and analyzed:

(1) A *horizontal company* is a member of one of the "presidents' councils" (*shachokai*), with the exception of those at the top of their vertical *keiretsu* group.
(2) An *independent* company belongs to none of these categories.
(3) A corporation is *vertically integrated* when another company owns over 20% of the shares, or when the main customer owns over 10% of the shares.
(4) A *core company* is a corporation heading the 20 largest industrial groups in the manufacturing industry listed on the Kigyo Keiretsu Soran.

Core companies can either belong to a horizontal group (i.e. be member of a *shachokai*, and at the same time be at the top of their respective group, such as Toyota) or be independent (i.e. without membership of a *shachokai*, but on top of their own group, for instance Sony). For the analysis of personal networks, it turned out that the vertical dimension (the comparison of core and vertically integrated

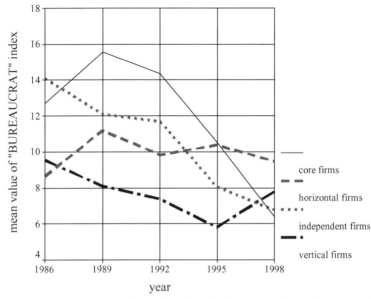

Fig. 3. Amakudari Networks, Investigated with Respect to Group Structure. *Source:* Author's estimations.

firms) is more important than the horizontal dimension (member or non-member of a horizontal *keiretsu*) (Moerke, 2000, p. 35).

Figure 3 reveals that amakudari networks have remained relatively stable for the "Big six," "horizontal" corporate entities. The other corporations have decreases in their amakudari networks with statistically significant differences (2.05) for the core vertical company comparison.

An interesting finding is that subsidiary and other vertically integrated firms started to appoint increasing numbers of ex-bureaucrats again after 1995. This development likely has its roots in the same mechanism found in the links to the financial institutions and was demonstrated in the research of development activities examined by Görtzen (2000). The company at the top of a vertical group assumes "responsibility" for the group's relationship management, and it ensures the flow of information. However, in seconding personnel, core firms have additional scope to control and influence their subsidiaries and subcontractors, as well as reducing personnel costs.

To make the changes even more visible, the mean values of network density for each subgroup were calculated over two different time spans, and their differences tested for statistical significance. Table 5 provides the results. The fact that the

Table 5.   Comparing the Average *Amakudari* Network with Respect to Group
Structure.

Keiretsu Structure	1985–1991	1992–1998
Horizontal companies	9.92	10.41
Core companies	14.25	10.41[**]
Independent companies	12.93	8.82[**]
Vertical companies	8.64	6.82

Source: Author's calculation.
** Significant at the level of 0.05.

links to state institutions have undergone considerable change only in core and independent firms may be interpreted as a further indication of the declining influence of industrial policy.

An important step would be to investigate in greater detail if these results apply to all industries (or are only specific to one or two). Based on the size of the sample ($n = 77$ per year), a further division of specific subsamples is not practicable (for instance, to enable examination of the difference between horizontal firms in the automotive, machine tool and electronics industries, etc.). Such a step would result in sub-subsamples of one, three, or four companies, thus making statistical analysis impossible. Therefore, we conclude: Group organization features are also of significance for *amakudari* networks: H4 is confirmed. To check for the impact on the industry of interference, group dummies will be integrated into the regression.

Amakudari Networks and Corporate Success

One aim of this investigation was to clarify whether there is a positive correlation between corporate economic performance and the intensity of amakudari networks. Findings from this study help to establish an answer to the question, "What are the benefits of *amakudari*?" as well as to determine whether *amakudari* bureaucrats tend to descend into wealthy corporations for their own safety and advantage.

To further success factors explore, a performance criterion composed of certain indices was used and applied to the sample. The first test was to see whether there was a correlation between economic success criteria and amakudari networks. However, neither the test for the whole time span nor the test for every single year provided sufficient statistical evidence for a straightforward correlation.

The second step was to define two groups that differ with regard to their economic results. We identified the so-called "Top 15" as the best-performing and the "Bottom 15" as the worst-performing companies. These two subsamples

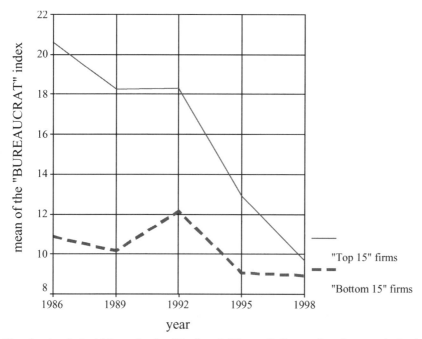

Fig. 4. Amakudari Networks for "Top" and "Bottom" Companies. *Source:* Author's estimations.

were then examined with respect to their amakudari networks. The investigation of the impact of the industry type showed remarkable stability in the pharmaceutical sector, while the companies in the other three categories differed dramatically. For this reason, the examination of links with the government bureaucracy for companies with "better" and "worse" economic performances was carried out without the pharmaceutical branch. Figure 4 presents a graphic overview of the comparison overtime. The differences between the two subgroups are clear and, at least in the first half of the period, statistically quite dramatic ($P < 0.05$). It is apparent that "good" companies, by accepting *amakudari* bureaucrats, initially considered it constructive to cultivate their ties with the authorities. However, from 1992 onwards, when scandals occurred, and it became obvious that ministerial bureaucracy was unable to either solve or forecast problems, the "good" companies radically reduced their amakudari networks. Thus, in 1998, a balancing out of the values can be noted, and the differences between the subgroups are no longer as significant. A Mann-Whitney test was applied for comparison of the year 1998, because the samples were insufficient for the *t*-test.

The values of the bottom 15 can also be explained by group structure. A disproportionately large number of vertically integrated companies are represented in the group of "bad" companies, which have fewer ex-bureaucrats on their boards for the same reasons as the core companies.

In conclusion, we can say that in the past, good corporations had closer *amakudari* networks (which partly confirms H5a) but that these networks have subsequently been reduced (confirming H5b).

Integration of Findings: The Amakudari Network Production Function

Following clarification of several details, this paragraph aims to establish the initiator of and driving force behind the *amakudari* process – the state and its bureaucratic institutions, or the corporations? Can a paradigm shift from the former to the latter be seen? In order to reach a conclusion, we have to return to a fundamental question, "What are the benefits of appointing ex-bureaucrats to the boards of directors? Do they have a (measurable) effect?"

In this last step, a production function was used to answer these questions, integrating aspects such as group membership and industry. The classical production function assumes that output is mainly determined by capital and labor. Based on the "Cobb Douglas" function, the equation reads as follows:

$$X = \alpha_0 \times C^{\alpha_1} \times L^{\alpha_2}, \tag{1}$$

where X = sales; α_0 = constant;[16] C = capital; L = labor (number of employees). Because companies operate in different environments, what is viewed as capital can be subject to a number of interpretations. For the purpose of this analysis, the Cobb Douglas function was adopted with "capital" being defined as social capital, i.e. the networks and knowledge of the appointed ex-bureaucrats. When replacing C (capital) by "AN" (*amakudari* networks), the Cobb-Douglas function can be written in the following log linear way:

$$\ln X = \ln\alpha_0 + \alpha_1 \ln L + \alpha_2 \ln AN. \tag{2}$$

In this analysis, a regression using the ordinary least-square method (OLS regression) was estimated. In light of the existence of panel data, dummy variables were used for each year. To integrate industry and *keiretsu* effects, the respective dummy variables were integrated into the equation. The estimation for the whole period resulted in the following:[17]

$$\ln X = \underset{(74.32)}{10.625} + \underset{(66.84)}{0.987\ln L} + \underset{(6.35)}{0.052\ln NB}, \tag{3}$$

where $(\ldots)$ = t-values; $R^2 = 0.943$; DW $= 2.056$; $N = 1077$.

The equation shows that links with the bureaucracy have a significant and positive influence on sales. The influence of labor on sales is understandably higher. Any other finding would be a considerable surprise. This equation very much reinforces the view that companies indeed chose bureaucrats according to their own requirements – a positive relation with sales is otherwise difficult to explain.

In the next step, a regression was run over the two time spans previously defined. By comparing the "bubble" period with the period of "crisis" in Japan, the characteristics of the relationship between corporations and state institutions became clearer. Consequently, we could answer the question as to who takes the initiative. The answer is linked to the question of the status of present-day Japan's position as being either developmental or post-developmental.

Table 6 provides the results for the regression run separately for the "bubble period" (1985–1991) and "crisis period" (1992–1998).

Not only did the impact of labor on sales increase, but also the influence of the networks with bureaucratic institutions increased. When one recalls that the extent of the amakudari networks has weakened over time, the logical conclusions are that:

(1) In the "bubble" period, sales were not a problem.
(2) In the latter half of the 1990s, Japanese companies became more aware of their resources. This includes the appointment of personnel to the board. People were selected with increasing attention to their abilities.

In summary, one cannot say that the state as an actor has vanished, but the data very much support the view that, particularly in the latter half of the period under analysis, a shift has taken place in which companies are now the main actors in the game. This supports Hypothesis 6.

Table 6. Amakudari Network Production Function, in Two Time Spans.[a]

Sales = Function of	1985–1991 (Bubble Period)	1992–1998 (Crisis Period)
–Constant (*t*-value)	10.691 (57.77)	10.822 (50.90)
–Labor (*t*-value)	0.977 (50.36)	0.996 (44.92)
–Amakudari network (*t*-value)	0.039 (3.76)	0.065 (4.98)
R^2	0.950	0.937
DW	1.985	1.932
N	539	538

Source: Author's calculation.
[a] All $\alpha < 0.001$.

CONCLUSION

The objective of this chapter was to research changes in government-business relationships in Japan, particularly in the amakudari process and amakudari networks formed by companies. To achieve this, the biographical data from the boards of directors of 77 of the largest companies in the manufacturing sector (a total of 10,000 individuals) were analyzed in respect to their ties to state bureaucratic institutions. An index was developed to indicate whether or not a director had worked with a state institution, and also to reflect the regulatory power of the institutions from which the directors originated, as well as directors' positions in the hierarchical structure of the board. The time period analyzed was from 1986 to 1998. The background to this study is a Japanese economy in long-term crisis where former success factors seem to have become obsolete, and ongoing deregulation enables or requires companies to take the initiative.

In summary, we can say that in the period under examination, *amakudari* networks became weaker. This applied to three of the four industries we studied. The one exception was the highly regulated pharmaceutical sector, where amakudari networks have remained the most constant, albeit lowest in numbers. The investigation also found that group structures are of significance. While all other subgroups were reducing their amakudari networks, the Big Six *keiretsu* firms continued to be receptive to *amakudari* descent. An investigation of the links between corporate success and amakudari networks revealed that successful corporations – once considered optimal locations for the secondment of ex-bureaucrats – have reduced their networks dramatically. The success of a company is now largely irrelevant in terms of appointments. The most interesting point, however, became evident only after integrating all industry and *keiretsu* effects into a production function. We found that amakudari networks did have a greater impact on sales in the latter half of the investigation period, leading to the interpretation that Japanese corporations are now able to make decisions regarding the appointments of ex-bureaucrats to the boards of directors more freely, and tend to select those individuals offering optimal access to resources required by the company.

NOTES

1. Cf. in particular Pempel's essay "Regime Shift: Japanese Politics in a Changing World Economy." The question regarding the actual (or optimal) direction of changes generated a wide range of opinions. The next question is whether there is an ideal model to follow. The Anglo-Saxon system frequently recommended (e.g. Nakatani, 1997; Vaubel,

2002) is, of course, criticized following the Enron and WorldCom bankruptcies (or even before; cf. Ronald Dore's (1999) harsh argumentation).

2. Although there are different forms of "administrative guidance," the common aspect is that the enterprises were not obliged to follow the advice provided by the bureaucracy, but were de facto better off doing so because otherwise the bureaucratic institutions would find ways to punish the corporations by delaying or simply failing to respond to requests, etc. (cf. Foljanty-Jost, 1989; Johnson, 1982).

3. Literally: "descending from heaven." Following their retirement from public service, high-ranking bureaucrats frequently occupy positions in management or directorships in companies after a legally specified interval of two years (Johnson, 1982; Moerke, 2000; Schaede, 1995; Usui & Colignon, 1997, 1999 and others). In the literature, "ascending" or "amaagari" is provided as the counterpart to "descending from heaven." This means the temporary secondment of personnel from private companies to state authorities. This procedure enables an interchange between authorities and citizens; those sent to government service are deemed to be officials for the duration of their secondment (Tsutsuumi & Yamaguchi, 1997, p. 47).

4. And was, therefore, examined a number of times. Cf. for instance Johnson (1982) for an analysis of MITI; or Göseke's (1997) investigation of JETRO.

5. Using the example of Sumitomo Metal who tried to resist MITI's orders and failed, Johnson (1982, p. 271) showed that there was a time when private enterprises could not afford to ignore the ministry's wishes and demands.

6. A more recent example is provided by the bridge and road system: The Honshū-Shikoku Bridge Authority that runs the relatively new Akashi Kaikyo Bridge "is currently forced to spend 200 yen for every 100 yen it churns out in revenue" because the number of users is far behind the estimations (Yoshida & Naito, 2001).

7. Especially Johnson (1982), but also Yamamura (1997).

8. Cf. Pfeffer and Salancik's (1978) contribution "The external control of Organizations. A Resource Dependence Perspective," as referenced to in Schaede (1995, p. 300), and in Kieser (1999, p. 164).

9. Usui and Colignon provide an exemption for they explicitly look for change in theirs papers.

10. This has a strong influence on corporate governance mechanisms. Cf. the paper of C. Pochet in this volume.

11. Pharmaceuticals remains a sensitive case, but with recent M&A (Mitsubishi Tokyo Pharmaceutical's merger with Welfide, or Chugai and Roche's agreement) things change, e.g. the market is no longer isolated.

12. Johnson (1982, p. 231) names three: the "Five year plan for economic independence" (1956–1960), the "New long-term economic Plan" (1958–1962), and the "National income doubling plan" (1961–1970), a more recent example is the "e-Japan Initiative" by Prime Minister Mori.

13. Johnson (1982, p. 230).

14. Göseke (1997) shows clearly that import promotion is more or less the fig leaf for the export promotion still carried out by JETRO.

15. This small survey addressed 50 people from management positions in private companies, newspapers/journals, and research institutions in Japan. It was conducted in July and August 2002.

16. Meaning the intersection with the *y*-axis.

17. For all shown coefficients, $\alpha < 0.001$.

REFERENCES

Albach, H., Görtzen, U., Miarka, T., Moerke, A., Westphal, T., & Zobel, R. (1997). Documentation of the "kaisha" database – The database of the annual reports of Japanese corporations. *Discussion Paper FS IV 97–39*. Berlin: Science Center for Social Research.

Aoki, M. (1988). *Information, incentives, and bargaining in the Japanese economy*. Cambridge: Cambridge University Press.

Blechinger, V. (1998). Slim on the way into the 21st century? The administrative reform program of the Government of Hashimoto. *Japanmarkt*, February, 17–18.

Blechinger, V. (2000). Corruption through political contributions in Japan. Paper, submitted for a TI workshop on "Corruption and Political Party Funding." La Pietra, Italy.

Calder, K. (1989). Elites in an equalizing role. Ex-bureaucrats as coordinators and intermediaries in the Japanese government-business relationship. *Comparative Politics, 21*, 379–403.

Dore, R. (1999). Japan's reform debate: Patriotic concern or class interest? Or both? *Journal of Japanese Studies, 25*, 65–89.

Foljanty-Jost, G. (1989). Informelles Verwaltungshandeln. Schlüssel effizienter Politik oder Politik ohne Politiker? [Informal administrative behavior: Key to efficient policy implementation or policy without politicians?]. In: U. Menzel (Ed.), *Im Schatten des Siegers* (pp. 171–190). Frankfurt/Main: Suhrkamp.

Görtzen, U. (2001). *Wissensgenerierung und -verbreitung als Wettbewerbsfaktor. Eine empirische Analyse am Beispiel japanischer Industrieaktiengesellschaften* [Knowledge creation and dissemination as a factor of competition. An empirical analysis of Japanese industrial stock corporations]. Wiesbaden: Deutscher Universitätsverlag.

Göseke, C. (1997). *Information gathering and dissemination. The contribution of JETRO to Japanese competitiveness*. Wiesbaden: Deutscher Universitätsverlag.

Hirata, M. (1996). Die japanische torishimariyaku-kai. Eine rechtliche und betriebswirtschaftliche Analyse [The Japanese "torishimari-kai." A legal and economic analysis]. *Zeitschrift für Betriebswirtschaft, 3*, 1–28.

Johnson, C. (1989). Wer regiert Japan? Ein Essay über die staatliche Bürokratie [Who governs Japan? An essay on the state bureaucracy]. In: U. Menzel (Ed.), *Im Schatten des Siegers* (pp. 225–255). Frankfurt/Main: Suhrkamp.

Kieser, A. (Ed.) (1999). *Organisationstheorien* [Organizational theories]. Stuttgart: Kohlhammer.

Kim, H. (1996). International colloquium on "the civil service and economic development: The Japanese experience. In: The World Bank (Ed.), *The Civil Service System and Economic Development* (pp. 3–37). Washington, DC: World Bank.

Koyama, K. (1996). *Sengo keizai wo sasaeta hitobito* [The men who supported the postwar economy]. Tokyo: Shoji homu kenkyukai.

Lincoln, J. R., Gerlach, M. L., & Ahmadjian, C. L. (1996). Keiretsu networks and corporate performance in Japan. *American Sociological Review, 61*, 67–88.

Miyamoto, M. (1996). *Die Zwangsjackengesellschaft* [The straitjacket society]. Düsseldorf: Metropolitan-Verlag.

Moerke, A. (1999). Performance and corporate governance structure of Japanese keiretsu groups. In: H. Albach, U. Görtzen & R. Zobel (Eds), *Information Processing as a Competitive Advantage of Japanese Firms* (pp. 211–238). Berlin: Edition Sigma.

Moerke, A. (2000). *Organisationslernen über Netzwerke. Die personellen Verflechtungen von Führungsgremien japanischer Aktiengesellschaften* [Organizational learning through networks.

An empirical analysis of personnel networks in the boards of directors of Japanese stock corporations]. Wiesbaden: Deutscher Universitätsverlag.

Moerke, A., Görtzen, U., & Zobel, R. (2000). Grundlegende methodische Überlegungen zur mikroökonomischen Forschung mit japanischen Unternehmensdaten [Fundamental considerations for micro-economic research with Japanese corporate data]. Discussion Paper FS IV 00–07, Wissenschaftszentrum für Sozialforschung, Berlin.

Nakano, K. (1998). Becoming a "policy" ministry: The organization and amakudari of the Ministry of Posts and Telecommunications. *Journal of Japanese Studies, 24*, 95–117.

Nakatani, I. (1997). A design for transforming the Japanese economy. *Journal of Japanese Studies, 23*, 399–417.

Pauer, E. (1995). Die Rolle des Staates in Modernisierung und Industrialisierung [The role of the state in modernization and industrialization]. In: G. Foljanty-Jost & A. M. Thränhardt (Eds), *Der schlanke japanische Staat* (pp. 28–47). Opladen: Leske+Budrich.

Pempel, T. (1997). Regime shift. Japanese politics in a changing world economy. *Journal of Japanese Studies, 23*, 333–361.

van Rixtel, A. (1995). *Amakudari in the Japanese banking industry: An empirical investigation. European network and the Japanese economy.* Unpublished manuscript, CEPR/Science Center for Social Research, Berlin.

van Rixtel, A., & Hassink, W. H. (1998). Monitoring the monitors: Amakudari and the ex-post monitoring of private banks. Discussion Paper DP No. 1785, CEPR (Center for Economic Policy Research), London.

Samuels, R. J. (2001). Kishi and corruption: An anatomy of the 1955 system. JPRI Working Paper 83, Cardiff, CA.

Schaede, U. (1994). Understanding corporate governance in Japan: Do classical concepts apply? *Industrial and Corporate Change, 3*, 285–323.

Schaede, U. (1995). The 'old boy' network and government-business relationship in Japan: A case study of 'consultative capitalism'. *Journal of Japanese Studies, 21*, 293–317.

Schaede, U. (2000). *Cooperative capitalism. Self-regulation, trade associations, and the Antimonopoly Law in Japan.* Oxford: Oxford University Press.

Schaede, U., Hoshi, T., & McMillan, J. (1997). *Kisei kanwa – Japanese deregulation. What you should know. Deregulation and Japanese corporate governance?* Japan Information Access Project Report.

Takahashi, T. (1995). Seiji keizai taisei – dokukinhō – zaikai [The system of government and economy; the Anti-Monopoly Law, and financial circles]. In: T. Takahashi (Ed.), *Corporate Governance – Nihon to Doitsu no Kigyō Shisutemu* [Corporate governance – The Japanese and German company system] (pp. 185–195). Tokyo: Chuo keizaisha.

Tsutsuumi, K., & Yamaguchi, J. (1997). *Kanryō amakudari hakusho* [White paper of the amakudari bureaucrats]. Tokyo: Iwanami.

Ueki, K. (1996). Die Kontrolle des Submissionsbetrugs (Dango) nach dem japanischen Anti-Monopol-Gesetz. *Zeitschrift für Betriebswirtschaft, 66*, 735–750.

Usui, C., & Colignon, R. (1997). *The ties that bind the Japanese polity and economy – Amakudari.* Annual Meeting of the Association of Japanese Business Studies, Washington, DC.

Usui, C., & Colignon, R. (1999). *Serial retirements of administrative elites – wataridori.* Association of Japanese Business Studies Twelfth Annual Conference, Best Papers Proceedings (pp. 43–60). Salt Lake City, UT: Association of Japanese Business Studies.

Vaubel, D. (2002). Japan goes normal. Talk delivered at the 9th Conference of the German Economy on Asia and Pacific Affairs, July 5, Tokyo. Mimeo.

Yamamura, K. (1997). The Japanese political economy after the "bubble": Plus ça change? *Journal of Japanese Studies, 23*, 291–331.

Yoshida, R., & Naito, Y. (2001). Inefficient public works project creaking under debt burden. *The Japan Times*, February 6, p. 3.

Zobel, R. (2000). *Beschäftigungsveränderungen und Organisationales Lernen in der japanischen Industrie* [Changes in employment patterns and organizational learning in Japanese stock corporations]. Doctoral dissertation, Humboldt University, Berlin.

THE WINDS OF CHANGE IN JAPANESE TRADE POLICY: TEXTILE MULTINATIONALS AND INTRA-INDUSTRY CLASHES OVER MARKET PROTECTION

Saadia Pekkanen and Mireya Solis

ABSTRACT

This analysis of the Japanese textile sector illustrates how intra-industry cleavages are becoming an integral feature of Japanese trade policymaking. In the past, a pattern of cross-sectoral variation in trade policy could be observed, as the government protected declining industries at home and sought to open foreign markets for the competitive export sector. The internationalization of Japanese firms, however, has radically affected the articulation of corporate trade policy preferences. There is an ongoing breakdown in solidarity among industry members based on their degree of multinationality and/or their reverse importing strategies. These clashes put contradictory pressures on the Japanese government, making it more difficult to predict the course of trade liberalization in Japan.

Japanese Firms in Transition: Responding to the Globalization Challenge
Advances in International Management, Volume 17, 89–111
© 2005 Published by Elsevier Ltd.
ISSN: 0747-7929/doi:10.1016/S0747-7929(04)17004-2

1. FROM CROSS-SECTORAL TO INTRA-SECTORAL CORPORATE PRESSURES

Significant changes in Japan's business environment over the past few decades have led to equally important transformations in the interactions between Japanese firms and their government counterparts. There is substantial variation in both strategy and performance within industries, and, as this paper undertakes to demonstrate through a close study of the textile industry, this is reflected in the increased complexity of Japanese policymaking for both the economics and the business sector.

In the past, a well-established pattern of cross-sectoral variation in Japanese trade policy could be observed. The government granted trade protection at home to declining industries, while at the same time it strove to open foreign markets to the competitive Japanese export sector. Today, the government confronts harder political choices on whether or not to supply the protection due to the growing divergence in corporate trade preferences *within* the same sector. These intra-sectoral differences arise from the fact that there is an ongoing breakdown in solidarity among industry members based on the degree of multinationality of Japanese firms and/or the strategies they follow vis-à-vis the domestic market. Indeed, in some industries, these intra-industry divisions are the result of upstream and downstream multinationals openly clashing over reverse imports and the protection of the domestic market. We illustrate our argument with a close look at the textiles case, long one of the most supported and politicized sectors in the Japanese economy. Within the textiles sector, there is little question that the sharp appreciation of the yen and a decade of domestic recession have fostered the internationalization of Japanese firms that are willing to disregard old conventions on "reverse imports." This has had led to diametrically opposed political pressures on the Japanese government, and hence the bifurcation in Japanese trade policy as a whole. We offer a political analysis of how Japanese textile firms articulate these varied trade preferences and lobby politicians and bureaucrats to tilt trade policies in their favor. As traced in detail, the bifurcation in the preferences of Japanese textile makers hinges not only on the degree of their corporate internationalization, but also on the role assigned by related Japanese MNCs to the home market in their worldwide marketing strategies.

By focusing on Japanese firm preferences, our overall contention is that the direction of Japanese trade policy is less likely to be determined by *gaiatsu* and more by the rift in the Japanese business community. The ongoing changes and divergences in firm preferences about trade liberalization, especially within the same sector, have important consequences for the future of Japan's trade policy. While we focus primarily on the textiles sector, the larger implication of our research is that such stark cleavages in the political preferences of firms are going to become a common and visible feature of the Japanese economy. These cleavages are increasingly going to come to the fore, especially as Japan struggles to adapt to the expanding scope of the legal rules of the WTO. The increased number of players that have now been brought into the trade game and that are willing to articulate their differences boldly, whether across sectors or within sectors, greatly complicates the making of Japanese trade policy. Whereas, before, industry associations generally tended to articulate one consistent position for the entire industry, this is becoming increasingly less frequent. The fault lines within sectors are becoming increasingly divisive and pit industry actors against each other in a visible and confrontational manner. In turn, such bifurcated corporate preferences put contradictory pressures on the Japanese trade-policy establishment, making it difficult to predict which constituency the government is likely to respond to. From the perspective of Japan's trade partners, we believe the divisiveness at the domestic policymaking level should temper any hopes for a smooth process of trade liberalization in the near future.

The remainder of the paper is in three parts. In the first section, we show how Japan has attempted to make the WTO the centerpiece of its trade diplomacy, using legal trade remedies both to open markets abroad and, simultaneously, to protect sensitive sectors at home. The legal activities of the Japanese government, in terms of both complaining and defending, reflect very well the conventional cross-sectoral pressures evident in the Japanese economy at a very broad level, and help to showcase our case study of the textiles sector where the trend towards intra-sectoral pressures is quite clear

Second, then, we turn to a detailed analysis of the internationalization of Japanese textile firms and the raging controversy over reverse imports. We focus on the textiles sector because, traditionally, it is considered to be one of the most protected sectors and the one where we should expect to see continued and consistent levels of government protectionism. Yet even within this sector, there are significant developments that we believe are a harbinger of changes to come across the manufacturing range in Japan. While textiles are often portrayed as a declining sector with homogenous corporate demands for protectionism, the reality is that there are considerable differences in the preferences of different firms with respect to liberalization. Even as some firms in the sector continue to demand protectionism as in the past, the most recent agents of Japanese multinationalism (apparel makers) have unabashedly challenged the principle of orderly importation and in so doing have politicized Japanese trade policy to an unprecedented degree. Such stark differences are more likely to increase rather than disappear anytime in the near future. In fact, they are already making an appearance across a range of policy issues. The resulting divergent corporate preferences came to a head in the Sino-Japanese conflict in 2001, for example, which illustrates the tangible and contradictory pressures on Japanese trade policy, especially in a WTO world.

In the last section, we highlight the larger applicability of our model, by stressing the burgeoning impact of divergent corporate preferences on the course of Japan's liberalization prospects.

2. JAPANESE CROSS-SECTORAL PRESSURES AND THE WTO

In this section, we focus on Japan's activities at the WTO, in terms of legal complaints and defenses mounted by the Japanese government in the formal dispute settlement processes. Even though we stress the importance of a trend towards intra-sectoral pressures as a whole, our larger goal in this section is to show that cross-sectoral pressures continue to be an important determinant of Japan's trade diplomacy. Such pressures are reflected almost evenly in Japan's legal activities from 1995 to the present in the WTO, which has become the forum of choice for handling disputes with Japan's trade partners. This macro-analysis helps set the stage for a detailed look at the textile industry in the next section, where the bifurcation of firm preferences at an intra-sectoral level is fast becoming a prominent feature in the domestic trade policymaking environment, and may well overturn the classic cross-sectoral pressures in importance in the long run.

As a first cut, an examination of the universe of Japan's involvement in legal cases at the WTO lends credence to the view that Japanese trade policy is itself split on behalf of its industries (Pekkanen, 2001a, b). Between the start of the WTO system in January 1995 through to the end of 2001, Japan was involved, as either complainant or defendant, in a total of 18 cases. Overall, one analytical perspective suggests that there is a both an offensive and defensive aspect to Japan's WTO strategy. On the offensive side, the legal rules of the WTO, which are designed to promote liberalization and transparency in trade relations, are used by the Japanese government to try and challenge, not always successfully, foreign measures and practices that affect the economic fate of its multinational or export-oriented firms. Here, the WTO cases include specifically those carried out on behalf of the Japanese automotive and steel industries. On the defensive side, the legal rules also allow the Japanese government to try and protect or safeguard, again not always successfully, the interests of its domestically oriented industries. Here, WTO cases such as those involving agriculture, leather, consumer photographic film, and textiles stand out. Both the offensive and defensive aspects of the strategy are discussed below in more detail.

On the offensive side of the equation, the Japanese government is strongly interested in "fair and free trade" for its multinational or export-oriented firms. Some statistical evidence on this score makes the point rather nicely. Seven of the eight complaints by Japan at the WTO were concerned with the fate of the automobile or the steel sector.[1] Needless to say, apart from their sheer size, these industries are among the most multinational and/or export-oriented in the Japanese economy. Although specific information on which corporations lobbied the government is not available, there is little indication, contrary to the textile sector, that there were divisive intra-sectoral splits in either the automobile or steel sectors as Japan moved towards formal legal activity in the WTO. Nor is there any justification for individual firms to oppose the search for liberalization measures abroad as almost all the firms in such sectors are interested in sustained market access abroad. A closer look at these cases is helpful.

Among the automobile cases, the Japanese government has struck out against what it deems to be discriminatory measures in both the developed and the developing world, including the United States, Brazil, Indonesia, and Canada. The story begins with Japan's first case at the WTO concerning retaliatory tariffs imposed by the United States Trade Representative (USTR) in May 1995 (WTO WT/DS6). Japan simply did not wish to engage the U.S. on such "aggressively unilateral" actions on the part of the USTR as it had done for most of the postwar period. Instead, the Japanese side found such behavior intolerable in a rule-based WTO world.[2] More importantly, armed with the legal weapons of the WTO, the Japanese government, in contrast to its past, was willing to confront the U.S. actions (Abels, 1998). Largely because of the legal challenge issued by Japan to U.S. actions that were in clear violation of the rules, the U.S. came to an agreement. Noticeably, the Auto agreement that resulted in the aftermath of the WTO challenge did not have any quantitative measures (ACCJ, 1997, p. 101). Japan also went on to issue an indirect challenge to the U.S., by filing a case against Canada (WTO WT/DS139/R, WT/DS142/R; WTO WTO/DS139/AB/R, WT/DS142/AB/R).[3] At issue here was the favoritism accorded by the Canadian government to the big three U.S. makers. This was a violation of the most-favored-nation treatment that is one of the two pillar principles of the WTO system. Here, too, Japan managed to get a WTO decision that held up its complaints, and this constituted a clear legal victory for its automobile manufacturers who had long complained about the differential treatment in the Canadian market. It was similarly able to prevail against the Indonesian government's National Car Program that discriminated against Japanese firms in favor of domestic ones. This, as the Japanese side articulated in its legal case, was a clear violation of the national treatment clause that is another pillar of the WTO system (WTO WT/DS54/R, WT/DS55/R, WT/DS59/R, WT/DS64/R; WTO WT/DS54/15, WT/DS55/14, WT/DS59/13, WT/DS64/12).[4]

In addition, another case is pending resolution concerning Brazilian measures in the automotive industry that affect the economic interests of Japanese firms (WTO WT/DS51).

A similar story about multinational and export-oriented interests in the making of Japanese trade policy is seen in the steel case. Here, too, the Japanese government has taken steps to deal with market access issues abroad on behalf of its home firms. Its major venue of complaint on behalf of the steel industry has been in the area of antidumping, and its chief target of complaints has been the U.S. Japan's first formal complaint against U.S. antidumping measures was concerned with a little-known measure called the U.S. Antidumping Act of 1916 (WTO WT/DS162/R; WTO WT/DS136/11; WTO WT/DS/162/14). In essence, this measure prohibited dumping undertaken in the U.S. provided that such dumping is carried out with the intent of destroying or injuring U.S. industries. In addition to giving the right to the U.S. government to impose fines or imprisonment, the 1916 Act also gave injured parties the right to sue for and receive treble damages in U.S. federal courts. In the aftermath of the Asian financial crisis in 1997, some U.S. steel companies made moves to attempt to use this Act to defend their interests. But so did the Japanese government, on behalf of its Japanese steel industry. Despite the fact that it had hardly been used, the Japanese government challenged the very essence of its existence, and prevailed in having it declared illegal under the WTO rules.

This case was essentially a warm up to other cases, where the economic interests of Japanese, as well as U.S., steel firms were more clearly at stake. Seeking a rule-based resolution, Japan moved to challenge U.S. government antidumping calculations that impeded the interests of its hot-rolled steel industry (WTO WT/DS184/R; WTO WT/DS184/AB/R). Although Japan prevailed in some of its legal arguments, the results were weaker than it wanted because the WTO ultimately refused to rule on the issue of duty reimbursement. But this weak legal outcome has not deterred Japan from filing other antidumping complaints at the WTO against the U.S. on behalf of its steel industry. In conjunction with other countries, it has also recently moved to challenge a U.S. provision, the "Byrd Amendment," that allows antidumping or countervailing duties collected in U.S. unfair trade cases to be given to injured U.S. domestic companies (WTO WT/DS217/1). This case is still pending resolution, and meanwhile reports have emerged that the Japanese government may well be considering filing another complaint at the WTO against U.S. antidumping measures that target imports of surface-treated sheet steel.[5]

On the defensive side of Japan's WTO strategy, the Japanese government very often seeks to protect or safeguard domestic interests. While some cases such as agriculture are not surprising in this respect, given the domestic electoral clout wielded by agriculture-related businesses, others such as leather, consumer photographic film, and especially textiles merit closer attention. In each of these cases, the Japanese government has shown how legal rules can be used to thwart pressures for liberalization or even transparency.

In the leather case, the Japanese government has long been accused of shielding domestic interests, although it is widely understood that it does so for sociocultural, not electoral, reasons (GATT BISD 26th Suppl. 1978–1979; GATT BISD 27th Suppl. 1979–1980, GATT BISD 31st Suppl. 1983–1984). While it came to bilateral agreements with its trade partners in the past because of visible protectionism, its trade partners, especially the U.S., became increasingly dissatisfied with such arrangements. It was no surprise that Japan suffered a legal setback in this case early on, with a GATT Panel finding its visible measures in violation of the rules. The conclusion was still that Japan intentionally maintained import restrictions in order to restrict leather imports, including those of the U.S. Faced with this legal onslaught, Japan subsequently moved to make its measures GATT/WTO legal, thereby making its continued protectionism almost unassailable under the existing rules as the EU is finding out at present.[6]

A more compelling case of political pressures is found in the high-profile consumer photographic film or Fuji-Kodak case (Komuro, 1998; WTO WT/DS44/R). This was among the clearest cut cases in which adherence to a set of substantive legal rules by the Japanese side led to an outright dismissal of a U.S. case that Japan's consumer photographic and film sector was exclusionary and discriminatory. Many of the U.S.'s charges against Japan could be legally ascertained in the context of the WTO rules. Even more importantly, none could be satisfactorily shown to cause harm to U.S. interests. The Japanese government walked away with a legal victory on behalf of the Fuji Corporation, which continues to dominate the domestic market.[7]

3. THE TEXTILE MNCS: FOREIGN PRODUCTION AND THE POLITICIZATION OF JAPAN'S TRADE POLICY

As noted in the preceding section, the WTO's legal rules have presented Japan with opportunities to open up markets abroad (steel and automobiles), and to protect in-efficient industries (leather) or widespread domestic practices (photographic film). In the area of textiles, the WTO is expected to significantly transform the rules of in-ternational trade by phasing out the lynchpin of textile protectionism: the Multifiber Agreement (MFA). Indeed, the textiles trade was given a ten-year transition period, and by 2005 it will be fully incorporated into the disciplines of the WTO. Certainly, these international changes in textile trade rules are important, but we argue that in order to fully explain Japan's use of trade remedies (or lack thereof), we need to trace the sources for divergent corporate preferences on textile trade liberalization. In particular, foreign production and reverse imports have profoundly divided the Japanese textile establishment, and have in many ways prevented the Japanese government from articulating a consistent policy on textile trade.

3.1. Who are the Japanese Textile MNCs?
Shifting Composition of Textile FDI Flows

Among Japanese manufacturers, textile firms pioneered the move to manufacture in foreign countries. Despite its old vintage, Japanese textile offshore investment has experienced important changes over time. The most significant transformation has centered around the composition of textile FDI flows. Indeed, this brief overview of Japanese textile overseas investment will show that the oldest manufacturing transnational corporations – the spinners – have been displaced as the core investors abroad by synthetic fiber makers and more recently by apparel companies (Solis, 1998). Moreover, these changes in the composition of foreign direct investment have had far-reaching implications on trade policy, as we will demonstrate later on.

In the prewar period, Japanese cotton spinning firms had opened numerous factories in China, and by the late 1950s, these upstream enterprises were already investing actively abroad. In embarking on foreign production, the spinners were not simply responding to wage hikes in Japan. These enterprises were also eager to cater to protected local markets, to gain access to key raw materials (cotton and wool) thereby bypassing the strict limits on foreign exchange, and to ship to offshore factories part of the redundant capacity at home (Take, 1982, p. 17). Many of these incentives (rising labor costs, export market closure, and domestic excess capacity) worked as well for the other upstream textile oligopolists: the synthetic fiber makers, who became active investors in the mid-1960s (Yoshioka, 1979, pp. 23–24). Upstream overseas investments in both natural and synthetic fibers picked up to produce the first textile boom in 1973.

However, the textile FDI boom was short-lived. In the aftermath of the oil shock, the Japanese government imposed emergency capital controls. The synthetic fiber makers were furthered discouraged from investing abroad by the serious economic recession they faced at home with the rise of energy costs (for the first time recording operating losses), and the dismal performance of some of their offshore factories.[8] New overseas investment capital dried up, and the upstream oligopolists divested as well from several of their offshore plants (Horaguchi, 1992).

Despite the freezing of foreign investment plans in the aftermath of the oil shock, the transnationalization of the Japanese textile industry had reached unrivaled dimensions. For instance, between 1965 and 1974, textile FDI represented close to 30% of all Japanese manufacturing overseas investments (Solis, 2003). It is important to note that in this first stage in the offshore expansion of Japanese textile producers, the most active investors by far were the upstream oligopolists. As of 1977, synthetic fiber making, spinning, and weaving totaled $537.5 million, equivalent to 53% of all Japanese textile investment. FDI in natural fibers (especially cotton spinning and weaving) amounted to $311.8 million or 31% of the total. Moreover, upstream firms played this leading role in FDI thanks to the active support of their domestic partners: the general trading companies. As of 1977, more than half of all overseas affiliates of Japanese textile oligopolists were joint ventures with the traders (Nihon Kagaku Seni Kyokai, 1978).

In sharp contrast, midstream and downstream textile sectors played a marginal role in the offshore expansion of this industry. The FDI amounts for knitting and dyeing were more modest: $77 million or 7.6% of total textile FDI. Investment amounts in downstream processing were particularly small ($26 million) representing less than 3% of all textile overseas investments (Nihon Kagaku Senii Kyokai, 1978).

3.2. The Second Boom in Japanese Textile FDI

The marked appreciation of the yen in the aftermath of the 1985 Plaza Agreement generated a second boom in overseas textile investment. For example, in 1985, textile FDI amounted to only $28 million, but two years later, it sharply increased to $206 million and peaked in 1991 with $1 billion. The sheer dimensions of the second textile FDI boom are staggering: between 1985 and 1999, overseas investment projects in this industry were worth $7.3 million, whereas the first expansionary period (1964–1975) had merely generated an investment outflow of $861 million.[9] There are, however, important differences between the two phases of accelerated expansion in textile overseas investments. In the more recent wave of expansion, upstream companies have been left behind by apparel firms, retailers, and general traders who seek to produce low-cost clothing in neighboring Asian countries, and import them back to Japan.

Yen appreciation and cross-national labor cost differentials affected the most labor-intensive sectors of the industry, and the threat of growing import penetration by foreign labels pressured downstream companies to respond with overseas manufacture.[10] For instance, in a MITI survey of textile firms' FDI, 78% of the 233 overseas investment cases recorded between 1988 and 1992 were in apparel. The shares of other sectors that had previously dominated Japanese FDI were minor: 6% for spinning, 6% for weaving, and 7% for dyeing.[11] Fiber-making overseas investment seems to have lost steam altogether, since only one case was reported in this survey (MITI, 1994, p. 176).

Table 1 provides us with a more detailed profile of the textile multinationals. This comparison across Japanese textile subsectors reveals significant differences in the internationalization paths of Japanese enterprises operating in different segments of the industry. The large upstream producers (as measured by their capital stock and workforce) went overseas early on (1960s and 1970s), and most of them established sophisticated production and distribution networks with numerous offshore affiliates. Yet, with the important exemption of Toray, the upstream producers still relied mostly on domestic production to supply the Japanese market (note the modest foreign production ratios).

The multinationalization of the mid- and downstream sectors of the textile industry evolved along very different lines. Enterprises operating in these subsectors tend to be smaller, especially the apparel makers (although there are important exemptions to this pattern such as World Company and Gunze). Moreover, most of these enterprises only ventured into foreign production very recently (post-1985 *endaka*), and many of them operate a limited number of overseas affiliates (again with some exemptions such as Iris, Gunze, and Wacoal). Yet, despite this recent internationalization and the smaller scale of their FDI network, the degree to which foreign production has displaced domestic manufacture for many of the downstream multinationals is remarkable (note in Table 1 the very high foreign production ratios for apparel makers, frequently in the 50–100% range).[12]

Concerns over hollowing-out and uncontrolled reverse importing in apparel, therefore, have generated new political divisions within the textile industry. The MITI survey clearly reveals important divergences in the corporate strategies of upstream and downstream textile multinationals. With the exception of apparel companies, all Japanese textile multinationals report that they aim to capture local markets through FDI. In sharp contrast, the main goal of clothing firms is to ship back to the home market garments manufactured abroad. In the MITI survey, more than two-thirds of the apparel makers planned to sell most of their offshore production in Japan (MITI, 1994, p. 211). As will be discussed in more detail in the following section, "reverse imports" have politicized further the debate on textile trade protection in Japan by pitting upstream and downstream firms against one another on the use of trade remedies, and by even weakening the solidarity of upstream firms as some of the best established companies (Toray) have opted for reverse importing as well.

Not surprisingly, Japanese apparel makers have mostly relocated in low-wage neighboring Asian countries, and one country in particular – China – has emerged as a veritable production hub for the Japanese apparel industry. Official FDI

Table 1. A Profile of the Textile Multinationals (Year 2000, Million Yen).

Company Name	Oldest Subsidiary Listed	Capital Stock	Number of Employees	Number Overseas Subsidiaries	FDI Balance	Foreign Production Ratio (%)
Fiber companies						
Asahi Kasei Kogyo	1969	103,388	14,720	29	n.a.	n.a.
Kuraray	1984	78,659	4,621	13	29,068	n.a.
Mitsubishi Rayon	1971	53,229	4,482	22	n.a.	n.a.
Toray	1964	96,937	9,510	50	166,962	24.1
Unitika	1961	23,798	2,970	14	9,066	1.8
Teijin	1970	70,787	5,887	26	n.a.	n.a.
Spinning firms						
Kanebo Boseki	1970	18,730	1,105	11	6,524	n.a
Nisshin Boseki	1974	27,587	4,935	14	20,465	5.6
Toyobo	1952	43,341	5,496	21	16,575	14.1
Kurabo	1959	22,040	2,259	10	10,200	6.0
Fuji Boseki	1968	5,400	1,313	3	1,300	15.0
Shikibo	1974	10,358	1,418	6	4,200	n.a.
Daiwa Boseki	1972	18,181	848	6	n.a	n.a.
Midstream firms						
Tokai Senko	1964	4,300	795	4	3,327	28.7
Koyo Senshoku	1994	9,500	467	2	n.a.	n.a.
Sakai Ovex	1996	4,153	782	2	2,580	0.0
Kawashima Orimono	1986	8,277	777	8	n.a.	1.0
Nippon Keori	1990	6,465	1,176	3	n.a.	n.a.
Otsu Keori	1995	100	320	2	n.a.	n.a.
Miyuki Keori	1979	1,815	335	2	541	5.3
Downstream firms						
Iris Co.	1991	2,000	83	8	n.a.	15.0
Atsumi Fashion	1990	40	115	2	n.a.	65.0
Gunze	1971	26,071	3,265	10	n.a.	2.0
Co-cos Nobuoka	1994	1,695	255	2	293	80.0
Kojima Iryo	1991	500	6	3	483	100.0
Jichido	1991	2,982	429	2	290	64.2
Hirota	1994	270	329		100	68.0
Flex Japan	1990	195	450	5	n.a.	56.3
World Company	1987	110,300	2,356	7	2,841	n.a.
Wacoal	1968	13,260	5,070	15	n.a.	9.0

Sources: Toyo Keizai (2001).

statistics in fact do not capture the complexity of Japanese apparel production networks in China (Solis, 2003). Japanese apparel makers are importing back to Japan garments manufactured not only in their Chinese factories, but also directly commissioned to Chinese producers through non-equity arrangements.[13] Currently, 70% of all Japanese apparel imports originate in China, and most of them were either produced or commissioned by a Japanese company (*Nihon Kagaku Senni Kyôkai*, 2001, pp. 122–123). Consequently, the fragile domestic consensus on avoiding overt protection is being undermined by the import avalanche.

4. THE BATTLE OF THE MULTINATIONALS: TRADE REMEDIES AND REVERSE IMPORTS

For close to half a century, a sophisticated system of quantitative restrictions operated in textile international trade. This protectionist regime first developed with GATT's adoption of the market disruption principle, allowing quantitative restrictions to counter sudden import surges that were not attributable to dumping or foreign subsidies. Quickly, industrialized nations developed a quota system for the international trade of natural fibers (the 1962 Long Term Agreement on Textiles – LTA), and later on applied the same principle to the trade of synthetic fibers (Cline, 1987, pp. 146–147). The Multi-Fiber Agreement (MFA) signed in 1974 remained in force until the mid-1990s.

The Uruguay Round produced the first major breakthrough in the liberalization of textile trade: the Agreement on Textiles and Clothing. With this new agreement, the MFA restrictions will be eliminated over a period of 10 years (1995–2004). Nevertheless, textile trade was not completely liberalized. The most blatant form of protectionism – quotas – will no longer be acceptable, but industrialized countries have imposed instead high tariffs on textile products (well above the manufacturing average) and have increasingly relied on safeguards and antidumping charges to keep textile imports at bay (Schott, 1994, p. 57; Spinanger, 1999; Reinert, 2000).

Japan's textile trade policy sharply deviates from this pattern of overt protectionism in the developed world. Japan has never imposed MFA restrictions, and its tariffs on textile products are among the lowest among industrialized nations. Consistently, the Japanese government has rejected the petition of upstream textile producers for *explicit* trade barriers. For example, during the first sharp increase in textile imports in the aftermath of the 1973 oil shock, spinners and weavers demanded that MITI use administrative guidance to moderate import growth, create a surveillance committee on imports, impose MFA restrictions, and pursue bilateral talks with foreign countries on the question of "orderly imports"

(Ito, 1993, p. 180; Yamazawa, 1988, p. 415). MITI, however, refused to endorse this package of open trade restrictions, arguing that such an approach in a trade-surplus country would call for retaliation from trade partners.

Protectionist sentiment in the Japanese textile industry increased once more in the late 1970s as the synthetic textile subsector also began to suffer from waning international competitiveness. During 1978–1979, the man-made textile subsector and the labor union *Zensen* supported the cotton spinners' and weavers' demands for trade protection. The broader consensus on the need for some form of relief from import competition allowed the Japan Textile Federation (the umbrella industry federation) to request MFA quotas and the elimination of the generalized system of preferences (GSP). Sensing this wider consensus, MITI agreed to informal measures, unofficially asking both South Korea and Taiwan to restrain their exports. However, the ministry remained adamant on its refusal to impose MFA quotas or phase out the GSP (Friman, 1990, pp. 126–131).

MITI's stand reflected its concern with negative international reaction to a protectionist shift in Japan's textile trade policy. In keeping with our general theme, MITI's position was also influenced by the fact that the textile subsectors could not present coherent demands on the actual implementation of MFA quotas. For example, there were open disagreements on the appropriate trigger for quantitative restrictions. The cotton weavers called for quotas whenever imports represented 10% of domestic production, whereas labor was prepared to endorse quantitative restrictions only when foreign goods amounted to 30% of domestic consumption. However, the upstream producers (both cotton and synthetics) were willing to forego explicit ceilings provided that quotas would be promptly implemented in the case of severe import surges (Friman, 1990, p. 133).

The lack of more overt tariff or quota protection continued to strain government-business relations. Impatient with the lack of progress on the MFA front, the spinners tried a different approach and filed an antidumping suit against South Korea and a countervailing suit against Pakistan in 1982. Since MITI bureaucrats did not dismiss these industry moves outright, the spinners used the threat of the pending suits to bring their foreign counterparts to the negotiating table: in March 1983, South Korea announced a VER, and the next summer, Pakistan agreed to eliminate export subsidies (Friman, 1990, pp. 134–135). A new pattern of import protection had thereby been established: cross-national industry accords to avoid legal action.[14]

In the past 15 years, import competition in textiles has increased dramatically, and the industry demands for overt protection have consequently become more vocal. Although the man-made fibers market remained relatively immune to import competition (with a moderate import penetration ratio of 8.7% in 1992), cheaper foreign goods have flooded most textile subsectors. For instance, imports as a

Table 2. Reverse Imports in the Textile Industry (1994, Percentages).

Product	China	NIES	Entire World
Yarn	0	7.3	6
Cloth	0	0	4
Knitted outerwear	10.4	3.3	6
Knitted underwear	11.4	20	15.4
Fabric outerwear	58.7	8.1	29.2
Fabric underwear	7.3	n.a.	7.3
All textiles	22.5	6.2	12.7

Note: Reverse imports are broadly defined to include products manufactured in Japanese offshore
   factories or commissioned by Japanese companies to local producers (through subcontracting
   and/or technological transfer). Share of reverse imports over total imports.
Sources: MITI, Sekai Sennii Sangyo Jijo, 1994.

percentage of domestic consumption represented 36% for cotton yarn and 39%
for cotton fabric in the early 1990s. However, the import penetration ratios reached
unprecedented heights in the apparel industry: 76% for knitted sweaters and 59%
for cotton outerwear, to name but a few cases (MITI, 1994, p. 159).

Reverse imports have been largely responsible for the ever-widening trade deficit
this sector is currently experiencing. Table 2 shows that Japanese enterprises are
directly responsible for close to 13% of all textile imports into Japan. Moreover,
the sharp differences on the importance of reverse imports by textile subsector
support our argument on the saliency of intra-industry clashes over domestic
market protection. The role of Japanese companies is very prominent in the import
of apparel (30% of fabric outerwear and 15.4% of knitted underwear), but only
very modest in the midstream and upstream sectors of the industry (Japanese
companies' reverse imports represent a mere 4% of total imported cloth and 6%
of all yarn and fiber imports).

Since upstream and downstream textile multinationals have concentrated their
overseas investments in different regions, the importance of reverse imports also
varies sharply by country of origin. For example, reverse imports into Japan from
industrialized markets are marginal (3% for Europe and 7% for the U.S.). However,
the one country that apparel makers and retailers have recently targeted – China –
plays a disproportionate role in reverse importing (Table 2). MITI estimates that
more than 20% of all textile imports from China are in fact reverse imports, and
the role of Japanese enterprises in apparel imports from China is extraordinarily
high: close to 60%.[15] These key differences in the marketing strategies of Japanese
textile multinationals have fueled open political clashes among textile subsectors,
and complicated the bureaucratic task of trade-policy formulation.

Indeed, this wave of reverse imports directly contradicts MITI's longstanding policy against importing textile products back to Japan. The role of the Japanese government in discouraging reverse importing during the first textile FDI boom was in no way minor. According to Yoshimatsu (2000, p. 152), in the early 1970s some "firms were required to submit sworn documents that they would not re-import textile products to Japan." Moreover, throughout the postwar period, the textile industry was subject to special capital controls requiring closer government supervision. The rationale behind the more restrictive approach towards Japanese textile FDI was the pernicious effect of unrestrained reverse imports (Solis, 2003). MITI continues to defend the need for special restrictions in sectors where there is concern about a "boomerang effect" (another term for reverse imports).[16] Quite consistently, MITI attempted to minimize the disruption of reverse imports, and the upstream oligopolists went along with this policy.

Past accusations that Japanese FDI had the perverse effect of increasing import penetration could be easily dismissed, because most imports did not originate from countries where Japanese companies were actively investing (Yoshioka, 1978). This is no longer the case, as noted above.[17] As Japanese factories abroad are increasingly geared towards serving the home market, the domestic alliance that had sustained a relatively stress-free transnationalization strategy looks increasingly fragile. The cracks are evident in the renewed battle for trade protection, as former allies (spinners, fiber-makers, and general traders) are now set apart by conflicting interests.

Upstream textile firms have renewed their efforts to stop the import avalanche. They were particularly disenchanted when MITI announced in 1994 the procedures to request quota relief. MITI announced that MFA implementation would be contingent on several policy considerations: the role of reverse imports, the likelihood that Japanese companies would use temporary import relief to regain competitiveness, and the consequences of quota implementation for Japan's trade relations with exporting nations. The upstream enterprises complained that whereas, in Europe, numerical ceilings automatically trigger quotas, in Japan this remained an exercise of bureaucratic discretionary power (*Nihon Keizai Shimbun*, November 25, 1994).

Consequently, the textile protectionist lobby shifted gears and explored instead the use of new WTO rules to forestall imports: safeguard provisions. Since the establishment of the WTO in 1995, a new dynamic has set in. The industry federations of spinners and weavers have frequently requested the implementation of safeguards (usually against imports from China); the Chinese government has usually responded with a pledge of self-restraint, and the Japanese bureaucracy has used this informal commitment to delay the implementation of quotas (*Nihon Keizai Shimbun*, November 7, 1996). Therefore, the Japanese state has remained adamant about imposing quantitative restrictions (either old-style MFA restrictions or new transitional safeguards) and has continued to prefer bilaterally negotiated export restraints.

The government's concern with foreign retaliation does not seem to be the only reason behind the absence of overt trade protectionism, even as the domestic market is engulfed by imports. We argue that divergent corporate preferences have played a powerful role in the evolution of Japan's textile trade policy. Domestic divisions among textile subsectors and companies have acted as an important check on Japan's protectionist lobby. The most active overseas investors in the latest textile FDI boom (apparel makers and traders) have emerged as the most vocal supporters of free-trade policies. Interestingly, even the general trading companies, in the past loyal allies of the spinners in their overseas investment projects and domestic marketing strategies, have also imported back to Japan large amounts of clothing items and have even explored new cross-national alliances. For instance, Marubeni broke with past practice in 1995 when it co-invested with a Korean spinner in Indonesia. This represented the first time that a Japanese general trading company teamed up with a rival foreign upstream firm (*Nihon Keizai Shimbun*, August 10, 1995).

The breakdown of industry solidarity is evident even among the upstream enterprises themselves. Some well-established fiber companies have been prepared to disregard old injunctions against reverse imports in order to defend their domestic market share. Toray's president justified this move that shook the textile establishment: "We would rather fill the market with foreign-made Toray products than sit back and see imports from foreign companies eating away the market share" (*Nikkei Weekly*, March 20, 1995).[18] The more visible role of Japanese companies feeding the nation's textile trade deficit via reverse imports has not gone unnoticed by Japan's trade partners. In fact, China has skillfully played this card to divert Japanese pressures on export caps. Chinese officials have reportedly admonished Japanese trade bureaucrats to put their own house in order (i.e. restrain the behavior of Japanese companies in China) if they wish to temper the flow of imports back into the Japanese market (*Nihon Keizai Shimbun*, May 18, 1995).

Throughout the 1990s, old conventions on FDI and orderly importation have been pushed aside. The post-endaka FDI boom witnessed the emergence of a whole new class of multinationals (the apparel-makers) that for the first time deliberately challenged the longstanding MITI rule against reverse importation. The signs of change in the political economy of textile trade policy are unequivocal. Upstream and downstream MNCs are now openly articulating clashing preferences on trade policy. MITI must engage in a new balancing act as it seeks to accommodate both textile sectors, while at the same time it is mindful of the negative reaction from trade partners to overt protectionism.

Remarkably, Japan has not invoked overt protectionist measures despite the fact that the domestic market is increasingly engulfed by imports. In the past, MITI was capable of checking import growth (and appeasing the upstream oligopolists) by launching informal cross-national negotiations (e.g. with South Korea and Pakistan). This formula is no longer capable of stopping the import avalanche, since Japanese downstream producers are openly targeting their home market from their offshore factories. The Japanese textile industry today is divided in different multinational segments with sharply divergent strategies concerning the domestic market.

Intra-industry divisions complicate trade policymaking. It is no longer possible to appease entire industrial sectors by supplying overt or covert import protection, since different subsectors have clashing trade-policy preferences, and there is even variation in the response of some firms within a given subsector (the Toray case). Moreover, reverse imports (and the ensuing intra-industry tensions) can be used by Japan's trade partners to divert protectionist measures.

Imports from China (where Japanese downstream textile makers have largely relocated) have figured prominently in the domestic debate over the appropriate trade regime for textiles. As shown in the following section, trade tensions between Japan and China escalated in the spring of 2001 when, for the first time, Japan imposed safeguards against some agricultural products. Although the Japanese government considered the application of similar measures on textiles, in the end it refrained from doing so. Revealingly, divergent corporate preferences (i.e. the opposition of the apparel industry) explain the different trade tactics employed by Japan vis-à-vis China.

5. FROM CORPORATE PREFERENCES TO TRADE SAFEGUARDS: JAPAN-CHINA DISPUTE

The year 2001 showed how important divergences in corporate preferences could be for the making and direction of Japan's trade policy as a whole. As China has risen in economic prominence, the specter of cheap imports from an up-and-coming China along with other Asian countries has loomed large over the landscape of the Japanese economy. From mushrooms to textiles, the impact on domestic Japanese firms has been wrenching.[19] The impact has also been magnified politically under the dour economic conditions. It is not surprising that one of the key agendas for Japan's trade policy today is the issue regarding the invocation of trade remedies, such as antidumping and safeguard measures, to protect home industries, especially as countries like China appear set to rely on such measures in the near future. Nowhere is this better illustrated than in the Sino-Japanese trade dispute that continued even after China joined the WTO. Nowhere also is it more clear that the cleavage between firm preferences is going to be a key feature of the Japanese economy in the near future.[20]

In 2001, a basic Sino-Japanese tussle over Chinese antidumping measures spilled over over into other areas and escalated to a full-scale trade war. The story begins as a range of producers began to demand import protection. The charge was led, not surprisingly, by the agricultural sector, followed thereafter by the textiles sector. At the end of January 2001, the Agricultural Ministry began to investigate conditions in nine agricultural products in China.[21] About a month later, the newly constituted Ministry of Economy, Trade, and Industry (METI), also began to entertain requests from textiles producers, specifically the Towel Industrial Association, for safeguard action.[22]

At the end of March, Japan announced safeguard action against three Chinese agricultural products, namely spring onions, shiitake mushrooms, and igusa rushes that would go into effect for a 200-day period from April 23. This would involve tariffs of up to 266% on trade in the three agricultural goods worth approximately $100 million. Since these safeguard actions were consistent with WTO rules, and China was poised to join the WTO, the Japanese side did not expect a rash reaction from China. But China condemned these moves as being against the rules of fair play and asserted that there could be adverse consequences for trade relations between the two countries.[23]

Once safeguard actions were taken on agricultural products, the protectionist floodgates were open.[24] METI then began safeguard investigations in the towel industry in the middle of April.[25] No doubt encouraged by such government actions, Japanese necktie producers also complained similarly of losing turf in their home market to foreign producers and sought to invoke textile safeguards.[26] But there was another side to the story, one that echoes our major contention about burgeoning cleavages in corporate preferences. Replicating the political game of the 1990s, Japanese apparel makers and retailers with extensive foreign operations abroad rushed to nullify the protectionist demands of upstream and midstream textile firms. Indeed, one of the rising stars in the Japanese apparel industry – Uniqlo – has championed the cause for free trade. This should come as no surprise, since most of Uniqlo's products originate in China.[27] The head of Fast Retailing Co. (who owns the Uniqlo brand) has no qualms about the effects of liberalizing textile trade: "There is no need for Japan to have all kinds of industries."[28]

The cleavages within the textiles industry also spilled over into the broader Japanese business community as China took retaliatory actions. Even as the two sides continued talks, China retaliated against the agricultural safeguards by imposing punitive tariffs of 100% on imported Japanese cars, mobile phones, and air conditioners valued at around $500 million.[29] These multinational business interests were then pitted against agricultural and textiles interests. As successive talks failed, Japan began to consider compensation for the Japanese companies affected by Chinese import restriction policies.[30] Japan also took some conciliatory moves, such as delaying its decision regarding import restrictions on towels from China. This goodwill measure could be attributed to the fact that import levels had stabilized, but perhaps more importantly to the absence of a domestic consensus in Japan supporting the textile safeguards in the first place.[31] The goal for the talks was to have a resolution before the beginning of November, at which point Japan would decide on renewing the controversial import tariffs on Chinese agricultural goods for up to four years.[32] The talks failed to achieve a breakthrough. As the safeguard restrictions expired, and China refused to consider the Japanese proposal for "orderly trade," Japan could only agree to put off moving the four-year limit until late December.[33] In December 2001, finally the two sides came to an agreement, although both have their eye on using the WTO framework in the near future.[34]

6. CONCLUSIONS

There is little question that changes in the Japanese economy, particularly the ongoing internationalization of Japanese firms, have very important consequences for government-business interactions as a whole, and more specifically for Japan's trade-policy choices. The dual nature of the Japanese economy, that is an efficient competitive sector coexisting with an inefficient non-competitive sector at the broadest macro-level, is well understood. The political preferences of businesses in such sectors, and especially the stark differences in their preferences regarding market opening, can serve both to retard and to propel the course of trade liberalization. As discussed in the first section, Japan's activities at the WTO speak to exactly this point. The legal activities in the dispute settlement processes make clear that, at the broadest level, Japan is engaged in a two-pronged strategy. On the offensive, Japan can challenge its trade partners on behalf of its competitive multinational and export-oriented firms. On the defensive, however, Japan seeks to safeguard non-competitive domestic businesses from foreign pressures, although it cannot do so permanently.

This dual-economy paradigm is also, as we have argued, becoming relevant within sectors rather than just across them. In fact, our main contention is that divisions within industries are more likely to burgeon in importance as far as the future of Japanese trade liberalization is concerned. Political pressure can become more acute for a government when firm preferences diverge even within the same sector, as detailed in the textile case. Conflicting trade demands within one industry are particularly taxing for governments in representative democracies, since they have to assess the political merits of visibly supporting some constituents over others.

In textiles, for example, even as many members of the Japan Towel Industrial Association asked METI to invoke a WTO safeguard against China and Vietnam for three years, others in the same industry were asking the government not to invoke such restrictions. Their rationale for such resistance was that they also manufactured towels in China.[35] Clearly, foreign production and reverse imports have emerged as one of the most contentious issues in the textile industry. Other sectors might be facing the same kinds of divisions, which again complicates government trade policy. This is even true for agriculture, long one of the most protected and least efficient businesses in the Japanese economy. When the Japanese government bowed to political pressures and acquiesced in the imposition of temporary safeguards on Chinese leeks, mushrooms, and rushes in April 2001, many trading houses, distributors, and others opposed the import curbs because it hurt their economic interests directly. It was, after all, Japanese firms that introduced seed species more suited for Japanese tastes abroad, undertook instructions of foreign farmers on appropriate cultivation and quality-control techniques, and generally led the charges for reverse imports in Japan.[36]

Divisions along these lines are also going to be increasingly prominent across a range of tradable sectors – automobiles, steel, and electronics – with cleavages not just between upstream and downstream firms but also between producers and retailers. These stark differences among warring corporate interests have now visibly spilled over into the political policymaking process and will, in our view, largely determine the fate of trade liberalization in the near future.

NOTES

1. Figures are calculated by authors based on dispute settlement data at www.wto.org.
2. Interviews with senior MITI (METI) officials, 1997, 1998.
3. Japan was followed by the EU in this complaint.
4. Japan was also joined in this complaint by both the EU and the U.S.
5. *The Japan Times*, 24 January 2002.
6. Interview, Ministry of Foreign Affairs, 1999.
7. One of the key issues was the degree of foreign shares of the domestic market, but the Japanese side maintained that both Kodak and Fuji had similar shares in third markets and an equally large share of their respective home markets.
8. For example, the average after tax profit rate of Japanese textile factories overseas plummeted from 7.8% in 1972 to 0.8% in 1974 (Okamoto, 1988, p. 81).
9. The share of total manufacturing FDI has remained small (3%) due to the massive overseas investments carried out by other Japanese sectors adversely influenced by the yen appreciation (electronics and automobiles).

10. In 1988, the hourly labor cost in the textile industry was of $14 in Japan, $3 in Korea, and less than $1 in Malaysia, Philippines, Thailand, China and Indonesia (Dicken, 1992, p. 248).

11. Unfortunately, more complete FDI statistics (with a breakdown by textile subsector) are no longer available since the Japan Chemical Fiber Association has stopped printing them in their yearbook.

12. In sharp contrast to the recent activism of downstream textile firms, midstream companies (weavers and dyers) have exhibited little appetite for foreign production. In the late 1990s, there were only three dyeing firms with investments abroad (a total of eight affiliates). Similarly, very few weavers have established overseas affiliates (the most important four are listed in Table 1: Kawashima Orimono, Nippon Keori, Otsu Keori, and Miyuki Keori). Interestingly, most of the midstream producers also ventured overseas for the first time in the aftermath of the yen appreciation, but they were never as active as the downstream producers in their FDI strategies.

13. These non-conventional practices include ¨compensatory trade" (whereby a Chinese company repays machinery imports from Japan with sewing operations) and ¨specialized lines" (reserving the output from the production line of a factory abroad) (MITI, 1994).

14. This pattern proved stable: in 1988, the textile industry filed a second antidumping suit against Korea (knitted sweaters) in 1988. Once more, MITI encouraged an informal settlement, which resulted on Korean VERs in February 1989 (Yoshimatsu, 2000, pp. 137–138).

15. MITI defines reverse imports to include items directly manufactured in Japanese offshore factories or commissioned by Japanese firms through subcontracting arrangements or technological transfer. In the case of apparel in particular, subcontracting has been the most common arrangement for reverse importing (52% of the total) followed by joint ventures (25%) and technological transfer (23%) (MITI, 1994, p. 202). Fast Retailing Co. (and its Uniqlo brand) is perhaps the best-known example of the aggressive use of subcontracting arrangements in China to rapidly capture market share in Japan. As will be discussed later on, this Japanese retailer has emerged as one of the most vocal opponents to textile trade restrictions.

16. MITI response to a written questionnaire submitted by one of the authors (December 2001).

17. For instance, 58% of apparel imports from both China and ASEAN are carried out by Japanese companies MITI (1994, pp. 197–198).

18. Toray's bold actions may reflect the larger role that foreign production plays in its overall activities when compared with other upstream firms (Table 1).

19. *The Economist*, 10 February 2001; *Nihon Keizai Shinbun*, 15 March 2001.

20. *Mainichi Shinbun*, 4 July 2001.

21. *Mainichi Shinbun*, 23 January 2001.

22. *Mainichi Shinbun*, 26 February 2001; Daily *Yomiuri*, 18 February 2001; *Financial Times*, 26 February 2001.

23. *Mainichi Shinbun*, 31 March 2001, 6 April 2001, and 17 April 2001; The *Business Times Singapore*, 16 April 2001; *New York Times*, 17 April 2001.

24. *Mainichi Shinbun*, 17 April 2001.

25. *Mainichi Shinbun*, 6 April 2001. The Japanese towel association claimed that 60% of the domestic demand was being met by foreign products.

26. *Mainchi Shinbun*, 13 April 2001.

27. *Mainichi Shinbun*, 8 May 2001 and 22 May 2001. Interview, Riwa Sakamoto, Deputy Director, Manufacturing Industries Bureau, METI, March 2001.
28. *Asahi News*, 26 February 2001.
29. *New York Times*, 20 June 2001; *Financial Times*, 20 June 2001 and 22 June 2001; *Daily Yomiuri*, 20 June 2001.
30. *Wall Street Journal*, 5 July 2001; *Financial Times*, 20 August 2001; *http://www3.nikkei.co.jp*, 24 September 2001.
31. *Financial Times*, 12 October 2001.
32. *Daily Yomiuri*, 4 November 2001; *Yomiuri Shinbun*, 8 November 2001; *Japan Times*, 9 November 2001.
33. http://news.bbc.co.uk, 8 November 2001.
34. Interview, Senior METI Official, December 2001.
35. *The Daily Yomiuri*, 29 May 2001.
36. *The Daily Yomiuri*, 8 May 2001.

REFERENCES

Abels, T. M. (1998). The World Trade Organization's first test. The United States – Japan auto dispute. *UCLA Law Review, 44*, 467–526.

ACCJ (American Chamber of Commerce in Japan) (1997). *Making trade talks work: Lessons from recent history*. Tokyo: The American Chamber of Commerce in Japan.

Cline, W. R. (1987). *The future of world trade in textiles and apparel*. Washington, DC: Institute for International Economics.

Dicken, P. (1992). *Global shiji – The internationalization of economic activity*. London: Paul Chapman.

Friman, R. H. (1990). *Patchwork protectionism: Textile trade policy in the United States, Japan, and West Germany*. Ithaca: Cornell University Press.

Horaguchi, H. (1992). *Nihon kigyô no kaigai chokusetsu tôshi: Ajia e no shinshutsu to tettai* [Overseas investment of Japanese firms: Expansion and withdrawal from Asia]. Tokyo: Tokyo Daigaku Shuppankai.

Ito, M. (1993). Senii [Textiles]. In: MITI (Ed.), *Tsushôsangyô Seisakushi* [History of Trade and Industrial Policies] (pp. 165–195). Tokyo: MITI.

Komuro, N. (1998). Kodak-Fuji film dispute and the WTO panel ruling. *Journal of World Trade, 32*, 161–217.

MITI (1994). *Sekai senii sangyô jijô. Nihon no senii sangyô no ikinokori senryaku* [Condition of the world textile industry. Survival strategy for Japan's textile industry]. Tokyo: MITI.

Nihon Kagaku Senii Kyôkai. *Senii handobukku* [Textile handbook]. Tokyo: Nihon Kagaku Senii Kyôkai. Various issues.

Okamoto, Y. (1988). Takokuseki kigyô to Nihon kigyô no takokusekika [Transnational corporations and the transnationalization of Japanese corporations]. *Keizaigakuron, 54*, 67–92.

Pekkanen, S. M. (2001a). Aggressive legalism: The rules of the WTO and Japan's emerging trade strategy. *The World Economy, 24*, 707–737.

Pekkanen, S. M. (2001b). International law, the WTO, and the Japanese state: Assessment and implications of the new legalized trade politics. *The Journal of Japanese Studies, 27*, 41–79.

Reinert, K. A. (2000). Give us virtue. *The World Economy, 23*, 25–55.

Solis, M. (1998). *Exporting losers: The political economy of Japanese foreign direct investment*. Ph.D. dissertation, Harvard University, Government Department.

Solis, M. (2003). Adjustment through globalization: The role of state FDI finance. In: U. Schaede & W. Grimes (Eds), *Japan's Managed Globalization: Adapting to the 21st Century* (pp. 101–123). Armonk, NY: M. E. Sharpe.

Spinanger, D. (1999). Textiles beyond the MFA phase-out. *The World Economy, 22*, 455–476.

Take, K. (1982). Waga kuni senii sangyô to kaigai tôshi [Our country's textile industry and overseas investment]. *Kaigai Tôshi Kenkyû Jôhô, 8*, 4–28.

Toyo Keizai (2001). *Kaigai shinshutsu kigyô sôran* [Comprehensive survey of firms' overseas expansion]. Tokyo: Toyo Keizai.

Yamazawa, I. (1988). The textile industry. In: M. Okuno & K. Suzumura (Eds), *Industrial Policy of Japan* (pp. 395–423). Tokyo: Academic Press.

Yoshimatsu, H. (2000). *Internationalization, corporate preferences, and commercial policy in Japan.* London: Macmillan.

Yoshioka, M. (1978). Overseas investment by the Japanese textile industry. *The Developing Economies, 18*, 3–44.

Yoshioka, M. (1979). Senii sangyô ni okeru kaigai tôshi [Overseas investment in the textile industry]. In: H. Kitamura & T. Mori (Eds), *Waga Kuni no Kaigai Tôshi to Kokusai Bungyô o Meguro Shomondai* [Problems Surrounding our Country's Overseas Investment and International Division of Labor] (pp. 67–113). Tokyo: Institute of Developing Economies.

PART II: INTER-ORGANIZATIONAL RELATIONSHIPS

This section focuses on changes in inter-organizational relationships. McGuire and Dow survey *keiretsu* to understand how domestic economic pressures have altered debt and equity ties among members. With the failure of many Japanese financial firms, it would be reasonable to expect that debt ties might weaken, or that equity ties might increase as healthy firms seek to stabilize their position by strengthening their relationships. They find that equity ties have strengthened but that debt ties have remained stable, suggesting that Japanese firms use a variety of ties and that the particular configuration can be altered in response to evolving circumstances.

Rose and Ito point out how M&As allow for more rapid downsizing and efficiencies through scale economies, while minimizing the likelihood of large-scale layoff and that M&A activity in Japan appears to be associated with a shift in operation focus from growth to reducing organizational costs. This is noteworthy because it suggests a movement away from Abegglen and Stalk's (1985) "winner's competitive cycle," which is predicated on growth to ameliorate the effects of treating labor as a relatively fixed cost. Rose and Ito draw parallels between the banking industry's experiences now and during the banking crisis of the 1920s. Their analysis serves as an admonition that historical analysis is neither irrelevant nor obsolete: Current conditions and behaviors may be neither new nor unique.

Guillot and Lincoln investigate two types of collaborative partnerships – dyadic and network. Through a detailed comparative case study of Sanyo and Matsushita, they conclude that network embeddedness may offer benefits but are cautious in their support, acknowledging that networks entail greater costs and structural rigidities that may make them more difficult to manage efficiently in an increasingly dynamic competitive environment.

Hoetker's paper concludes the section by questioning the West's monolithic model of "Japanese-style" supply relationships, which implies that supply relationships are an inevitable outcome of unique environmental conditions. Noting that the model is actually a description of the Japanese automotive industry, he finds a significantly different set of supply relationships in the notebook computer industry, thereby debunking the myth of a monolithic model. He demonstrates the importance of surfacing the unique characteristics inherent in an industry's competitive environment. Hoetker's larger message is that context matters and cross-national research needs to be tempered by theorizing and research design that is equally sensitive to within-country differences.

KEIRETSU ORGANIZATION IN A CHANGING ECONOMIC CONTEXT: THE EVOLUTION OF DEBT AND EQUITY TIES AMONG KEIRETSU FIRMS

Jean McGuire and Sandra Dow

ABSTRACT

This paper examines the evolution of debt and equity ties among keiretsu firms between the early 1990s and the later part of the decade. During this time frame, the stable shareholding relations characteristic of the Japanese inter-corporate network faced significant pressures from the opening of the Japanese equity market and globalization of financial markets. We investigate whether the traditional "stakeholder model" of the Japanese firm is threatened by North American "shareholder" models. Using multiple measures of keiretsu ties, our analysis suggests this is not the case. Overall, we provide evidence of strengthening ties, although in the case of equity, there has been an evolution away from institutional investors.

INTRODUCTION

Advantages of the Japanese keiretsu organization at times seem to have reached mythical proportions. At least throughout the 1980s and 1990s, it was rare to find

Japanese Firms in Transition: Responding to the Globalization Challenge
Advances in International Management, Volume 17, 115–138
Copyright © 2005 by Elsevier Ltd.
All rights of reproduction in any form reserved
ISSN: 0747-7929/doi:10.1016/S0747-7929(04)17005-4

studies that suggested membership was not enviable. Indeed, throughout the 1980s, the keiretsu system was charged with creating unfair trading practices between Japan and the United States. In spite of this, empirical evidence regarding the nature of the ties that bind keiretsu members together, their very cohesiveness, and indeed the successes they may have created do not in fact yield unanimity of opinion. For example, numerous studies have been unable to verify superior profitability of keiretsu. Nor is the export record of leading member firms enviable. Indeed, perhaps somewhat conveniently, scholars interested in Japan's economic success justified their hypotheses by explaining that depressed short-term profitability promoted enhanced long-term growth. While, without a doubt, there is merit to this argument, recent economic upheaval in Japan and increasing global competitiveness have perhaps made the "long-run" arrive earlier than anticipated and with unexpected outcomes.

Although Japanese keiretsu organization has been seen as a source of competitive advantage for Japanese firms (Aoki, 1990; Williamson, 1991a), the maintenance of keiretsu organization in the context of economic and regulatory change has recently been challenged (Johnston, 1995; Kim & Hoskisson, 1996; McGuire & Dow, 2002). The bursting of the economic bubble that occurred in the 1991–1992 period significantly altered the economic context in which Japanese firms operated (Geringer, Tallman & Olsen, 2000). Indeed, Ito (1997) and Dow and McGuire (1999) suggest that the characteristics of the Japanese industrial system which have contributed to the growth of the Japanese economy may now act as constraints. Nevertheless, evidence for the persistence of equity links in keiretsu is relatively consistent (Gerlach, 1992a; Johnston & McAlevey, 1998; McGuire & Dow, 2002). With few exceptions, however, most studies of modern keiretsu ties have focused on either debt or equity links. This study builds upon existing research by examining the evolution of both debt and equity ties during the 1991–1997 period to assess the extent to which such ties have remained stable in the context of changing financial and competitive environments.

KEIRETSU TIES IN THE JAPANESE ECONOMY

Keiretsu groupings have long represented the industrial infrastructure of Japan. These groupings originated from the zaibatsu groups that dominated the Japanese economy until the end of World War II when the allied forces dismantled the zaibatsu by removing firm management and breaking up ownership ties. To avoid the reestablishment of these groups, regulation limited ownership stake in firms to 10% of outstanding shares (Aoki, 1992; Argy & Stein, 1997; Miyashita & Russell, 1994). By the 1950s, however, zaibatsu groups re-emerged as keiretsu. Estimates place 89 of the 200 largest firms in Japan within one of these groups (Hoshi, Kashyap & Scharfstein, 1991).

Although keiretsu ties are complex, involving financial ties, personnel exchanges, buyer-supplier relationships, and historical ties, this analysis focuses primarily upon financial interlocks. These financial relationships are characterized by close ties with banks and by a closely linked network of reciprocal shareholdings. Personnel ties, memberships on president's councils, and buyer-seller relationships, reinforce these financial ties. Recent changes in the economic context, however, have placed significant pressures on the debt and equity ties that have formed the economic basis of Japanese keiretsu.

Keiretsu typically revolve around a main bank and its affiliated financial institutions (e.g. insurance and trading companies). Non-financial membership is diverse, originating from a wide range of major industrial sectors (Argy & Stein, 1997; Miyashita & Russell, 1994). Within-group shareholdings are significant, ranging from 23 to 42% (Gerlach, 1992a). Major shareholders are typically the main bank and its affiliates and other associated firms. Much of this shareholding is reciprocal, resulting in a complex network of mutual dependence (Johnston & McAlevey, 1998; Prowse, 1992; Sheard, 1994a).

Perhaps as a result of the earlier limitations imposed on ownership, these equity ties do not imply high individual ownership stakes. Rather, keiretsu firms exhibit a "dispersed yet concentrated" ownership structure. Further, keiretsu shareholdings tend to be reciprocal. In contrast to the control implied by uni-directional ties, reciprocal ties imply a mutual dependence which fosters cooperation and mutual forbearance (Prowse, 1992; Sheard, 1994a). Equity ties are complimented by other transactional links that reinforce the mutual interests of corporate stakeholders, for example buyer-seller relationships, lending ties and exchanges of personnel. As a result, keiretsu shareholdings differ from the "arm's length" relationship found in North America. Rather, keiretsu shareholdings reinforce historical ties and other financial links to form a stable constituency on which the firm can rely (Johnston & McAlvey, 1998).

In addition to equity ties, main banks have traditionally provided a significant portion of the debt financing of keiretsu firms. The bank-centered nature of the keiretsu is deeply rooted in their history. As noted earlier, the major horizontal keiretsu are organized around a main bank. Although reliance on bank debt is characteristic of Japanese firms (Corbett, 1994), keiretsu firms rely more heavily upon bank financing than do non-keiretsu firms (Gerlach, 1992b; Hoshi et al., 1991; Prowse, 1992). Typically, the main bank may account for 10–20% of a firm's financial borrowing (Flath, 1993). Total group lending can run as high as 63% (Gerlach, 1992a). Lending ties are also more stable among keiretsu firms (Gerlach & Lincoln, 1992). Thus, keiretsu firms are more closely tied to their banking partners than are non-keiretsu firms. As with equity ties, other forms of links reinforce lending ties, most importantly equity holdings. The main bank and its affiliates are major shareholders in group firms, typically accounting for 15–30% of outstanding shares (Hoshi, 1994). These ties are also reciprocal, with firm holdings in banks and financial institutions sometimes exceeding bank shareholdings (Sheard, 1994a).

Benefits of Keiretsu Organization

Most discussions of keiretsu organization emphasize how this distinctive brand of industrial organization results in a set of interrelated and stable financial stakeholders. In turn, researchers have identified several potential benefits of keiretsu organization. A major benefit of keiretsu membership is that it insulates the firm from market and financial risk. Stable reciprocal shareholders are less likely to sell their shares in response to poor performance (Nakatani, 1984; Prowse, 1992; Sheard, 1994a). This insulation from market pressures is augmented by Japanese corporate governance practices which make it very difficult for outside shareholders to impact corporate governance (Sheard, 1994a). As both shareholders and lenders, banks are likely to work with financially troubled firms by providing managerial assistance, extending payment terms, purchasing inventory, etc. (Aoki, 1994; Sheard, 1994b, c). Group firms may also assist in research and development activities or other risky ventures (Gerlach, 1992b). Close relationships with banks and other lenders provide the firm with ready access to financing (Frankel, 1991; Nakatani, 1984; Sheard, 1994b). As a result, keiretsu firms may have greater financial flexibility than do North American firms.

The risk-reduction benefits of the keiretsu extend to creditors and shareholders as well. The reciprocal monitoring by a closely connected set of financial stakeholders described earlier opens the firm to wide-ranging scrutiny which once again serves to reduce risk for these stakeholders (Kim & Limpaphayom, 1998; Sheard, 1994b, c). Risk is further diminished by the assistance given to troubled firms by other group members (Hoshi, 1994; Sheard, 1994c). As a result, opportunistic behavior is also limited in the keiretsu setting. Many scholars argue that through the share cross-holding mechanism, the keiretsu system allows the group collectively to monitor and control members (see for example, Gilson & Roe, 1993, among others).

In essence, keiretsu organization affords members financial stability and more ready access to financing. The importance of these benefits can be understood in terms of the strategic challenges facing Japanese firms at the time of the rebirth of the keiretsu. During the post-World War II period, Japanese industry faced severe challenges in developing global competitiveness. As a result, Japanese firms required access to large amounts of capital to develop their competitiveness. Prior to the 1980s, however, regulation virtually eliminated access to non-bank financing in Japan, and foreign investment faced significant regulatory barriers (Campbell & Hamao, 1994; Ueda, 1994; Weinstein & Yafeh, 1998). In this context, financial stability and insulation from short-term performance pressures were critical for the continued competitiveness of Japanese firms. Stable shareholdings and close ties with banks provided a ready pool of "patient capital" that encouraged long-term investment. Reciprocal monitoring by firms and financial institutions reduced risks to holders of debt and equity. Access to stable domestic markets associated with keiretsu membership also encouraged long-term investment.

MODERN KEIRETSU TIES

Despite these traditional advantages, scholars have begun to question whether the value of keiretsu membership may have diminished in the context of changes in credit and equity markets (Johnston, 1995). Although keiretsu ties may have been instrumental to the growth of the Japanese economy in the context of regulation and closed financial and product markets, its benefits may have eroded in the context of deregulation and more open competition.

Recent attention has focused on the costs of keiretsu membership. Researchers have long acknowledged the lower financial performance of keiretsu firms (Aoki, 1990; Nakatani, 1984; Sheard, 1991). Although the traditional argument has been that this lower short-term performance is offset by greater long-term benefits and flexibility, the validity of this argument in the context of the recent Japanese economic downturn is uncertain. Studies have increasingly documented the costs of keiretsu membership. For example, Weinstein and Yafeh (1998) found that keiretsu firms incur higher costs of debt. Geringer et al. (2000) as well as Lawrence (1991) provide no evidence that keiretsu membership facilitates foreign entry or export development. Indeed, Geringer et al. (2000) found that means for keiretsu firms are significantly lower than those for independent firms along all dimensions of foreign market entry used. More rare, however, is the questioning of the nature of the ties themselves. Nonetheless, Miwa and Ramseyer (2000) study the Japanese automobile industry and discover that the strength of group ties appears much less than what is claimed by many scholars of the keiretsu system. Miwa and Ramseyer (2000) further note that membership appears not to be stable in the automobile industry, particularly among second and third tier firms. Similar evolutions may be occurring in horizontal keiretsu. In contrast to common assumptions of management stability, Roe, Ramseyer and Romano (1993) note the increasing frequency of management turnover, including forced turnover. Roe et al.

(1993) further note that the subtle balance and trade-offs among debt and equity holdings may be changing. Others, such as Cowling and Tomlinson (2000), allude to past successes of Japanese multinationalization as a precursor to the weakening of the domestic keiretsu system.

These arguments raise the important question of whether the traditional debt and equity ties linking keiretsu members can be maintained in the context of changes in the Japanese economy. The following paragraphs will outline these changes and their implications for keiretsu organization.

Evolution of Japanese Equity Markets

The stable shareholding relations characteristic of the Japanese inter-corporate network may face important pressures from the opening of the Japanese equity market and globalization of financial markets. Deregulation of equity markets has encouraged foreign investment in Japan (Ahmadjian & Robbins, 1999; Weinstein & Yafeh, 1998). Such foreign investment, particularly by institutional investors, may place increased performance pressures on Japanese firms. In essence, the traditional "stakeholder model" of the Japanese firm may be threatened by North American "shareholder" models (Thomas & Waring, 1999). One of the traditional strengths of keiretsu has been their role as a "buffer" against market downturns, which allow the firm to develop long-term competitive strengths.

In doing so, however, non-competitive firms may survive with the support of more competitive partners. Johnston (1995) argues that such insulation from competitive pressures places keiretsu firms at a strategic disadvantage. More significantly, however, increased performance pressures may limit the willingness of stronger firms and financial institutions to support less competitive partners. Ahmadijian and Lincoln (2001) and Miwa and Ramseyer (2000) argue that buyer-supplier relations in the automobile industry are evolving away from "hybrid" network ties toward full integration or arms' length transactions. Hybrid financial ties among keiretsu members might well coincide with the dilution of keiretsu ties.

Despite these arguments, both Gerlach (1992b) and Johnston and McAlevey (1998) provide evidence of the persistence of stable shareholdings. Indeed, Johnston and McAlevey (1998) provide evidence of re-establishment of cooperative shareholding arrangements, particularly during more recent time periods. McGuire and Dow (2002), however, find greater movement toward North American ownership structures among keiretsu firms than among independent firms.

In the context of evidence pointing toward increased efficiency in the Japanese stock market (Korkie & Naamura, 1997), these contradictory findings suggest that the evolution of the ownership structure of Japanese firms may be more complex than a simple evolution toward greater or less stability of traditional patterns of shareholdings. Furthermore, Miwa and Ramseyer (2000) observe that second and third tier firms never enjoyed the strength of continuous relationships through time. Thus, any examination of the weakening of the keiretsu system may focus primarily on those ties that were of less importance in the first place. Further, the entrance of new categories of shareholders, for example foreign investors, must be considered. There has been little empirical examination of the impact of foreign investment in Japanese firms. Since outside investors may find it difficult to influence the strategic or performance objectives of keiretsu firms, changes in ownership patterns may not necessarily imply modification of the traditional performance patterns of Japanese firms (e.g. Ahmadjian & Robbins, 1999). Sheard (1991) suggests that the increased foreign involvement of Japanese firms and financial institutions may also contribute to the evolution of Japanese industrial organization by familiarizing Japanese firms with alternative modes of doing business.

Changing Banking Relationships

There have also been significant changes in the role of banks in the Japanese economy. First, the Asian economic crisis may have severely strained the financial resources of Japanese banks to maintain the debt and equity holdings thought to insulate Japanese firms from financial pressure. Indeed, diminished reliance on bank financing preceded the Asian crisis, coinciding with the move toward re-regulation of the Japanese economy. Nonetheless, the Japanese banking industry was particularly hard hit by declines in the Japanese equity and real-estate markets, as well as declines in most Asian economies.[1] The Asian crisis affected both the domestic investments in loans, real estate, and equity held by Japanese banks, and their substantial investment in other Asian markets. Official estimates of losses in this period are $600 billion (Asian Wall Street Journal, 1995) The Japanese government acknowledges that bad debts for Japanese banks as a result of the Asian crisis are today valued at $345 billion, although private analysts suggest the true figure may be two to four times this amount (Wiseman & Cox, 2002). These financial pressures may make it increasingly difficult for Japanese firms to maintain non-performing loans or poorly performing equity in their portfolios.

Regulatory change in the 1980s and again in the early 1990s significantly reduced traditional dependence on banks for debt financing (Campbell & Hamao, 1994; Weinstein & Yafeh, 1998). Prior to these reforms, access to bonds and other forms of non-bank debt was limited. Indeed, regulations regarding interest ceilings and collateral requirements virtually eliminated access to the bond market for Japanese firms (Campbell & Hamao, 1994; Ueda, 1994). This deregulation has continued into the late 1990s and beyond. Gibson (1998) refers to these changes as "big bang" deregulation. This continued deregulation suggests that reduced use of debt may be just the "tip of the iceberg" of the changing patterns of capital structure in Japan.

Given these costs, the use of non-bank financing has increased dramatically. The percentage of bank borrowing by Tokyo Stock Exchange listed firms decreased from 90% in 1980 to 50% in 1991 (Campbell & Hamao, 1994; Hoshi, 1994; Weinstein & Yafeh, 1998). Although it might be expected that non-keiretsu firms would be more aggressive in moving into the bond market when compared to keiretsu firms, empirical evidence on this topic is mixed (Campbell & Hamao, 1994; Hoshi et al., 1991). Prowse (1990) and Weinstein and Yafeh (1998) provide evidence of reduced reliance on bank funding for firms with higher potential growth opportunities. Such firms probably have greater alternatives to bank financing.

Despite earlier findings of lower cost of capital for Japanese firms (Frankel, 1991), more recent evidence has found that the cost of this bank-centered system is significant. Weinstein and Yafeh (1998) provide evidence for the significant costs of bank debt incurred by main bank firms. The costs of this system may become increasingly onerous in the context of global competition.

Roe et al. (1993) further suggest that any weakening of debt ties may erode equity ties as well. If indeed equity ties serve to reinforce lending relationships, reductions in lending positions may make equity investments less attractive for banks and financial institutions. In view of the monitoring role of group banks (Gibson, 1998; Sheard, 1994b), this may have repercussions for non-bank shareholdings as well.

The focus of the current research, however, is the extent to which changes in the Japanese context have resulted in significant changes in keiretsu ties. Still today in Japan, financial stakeholders remain relatively homogeneous. Therefore, Gerlach (1992b) argues that the substitution of one form of financial tie for another may have little substantive impact on the firm. Indeed, his empirical analysis shows that declining reliance on capital borrowed from group financial institutions is offset by an increase in the proportion of group-owned equity capital (Gerlach, 1992b). Hoshi's findings (Hoshi, 1994) also support substitution of group debt for other forms of group-centered financing. Thus, previous studies focusing on one type of tie, for example ownership or lending ties, may not tap the interdependent evolution of the many links among keiretsu firms.

Understanding of the evolution of keiretsu ties is particularly important given changes in financial and strategic demands facing keiretsu members. The banking and equity ties traditionally linking keiretsu members may be increasingly difficult to maintain. We noted earlier that a major benefit of keiretsu membership is the financial stability and reduced risk made possible by keiretsu membership. Our earlier discussion suggests that the benefits of keiretsu membership may have diminished in recent years. In essence, Kim and Hoskisson (1996) and Weinstein and Yafeh (1998) argue that the costs of Japanese inter-corporate networks may become more prominent in the context of increased competition and the globalization of financial markets, with their benefits attenuated. Building upon Porter's (1990) argument for the role of strong domestic competition in building globally competitive firms, potential insulation of keiretsu firms from product-market pressures may increasingly hamper the ability of keiretsu firms to face more open competition. More recently Sakakibara, Porter and Takeuch (2000) suggest that the successes of the Japanese economy are not so much due to the context and uniqueness of industrial organization found in that country, as to the success of a few select industries.

RESEARCH PROPOSITIONS

Financial ties among keiretsu firms involve both debt and equity holdings. As discussed earlier, both types of ties may have come under pressure in recent years. For discussion purposes, we present three alternative scenarios regarding the evolution of debt and equity ties. The first scenario is one of "no change" along either dimension of inter-corporate linkages. This resistance to change can result from several sources. At the most "macro" level, inter-corporate ties are congruent with the collectivist nature of the Japanese culture (Bappa, 2000; Hofstede, 1991; Steensma, Marino, Weaver & Dickson, 2000). Thus, keiretsu ties may be resistant to pressures for change. Moreover, we noted earlier that financial interlocks are only one dimension of keiretsu ties. In the context of the multi-dimensional ties that link keiretsu members, financial ties may reinforce other types of links. For example, financial ties may facilitate buyer-supplier relations or collaborative research and development activities (Ahmadijian & Lincoln, 2001). As a result, financial ties may be less subject to purely financial logic in the Japanese context than they might be in North America. This view is supported by Moerke (2004), who finds that in general, links to government bureaucracy diminished after 1992, with the exception of members of horizontal keiretsu, where government influence actually increased.

Second, both equity and debt ties may have dissipated in the context of the economic changes outlined above. Although our discussion of changes in the Japanese equity markets provides a theoretical basis for this argument, there has been limited empirical support for this perspective. As noted earlier, existing research on this topic has found equity ties to be relatively stable. Indeed, there is evidence that when taken in the context of both debt and equity ties, equity links may have strengthened among keiretsu firms (McGuire & Dow, 2002).

However, debt and equity ties have been subject to different pressures and may have responded differently to these pressures. Indeed, debt and equity ties differ in several important characteristics that might influence their resistance to outside pressures. The empirical evidence cited earlier suggests that equity ties may have been more resistant to change than banking relationships. However, the theoretical basis for the resistance of equity ties and the dissipation of lending ties has yet to be fully articulated. It is therefore important to explore more fully the theoretical bases for differences in the stability of debt and equity ties.

In many ways, equity links represent "weak ties" (Granovetter, 1973) between firms. As noted earlier, relatively small stakes held by larger numbers of firms characterize inter-firm equity ties. Further, equity holdings imply less of an active monitoring role than does debt, especially bank debt, particularly when reinforced by other forms of banking relationships such as maintenance of corporate accounts, providing assistance for import and export activities, and the like. Thus, even a relatively small reduction in holdings may have, or be perceived as having, a significant impact on ties between the two firms. This may not be the case for bank debt, where the relatively high levels of debt financing may allow the firm to reduce lending ties without substantively altering the nature or significance of the tie or other forms of financial involvement. Finally, unlike debt, equity ties are often reciprocal. The reciprocity of equity ties may also contribute to their durability (Williamson, 1983, 1991a, b). Reciprocal ties may tend to be more stable than unidirectional ties due to mutual forbearance. Finally, keiretsu firms may find it difficult to attract outside equity. Dewenter, Novaes and Pettway (2001) argue that outside investors face significant information asymmetries in assessing keiretsu firms. The complexity and opaque nature of keiretsu relationships make it more difficult to assess potential investment in keiretsu firms. Outside investors would also face significant difficulties in playing a role in corporate governance. These challenges may make investment in keiretsu firms less attractive for outside investors, leading to stability of keiretsu shareholdings.

Although these arguments suggest the greater "durability" of equity ties, it is important to acknowledge several possible counter-arguments. The costs of reliance on bank funding may become particularly burdensome in the context of the continued deregulation in Japan. Finally, evidence concerning the "costs" of bank financing may imply greater benefits to reducing reliance on bank financing than reducing equity ties. As pointed out by Sakakibara et al. (2000), untangling of reciprocal shareholding, and in particular bank-sourced holdings, might serve to actually strengthen the Japanese competitive position by subjecting firms to market scrutiny. Nevertheless, implementation of regulatory reform has been slow with tremendous resistance encountered from the "iron triangle" comprising backbench and local politicians, businesses, and the administrative departments. Indeed, Kawamoto (1999) cites as an example the slowness of financial institutions to deal with bad loans. Although lending ties are deeply embedded in the bank-centered organization of the keiretsu, they run, for the most part, from the bank to the firm. Even if other types of ties reinforce lending ties, the mutual dependence implied by equity ties may differ from the lender-client relationship of main bank financing. Particularly in the context of lower-cost alternatives, firms may be more willing to reduce reliance on bank debt. These reductions in lending may have a limited impact on the nature of the ties between firms and banks. Although Gibson (1998) suggests that reductions in lending may make equity investments less attractive for banks, we noted earlier that firms hold significant portions of bank equity. It is likely that banks would prefer to maintain a "balanced" equity position with partner firms. Even in the context of reduced lending ties, equity holdings would serve to maintain bank ties.

Despite these countervailing arguments, this discussion suggests that equity ties among keiretsu firms may have remained stable, while lending ties may have dissipated. Indeed, it is possible that equity ties may have strengthened. If keiretsu firms are less attractive to outside investors, keiretsu firms may have found themselves increasingly reliant on in-group holdings, while independent firms were better able to attract a broader range of investors. The economic pressures noted earlier may have elicited a "circling the wagon" reaction.

However, this discussion has tended to assume that keiretsu ties are homogeneous in nature and strength. This is not the case. Firms differ in the extent to which they are "core" members of the keiretsu, with many firms being more closely or loosely tied to the group. Evidence from buyer-seller networks suggests that stronger ties may be particularly relevant to firms in the core of the keiretsu (Ahmadijian & Lincoln, 2001; Miwa & Ramseyer, 2000). Closely tied firms feel particular pressure to maintain keiretsu ties and support group firms, particularly in the context of economic downturn. They may also be less attractive investment targets for outside investors. Greater evolution of keiretsu ties may be evident among more peripheral firms. Empirically, however, most research has focused on firms with clear keiretsu affiliations.

Although we acknowledge that the theoretical and empirical evidence is far from clear, we feel that the argument for reductions in debt ties, and the stability or possible strengthening of equity ties, has significant theoretical and empirical support. In general, we suggest that keiretsu ties have evolved over time, in response to regulatory changes in the Japanese economy as well as heightened competitiveness in a global context. It might be the case that in order for Japanese firms to survive, and indeed thrive, the best of both worlds will have to be incorporated. Strategically, this might mean that Japanese firms may have to respond more to shareholder demands and rely less on traditional stable shareholdings. Pressures on the banking sector might eventually lead to real declines in debt financing, although as noted earlier, so far such changes have been more cosmetic than actual. The preceding discussion suggests the following hypotheses:

Hypothesis 1. Recent economic pressures and regulatory changes have led to the weakening of debt ties among Keiretsu firms during the 1992–1997 time period.

Hypothesis 2. Equity ties among keiretsu firms have remained stable or strengthened during the 1992–1997 time period.

Sample

Data on keiretsu affiliation, group borrowing, and group shareholdings are obtained from *Japanese Company Handbook* and *Industrial Groupings in* Japan for the years 1990–1991 and 1996–1997. These biannual references are the accepted source of information regarding group membership and ties and have been used in previous studies (Geringer et al., 2000; Paker & Hodder, 2002). We use classification as a member of the six major horizontal keiretsu, as listed in *Industrial Groupings in Japan* for each year to identify keiretsu firms. Additional financial data used to measure keiretsu ties and as control variables are taken from the Worldscope database for 1992 and 1997. The final sample consists of 660 keiretsu firms in 1992 and 700 keiretsu firms in 1997. In order to control for changes in economic context, performance data, specifically return on assets, are measured as a five-year average. Thus, we are able to capture performance in the 1987–1991 period, as well as performance over the 1992–1997 period.

Given that the shocks to the Japanese economy were both regulatory and economic in nature, it is difficult to precisely identify an exact cutoff between economic regimes. Selection of any cutoff point involves compromise and trade-offs. However, yearly samples were selected to reflect two distinct economic and regulatory environments in Japan. The earlier time period was one of "boom" markets in Japan. Although this period includes the 1987 market decline, Johnston and McAlevey (1998) and Sheard (1991) note that the market crash was more limited and had a short-lived impact on the Japanese market. Indeed, the period 1988–1989 was one of extraordinary growth of the Nikki Stock Average (Johnston & McAlevey, 1998). Both OECD and IMF data suggest 1991 as a pivotal year in the Japanese economy. Data from the OECD and the International Monetary Fund

(Bayoumi, 1999; OECD, 1998) show that this time period was one of growth and expansion in the Japanese economy along most economic indicators. The later period, in contrast, was one of substantial financial pressures on Japanese firms and financial institutions. The IMF notes that despite some signs of recovery in 1996, the Japanese economy continued its recessionary tendencies. Further, Geringer et al. (2000) empirically identified 1987–1991 and the post-1992 period as distinct "strategic" time periods. The two time periods also tap differences in the regulatory environment. Although the early regulatory changes had occurred prior to 1991, this process had not been finalized and may have had uncertain immediate impact (Campbell & Hamao, 1994; Ueda, 1994; Weinstein & Yafeh, 1998). The later time period encompasses the post-regulatory period, including those changes occurring in the early 1990s. Although selection of an earlier time period might have better coincided with the formal implementation of the earlier changes, examination of the impact of the change in economic conditions would have been impossible. Given that our sources on Japanese firms are usually published on a biannual basis, we felt that the two periods selected provided the best "window" for examining change in keiretsu ties.

Methodology

In order to examine evolution of keiretsu ties over time, binomial logistic regression was employed. First, we compared keiretsu firms with independent firms in 1992 and repeated the analysis for 1997. This procedure allowed us to evaluate whether or not keiretsu members are more or less distinguishable from independent firms over time. At this stage in the analysis, the following variables commonly used as keiretsu classifiers in addition to control variables were employed:

(1) *Dummy dependant variable.* The dummy dependant assumes a value of 0 if the firm is independent and 1 if the firm is a keiretsu member.
(2) *Ownership ties.* We used traditional ownership measures of 5% ownership and institutional ownership.
(3) *Lending ties.* To measure more closely the reliance of keiretsu firms on bank financing, we measured the percentage of short-term debt to total debt. Most short-term debt is bank debt, particularly in Japan (Dow & McGuire, 1999; Kanatas & Qi, 2001).
(4) *Subsidiary investment intensity.* Investment in subsidiaries as a percentage of total assets was used.

Control variables: We controlled for firm size (log of net sales) and leverage (debt/equity). Further, the firm's financial performance may influence patterns of debt and equity. We therefore controlled for the firm's five-year average ROA. As noted above, firm profitability also allows us to take into account changes in the general economic environment. Finally, we controlled for industry affiliation with dummy variables.

The second part of our analysis focuses on keiretsu membership over time. At this point, we directly examined the strength of keiretsu ties over time using binomial logistic regression. The sample at this point was restricted to keiretsu firms observed in 1992 and 1997. The following variables were used in this analysis:

(1) *Dummy dependant variable.* The dummy dependant took on a value of 0 if the year is 1992 and is assigned a value of 1 if the year is 1997.
(2) *Group equity ties.* Equity ties among keiretsu firms were measured by the percentage of equity held by group members.
(3) *Outside holdings.* Ahmadijian and Lincoln (2001) suggest that keiretsu members attempt to reinstate their control or increase stockholdings as a defense against greater dilution of keiretsu ownership. We therefore subtracted the percentage of group holdings from the shareholdings of the 10 largest shareholders in the firm to arrive at a measure significant outside shareholdings.
(4) *Ownership ties.* We used traditional measures of institutional ownership and foreign ownership.
(5) *Group lending.* The total amount of group lending as a percentage of total borrowing was used.
(6) *Bank debt.* As in the previous analysis, to measure more closely the reliance of keiretsu firms on bank financing, we measured the percentage of short-term debt to total debt.
(7) *Subsidiary investment intensity.* Investment in subsidiaries as a percentage of total assets is used.
(8) *Strength of group affiliation.* The previous measures focused on the "financial" dimensions of keiretsu ties. However, keiretsu ties involve more tacit and historical links not tapped by equity and debt ties. *Industrial Groupings in Japan* also provides a more "subjective" evaluation of the strength of ties, measured on a scale of 1–4. An implicit assumption of this analysis is that changes in financial ties imply changes in the strength of keiretsu affiliation. We therefore used this measure as the strength of group affiliation. Despite extensive effort to obtain clarification on the calculation of this variable through colleagues and Dodwell Publications, we were unable to do so. Those familiar with the publication noted that it reflected both financial ties and the more subjective evaluation of Dodwell Publications of the strength of the tie. Additional analysis of this variable (available from the authors) showed that 46% of the variance of the tie strength was explained by our control and

financial tie variables. This would seem to confirm the inclusion of subjective and historical factors in assessing overall tie strength. We feel that the theoretical importance of assessing tie strength independent of our predictive variables, and the importance of non-financial ties to understanding keiretsu membership, outweighs the lack of information regarding its development.

(9) *Keiretsu membership.* Anecdotal evidence suggests that the six major keiretsu may differ in the stability of their membership. Specifically, strong historical links among the older, more entrenched Mitsubishi, Mitsui, and Sumitomo groups mbe particularly resistant to change (Levinson, 1992). We therefore included dummy variables to represent keiretsu affiliation.

Control variables: Again, we controlled for firm size (log of net sales), leverage (debt/equity) and profitability (five-year ROA average).

RESULTS

Keiretsu vs. Independent Firms in 1992 and 1997

The results of the binomial logistic regression predicting keiretsu affiliation vs. classification as an independent firm in either 1992 or 1997 are presented in Tables 1 (1992) and 2 (1997). We make use of our control variables and traditional measures of keiretsu ties: short-term debt usage; subsidiary investment intensity; 5% ownership and institutional ownership. These variables have been shown to be good predictors of keiretsu membership (Dow & McGuire, 1999) and distinguish group members from those classified as independent firms.

The classificatory power of the model is high for both years with little difference between the level of correct prediction as a keiretsu in 1992 vs. 1997. Nevertheless, it seems in both 1992 and 1997 that the model is relatively poor in predicting non-keiretsu membership with a correct rate of only 55.28% in 1992 and 58.27% in 1997. As would be expected, there is greater homogeneity among keiretsu membership. These results also suggest that the dominance of the keiretsu system in Japan spills over to those classified as independent firms. In terms of predicting keiretsu membership in 1992 and 1997, our variables are stable, with the exception of institutional investment. In 1992, greater institutional investment is significantly associated with membership, while in 1997, the tendency is reversed. This finding hints at the possibility that keiretsu ties have changed over time, and in particular, the nature of equity ties among members may have evolved. In so far as debt ties are concerned, however, short-term debt remains a predictor of keiretsu membership

Table 1. Probability of Keiretsu Membership vs. Independent Grouping (1992).

Variable	Coefficient	Standard Error	Wald	Significance
Constant	2.6646	14.0100	0.0362	0.8492
5% Ownership	0.0313	0.0111	7.9533	0.0048
Institutional ownership	0.0367	0.0175	4.4112	0.0357
Lending ties	0.0124	0.0062	4.0478	0.0442
Subsidiary investment	−0.1580	0.0313	25.0906	0.0000
ROA 5-year average	−0.1677	0.0883	3.6053	0.0576
Debt–equity	0.0016	0.0013	1.4341	0.2311
Firm size	0.2852	0.1332	4.5854	0.0322
Industry 1[a]	−3.5080	13.9733	0.0630	0.8018
Industry 2[a]	−5.8578	13.8807	0.1781	0.6730
Industry 3[a]	−6.9038	13.8793	0.2474	0.6189
Industry 4[a]	−0.1710	1.3704	0.0156	0.9007
Industry 5[a]	−4.6853	13.9134	0.1134	0.7363

Note: Dependant variable: 0 if independent; 1 if keiretsu member. −2 log likelihood: 301.089. Goodness of fit: 422.371. Chi-square: 249.937 12 df. Significance: 0.0000. Percentage correct keiretsu membership: 98.36% (*n* = 359). Percentage correct independent firm: 55.2% (*n* = 68).
[a] Dummy variables indicating industry affiliation.

Table 2. Probability of Keiretsu Membership vs. Independent Grouping (1997).

Variable	Coefficient	Standard Error	Wald	Significance
Constant	4.6417	19.3169	0.0577	0.8101
5% ownership	0.0350	0.0120	8.5491	0.0035
Institutional ownership	−0.0508	0.0171	8.8217	0.0030
Lending ties	0.0186	0.0064	8.5320	0.0035
Subsidiary investment	−0.1750	0.0321	29.6237	0.0000
ROA 5-year average	0.0688	0.0815	0.7120	0.3988
Debt–equity	0.0005	0.0007	0.5333	0.4652
Firm size	0.4566	0.1341	11.5894	0.0007
Industry 1[a]	−7.9458	19.2882	0.1697	0.6804
Industry 2[a]	−8.9604	19.2671	0.2163	0.6419
Industry 3[a]	−9.7960	19.2670	0.2585	0.6111
Industry 4[a]	−4.2869	3.2232	1.7690	0.1835
Industry 5[a]	−4.7954	19.0689	0.0632	0.8014

Note: Dependant variable: 0 if independent; 1 if keiretsu member. −2 log likelihood: 291.605. Goodness of fit: 358.730. Chi-square: 269.751 12 df. Significance: 0.0000. Percentage correct keiretsu firms: 97.25 (*n* = 354). Percentage correct independent firms: 58.27% (*n* = 74).
[a] Dummy variables indicating industry affiliation.

through 1997, and if anything, the magnitude of the coefficient suggests that this tie has strengthened.

EVOLVING KEIRETSU TIES

In order to evaluate more directly the evolution of keiretsu ties through time, we eliminated independent firms from the analysis and focused solely upon keiretsu membership. Given the shift in importance of institutional investment between 1992 and 1997, we proposed that subtle changes in group ties might be captured by breaking down equity holdings into group shareholding, foreign ownership, and outside blockholders. Furthermore, as a direct test of the strength of keiretsu membership, we included the tie strength variable. Table 3 presents descriptive statistics for selected variables for 1992 and 1997.

As indicated in Table 3 changes in the strength of keiretsu ties occurred over the 1992–1997 period. Group borrowing declined somewhat overall, but use of short-term debt increased, which is suggestive of keiretsu members looking to the outside for debt financing. In terms of equity ties, group shareholding declined during the period, as did overall ownership concentration, as measured by 5% holdings and institutional investment. In spite of such declines, we observe that outside equity holdings are somewhat weaker in the later period, and foreign ownership is markedly higher. Subsidiary investment also rose during the period. Tie strength, which is presumed to approximate the overall strength of the keiretsu relationship, is slightly higher in the later period. These results are a challenge for coherent interpretation. On the one hand, traditional keiretsu ties along some

Table 3. Descriptive Statistics.

Variable	*N* 92	*N* 97	*M* 97	S.D. 97	*M* 92	S.D. 92
Group holdings	381	372	23.9769	14.4740	24.4155	15.3149
Group borrowing	318	336	29.1000	15.5955	30.9123	15.1523
5% ownership	445	441	20.4760	17.6165	22.2454	17.7212
Institutional ownership	445	441	23.1542	8.5867	24.9240	9.2156
Foreign ownership	445	441	7.8249	8.6070	4.0506	5.9477
Tie strength	455	444	2.73	1.03	2.62	1.02
Outside equity holdings	381	372	18.2059	8.9330	19.8294	8.8821
Size	455	445	14.3057	1.4229	14.2014	1.3902
Lending ties	454	445	47.9777	29.3467	42.4950	27.7749
Subsidiary investment	454	442	9.7350	20.9674	8.9981	18.3862
ROA 5-year average	448	445	1.8512	1.8865	3.3613	1.8112
Debt–equity ratio	455	445	269.9914	637.2936	259.6031	590.5882

dimensions have weakened. Those ties presumed to differentiate keiretsu members from independent firms (ownership concentration, group holdings, and group borrowing) weakened over time. This weakening of ties appears to have been offset by stronger subsidiary investment and a lessening of the importance of overall outside equity but significantly more pronounced foreign ownership. Whether these general tendencies sufficiently differentiate the 1992 keiretsu member from those profiled in 1997 is an empirical question.

Binomial logistic regression was again used to assess the evolution of debt and equity ties over the two time periods with attention now solely focused upon keiretsu members. Results are contained in Table 4. In these regressions, the dummy dependant variable was assigned a value of 0 to indicate 1992, while 1 designates the year 1997.

Table 4. Probability of Keiretsu Membership in 1997 vs. 1992.

Variable	Coefficient	Standard Error	Wald	Significance
Constant	5.8657	1.7139	11.7138	0.0006
Institutional ownership	−0.0303	0.0141	4.5963	0.0320
Subsidiary investment	−0.1152	0.0429	7.2007	0.0073
Lending ties	0.0143	0.0049	8.3419	0.0039
Group holdings	−0.0418	0.0100	17.5801	0.0000
Outside holdings	−0.0331	0.0154	4.6150	0.0317
Foreign owners	0.1541	0.0216	50.7716	0.0000
Group borrowing	−0.0087	0.0077	1.2852	0.2569
Tie strength	0.3745	0.1168	10.2734	0.0013
Mitsubishi[a]	0.2101	0.3398	0.3822	0.5364
Sumitomo[a]	0.3513	0.3527	0.9923	0.3192
DKB[a]	0.1120	0.3676	0.0929	0.7606
Fuyo[a]	0.0725	0.3462	0.0439	0.8341
Mitsui[a]	0.2732	0.3958	0.4763	0.4901
ROA 5-year average	−0.7562	0.0827	83.5618	0.0000
Debt–equity	−0.0003	0.0002	3.1012	0.0782
Firm size	−0.2909	0.1059	7.5466	0.0060
Industry 1[b]	−0.0667	0.5782	0.0133	0.9081
Industry 2[b]	0.6422	0.5193	1.5293	0.2162
Industry 3[b]	0.5844	0.5093	1.3166	0.2512
Industry 4[b]	0.7859	0.6483	1.4698	0.2254
Industry 5[b]	0.7820	0.5800	1.8177	0.1776

Note: Dependant variable: Year (1992: 0; 1997: 1). −2 log likelihood: 638.303. Goodness of fit: 864.283. Chi-square: 238.070 21 degrees of freedom. Significance: 0.0000. Percentage correct 1997 = 79% (n = 239). Percentage correct 1992 = 78.88% (n = 261). Overall percentage correct = 78.99%.
[a] Dummy variables indicating keiretsu affiliation.
[b] Dummy variables denoting industry affiliation.

The model is highly significant and correctly classifies nearly 80% of observations in both years. Neither specific keiretsu affiliation (i.e. membership in one of the six major groupings) nor particular industrial classification has a bearing on whether the firm is drawn from the 1992 or 1997 sample. Thus, we can conclude that changes that are observed are keiretsu and industry-wide. Other control variables: profitability, the debt-equity ratio, and size are significant determinants of classification, and higher values all favor 1992 firms over 1997 firms. It is perhaps worth mentioning that declining profitability and reduced overall indebtedness suggest a less competitive environment in 1997 on the one hand, and a move away from traditional financing sources for keiretsu firms on the other.

The focus of the present research is on the strength of keiretsu ties over time. Our preliminary analysis, which discriminated between keiretsu and independent firms in the two time periods, suggests that the ties have evolved over time, although the terms "weakening" or "strengthening" greatly oversimplify what we observed. In terms of equity ties, the probability a firm is drawn from the 1997 sample of keiretsu firms is increased as foreign ownership rises. Greater levels of group holdings, outside shareholders, and institutional investment significantly favor classification among the 1992 group of firms. It is difficult to judge, based solely on these coefficients, whether equity ties strengthened over time. Certainly, we cannot reject outright the hypothesis that equity ties remained stable or strengthened over time, since clearly the ties evolved over time. There is less dependence on the group but, at the same time, less involvement of outside blockholders and greater foreign presence. These results could hint at a regrouping of inter-related shareholders who, in terms of numbers, have less presence but perhaps, in terms of impact, remain a significant driving force in the keiretsu system. Certainly, the result that greater tie strength is coincident with the probability of 1997 keiretsu membership supports this conjecture. Rose and Kiyohiko (2004) reach a similar conclusion that while cross-holding of equity has declined in the 1990s, keiretsu ties remain strong at the corporate level. Anecdotal evidence is also suggestive of the possibility that ties have changed over time. Toyota group's increased cross-shareholding and move toward a holding company structure can be viewed in this way – as a response to the loss of support from group banks (Mitsui, Sanwa, and Tokai) in terms of both debt and equity.[2]

Turning to debt ties, a somewhat clearer pattern emerges. Greater use of short-term debt favors classification as a 1997 keiretsu member, but at the same time, the level of group borrowing does not significantly determine classification as either a 1992 keiretsu firm or a 1997 keiretsu firm. Taken together with the declining importance of overall debt financing as measured by the debt/equity ratio in 1997 relative to 1992, these results are suggestive of strengthening debt ties.

CONCLUSIONS AND IMPLICATIONS FOR FUTURE RESEARCH

This paper has examined the evolution of debt and equity ties among keiretsu firms between the early 1990s and the later part of the decade. In contrast to studies focusing on only one type of tie, our analysis has allowed us to examine patterns of both debt and equity holdings. Results suggest that equity and lending ties have evolved in the more difficult context of the later time period. The results also provide evidence for the stability (and indeed strengthening) of equity ties, while debt ties have remained stable or even strengthened in the context of financial pressures and the increased availability and attractiveness of alternative forms of non-bank financing. The latter may be due to the slowness of lending institutions to respond to the current economic situation and changes in regulation.

These results highlight the need to examine the evolution of multiple ties which link keiretsu firms. Our study, for the most part, examined only debt and equity ties. Use of the tie strength variable did, however, permit some latitude in evaluating something other than purely financial ties. Our findings are consistent with those of Moerke (2004), for example, who notes an overall decline in dependence upon links to government bureaucracy for most Japanese firms, while observing that members of horizontal keiretsu appear to have fortified such linkages during the 1990s. This result suggests the importance of examining other types of transactional ties in future research. Debt and equity links may serve to substitute, or to cement other types of ties (for example buyer or supplier relationships). Personnel ties should also be considered. Indeed, in the context of reductions in lending ties, personnel exchanges between banks and group firms may become particularly important.

It is important that future research examine degrees of inclusion in the keiretsu. Research distinguishing between keiretsu and independent firms has created a false dichotomy and has ignored the presence of large numbers of firms less closely tied with a keiretsu. Although the difficulties in assessing strength of affiliation are significant, it may be of considerable importance in understanding the structure and implications of keiretsu membership. Guillot and Lincoln (2004) emphasize precisely this point in their comparison of Matsushita Electric Industrial and Sanyo Electric. Matsushita successfully enriched its keiretsu ties with suppliers by encouraging and sharing innovation. Their study is yet another example of the fact that strong network ties with keiretsu members which extend beyond purely financial links produce substantial benefits to the core firm as well as more strongly affiliated members.

Finally, this study does not examine changes in the strategic or performance implications of keiretsu affiliation. As noted earlier, in the absence of differences in stakeholder demands, changes in keiretsu ties may only imply the replacement of one form of link with another. Understanding the evolution of Japanese industrial organization requires investigation as to whether these economic changes have, indeed, changed the demands and pressures placed on Japanese firms. Second, it is important to investigate whether any changes in stakeholder demands have led to modifications in the performance and strategic characteristics of Japanese firms. In this respect, inclusion of stakeholder theory in the more corporate governance-based research, which has dominated examination of Japanese industrial organization, may provide a significant advancement in our understanding of the evolving Japanese context.

NOTES

1. Rose and Kiyohiko (2004), in a companion article in this volume, trace the history of bank merger activity in Japan to the present day.
2. We thank an anonymous reviewer for this example.

REFERENCES

Ahmadijian, C., & Lincoln, J. (2001). Keiretsu, governance, and learning: Case studies in change from the Japanese automobile industry. *Organization Science, 12*, 683–701.

Ahmadjian, C., & Robbins, G. (1999). Foreign share ownership and corporate behavior in Japan. Paper presented at the Academy of Management Meetings, Chicago.

Aoki, M. (1990). Toward an economic model of the Japanese firm. *Journal of Economic Literature, 8*, 1–27.

Aoki, M. (1992). A bargaining game-theoretic approach to the Japanese firm. In: P. Sheard (Ed.), *International Adjustment and the Japanese Firm* (pp. 30–49). St. Leonard, Australia: Allen & Unwin.

Aoki, M. (1994). Monitoring characteristics of the main bank sysem: An analytical and developmental view. In: M. Aoki & H. Patrick (Eds), *The Japanese Main Bank System* (pp. 109–141). Oxford: Oxford University Press.

Argy, V., & Stein, L. (1997). *The Japanese economy*. New York: New York University Press.

Asian Wall Street Journal (1995). Japan discloses enormous sum of bad loans. June 7, 1.

Bappa, A. (2000). The Japanese family: An institutional logic for Japanese corporate networks and Japanese management. *Academy of Management Review, 25*, 409–415.

Bayoumi, T. (1999). *The morning after: Explaining the slowdown in Japanese growth in the 1990s.* International Monetary Fund.

Campbell, J., & Hamao, Y. (1994). Changing patterns of corporate financing and the main bank system in Japan. In: M. Aoki & H. Patrick (Eds), *The Japanese Main Bank System* (pp. 325–34). Oxford: Oxford University Press.

Corbett, J. (1994). An overview of the Japanese financial system. In: N. D. M. Prevezer (Ed.), *Capital Markets and Corporate Governance* (pp. 306–324). Oxford: Oxford University Press.

Cowling, K., & Tomlinson, P. P. (2000). The Japanese crisis – A case of strategic failure. *The Economic Journal, 110*, F358–F381.

Dewenter, K., Novaes, W., & Pettway, R. (2001). Visibility vs. complexity in business groups: Evidence from Japanese Keiretsu. *Journal of Business, 74*, 79–100.

Dow, S., & McGuire, J. (1999). The sources and advantages of Japanese industrial organization. *Asia Pacific Journal of Management, 16*, 47–74.

Flath, D. (1993). Shareholdings in the Keiretsu, Japan's financial groups. *The Review of Economics and Statistics, 75*, 249–258.

Frankel, J. (1991). The cost of capital in Japan: An update. *Business Economics, 26*, 25–31.

Geringer, J. M., Tallman, S., & Olsen, D. (2000). Product and international diversification among Japanese multinational firms. *Strategic Management Journal, 21*, 51–80.

Gerlach, M. (1992a). The Japanese corporate network: A block model analysis. *Administrative Science Quarterly, 37*, 105–139.

Gerlach, M. (1992b). *Alliance capitalism: The social organization of Japanese business.* Berkeley: University of California Press.

Gerlach, M., & Lincoln, J. (1992). The organization of business networks in the United States and Japan. In: R. Eccles & R. N. Nohiria (Eds), *Networks and Organizations* (pp. 491–520). Cambridge, MA: Harvard Business School Press.

Gibson, M. (1998). "Big bang" deregulation and Japanese corporate governance: A survey of the issues. *Board of Governors of the Federal Reserve System International Finance Discussion Papers.* Washington, DC.

Gilson, R. J., & Roe, M. J. (1993). Understanding the Japanese Keiretsu: Overlaps between corporate governance and industrial organization. *Yale Law Journal, 102*, 871–884.

Granovetter, M. (1973). The strength of weak ties. *American Journal of Sociology, 78*, 1360–1380.

Guillot, D., & Lincoln, J. R. (2004). Dyad and network: Models of manufacturer-supplier collaboration in the Japanese TV manufacturing industry. *Advances in International Management, 17*, 161–190.

Hofstede, G. (1991). *Cultures and organization.* New York: McGraw Hill.

Hoshi, T. (1994). The economic role of corporate grouping and the main bank system. In: M. Aoki & M. Dore (Eds), *The Japanese Firm: Sources of Competitive Advantage* (pp. 285–309). Oxford: Oxford University Press.

Hoshi, T., Kashyap, A., & Scharfstein, D. (1991). Corporate structure, liquidity, and investment: Evidence from Japanese industrial groups. *The Quarterly Journal of Economics, 106*, 33–59.

Ito, T. (1997). Japan's economy needs structural change. *Finance and Development, 34*, 16–19.

Johnston, S. (1995). Managerial dominance of Japan's major corporations. *Journal of Management, 21*, 191–209.

Johnston, S., & McAlevey, L. (1998). Stable shareholdings and Japan's bubble economy: An historical overview. *Strategic Management Journal, 19*, 1101–1107.

Kanatas, G., & Qi, J. (2001). Imperfect competition, agency, and financing decisions. *The Journal of Business, 74*, 307–338.

Kawamoto, A. (1999). Unblocking Japanese reform. *The OECD Observer*, March.

Kim, H., & Hoskisson, R. (1996). Japanese governance system: A critical review. In: S. B. Prasad (Ed.), *Advances in International Comparative Management* (Vol. 11, pp. 165–190). Greenwich, CT: JAI Press.

Kim, K., & Limpaphayom, P. (1998). A test of the two-tier corporate governance structure: The case of Japanese keiretsu. *The Journal of Financial Research, 21*, 37–51.

Korkie, B., & Naamura, M. (1997). Block holding and keiretsu in Japan: The effects of capital markets liberalization measures on the stock market. *Journal of International Money and Finance, 16*, 113–140.

Lawrence, R. Z. (1991). Efficient or exclusionist? The import behavior of Japanese corporate groups. *Brookings Papers on Economic Activity, 1*, 311–331.

Levinson, H. (1992). Keiretsu relations changing. *Japan Times*, Weekly international edition, 18.

McGuire, J., & Dow, S. (2002). The Japanese Keiretsu system: A comparative analysis. *Journal of Business Research, 55*, 33–40.

Miwa, Y., & Ramseyer, J. M. (2000). Rethinking relationship-specific investments: Subcontracting in the Japanese automobile industry. *Michigan Law Review, 98*, 2636–2667.

Miyashita, K., & Russell, D. (1994). *Keiretsu: Inside the hidden Japanese conglomerates*. New York: McGraw-Hill.

Moerke, A. (2004). The changing trend in links between bureaucracy and the private sector in Japan. *Advances in International Management, 17*, 61–90.

Nakatani, O. (1984). The economic role of financial corporate grouping. In: M. Aoki (Ed.), *The Economic Analysis of Japanese Firms* (pp. 227–258). Amsterdam: North Holland.

OECD (1998). *OECD economic outlook*. Paris: OECD.

Paker, B., & Hodder, J. (2002). Japanese capital structure during a turbulent period. *Social Science Research Network Electronic Paper Series*.

Porter, M. E. (1990). *The competitive advantage of nations*. New York: Free Press.

Prowse, S. D. (1990). Institutional investment patterns and corporate financial behavior in the United States and Japan. *Journal of Financial Economics, 27*, 43–66.

Prowse, S. D. (1992). The structure of corporate ownership in Japan. *Journal of Finance, 47*, 1121–1140.

Roe, M. J., Ramseyer, J. M., & Romano, R. (1993). Some differences in corporate structure in Germany, Japan, and the United States. *Yale Law Journal, 102*, 1927–1950.

Rose, E. L., & Kiyohiko, I. (2004). M&As in the Japanese banking industry: Past and future. *Advances in International Management, 17*, 141–160.

Sakakibara, M., Porter, M. E., & Takeuch, H. (2000). *Can Japan compete?* New York: Basic Books and Perseus.

Sheard, P. (1991). The economics of Japanese corporate organizations and the structural impediments debate: A critical review. *Japanese Economic Studies, 19*, 30–78.

Sheard, P. (1994a). Interlocking shareholdings and corporate governance. In: A. Aoki & M. Dore (Eds), *The Japanese Firm: The Sources of Competitive Strength* (pp. 310–349). Oxford: Oxford University Press.

Sheard, P. (1994b). Reciprocal delegated monitoring in the Japanese banking system. *Journal of Japanese and International Economics, 8*, 1–21.

Sheard, P. (1994c). The governance of financial distress. In: M. Aoki & H. Patrick (Eds), *The Japanese Main Bank System* (pp. 188–230). Oxford: Oxford University Press.

Steensma, K., Marino, L., Weaver, M., & Dickson, P. H. (2000). The influence of national culture on the formation of technology alliances by entrepreneurial firms. *Academy of Management Journal, 43*, 951–973.

Thomas, L. G., & Waring, G. (1999). Competing capitalisms: Capital investment in American, German, and Japanese firms. *Strategic Management Journal, 20*, 729–748.

Ueda, K. (1994). Institutional and regulatory frameworks for the main bank system. In: M. Aoki & H. Patrick (Eds), *The Japanese Main Bank System* (pp. 89–108). Oxford: Oxford University Press.

Weinstein, D., & Yafeh, V. (1998). On the costs of a bank-centered financial system: Evidence from the changing main bank relations in Japan. *The Journal of Finance, 53*, 635–672.

Williamson, O. E. (1983). Credible commitments: Using hostages to support exchange. *American Economic Review, 73*, 519–537.

Williamson, O. E. (1991a). Comparative economic organization: The analysis of discrete structural alternatives. *Administrative Science Quarterly, 36*, 269–296.

Williamson, O. E. (1991b). Strategizing, economizing, and economic organization. *Strategic Management Journal, 12*, S75–S94.

Wiseman, P., & Cox, J. (2002). Japan may fumble bank reform again. *USA Today*. Retrieved October 27, 2002, from www.usatoday.com/money/markets/world/2002–10–27-japan_x.htm.

M&As IN THE JAPANESE BANKING INDUSTRY: THE MORE THINGS CHANGE?

Elizabeth L. Rose and Kiyohiko Ito

ABSTRACT

Recently, Japanese commercial banks have experienced increased merger and acquisition (M&A) activity. M&As allow rapid downsizing and increased scale economies, while avoiding massive layoffs. Faced with the pressures of globalization and a difficult domestic economic environment, some Japanese banks appear to have shifted their operational focus from developing growth-enabling core competencies to reducing organizational costs. Keiretsu relationships are changing accordingly, with individual groups adapting in different ways. Most Japanese banks experienced extensive M&A activity at earlier points in their corporate histories. The recent flurry of M&As in the banking sector is nothing new, but rather a resurgence of past practices.

INTRODUCTION

Domestic mergers and acquisitions (M&As) in Japan increased by a factor of up to 10 during the last decade of the 20th century (Alexander, 2000). Banks have not been immune to large-scale M&A activity in this post-"bubble" economy. After decades of tight governmental control over the financial sector, a considerable number of banks have failed. Naturally, this upheaval in the banking industry

Japanese Firms in Transition: Responding to the Globalization Challenge
Advances in International Management, Volume 17, 139–157
Copyright © 2005 by Elsevier Ltd.
All rights of reproduction in any form reserved
ISSN: 0747-7929/doi:10.1016/S0747-7929(04)17006-6

has had a strong negative effect on other industries, and on the economy as a whole. Many banks have dealt with their problems in the current *Heisei* recession through consolidation. The purpose of this paper is to study M&As in the Japanese banking sector, based on a typology for M&As suggested by Bower (2001), with the intent of understanding more about the changing nature of business strategy in Japan.

There is an extensive literature on the main bank system in Japan (e.g. Aoki & Patrick, 1994; Hoshi, Kashyap & Scharfstein, 1990; Weinstein & Yafeh, 1998). Our primary focus in this paper is on the more recent, and less-documented, M&A activities among banks. We discuss the nature of banks' current M&A strategies, along with reasons for the lack of M&As between the end of World War II and the *Heisei* recession. We also overview the history of M&As in Japan, particularly in the banking industry, and discuss similarities and differences between pre-World War II M&As and those of the post-bubble economy. The recent mergers among banks have led to some changes. We discuss the implications of these changes with respect to the macro-level issue of industrial structure and the micro-level issue of employment practices.

This paper is organized as follows. In the next section, we introduce categories of M&As. We also analyze the effect of consolidation in the banking industry and describe the evolving strategies of Japanese banks. The third section reviews post-World War I M&A activities, the role of the Ministry of Finance (MOF), and the development of the Japanese banking sector's institutional and regulatory structures, and draws comparisons with the financial environments in other countries. In the fourth section, we consider the impact of recent bank M&As on Japan's industrial group structure. The last section presents a summary and our conclusions.

RECENT M&As IN THE JAPANESE FINANCIAL SECTOR

Value Creation from Downsizing

There is a large literature on the effects of M&As. Much of the research in this area considers issues of value creation through M&A (e.g. Kitching, 1974; Ravenscraft & Scherer, 1989; Seth, 1990). Recently, Bower (2001) discussed M&A activities in U.S. firms, identifying five rationales for undertaking such a strategy. The five categories of M&A motivation are:

(1) to deal with overcapacity through consolidation in mature industries;
(2) to roll up competitors in geographically fragmented industries;

(3) to extend into new products or markets;

(4) to substitute for R&D;

(5) to exploit eroding industry boundaries by inventing an industry.

Banking is a mature industry. The expansion during Japan's bubble economy resulted in extensive overcapacity, given the current environment of slow (or negative) growth. Thus, bank mergers in Japan are generally well described by Bower's Category 1, as they represent defensive measures aimed at consolidating, downsizing, and obtaining scale economies.[1] Under these conditions, mergers and/or acquisitions offer considerable potential for the synergies that form such a strong focus of the M&A literature (e.g. Chatterjee, 1986; Datta, 1991; Harrison, Hitt, Hoskisson & Ireland, 1991; Lubatkin, 1983). Merged banks increase their size, while having the opportunity to close redundant branches and offices. The resulting firm has a greater market share and more clout. In the process of consolidation, the new organization should be able to develop a more efficient operation, utilizing the most skilled managers from the original firms. Following extensive M&A activity, the industry as a whole has less excess capacity.

The issue of excess capacity, at the levels of both the firm and the industry, is important. In the absence of firm-specific, unique financial products and services, a bank's performance is directly related to the size of its total deposits. When banks are similar in terms of size, products offered, and the amount of non-performing assets, internal cost cutting becomes crucial to the restructuring effort. This is the situation in which many of Japan's surviving banks have found themselves at the start of the 21st century.

This is a very new situation for these organizations. Due to the strong protection afforded the banks by MOF, through its regulatory control, more than 40 years passed following World War II without a single Japanese bank suffering a net loss. Such a lucrative business environment tends to create bloated organizations, staffed by highly compensated employees, many of whom may not be particularly productive. Arguably, this was the case for the banking sector in Japan. A recent government survey indicated that the average salary of managers in banks and insurance firms is approximately 30% higher than those of managers in manufacturing firms (Statistics Bureau, Ministry of Public Management, Home Affairs, Posts and Telecommunications, 2003).

It is not surprising, then, that M&A activity has picked up in the Japanese banking sector. Following the merger of such bloated banks, the resulting organization might be expected to slim down by shedding excess employees. However, Spindle (1998, p. A18) noted that, in Japan, ". . . mergers often disappoint investors because they seldom lead to the mass layoffs that might improve profits." Mass layoffs are viewed differently in Japan, compared with many other business environments. Large-scale layoffs, such as those generally associated with U.S. downsizing, would have devastating effects on a bank. The organization would risk a mass exodus of depositors, because customers would be reluctant to maintain their accounts in a bank displaying such signs of weakness. Large-scale layoffs would also have a strong negative impact on the bank's longer-term future. Highly skilled potential employees have employment choices, and are unlikely to opt to work for companies that lay off employees as a matter of course, given Japan's still nascent secondary labor market. Therefore, during past recessions (e.g. the oil crises in the 1970s), many Japanese firms chose to downsize slowly, relying primarily on natural attrition, the freezing of new hires, and the encouragement of early retirements.

Natural attrition is hardly a quick and effective cost-cutting measure; large-scale layoffs are much more efficient. In the face of the current *Heisei* recession, though, there has been a clear need for more dramatic action. Over the years, the excess capacity in the Japanese banking industry had become quite substantial. By 1990, 114 publicly traded banks in Japan had a total of 13,738 domestic branches, in a geographic region approximately the size of California. In addition, approximately 24,000 post offices offer postal savings transactions. When the economy slowed, reductions in branches and personnel were needed rather desperately, to generate economies of scale. Natural attrition alone would not suffice.

In such a situation, M&As can provide assistance with the difficult problem of downsizing, offering a solution that falls between natural attrition and massive layoffs. One positive outcome of M&A activity is the achievement of scale economies in various business activities; the scale economies associated with human resource management (HRM) are particularly critical in a recession. These can be demonstrated with respect to the processes of recruitment and downsizing. Consider a potential merger among n banks, all of which are relatively similar in size, with approximately the same number of branches throughout Japan, generally in the same cities. Given their comparable sizes and the fairly standardized HRM practices in the Japanese financial sector, we can assume that each bank, separately, would expect to hire approximately X new employees and have approximately Y retirees each year. Thus, the independently operating banks would be expected to take on nX new employees and lose nY employees to retirement, on an annual basis. If the banks merge, the new organization will have n branches in each of the cities, offering identical financial products and services. Often, the branches of the former competitors are located in very close proximity to each other. There is little merit in operating n separate branches and buildings, in virtually identical locations, following the merger.

Before the merger, each independent bank would have had great difficulty consolidating. Closing a city branch would have been costly to the bank, causing it to lose customers to its rivals and damaging its reputation. After the merger of the n banks, however, the newly merged bank can eliminate all but one of the branches in each city, without losing customers. The new bank can cut costs by closing $n - 1$ of the branches in the city, and impose minimal inconvenience on its customers in the process. The cost savings resulting from the merger can be substantial. For example, assume that there are three banks, each with 10 branches (one in each of the same 10 cities) and a headquarters in Tokyo. Thus, there are 30 branches in 10 cities, plus three headquarters. Operating independently, if each bank closes five branches, the total number of closed branches for the three banks is 15. If they merge and close geographically redundant offices, they can close 20 branches and two headquarters in Tokyo. The merger results in minimal loss of customers or geographic coverage, with more branch closures and higher per-branch sales.

Given the reluctance to undertake large layoffs in Japan, closing $n - 1$ branches in each city will result in immediate and considerable overstaffing. Sustaining operations in each remaining branch is unlikely to require n times the former number of employees, particularly given the increasing use of automated transactions in the current environment. However, the newly merged bank has the opportunity to reduce its overstaffing situation much more quickly, compared with n independent organizations having closed (in total) the same number of branches. In the merged bank, nY employees will retire each year, while the number of new hires will be X, rather than nX. With the current demographics, retirees belong to the baby-boom generation, further accelerating the speed of the downsizing process, because Y can be substantially larger than X. While it is true that this workforce reduction is far from immediate, and a situation of excess employees may continue for quite a few years, the merged bank can downsize much more quickly than the individual banks.

The merged bank is able to take advantage of scale economies. The pre-merged banks cannot achieve the same result by remaining independent and simply reducing or freezing their hiring, partly because each branch needs a minimum number of staff to maintain its operation. In addition, a reputation for stable employment is critically important for large Japanese companies. The number of new employees hired by large companies is published annually, and prospective employees monitor these numbers closely. Large reductions in hiring have damaging reputational effects. In addition, substantial reductions in the number of new recruits result in discontinuities, causing disruptions to promotion and training schemes that ripple through the HRM function for decades (Odagiri,

1992). Merging the n former competitors provides a swift way to close excess branches, without the same level of negative publicity. The newly merged bank can justify a lower level of hiring, on the basis that it is a single entity, rather than a collection of n companies. Compared with the n separate and independent banks, the result of the M&A has a much better chance of having sufficient business volume per branch to remain profitable.

Thus, a benefit of M&A activity is a quicker reduction of excess employees, without having to resort to large and immediate layoffs. The tight nature of the secondary labor market in Japan means that immediate downsizing has not been a viable option for the past 50 years. Instead, firms appear to use M&As to downsize efficiently, avoiding the embarrassment of having to make emergency announcements of imminent action. In addition, the appearance of the post-merger mega-bank should signal stability and project a safer image to consumers. Internally, this may keep employees from jumping ship and working for other growing financial institutions. Externally, it may allow the new bank to attract more customers and more high-quality employees.

While M&As offer benefits of scale economies and more rapid downsizing, they also have serious drawbacks. Even when the strategic goal of the merger is clear, its implementation may be complicated. Firms have distinct organizational cultures (e.g. Smircich, 1983). Differences in the cultures of firms involved in M&As can result in misunderstandings and conflicts during and after the merger. It is notoriously difficult to integrate multiple established and entrenched systems (e.g. Shrivastava, 1986). These difficulties can have negative impacts on the value creation possible through M&A activity (Chatterjee, Lubatkin, Schweiger & Weber, 1992). The entrenchment may survive long after the merger has been completed; since 1971, the president of DKB has been selected alternately (*tasukigake*) from employees of the former Daiichi Bank and Kangyo Bank. In addition, the logistics of merging are complex. In April 2002, at Mizuho Bank, the incomplete integration of the computer systems of the three newly merged banks created chaos in customer account transactions from the first day of the new bank's operation. The process of merging firms can be time-consuming and politically charged, even when the amalgamating companies are in a mature industry and have values that are essentially similar (Bower, 2001).

Changing the Strategic Focus from Growth to Cost Cutting

Transaction cost theory posits that firms can organize their interdependence through hierarchy, markets, or contracts. Large Japanese firms have tended to rely less on pure hierarchy than their counterparts from other countries, particularly the U.S. Instead, the traditional Japanese industrial structure has been built on long-term supplier relationships and industrial groupings. Given the slow, and even negative, growth experienced by the Japanese economy since the 1990s, it seems reasonable to expect that some reshaping of the industrial structure will take place, as firms move to contain their operational and organizational costs.

Many Japanese firms have long had strong biases toward growth (Abegglen & Stalk, 1985). Managers have focused on the resource side of their operations, nurturing, developing, and protecting core competencies to sustain growth. As complex harmonizations of individual technologies and production skills, a firm's core competencies form the basis of its fundamental pattern of internal coordination and learning (Prahalad & Hamel, 1990). Japanese firms have tended to develop core competencies to encourage growth, generally viewing cost control as a secondary issue. In a booming economy, firms thrive by being able to add capacity ahead of demand, and they can afford to do so. However, in an economic environment characterized by sustained slow or negative growth, with external forces outside of the firm's control limiting the potential for expansion, such a strategy is unlikely to yield a superior performance. Given limited growth, cost control becomes paramount in the quest to improve the bottom line.

Prahalad and Hamel noted the need for Western firms to shift their strategic focus from cost-cutting to core competencies: "During the 1980s, top executives were judged on their ability to restructure, declutter, and de-layer their corporations. In the 1990s, they will be judged on their ability to identify, cultivate, and exploit the core competencies that make growth possible..." (1990, p. 79).

There now appears to be a switch in roles. Since the late 1990s, top executives in Japan began to be judged on their abilities to restructure, declutter, and de-layer their firms. The changing nature of Japanese business is related to a strategic shift from growth-generating core competencies to cost-controlling restructuring. The two strategies are certainly not mutually exclusive, but the balance between them and their priorities has shifted for many firms in Japan. New strategic priorities have been dictated by the changes in domestic macroeconomic conditions associated with increased global competition and the bursting of the bubble economy.

This has especially been the case for banks. They are particularly vulnerable in the changing economic conditions, partly because their own success is so dependent on the success of other sectors in the Japanese economy. In addition, the protection from MOF had provided an extremely favorable business environment for the banks. As a result, it can be argued that many of the large Japanese banks experienced great success for nearly half a century, without ever having had to develop firm-specific core competencies to sustain growth.

HISTORICAL DEVELOPMENT

M&As in the Banking Industry

Outside the financial sector, there has not generally been extensive, large-scale M&A activity in Japan. When undertaking diversification, Japanese managers have tended to exhibit a preference for establishing companies de novo, rather than purchasing existing firms. The typical explanation for the low level of M&A activity has been the nature of the country's corporate environment (Pettway, 1991). Japan's traditional corporate paternalism – illustrated by lifetime employment, limited labor mobility and secondary job markets, seniority-based wage systems, and company unions – has been seen as a major source of protection for the autonomy of individual enterprises. The decision to establish new subsidiaries, rather than rely on M&As, supports the expansion of existing management ranks, and avoids many of the human resource-related problems associated with the combining of previously separate firms.

Abegglen and Stalk (1985) described the conventional view of why Japanese firms have not made extensive use of M&As. The arguments include notions regarding the sale of a company's having implications of buying and selling people, and M&A activity's having a sense of social irresponsibility and immorality about it. Additional issues raised are the problems associated with combining two entrenched work forces, and there being little scope for the reduction of the work force. These points have some strong validity for the post-World War II environment. However, they do not provide an accurate reflection of the behavior of Japanese firms prior to World War II, especially in the banking industry.

Many Japanese firms create offspring, in the form of subsidiaries (Ito & Rose, 1994). Charts of corporate genealogy tend to expand through time, starting from a single organization to, sometimes, hundreds. Notable exceptions to this generalized pattern of expansion are firms in the financial sector, whose genealogical charts tend to contract through time, starting with many small firms and merging into a single, large organization, through repeated consolidations. Figure 1 shows the genealogical chart for Daiwa Bank, prior to its merger with Asahi Bank. It is interesting to note that Daiwa Bank experienced the lowest level of M&A activity among the large commercial banks in Japan. The other large banks (e.g. Mizuho, Sumitomo Mitsui, Tokyo-Mitsubishi, UFJ) were formed through much more extensive series of M&As, especially before World War II.

The government has officially recorded more than 5,000 banks since 1872, when the first modern banking law was enacted (Tokyo Bankers Association, 1998). As of the beginning of 2002, there were 137 commercial banks in Japan: seven city banks, 64 regional banks, seven trust banks, three long-term

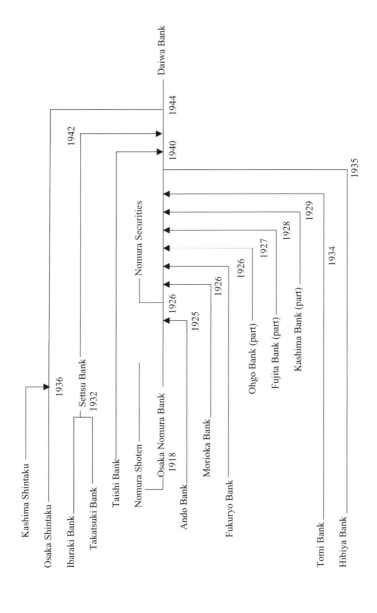

Fig. 1. Genealogy of Daiwa Bank. *Source:* Yakura & Ikushima, 1981.

credit banks, and 56 second association regional banks. This is a reduction of almost 2000 banks since 1901 (Sugiyama, 1974). More than 50% of these firms disappeared as a result of M&A activity.

The Post-World War I Era

The First World War ended in 1918. Because Japan was located far from the war zone and escaped physical damage, many Japanese companies benefited from the wartime economic boom. However, the boom ended quickly. By 1920, a post-war recession had begun. During 1920–1931, there were at least five recessions/depressions (*kyoko*) in Japan: *Sengo Kyoko* (1920), *Ginko Kyoko* (1922), *Kanto Great Earthquake Kyoko* (1924), *Showa Kinyu Kyoko* (1927), and *Showa Kyoko* (1930). The Japanese economy during the 1920s can be appropriately described as staggering along from one depression to another.

The first of these, the *Sengo Kyoko* (Post War Depression), had remarkable parallels with the *Heisei* recession of the 1990s. Shinomiya (1974) identified two main factors related to the cause of the *Sengo Kyoko*. First, Japanese firms made aggressive capital investments, aimed at growth, during World War I. This created production overcapacity in many industry sectors. Second, the huge profits generated during the war were used to make new capital investments and pay higher dividends. Firms did not work to improve their balance sheets, and held on to extra assets that were not productive. The overcapacity and nonproductive assets created severe financial problems in the face of the recession. The proposed causes for the *Sengo Kyoko* are almost identical to the reasons generally assumed to have created the post-bubble *Heisei* recession some 70 years later. They include overinvestment to satisfy growing demand, the assumption of too much debt to finance the overinvestment, lack of internal financial discipline and control, and the availability of abundant governmental financial support and credit extension. In both cases, large technological changes underlay economic trends: from textiles to heavy manufacturing for the *Sengo Kyoko* and from manufacturing to information technology for the *Heisei* recession. Interestingly, Shinomiya (1974), writing more than 15 years before the *Heisei* recession, used the overcapacity and overinvestment immediately following World War I to demonstrate the marked difference between pre- and post-World War II management in Japan, and suggested that managers in the post-World War II era had learned from the earlier experience. It appears that the bubble economy of the late 1980s erased the painful corporate memories of the experiences following World War I.

The economic turmoil after World War I caused many banks to fail. Figure 2 shows a time series plot of the number of bank failures per year in Japan, from

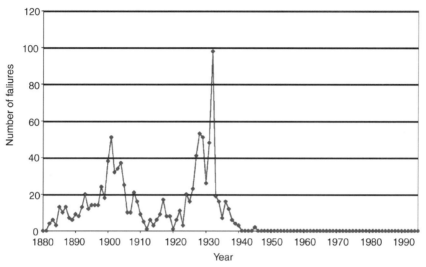

Fig. 2. Bank Failures in Japan.

1880 to 1995. These are banks that closed their doors and went out of business; banks that were rescued by other firms through acquisition are not included. The data demonstrate that Japan was not immune to the global economic difficulties following World War I. Between 1924 and 1934, 411 banks ceased their operations, including 98 firms in 1932 alone. It should be noted that the banking industry M&As that took place prior to World War II were mostly acquisitions of weak banks by stronger ones. Generally, local banks acquired other small, local banks in the same or adjacent territories (Sugiyama, 1974). These mergers created scale economies, providing the surviving banks with wider geographic coverage and more customers. Unlike the current merger activity, the pre-World War II M&As are well-described by Bower's Category 2: geographic roll-up.

Of course, the financial sector was not the only sector in trouble during the between-war period. Industry consolidation occurred throughout the Japanese economy. Despite claims that hostile takeovers have never worked in Japan (Spindle, 1998), many examples of such activity can be found between World War I and World War II. For example, the fierce personal rivalry between the heads of two railroad-based *zaibatsu* – Keita Goto of Tokyu and Yasujiro Tsutsumi of Seibu – led to a flurry of hostile takeovers in a variety of industries, including real estate, building management, transportation (railways, bus, and taxi), and department stores. The hostile takeover activity led other firms to take defensive measures, including cross-shareholding by friendly firms, which would later become such an integral part of the Japanese industrial system.

MOF and Consolidation in the Financial Industry

Having a financial system consisting of a small number of banks makes the job of regulating them relatively easy (Rosenbluth, 1989). Japan's Ministry of Finance (MOF) managed to accomplish just this, with some help from the global economic and political situation in the late 1920s. The financial crises precipitated by the bankruptcy of Suzuki Shoten in 1927 and heightened by New York's Black Monday in 1929 had important ramifications in Japan. They led to greater consolidation in the banking sector, which increased the power of the *zaibatsu* banks. The number of commercial banks in Japan decreased dramatically during the first four decades of the 20th century, from 1697 in 1905 to 427 by 1936. Over 950 banks closed their doors completely during this period, and another 1333 were either merged or acquired.

In 1936, the policy of one regional bank in each prefecture began to emerge. The next year, the emergency capital procurement law was enacted, in response to the budget deficit created by military expenditures. By 1943, the military's need for money was so great that it enacted legislation strengthening its authority to draw funds from private banks. The Bank of Japan, closely associated with MOF, provided a steady flow of loans to the banks during World War II, enabling them to maintain an outpouring of cash to support the military effort. By early 1945, mergers left one regional bank in each prefecture. Under military rule, the financial industry had become streamlined in a way that MOF could scarcely have achieved on its own. The number of ordinary banks in Japan fell from 377 in 1937 to 61 in 1945.

The Post-World War II Era

The Convoy System

After the cessation of military rule, MOF retained its extensive powers and provided considerable protection to financial institutions. Small banks had few incentives to give up their independence, as long as MOF stood behind them with an implicit guarantee of solvency. There was no credible danger of MOF's revoking its guarantee, as the small banks were well organized and politically influential in their support of the Liberal Democratic Party (Rosenbluth, 1989). The MOF protection was so strong that no commercial banks failed during the years from 1946 to 1997. None even suffered a loss for many decades. M&A activity virtually disappeared from the financial sector.

MOF's control over the banking industry was extremely effective at not allowing banks to fail. It accomplished this via the "convoy system," which is the term often used to describe a wide-ranging set of regulations in the Japanese financial sector

(Hoshi, 2001). The origin of the term is nautical and refers to ships traveling to a destination safely as a group. For the group of ships to remain together, the convoy must not travel any faster than the slowest of its member ships. The implication is that stronger, more seaworthy ships in the convoy provide assistance to weaker ships that may be endangered (e.g. by inclement weather, bad luck, or attack). Leaders are discouraged from moving too far ahead of the rest of the group. The convoy system suggests a unified command, in which each ship follows the instructions of the convoy leader, rather than operating independently of the other ships. As convoy leader, MOF used controls on interest; restrictions on branching, products, and service hours; and administrative guidance (*gyosei shido*) to control its fleet of banking institutions.

The use of such a controlling system is not completely unique to MOF. Breton and Wintrobe (1978) pointed out that, in addition to conducting open market operations, the central banks in many other countries also control their financial sectors using tactics that include switches to bank deposits, changes in bank or discount rates, variation in reserve requirements, and moral suasion. Breton and Wintrobe suggested that these various monetary instruments differ in their informational content, particularly with respect to what they convey to banks about the degree of restrictiveness or ease of the monetary policy being conducted by the authorities. The maximum amount of information is communicated through moral suasion, because its use is based on direct contact between the banks and the central bank.

Following World War II, MOF made extensive use of the convoy system to rescue insolvent banks. Until recently, it was very rare for either the Bank of Japan or the deposit insurance organization to participate directly in rescues. In most cases, MOF effected the rescues using indirect methods, such as administrative guidance. MOF has generally used a carrot-and-stick approach, providing incentives to rescuers by relaxing regulations, such as permitting participating banks to have increased numbers of branches. MOF has reportedly threatened to delay or refuse permission to offer new products, if financial institutions fail to cooperate in rescues. Similar to most other countries, the myriad of regulations governing Japan's financial markets provide banks with strong incentives to maintain good relations with MOF.

Rescues typically required the supporting bank to provide managerial and personnel assistance to its troubled compatriot, in addition to financial support. The pair of banks usually had some type of connection prior to the rescue, such as a genealogical link or membership in the same industrial group. The rescuing bank could expect to benefit from increased scale economies and, if the troubled bank had been a local rival, reduced competition. The rescuer would generally become the largest creditor or stockholder of the insolvent bank. Most of the time, the weaker bank ended up merged with its rescuer. (It should be noted that, since 1997, the pattern regarding which banks have initiated rescues has been much less clear. Only a few banks that have been the major shareholders of insolvent banks have undertaken de facto M&As. For example, Sumitomo Mitsui Bank acquired Hyogo Bank (Minato Bank), and part of Namihaya Bank's operation was transferred to Daiwa Bank.)

The convoy system broke down in the late 1990s, just when the banks were desperately in need of MOF's protection. Several developments in the financial sector contributed to the system's demise. First, deregulation in the 1980s reduced the regulatory rewards available for MOF to offer banks in exchange for assisting failing banks (Hoshi, 2001). The fact that less-regulated market conditions were governing banks' strategies meant that MOF had fewer carrots and sticks. Second, the post-bubble economic crisis weakened Japan's domestic financial institutions quite severely. Realistically, only a few banks remained in a good enough condition to be in the position to rescue others. Third, it became hard to justify the rescuing and sustaining of failed banks. The banking sector was characterized by extensive overcapacity. Like any other industry, such a situation implies the need for reduction. The operation of rescuing a bank is an expensive one that often involves taxpayers' funds; saving weak banks that really ought to have disappeared lacks economic justification.

The demise of the convoy system is evidenced by the collapses of Hokkaido Takushoku Bank (Japan's 10th largest commercial bank) in 1997, the Long-term Credit Bank of Japan in 1998, and many others. These banks failed due to bad loans made during the 1980s. After initial efforts to rescue them in the normal manner were unsuccessful, direct intervention by the government, the Bank of Japan, and the deposit insurance organization were required, in order to protect depositors. This scenario represented an enormous change to the way in which business had been done for a long time in the Japanese banking sector. In 1998, MOF was restructured. The rather sudden reappearance of bank failures and the perceived lack of proper supervision were widely perceived to be the reasons for this action.

Uniquely Japanese?
The convoy system lasted for 50 years following World War II, but this long-lived institutional setup is not unique to Japan. Cassess (1984) observed very similar preservations of financial sector systems in many other countries, including Belgium, Denmark, Finland, France, Germany, Italy, Mexico, Portugal, Spain, Sweden, Switzerland, the U.K., and the U.S. In the 1930s, banking-sector interventions happened almost simultaneously over a wide geographic area. Large banks had been hit particularly hard by the worldwide financial crisis and needed

a great deal of assistance from their central banks and governments. However, the interventions survived well beyond the crisis they were intended to solve.

There are several characteristics common to the financial systems in this diverse set of countries. First, most of the principal banking laws were adopted in the 1930s. Second, as a general rule, controlling power over the credit system was allocated to two bodies, one of which was a government institution and the other the central bank. Third, the introduction of the government institution increased the state's direct control over the banking sector. Finally, the institutions created in the 1930s remained virtually unchanged for a long time, despite the fact that some of the laws passed in the 1930s have since been changed or abrogated (Cassess, 1984).

There are, of course, differences among the national systems. This is demonstrated by comparing the banking systems in Japan and the U.S. For example, the government holds considerably more power in Japan. Until recently, MOF was responsible for functions similar to those performed by the U.S.'s Internal Revenue Service, along with some parts of the Department of Treasury, the Federal Reserve Board, and the Securities and Exchange Commission. However, despite the different degrees of control, the presence of close government control over the banking sector and its long-lived stability after World War II are nothing uniquely Japanese.

INDUSTRIAL GROUP CONSOLIDATION

The bank mergers announced since the late 1990s have brought changes in Japan's industrial structure. Six large industrial groups have dominated the post-World War II era: Mitsui, Mitsubishi, Sumitomo, DKB, Fuyo, and Sanwa. Each group has traditionally had its own main commercial bank: Sakura Bank for the Mitsui group, Tokyo Mitsubishi Bank for the Mitsubishi group, Sumitomo Bank for the Sumitomo group, DKB for the DKB group, Fuji Bank for the Fuyo group, and Sanwa Bank for the Sanwa group. The merger of DKB, Fuji Bank, and Industrial Bank of Japan to create Mizuho Bank has resulted in a close relationship between the DKB and Fuyo groups. Similarly, the merger of Sakura Bank and Sumitomo Bank has created a much closer relationship between the two very old former *zaibatsu* groups of Mitsui and Sumitomo.

Even after the bank mergers, it is hard to imagine the complete break-up of the industrial groups to which the banks belong. Newly merged banks seek to obtain scale economies through consolidation. They need to keep the business of the customers and member companies associated with the previously independent banks, and then find new customers, who may be independent or belong to other groups. While some *keiretsu* members are reducing their cross-share holdings of member firms at the individual firm level, the industrial groups do not appear to be breaking their corporate ties at the group level.

A "follow the leader" (Knickerbocker, 1973) or "herding" mentality is especially strong in the Japanese domestic market, whose large size had created stability, growth, and profitability in the past (Clark, 1979). Keeping up with rivals at the corporate and industrial group levels, in terms of size, is important in order to remain competitive. After several mega-bank merger announcements were made in 1999, some of the banks that had not been involved in recent large-scale mergers felt the need to pursue new ties with other banks, allowing them to gain scale economies and accelerate downsizing. Daiwa and Asahi Banks merged in 2002. The pressure appears to have been especially strong for Sanwa Bank, which merged with Tokai Bank in January 2002, creating UFJ. This merger may eventually benefit the Sanwa group as a whole, as it competes against much larger rival industrial groups.

Coincident with the merger activities among the large banks in Japan, many individual companies in industries as diverse as retailing, chemicals, construction, insurance, and oil have undertaken mergers. The structure of the *keiretsu* is gradually changing. However, while the old "Big Six" industrial groups may have made alterations to their group structures, it is too early to call this the demise of the Japanese industrial structure of the past 50 years. Constant change has long been the name of the game in Japan (Abegglen & Stalk, 1985).

In sum, difficult economic times force firms to adapt to a new environment and an altered future. The post-World War I depressions created a wave of M&As and industry consolidations. Survival of the fittest meant that the roots of some of the strongest post-World War II Japanese companies emerged during this time. Firms that outlasted the economic upheaval learned to be flexible in the context of a new business environment that required them to focus on innovative products and services that differed from the traditional product portfolios with which they were familiar. As a consequence, firms became stronger, more effective, and more flexible in the face of later environmental changes. Given the similarities between the situation following World War I and the current one, the *Heisei* recession may yet induce the emergence of firms that are better and stronger than before. Such results will certainly not be without struggles.

SUMMARY AND CONCLUSIONS

The industrial structure of the Japanese banking sector was seriously altered during the 1990s. Banks seem to have been changing their strategies, as the environment shifted – rather quickly – from a tightly regulated regime to a more free-market one. Downsizing and mergers were necessary adjustments, as economic realities forced banks to find better organizational forms. During the remarkably stable era following World War II, the strategy of Japanese banks was focused on growth. This focus was supported by an environment that, while heavily regulated by MOF, was always profitable.

The fundamental external changes meant that strategic adjustments were no longer optional for Japanese banks. Some failed to make the necessary changes quickly, relying too heavily on old assumptions and saddled by too many bad loans. The resulting M&A activity means that the Japanese banking industry has experienced dramatic changes in its industry structure. However, as discussed earlier, M&As and bank failures are not new to the financial sector in Japan; they simply experienced a 50-year hiatus.

The fact that many banks were slow to react to the changing environment is not surprising. When companies and managers have been accustomed to operating in a certain way for half a century, the practices, psychology, and assumptions of the organization tend to become enshrined as essentially sacred. Commercial banking has been among the most conservative industries in Japan, and few managers would dare to defile their bank's divine principles. Each firm's know-how has been imprinted on its organizational genes, which are the aggregate of its managers' strategic and operational mentalities – essentially, the bank's only way of doing business. Such firmly established organizational genes are difficult to change quickly.

Dynamic changes are the hallmark of a vibrant economy. Even one of the most protected industries could not escape the force of change in their economic environment. Based on Bower's (2001) typology, we have demonstrated how Japanese banks have used M&As to deal with their changing environments. The intentions of such a strategy have differed in different eras, depending on the prevailing economic and environmental conditions. In contrast with activities earlier in the 20th century, the recent large-scale M&As appear to be addressing the problem of severe overcapacity. The restructuring in the banking sector is a necessary process for providing financial stability in the Japanese economy.

NOTE

1. While nearly all of the mega-mergers among Japanese banks in the post-bubble economy fall primarily into Bower's Category 1, some have characteristics of Category 3. These include some mergers between banks and other financial-sector firms (e.g. trusts and insurance). In addition, Mitsubishi Bank's consolidation with the Bank of Tokyo allowed a greater expansion into new markets, building on the latter organization's strong focus on overseas operations.

ACKNOWLEDGMENTS

The order of the authors is determined by a stochastic method. We are very grateful to Shige Makino, Andreas Moerke, Tom Roehl, Adrian Tschoegl, Teri Ursacki-Bryant, three anonymous reviewers, and the participants at the *AIM* Special Issue Colloquium in June 2002, for suggestions that have improved this paper.

REFERENCES

Abegglen, J. C., & Stalk, G., Jr. (1985). *Kaisha, the Japanese corporation*. New York: Basic Books.
Alexander, A. J. (2000, September 22). Corporate restructuring in Japan: A review. *JEI Report, 36*.
Aoki, M., & Patrick, H. (Eds) (1994). *The Japanese main bank system: Its relevance for developing and transforming economies*. Oxford: Oxford University Press.
Bower, J. L. (2001). Not all M&As are alike – and that matters. *Harvard Business Review, 79*(3), 92–101.
Breton, A., & Wintrobe, R. (1978). A theory of "moral" suasion. *Canadian Journal of Economics, 11*, 210–219.
Cassess, S. (1984). The long life of the financial institutions set up in the thirties. *Journal of European Economic History, 13*, 273–294.
Chatterjee, S. (1986). Types of synergy and economic value: The impact of acquisitions on merging and rival firms. *Strategic Management Journal, 7*, 119–139.
Chatterjee, S., Lubatkin, M. H., Schweiger, D. M., & Weber, Y. (1992). Cultural differences and shareholder values in related mergers: Linking equity and human capital. *Strategic Management Journal, 13*, 319–334.
Clark, R. (1979). *The Japanese company*. New Haven, CT: Yale University Press.
Datta, D. K. (1991). Organizational fit and acquisition performance: Effects of post-acquisition integration. *Strategic Management Journal, 12*, 281–297.
Harrison, J. S., Hitt, M., Hoskisson, R. E., & Ireland, R. D. (1991). Synergies and post-acquisition performance: Differences versus similarities in resource allocations. *Journal of Management, 17*, 173–190.
Hoshi, T. (2001). The convoy system for insolvent banks: How it originally worked and why it failed in the 1990s (Working Paper). San Diego: Graduate School of International Relations and Pacific Studies, University of California, San Diego.
Hoshi, T., Kashyap, A., & Scharfstein, D. (1990). The role of banks in reducing the costs of financial distress in Japan. *Journal of Financial Economics, 27*, 67–88.
Ito, K., & Rose, E. L. (1994). The genealogical structure of Japanese firms: Parent-subsidiary relationships. *Strategic Management Journal, 15*(Summer), 35–51.
Kitching, J. (1974). Winning and losing with European acquisitions. *Harvard Business Review, 52*(2), 124–136.
Knickerbocker, F. T. (1973). *Oligopolistic reaction and multinational enterprise*. Boston: Division of Research, Graduate School of Business Administration, Harvard University.
Lubatkin, M. (1983). Mergers and the performance of the acquiring firm. *Academy of Management Review, 8*, 218–225.

Odagiri, H. (1992). *Growth through competition, competition through growth: Strategic management and the economy in Japan*. Oxford: Clarendon Press.

Pettway, R. H. (1991). Japanese mergers and direct investment in the U.S. In: W. T. Ziemba, W. Bailey & Y. Hamao (Eds), *Japanese Financial Market Research* (pp. 595–613). Amsterdam: North Holland.

Prahalad, C. K., & Hamel, G. (1990). The core competence of the corporation. *Harvard Business Review, 68*(3), 79–91.

Ravenscraft, D. J., & Scherer, F. M. (1989). The profitability of mergers. *International Journal of Industrial Organization, 7*, 101–116.

Rosenbluth, F. M. (1989). *Financial politics in contemporary Japan*. Ithaca, NY: Cornell University Press.

Seth, A. (1990). Value creation in acquisitions: A re-examination of performance issues. *Strategic Management Journal, 11*, 99–115.

Shinomiya, T. (1974). Fukyo tono tatakai [Fighting against recession]. In: K. Nakagawa, H. Morikawa & T. Yui (Eds), *Kindai Nihon Keieishi no Kisochishiki* (pp. 218–219). Tokyo: Yuhikaku.

Shrivastava, P. (1986). Postmerger integration. *Journal of Business Strategy, 7*, 65–76.

Smircich, L. (1983). Concepts of culture in organizational analysis. *Administrative Science Quarterly, 28*, 339–358.

Spindle, B. (1998). Merger boomlet takes hold in Japan. *Wall Street Journal*, April 13, A18.

Sugiyama, K. (1974). Ginko godo [Banks' M&As]. In: K. Nakagawa, H. Morikawa & T. Yui (Eds), *Kindai Nihon Keieishi no Kisochishiki* (pp. 229–230). Tokyo: Yuhikaku.

Statistics Bureau, Ministry of Public Management, Home Affairs, Posts and Telecommunications (Ed.) (2003). *Japan statistical yearbook*. Tokyo: Japan Statistical Association.

Tokyo Bankers Association (1998). *Hompo ginko hensen-shi* [The transition of Japanese banks]. Tokyo: Tokyo Bankers Association.

Weinstein, D., & Yafeh, Y. (1998). On the costs of a bank-centered financial system: Evidence from the changing main bank relations in Japan. *The Journal of Finance, 53*, 635–672.

Yakura, S., & Ikushima, Y. (1981). *Genealogical chart of Japanese major corporations*. Tokyo: Yuhikaku Press.

DYAD AND NETWORK: MODELS OF MANUFACTURER-SUPPLIER COLLABORATION IN THE JAPANESE TV MANUFACTURING INDUSTRY

Didier Guillot and James R. Lincoln

ABSTRACT

The analysis of manufacturer-supplier relationships in Japan has contributed significantly to the advancement of interorganizational theory. It has yielded broad evidence that long-term collaborative partnerships enable firms to exploit the incentive benefits of market-based exchange while reaping the learning and coordination benefits of internalization within a corporate hierarchy. In this paper, we go beyond the issues of trust and cooperation that have occupied much prior theory and research on supplier relations in considering another dimension along which collaborative agreements may be arrayed. We build on transaction and network theories, respectively, to propose two types of long-term collaborative ties: dyadic or bilateral governance and network embeddedness. A comparative analysis of collaborative relationships in product and process development between two Japanese TV manufacturing companies and their suppliers provides empirical evidence for the distinctive effect of network ties over dyadic relationships for collaborative knowledge-sharing.

Japanese Firms in Transition: Responding to the Globalization Challenge
Advances in International Management, Volume 17, 159–185
Copyright © 2005 Elsevier Ltd.
All rights of reproduction in any form reserved
ISSN: 0747-7929/doi:10.1016/S0747-7929(04)17007-8

INTRODUCTION[1]

Long-term interfirm partnerships are a conspicuous feature of the contemporary business landscape within and across industries in developed economies. This growing global reliance on patterns of cooperation that depart significantly both from arm's length market exchange and merger/acquisition has sparked much scholarly interest. Studies in macro-organizational theory (e.g. Powell, 1990), economic sociology (e.g. Granovetter, 1985; Podolny & Page, 1998), political science (e.g. Piore & Sabel, 1984), or economics (e.g. Williamson, 1985, 1996) document the positive effects of stable collaborations on such organizational processes and outcomes as organizational learning (Saxenian, 1994), diffusion of technology (Dyer & Nobeoka, 2000), risk sharing (Womack, Jones & Roos, 1990), or relation-specific investments (Asanuma, 1993; Williamson, 1996). This research shows how partnerships enable companies to acquire status (Stuart, Hoang & Hybels, 1999), to exploit the incentive benefits of market-based exchange while reaping the learning and coordination benefits of internalization within a corporate hierarchy (Lincoln & Ahmadjian, 1997), and thus to increase economic performance (Baum, Calabrese & Silverman, 2000).

While there is wide agreement that stable partnerships serve as viable governance structures with numerous benefits for corporate behavior and performance, there is little consensus on the precise nature and significance of relational forms of organization. Theorists in the transaction-cost economics tradition view them as hybrids, intermediate between the polarities of market and (administrative) hierarchy (Williamson, 1985, 1996). They are sustained by credible commitments and expectations of repeated exchange, as opposed to the force of competition, on the one hand, or internal auditing and order-giving on the other. In a similar vein, resource-dependence theorists discuss "bridging" strategies whereby firms in bilateral exchange relationships manage such dependencies through quasi-administrative devices such as director interlocks, joint ventures, and the like (Pfeffer & Salancik, 1978).

Yet other theorists see network organization as irreducible to a transaction-cost logic (Powell, 1990). Inherent in such forms, they argue, is reliance on trust and obligation – not legalistic or bureaucratic safeguards – to deter parties from exploiting windows of opportunities for short-term one-sided gains over the collaboration's course (Podolny & Page, 1998; Uzzi, 1996). Beginning, perhaps, with Dore's (1986) claim that norms of "good will" and reciprocal obligation abet opportunism in Japanese market transactions, a considerable stream of work shows how trust and reciprocity infuse commercial exchanges with superior information transfer and mutual learning properties than is typical of Western markets (Gerlach, 1992; Lincoln, 1990).

While much writing sees trust and obligation reducing transaction costs while averting the various perils associated with arm's length contracting and bureaucratic rigidity, less discussion has centered on the appropriate unit or level of analysis in the study of relational forms. From the perspectives of such prominent interorganizational theories as transaction-cost economics, agency theory, and resource dependence, it is the transacting *dyad* – the parties to a bilateral exchange. Williamson (1994, p. 85) is explicit on this: "Transaction cost economics is preoccupied with dyadic relations, so that network relations are given short shrift." Others, however, argue persuasively that analysis should be pitched at the *network* level and that dyadic exchange cannot be understood without taking into account its network "embeddedness," to use Granovetter's influential term. From the embedded network perspective, third party and other indirect ties shape the interaction between a pair of firms, such that attention confined to the pair is apt to blind the observer to processes operative at triad, clique, and network levels (Burt, 1992). The point is made in Uzzi's (1996) discussion of the role of indirect ties in the purchase-supply transactions in the New York garment industry:

In the firms I studied, third-party referral networks were often cited as sources of embeddedness. Such networks operate by fusion: one actor with an embedded tie to each of two unconnected actors acts as their go-between by using her common link to establish trustworthiness between them. The go-between performs two functions: he or she: (1) transfers expectations of behavior from the existing embedded relationship to the newly matched firms; and (2) "calls on" the reciprocity "owed" him or her by one exchange partner and transfers it to the other.

From Uzzi's perspective, then, the third- (and fourth, fifth, . . ., *N*th) party ties implied by network-embedded exchange render it superior to strictly dyadic exchange in limiting opportunism, as they create a cross-cutting web of trust and obligation, spreading information, sharing risks, and allocating resources. The embedding of pairwise transactions in a network promotes synergies across firm boundaries. As Uzzi (1996, p. 677) puts it: "thicker information on strategy, production know-how, and profit margins is transferred through embedded ties, thus promoting learning and integrated production in ways that the exchange of only price data cannot." Powell, Koput and Smithdoerr (1996) further frame the issue (p. 119):

Interorganizational collaborations are not simply a means to compensate for the lack of internal skills, . . . nor should they be viewed as a series of discrete transactions. . . . Firms deepen their ability to collaborate not just by managing relations dyadically, but by instantiating and refining routines for synergistic partnering. . . . Richard DiMarchi, Vice President for Endocrine Research at Eli Lilly and Company, emphasizes that the biggest mistake his company could make in managing research alliances is to treat them as "one-offs" – independent relationships pursued separately. Firms must learn how to transfer knowledge across alliances and locate themselves in those network positions that enable them to keep pace with the most promising scientific or technological developments.

Thus, where interorganizational learning and innovation is the goal, an embedded network strategy, such that a firm actively manages not only its direct dyadic ties with a given set of alters, but the connections among the alters as well, best taps the collective expertise of the network and synergistically enhances it in ways that benefit the whole.

In this chapter, we consider two models of governance – dyad, and network – in a study of manufacturer-supplier relations in the Japanese consumer electronics/electrical machinery industry. Specifically, we examine the sourcing strategies of two prominent companies – Matsushita Electric Industrial Co. and Sanyo Electric Co. Of the two, Matsushita's approach to supply-chain management is the development of its supplier pool as a *network*, so that shared and synergistic learning can take place, while Sanyo's strategy is essentially to manage its exchange relations with suppliers independently and sequentially, and to encourage competition among them. We will see that, associated with this difference in the level at which supply transactions are managed is a difference in the degree to which suppliers are delegated responsibility for product and process design, enabling them to co-develop and thereby learn in partnership with the parent manufacturer. These differences are roughly consistent with and extend the thesis of transaction-cost theory as to how variation in governance mode and organization form is pegged to relation-specific investment.

The chapter is organized as follows. We first review some theoretical arguments for dyadic and network modes of organizing exchange and for the differential impact of such modes on technological partnering between firms. We then provide some background on Matsushita Electric and Sanyo Electric as contrasting cases of supply-chain organization, focusing, in particular, on Matsushita's *kyoei-kai* or supplier cooperative association. There is no comparable association at Sanyo. Next, based on interviews we conducted in both firms, we examine how the nature of the part and the structuring of the supply transaction shape the role suppliers play in product and process development. Theoretical and practical implications of the results are then discussed.

THEORIES OF BILATERAL EXCHANGE

The distinction between dyadic and network forms is an important elaboration of extant theory on the management of purchase-supply relations. To date, most work is pitched at the dyad level: the customer-supplier pair. Such dyadically based exchange is presumed to take three organizational forms: arm's length market contracting, hierarchical internalization (e.g. vertical integration), and "relational contracting," i.e. high-trust, long-term, obligational exchange. Students of supply-chain structure in the automobile industry have devoted much attention to the propensity of Japanese firms, in contrast to American carmakers, to develop close, diffuse, and stable relations with their suppliers (Clark, 1991; Nishiguchi, 1996; Smitka, 1991; Womack et al., 1990). The same difference has been documented in the electronics industries (Sako, 1992). This is a logical extension of interorganizational theory, given that diffuse and trusting relations in the organization of exchange pose a challenge to the classic antinomy of market and hierarchy (Williamson, 1975, 1985).

With few exceptions (e.g. Powell et al., 1996; Uzzi, 1996), theorizing on the virtues of high-trust relational contracting has yet to tackle directly the question of what difference it makes if exchange relations with these qualities are dyadic, discrete, and sequential versus networked, simultaneous, and synergistic. Most studies that look beyond dyadic interactions to how the network of collaborative ties conditions its member firms' performance focus chiefly on strategic alliances between competitors (e.g. in R&D), neglecting ties formed across supply-chain stages (Dyer & Nobeoka, 2000 for an exception).

Dyad and network represent alternative frames of reference and levels of analysis for the assessment of cooperative interfirm relations. Transaction-cost and resource-dependence theory, as noted, view the transacting pair in isolation, divorced from the broader network in which it is situated or embedded. In such models, the parties strive to manage and stabilize their exchange, by (in the first case) forging credible commitments and (in the second case) installing bridging and co-opting devices (Baker, 1998; Lincoln, Gerlach & Takahashi, 1992). In practice, these comprise the same bundle of practices: equity stakes, board interlocks, reciprocal trade agreements, etc. Such cementing ties motivate the parties to invest in the relationship, thus creating and conserving assets whose value is largely confined to the immediate pair (Asanuma, 1989, 1993).

Bilateral governance strategies of this sort have both advantages and disadvantages. On the upside, they attenuate incentives for opportunism and foster hard-to-emulate capabilities. On the downside, by approaching partnerships in pairwise fashion as discrete and independent, such strategies give up economies of embeddedness, e.g. gains from synergistic learning and network-wide cooperation. The greater the connectivity and multiplexity of the network, the richer is the information flow, the faster is the learning, and the stronger are the normative safeguards against opportunism (Coleman, 1966). For instance, a firm may realize a one-time gain from cheating on a business partner, but if that partnership is deeply embedded in a network, the adverse reputational effects and loss of access to resource channels can be costly indeed.

Because the relational safeguards afforded by networks provide more protection against opportunism than pairwise commitments can provide, embedded partnerships allow for greater relation-specific investment. Applied to supply-chain organization – our present concern – network embeddedness motivates suppliers to invest in innovation and customization of products and services to the unique requirements of customers, and, conversely, motivates customers to share risks with suppliers and entrust high-level design and development responsibilities to them.

The merits of network governance for crisis management are clear as well. A compelling case of a supply network mobilizing to share risk and manage crisis was the Toyota supply network's response, chronicled separately by the *Wall Street Journal* (1997) and Nishiguchi and Beaudet (1998), to a catastrophic fire at an Aisin Seiki factory in 1997. The fire halted production of a key brake component used in number of Toyota models, thus bringing much of Toyota's assembly operation in Japan to an abrupt standstill. Yet, because of the fast response and tight coordination of the supply network as a whole, p-valve production was restored in a matter of days. Because Aisin was Toyota's sole source of the p-valve, suppliers of other parts had to convert their operations, a process requiring the collective mobilization of the network in sharing knowledge and transferring skills. Reitman (1997), the *Journal* reporter, comments that:

> The secret lay in Toyota's close-knit family of parts suppliers. In the corporate equivalent of an Amish barn-raising, suppliers and local companies rushed to the rescue. Within hours, they had begun taking blueprints for the valve, improvising tooling systems and setting up makeshift production lines.

A quote from a manager of one affiliated company, Toyoda Machine Works, also testifies to the network embeddedness of Toyota's supplier relations. "Toyota's quick recovery," he said, "is attributable to the power of the group, which handled it without thinking about money or business contracts" (Reitman, 1997).

The remainder of the paper is a study of dyadic and network strategies of managing purchase-supply transactions in the Japanese television manufacturing industry. Our core hypothesis is that supply transactions governed by network, rather than dyadic, forms motivate and facilitate knowledge-sharing, mutual learning, and relationship-specific investment.

THE CASE STUDIES: MATSUSHITA AND SANYO COMPARED

The Industry

The Japanese TV manufacturing industry is an interesting setting for a study of the organization of supply networks. First, while Japanese electronics has been the venue for some significant supply-chain research (e.g. Fruin, 1997; Hiramoto, 1994; Lincoln, Ahmadjian & Mason, 1998; Roehl, 1989; Sako, 1992), it is on the whole less studied than is the automobile industry and less well understood (see, e.g. Nishiguchi, 1996; Smitka, 1992; Womack et al., 1990). Second, the TV industry utilizes a large number of parts and subassemblies, which vary in complexity and value, and thus in how they constrain collaboration and exchange.

Japanese firms' incentives to pursue collaborations with positive sum benefits in terms of joint innovation, risk-sharing, and knowledge-sharing – versus gains to the core firm at the supplier's expense (e.g. lower labor cost) – are weaker in electronics than in autos (Asanuma, 1989). Japan's large electrical machinery and electronics makers are more integrated vertically and horizontally than the carmakers: Each embraces an array of product divisions, from relatively low-tech "white goods" (rice cookers, irons, washing machines) to high-tech computer and consumer electronic products (Beer & Spector, 1981; Shimotani, 1989). By comparison, the pattern in the Japanese auto industry is one of core firms, themselves fairly specialized in product line, diversifying through consignment ("*itaku*") pacts with *keiretsu* partners (Shioji, 1995). Hino, for example, is the Toyota Group truck producer, and Daihatsu is the specialist in minicars.

Moreover, while the auto firms are known to outsource high-value electronic and electrical parts, and even drive train components such as transmissions, the electronic/electrical machinery producers procure these internally, going outside for relatively low-value components such as plating, packaging, and the like.

Thus, the boundaries of the Japanese electronics firm are wider – encompass more diverse transactions – than is generally true of the automakers, which, by the nature of their business, are thrust into highly co-dependent vertical and horizontal ties. These higher-valued and more relation- and product-specific transactions ensure that supply transactions in the auto industry are organized less in arm's length fashion, more in terms of organization and network. Asanuma (1989, p. 6) concurs:

> [Auto firms develop and produce a single] . . . product which is in a relatively mature stage with respect to technology. By contrast, a typical original equipment manufacturer in the electric machinery industry produces many final products that are extremely diverse both with respect to the typical scale of production, . . . and regarding the degree of technological maturity.

Each electrical machinery plant thus specializes in one or more product lines, which share features with other plants in terms of core technology but differ in production scale and technological maturity. This heterogeneity of production operation and organization configures the network of vendors and subcontractors from which core manufacturers source parts and materials. The operating divisions of the core firm are fairly autonomous, retaining much of the responsibility for purchasing and procurement decisions.

We chose to focus on the television manufacturing operations of Matsushita and Sanyo. The two firms have similar product mixes – medium and large screen color television sets – and a similar representation of consumer electronic products in their overall product portfolios (roughly 65%) Both are headquartered in the Osaka metropolitan area of the Kansai region and thus access the same localized pool of suppliers and subcontractors. They have also been relatively similar in terms of position in the domestic consumer market for televisions, Matsushita leading in 1996 with 17% of total domestic sales, and Sanyo ranking fifth with an 11% share.

In April 1997, Matsushita implemented a form of organization, pioneered by Sony, that was then diffusing rapidly among large Japanese firms (Shimotani, 1997): the "in-house company system" (*sha-nai bunsha seido*). Most of Matsushita's existing divisions were grouped into the following four "internal companies." Audio-video, electrification-housing, air conditioning, and electric motors. The TV division of Matsushita is one of 13 divisions within the Audio Video Company (AVC) internal company. Sanyo did not formally adopt the in-house company form, but its 10 business headquarters played a similar role. However, the number of divisions under each such headquarters is smaller at Sanyo than at Matsushita. At Sanyo, the TV division had just one production plant in Japan, located in Daito, a suburb of Osaka. The division also had 16 TV production plants located abroad.

For the purposes of this study, a "supplier" is a firm providing parts, materials, or services to the television-manufacturing divisions of Matsushita or Sanyo located in Japan. As we explain below, suppliers can be independent companies, members of a customer-specific supplier association, or affiliated ("*keiretsu*") companies in which the customer has an equity stake and a degree of management control.

Methodology

Our interviews with Matsushita and Sanyo span a period of 8 years. The first interviews were in July of 1994 with members of the Corporate Purchasing Department in Osaka. Additional interviews were conducted in the summer of 1996. A questionnaire was then sent to managers of both firms' purchasing centers. Final sets of interviews with purchasing general managers at both Matsushita and Sanyo were conducted in the summer and fall of 1997 to monitor changes and clarify issues raised in the questionnaire and in the earlier interviews. Finally, we have consulted extensively with Professor Masahiro Shimotani of Kyoto University, an expert on Matsushita and its affiliated companies. Over the course of our research, Prof. Shimotani's assistance and advice have been invaluable.

The Matsushita Kyoei-Kai as a Case of Network Governance

Matsushita buys parts and materials from some 10,000 suppliers, accounting for roughly half of Matsushita's total sales. Most produce relatively low-value parts and services (packaging, molding, painting, plating). Few, if any, enjoy expertise and technology rivaling Matsushita's own, although that has changed as Matsushita's program of upgrading its elite (*kyoei-kai*) suppliers' capabilities has proceeded. Forty percent of these are proprietary suppliers from whom Matsushita obtains off-the-shelf, highly standardized products.

The remainder is a supplier-subcontractor, whose production is to some degree tailored to Matsushita's needs. Of the latter, 270 formed the Matsushita *kyoei-kai*, "mutual prosperity association" (Shimotani, 1997, 2002). The *kyoei-kai* is an elite group of suppliers, chosen for the quality and reliability of their products. They account for 33% of Matsushita's externally procured parts and materials. The *kyoei* membership, however, has declined over time. In 1984, there were 348 members from which Matsushita purchased close to 50% of its outsourced materials. Of the TV group's 24 *kyoei-kai* companies, two supply Matsushita plants with electric parts, 14 with structure parts, and 8 provide manual insertion and subassembly.[2] To become a *kyoei* member, a firm must: (1) have more than 100 employees; (2) maintain a trading relationship with Matsushita for more than 3 years; and (3) do more than 20 million yen per month of business with Matsushita. These criteria were set by the Matsushita Corporate Purchasing Department (Shizai Center), which oversees the *kyoei-kai*.

While most procurement decisions are decentralized to the operating division level, Corporate Purchasing is responsible for developing and implementing corporate policy toward the *kyoei-kai* and its member firms. In 1993, it began a "Revitalization Plan" aimed at developing the *kyoei-kai* as an efficient learning network of elite Matsushita suppliers. Corporate Purchasing sought to better measure and monitor the performance of the *kyoei* suppliers and assist them in: (1) raising their quality; (2) lowering costs by "rationalizing" (*gorika*) production; (3) improving delivery; and (4) increasing their involvement in design and development. The program features an elaborate system of grading suppliers on these performance dimensions along with numerous procedures for communicating Matsushita's expectations and enabling suppliers to meet them.

Matsushita Corporate Purchasing manages transactions between the Matsushita product divisions and their suppliers by helping the division maintain clear and detailed cost, quality, and technology standards, thus spelling out the objectives that the *kyoei* companies must achieve. *Kyoei* firms are encouraged to participate in the process and offer countermeasures. The ultimate objective is to move both division and suppliers down parallel learning curves in the achievement of lower cost and higher quality, reliability, and sophistication.

The *kyoei* motto is "trust and prosperity," and references to trust in supplier relations were frequent in our interviews with Matsushita. One upgrade in trust actively sought by Matsushita directly reduced its supplier-monitoring costs. A supplier making it through Matsushita's quality evaluation and ranking process was awarded Matsushita's Quality Independence Guarantee (QIG). Incoming parts and materials from QIG-certified supplier were presumed not to require inspection. Small *kyoei* suppliers required considerable assistance from Matsushita to meet the QIG standard. In 1995, Matsushita introduced a new evaluation system for its *kyoei* subcontractors based on four criteria: quality, suggestions, deliveries, and cost. Matsushita rates every supplier on a 4-point (A to D) scale. To remain in the association, a supplier must be graded "A" on each criterion. The evaluation led Matsushita to drop 31 subcontractors from the *kyoei-kai* and admit 8 new ones. The 24 members of the TV subgroup all passed the QIG screening.

The purpose of the *kyoei-kai* was to ensure the survival both of Matsushita and its best domestic suppliers. The association was founded in a time of growing competition in the consumer electronics market (Shimotani, 1997). Because Matsushita is an integrated and divisionalized company manufacturing many of its high-end parts, much of its outsourcing has been relatively low-value, low-tech items. The *kyoei-kai* was part of an Matsushita strategy to shift more product and process design responsibility for high-value components to Matsushita's elite domestic suppliers. Pressure to reduce costs and globalize operations had led Matsushita to diversify its supply base, encouraging low-end domestic suppliers to find new customers. Only suppliers in possession of specialized higher-tech skills would be retained. In the stringent economic environment of Japan in the 1990s, many manufacturers adopted this position with their domestic suppliers: Unless the suppliers acquired competencies not available at lower cost offshore, they would lose the business. Thus, Matsushita's challenge was to transform its domestic supplier base from producers of low-tech low-value materials to builders of complex components whose technology matched or surpassed Matsushita's own.

We asked our informants whether Matsushita produced in-house the same parts and materials it sourced from the *kyoei* association. They said that they did or at least were capable of doing so. Many Matsushita products are complex and require large capital investments for their manufacture. The *kyoei* companies are generally small and lack the plant, equipment, and skills necessary to produce complex, high-value components. However, under pressure from, and with the assistance of, Matsushita, *kyoei* firms had been increasing their investments in such capabilities.

Although the *kyoei-kai* routinely pressures Matsushita to increase its purchases from them, Matsushita's stance is that it cannot do so if equal value and quality exist at lower cost abroad. The long-term solution for both sides, Matsushita managers said, was to develop the capabilities of its best domestic suppliers through the *kyoei* structure and process so that they have a competitive advantage over the offshore suppliers, if not in cost, then in quality, technology, and customization.

Unlike Matsushita's old practice of minimizing supplier initiative and control by having them produce to detailed Matsushita-supplied blueprints, the company now expects *kyoei* suppliers to participate in early-stage design decisions. It is the product division's responsibility, with the support of Corporate Purchasing, to solicit clear and specific input from *kyoei* firms. For example, a division will begin with a set of drawings or paper or wood model and invite suggestions from suppliers as to product form and function. According to Matsushita, the *kyoei-kai* suppliers as a whole gain a competitive advantage from the early information they receive on Matsushita's product development plans and procurement needs.

The TV division delineates the tasks of the supplier in three areas: design and development responsibility understanding the target, and grasping the division's long-term product trajectory. If the division effectively communicates its expectations in these areas – through publication of specs, formal training, *shukko* (personnel) transfers, and the like, the suppliers can acquire a clear vision of what is required and can orient their products and processes accordingly. Since many of these organizational learning processes are similar across *kyoei* suppliers, there are benefits to them and to Matsushita from pooling and sharing know-how and experience.

As Matsushita's efforts to assist and motivate the *kyoei-kai* in acquiring special competencies bore fruit, it began reversing the teacher-student roles. A special headquarters team was charged with enabling Matsushita to absorb new technology from the most advanced suppliers. A small number of *kyoei* suppliers were developing technology that Matsushita itself did not have. One was a very precise method of gold plating that Matsushita said would take it five years to develop. Another was a novel method of plastic injection molding. A third was a technique of punching tiny sound holes directly into the TV cabinet plastic, thus eliminating the need for speaker holes and netting.

Matsushita will share *kyoei* suppliers' risks, assisting firms in difficulty when the problem is bad luck or bad management, and the core assets and capabilities of the firm remain strong. Corporate Purchasing managers told us that, if a drop in business with one Matsushita division threatened the survival of a *kyoei* member, they would help it find new business with another division. Moreover, Matsushita's policy of going abroad if a better price for the same quality could be had is softened, in practice, by the assistance it gives *kyoei* suppliers in moving their own production facilities overseas (often in the vicinity of Matsushita plants). Two *kyoei* suppliers we interviewed in Osaka told us that Matsushita had supported their forays into Asia in significant, if indirect, ways. Consequently, one of these suppliers said, its business, unlike that of many small and medium-sized Kansai firms dependent on large manufacturers, had expanded during the lean 1990s.

Matsushita, of course, benefits by absorbing some of its suppliers' risks. A manager of a *kyoei* member told us: "We know that Matsushita will do its best to help us if a problem – falling demand, for example – occurs. We are therefore confident and do not hesitate to make specific investments when possible."

So, Matsushita's *kyoei* program of upgrading the production capabilities and knowledge assets of its top suppliers has engendered closer ties and greater cooperation with fewer partners than was true in the past. Unlike the relative arm's length posture toward suppliers for which Matsushita had been known, the company is committed to helping suppliers adapt to the new procurement environment, thus strengthening the *kyoei* members as individual businesses and the *kyoei* organization as a whole.

The *kyoei-kai*, we suggest, is an example of network governance of purchase-supply transactions in the Japanese electronic industry. It has upgraded Matsushita suppliers' capabilities, as individuals and as a group, through training, quality rating, and information sharing. By organizing its best suppliers in a formal association governed by strict rules of entry and participation, Matsushita has moved beyond dyadic or bilateral ties.

We stress that the *kyoei-kai* is not merely a vehicle for superior management of Matsushita's dyadic relations with its best suppliers, but also one for managing the ties among the suppliers themselves, as testified in an interview we conducted with Osaka-based Chiyoda Container. Chiyoda has been a major Matsushita supplier for 40 years – Matsushita was its largest customer – and a *kyoei* member. It had a close working relationship with Matsushita and took care to protect Matsushita in its dealings with other customers, for example, by assigning different employees to Matsushita and the competitor in order to foreclose information spillovers. Indeed, managers at the Chiyoda factory we visited said that, out of loyalty to Matsushita, it did no business with Sanyo, although Chiyoda factories elsewhere did sell to Sanyo. Moreover, a product or technology that Chiyoda codesigned with Matsushita would not be offered to other customers as long as the patent was in force. Matsushita gave Chiyoda wide discretion in product and process design. The supplier, in turn, gave Matsushita suggestions on TV design that would increase packaging efficiency. Finally, Chioyda's business had gained directly from the horizontal ties that its *kyoei* membership had fostered. The trust and communication that existed in the *kyoei-kai* created opportunities for firms to do business and otherwise partner with one another.

In its work with the *kyoei-kai*, Matsushita has walked a fine line. On the one hand, it sought to reap the benefits of relationship-specific investment and network synergy by reducing costs and raising the speed and quality of its product and process development. However, given its policy on offshore production and procurement, Matsushita is concerned with avoiding excessive dependence on the *kyoei* suppliers and they upon it. Matsushita managers claimed that the *kyoei* program was in fact reducing supplier dependence rather than increasing it, for a demonstrated ability to meet Matsushita's lofty procurement standards would benefit the *kyoei* suppliers' reputations and thus their attractiveness to other customers. Yet, Matsushita was hardly blind to the risks of design collaboration and other forms of knowledge-sharing with suppliers who were at the same time serving competitors. As in Chiyoda's case, suppliers playing the most strategic roles in Matsushita product and process design (e.g. the plastic injection example) were prohibited from offering other firms the same technology during the first year of use by Matsushita or, in the case of a patented technology, until the patent expired.

Thus, Matsushita's drive to upgrade the knowledge and skill of its suppliers rests not only on more productive one-on-one procurement relationships but also on the cultivation of a tighter-knit, better-managed network wherein collective learning occurs through a web of horizontal ties. The *kyoei* strategy is the realization of a commitment to long-term, mutual and synergistic learning, and so enables suppliers to adopt new technologies and business methods, while exploring new markets for products as Matsushita divisions' domestic sourcing declines. Among suppliers, the *kyoei-kai* bolsters loyalty to Matsushita, opportunity and incentive to learn from one another, and willingness to invest in relation-specific assets, all the while enhancing competitive capability and reputation.

The Sanyo Electric Case

At Sanyo, suppliers are ordinarily not involved in product and process development until the latter stages. The Sanyo product development process, not atypical among Japanese technology firms, begins with one function (the R&D Division or the Design and Development division) taking the lead. A working group is then formed early on that draws in people from a cross-section of the organization (other product divisions such as semiconductors, audio-functional groups such as manufacturing, marketing and accounting, QC, and purchasing). Suppliers are not invited to join, but the purchasing managers know the suppliers and represent their interests and concerns to the group.

The involvement of suppliers in the Sanyo product development process is low. Sanyo develops the product, presents the specs to suppliers, some negotiation takes place, and the price is set. Sanyo people told us this generally was the norm in Japanese electronics. Matsushita, they said, was similar, but at the time of our interview, this was a reference to Matsushita's past practice, not its later strategy of promoting knowledge-sharing and mutual learning with an elite supplier pool developed and organized through the *kyoei-kai*. Sanyo engineers did say that stronger partnerships with suppliers in new product/process development was desirable, because it would permit them to focus on core products and technologies while delegating to suppliers the responsibility for parts and subassemblies. (Matsushita people voiced similar hopes for what the *kyoei* program would achieve.) Sanyo managers cited the fast product development and frequent remodeling cycles typical of electronics as the principal barrier to close collaboration with suppliers. The introduction of minor model changes every six months, and a full remodeling of the product range every year, they said, demanded that Sanyo engineers design the products and parts. Matsushita, of course, is under the same time constraints.[3] Echoing Sanyo's concerns, one Matsushita informant confided that some managers were frustrated with, and unsupportive of, the *kyoei* program. Given rising competitive pressures to shorten product development times, they felt that Matsushita could design and build products faster if it abandoned the effort to work with the *kyoei-kai* and, as in the past, made the parts itself.

While Sanyo has no formal supplier association similar to Matsushita's *kyoei-kai*, it nonetheless has long-term procurement relations with an elite set of suppliers. According to the director of purchasing for the TV division, Sanyo uses a total of 211 regular suppliers, of which 50 trade regularly with the TV division. Of these 50 firms, 30 are considered by Sanyo to be primary suppliers. In 1997, these suppliers represented 83.3% of total parts procurement for the Sanyo TV division. Some of these firms, such as Sanyo Denshi Buhin, are affiliated companies, but most are independents. At 30, Sanyo's elite supplier pool is quite comparable to Matsushita own elite pool (26 *kyoei* suppliers and 2 affiliated companies).

Yet a critical difference between Sanyo and Matsushita in their purchasing management is that Sanyo seeks to maximize competition among suppliers at each remodeling cycle, giving no preference to those who already have a piece of the business. Such competition is possible, because most of Sanyo's suppliers are parts manufacturers (*buhin meka*) rather than "set" manufacturers (*setto meka*).[4] Matsushita appeared less concerned with stimulating competition among its top suppliers than in working with them through the *kyoei* process to develop their abilities and stimulate cooperation. The Matsushita QIG system, for example, was not a rank-ordering of suppliers aimed at sparking competition but rather the criterion for selecting them into the *kyoei-kai*. A supplier who failed to make the grade was out.

Thus, the main sense in which Sanyo manages the relationships among its suppliers is the competition that it fosters among them. Such competition has well-known advantages in motivating suppliers to lower costs and raise quality and reliability in order to get and keep a manufacturer's business. But if the goal is the kind of knowledge-sharing, joint learning, and general cooperation that Matsushita seeks from in its *kyoei-kai*, the downsides to supplier competition are clear as well.

LEVELS OF COOPERATION AND MODES OF GOVERNANCE

In this section, we use a more systematic methodology to demonstrate: (1) that Matsushita shares more initiative and responsibility with suppliers in developing products and processes than does Sanyo; and (2) that Matsushita is most likely to share responsibility with suppliers when the latter are organized in embedded network fashion via either the *kyoei-kai* or *keiretsu*-type equity ties. For Matsushita, unlike Japan's principal automakers, organization by cooperative association and by *keiretsu* are alternative, not overlapping and reinforcing governance forms. We use Asanuma's (1989) methodology for gauging supplier initiative and responsibility-sharing with a manufacturer. A similar methodology has been applied to manufacturer-supplier relations in the Japanese automobile and electronics industries (Asanuma, 1989).

As noted, while Matsushita's daily decisions on parts procurement are made at the division level, the Shizai Center (Corporate Purchasing) has responsibility for managing Matsushita's supplier association (*kyoei-kai*) and for developing and implementing company-wide policy toward *kyoei* firms. SEI has no such purchasing center at the headquarters level; the TV division has sole charge of its suppliers.

The suppliers recorded in Table 1 are Matsushita and Sanyo's "strategic suppliers," according to the managers we interviewed. They account for approximately 80% of the two manufacturers' total purchasing/procurement costs. Our informants classified suppliers by: (1) type of product transacted; (2) type of governance structure; and (3) degree of cooperation and initiative in product and process design. We were able to cross-check the governance structure classification with archival data from published sources (Toyo Keizai, various years), providing information on equity relationships, membership in known *keiretsu* groups; and

Table 1. Classification of Parts and Suppliers According to the Degree of Initiative in Design of the Product and the Process and by Type of Governance Structure.[a]

	Parts Manufactured According to Drawings Provided by the Core Firm (DS)			Parts Manufactured According to Specifications Provided by the Core Firm ("Ordered Goods")	Parts Manufactured According to Drawings Provided by Suppliers (DA)		Parts Offered by Catalog ("Marketed Goods")
	I — The core firm provides minute instructions for the manufacturing process	II — Supplier designs the manufacturing process based on blueprints of products provided by the core firm	III — The core firm provides only rough drawings and their completion is entrusted to the supplier	IV — Core firm provides specifications and has deep knowledge of the manufacturing process	V — Intermediate region between IV and VI	VI — Although the core firms issues only limited specifications, it has limited knowledge concerning the process	VII — The core firm selects from a catalog offered by the supplier
PCBs	I (Matsushita = 4, Sanyo = 2)		A (Matsushita = 1)	A (Matsushita = 1)			
Electromechanical							
Resistances							A (Matsushita = 4), K (Matsushita = 2), I (Matsushita = 1, Sanyo = 3)
Switches							A (Matsushita = 4), K (Matsushita = 2), I (Matsushita = 1, Sanyo = 2)
Electronic parts							
Semiconductors						A (Matsushita = 1)	A (Sanyo = 2), I (Matsushita = 34, Sanyo = 36)
CR tubes						A (Matsushita = 1)	I (Matsushita = 3, Sanyo = 4)
Structure parts							
Cabinet		I (Sanyo = 2)	K (Matsushita = 3)				
Plastic parts		I (Matsushita = 5, Sanyo = 2)	K (Matsushita = 3)				
Subassembly	K (Matsushita = 8), I (Matsushita = 1, Sanyo = 1)						
Mold	I (Matsushita = 1, Sanyo = 1)	I (Matsushita = 1, Sanyo = 1)	K (Matsushita = 3)				

Sources: Interviews.

[a] A: Affiliated company; K: *kyoryoku* supplier; I: Independent supplier.

supplier association membership. Moreover, since interviews were done with different managers of the same company on different days, one informant's report could be compared with others. The responses were highly consistent.

Table 1 classifies Matsushita and Sanyo suppliers by the Asanuma scale. Each cell entry labeled "Matsushita" or "Sanyo" refers to one supplier. The scale distinguishes seven levels. At one extreme are Level I relations – the supplier's involvement in product/process development is minimal, and the core firm provides detailed and comprehensive instructions. At the other extreme are Level VII transactions – "marketed goods" – that involve no tailoring to customer needs and thus no investment in relationship-specific assets. At Level II, the customer wholly controls the process, and the supplier merely executes the customer's designs. At Level VI, the customer issues specifications, but the supply transaction is of the "black box" sort – the supplier's knowledge exceeds the manufacturer's knowledge, and the supplier controls both the product development and the manufacturing process. Few of either manufacturer's supplier relations are of this type. In the automobile industry, by contrast, many more parts such as seats, brakes, or injection systems are of this type (Ahmadjian & Lincoln, 2001; Asanuma, 1993; Nishiguchi, 1996). Levels III and IV are where the greatest customer-supplier cooperation and responsibility-sharing take place. Each firm is a knowledgeable and valued partner, and each must trust and depend on the other for the transaction to succeed.

Differences by Parts

Whatever the differences among manufacturers' procurement strategies and the modes of supply-chain governance, the nature of the part sourced to some extent conditions the customer-supplier collaboration. We can see from Table 1 that electronic and electro-mechanical parts are generally purchased ready-made and "off the shelf." Indeed, of the electro-mechanical components that Matsushita and Sanyo outsource, there is no variance: All are marketed goods. The purchase is thus a straightforward market transaction. The supplier monopolizes product design and production, and the customer selects from a catalog of products and models.

Of the remaining parts in the table, structure parts, printed circuit boards and subassemblies all involve customization to the customer's manufacturing and marketing requirements, so there is considerable customer involvement in their design and manufacture. For example, for electro-mechanical parts, located at the other end of the continuum, all subassemblies are sourced by Matsushita and Sanyo. At Level I, the supplier has little discretion or initiative. Product and process design is the customer's domain. Structure parts, printed circuit boards (PCBs) and molds all vary across Levels I, II, and III of the Asanuma continuum. All are ordered goods in which the customer provides drawings – product and process specification – but there is variation by manufacturer and governance form in the detail of those drawings and the discretion given the supplier.

Differences by Manufacturer

Within each class of parts, Matsushita's relationships with suppliers are more collaborative than Sanyo's relationships. Take the case of electronic parts. Both manufacturers buy many of them as "marketed" goods, requiring no customer-specific modification and thus little cooperation and communication between customer and supplier. Indeed, all of SEI's electronics parts purchases fall in this class. Yet, two Matsushita suppliers produce such parts in Level VI, "drawing-approved" fashion, sharing some product and process design responsibilities with Matsushita. Our informants said that Matsushita was reducing its "off-the-shelf" purchases, increasing reliance on drawing-approved ordered goods. The shift is consistent with Asanuma's (1989) dynamic take on supply-chain organization. In his words, drawing-approved parts and quasi-DA parts (structure parts) "mainly originate from two directions: from marketed goods type parts and from DS parts" (1989, p. 14). The change is in line with Matsushita's development and increased use of the *kyoei-kai*.

Further, in its purchases of PCB, structure parts, and mold types, Matsushita entrusts more discretion and control to suppliers than does Sanyo. Matsushita provides only rough drawings for the manufacture of PCB and structure parts. Sanyo, however, presents its suppliers with full blueprints. The difference is important, because the Level III parts (customer supplies rough drawings only) are quasi-"drawing accepted" in Asanuma's terms, implying greater customer-supplier sharing and asset/relationship specificity than are Level II ("blueprint supplied') parts. Our respondents at Matsushita told us that they had previously outsourced structure parts as Level II, but were now using Level III methods. Thus, Matsushita and Sanyo's sourcing strategies have diverged as Matsushita developed the *kyoei-kai* and, through it, distributed product and process responsibility to its top-rated suppliers.

Differences by Governance Form

We have established that, for the same complexity/customization of parts, Matsushita delegates more expertise and initiative to its suppliers than does Sanyo.

The question we address now is whether this contrast in sourcing strategy is attributable to a difference between the companies in the organizational form of supply transactions. Specifically, we hypothesize that the suppliers on whose expertise and control Matsushita is most dependent are organized in network form, as opposed to dyadic form.

Matsushita and Sanyo suppliers may be classified according to the following three governance modes:

(1) Independent suppliers: "Independent suppliers" are legally and administratively independent, not owned or controlled by the manufacturer (Matsushita or Sanyo) or combined in a supplier association established and maintained by the manufacturer. Of these, we focus on suppliers considered to be important trading partners. What is distinctive about supply relations of this sort is not that they consist of market contracting – their long-term, relationship-specific nature means that trust, reciprocity, and commitment structure them beyond what market governance generally implies. Rather, they are *dyadic*-what organization they have is specific to the transacting customer-supplier pair, and they thus lack "embedded network" character. Dyadic or bilateral organization includes the monitoring, incentive alignment, absorption, co-optation, and reciprocity processes given much attention in theories of organizational exchange such as transaction cost economics, agency theory, and resource dependence.

(2) Cooperative association (*"kyoryoku"*) suppliers: The second governance form is the organization of suppliers in a cooperative association set up by, and dedicated to, one manufacturer. The member suppliers are independently owned and managed but are committed to a long-term business relationship with the manufacturer and to making specific investments in that relationship. As noted, of the two manufacturers we studied, only Matsushita maintains a cooperative association, the *kyoei-kai*.

(3) Affiliated (*"keiretsu"*) companies: The third governance form is *keiretsu* or capital-related (*shihon kankei*) companies. *Keiretsu* in its narrowest sense is a network of companies linked to one another through stable purchase-supply agreements, partial ownership ties, and personnel exchanges. Supply relations in the electronics industry generally have fewer of the trappings of *keiretsu* than in the auto industry (Asanuma, 1984; Fruin, 1997, p. 99; Lincoln & Ahmadjian, 2001). Neither Matsushita nor Sanyo has forged the kinds of *keiretsu* connections common at Toyota and elsewhere in the auto industry. Other electronics/electrical machinery firms such as Hitachi, Toshiba, Mitsubishi Electric, and NEC have stronger *keiretsu* supply networks in this sense (Fruin, 1999; Lincoln et al., 1998; Lincoln & Ahmadjian, 2001).

Yet, Matsushita and, to a lesser degree, Sanyo lead a well-defined vertical *keiretsu* of another sort – the "Matsushita Group." These are independently managed firms in which Matsushita and Sanyo maintain equity stakes and on whose boards they have typically installed one or more directors. Such *keiretsu* affiliates serve to expand the parent firm's final product line and supply it with manufactured parts and services.[5] Indeed, in early 2002, Matsushita announced that it was folding in as wholly owned divisions several major affiliated companies, including Matsushita Kotobuki, Kyushuu Matsushita, and Matsushita Tsushin (communications). The principal reason given for the consolidation was that the affiliated companies had attained too much independence, and their product lines were inefficiently overlapping, and competing, with Matsushita Electric's own.

The *kyoei-kai* is a device for organizing Matsushita's top suppliers as a network, not as a set of individuals. As a formal governance structure, it encourages horizontal ties between *kyoei* members based on common membership, compliance with *kyoei*-rules (e.g. the QIG), and various knowledge-sharing and capability-enhancement activities.

Generally speaking, cooperative associations and *keiretsu* are not mutually exclusive governance forms. In the auto industry, for example, they consist of overlapping sets of firms (Sako, 1994). Supplier cooperative associations at Toyota and Nissan overlay a network of *keiretsu* equity stakes and personnel transfers. In the case of Matsushita and Sanyo, however, no overlap exists between the two.

On the face of it, the *kyoei-kai* would seem to be a closer approximation to the network mode of governance than are the *keiretsu* devices of equity ties and personnel dispatches. In the vertical keiretsu, unlike the horizontal keiretsu groups, the bulk of the quasi-administrative linkage is between manufacturer and supplier, not among the suppliers themselves, although such ties may well exist. Yet a cohesive keiretsu supply network, as Toyota's is known to be and as the Aisin fire case again confirms, also comprises not merely a series of "one-off" customer-supplier transactions but a genuine network in which productive third-party ties proliferate. Our information on the degree to which Matsushita and Sanyo manage their affiliated suppliers' horizontal relationships is limited, but it does appear consistent with the Matsushita Group's reputation in Japanese business circles as a prominent vertical *keiretsu* (Career Development Center, 2002; Dodwell, 2002; Shimotani, 2000) – that Matsushita and its affiliated firms together form a coherent and strategic cluster, collaborating with and supporting one another. Sanyo, however, appears to manage its affiliates in rather more sequential, dyadic fashion. While Sanyo has an expansive network of subsidiaries and affiliates, it does not appear in the usual published classifications as a well-known industrial *keiretsu* grouping. Further testimony to this point is a Sanyo purchasing manager's comment that "our purchasing strategy is to treat affiliated and independent suppliers equally.

No priority is given to affiliated companies over other suppliers and we always encourage competition among all our supply sources."

We acknowledge that our three-way classification of governance forms is also an ordering by internalization or absorption of the exchange within the boundaries of the customer firm. Transactions between Matsushita and Sanyo and the affiliated companies, which they partly own and control, are most "absorbed" in this sense; transactions between Matsushita and its *kyoei* suppliers are at an intermediate level, Again, in contrast with the automotive companies, the *kyoei-kai* is in lieu of, not on top of, *keiretsu* governance. Exchanges with the independent suppliers are least absorbed. In contrast, both *keiretsu* and *kyoei* governance may be considered network forms in the sense that the manufacturer is actively involved in the cultivation and orchestration of horizontal, cross-supplier ties. Transactions between the manufacturers and their independent suppliers are more dyadic in nature, however strong they are in a long-term, relational contracting sense. If absorption of the transaction is the salient dimension along which governance forms may be arrayed, we expect the collaboration to be closer between the manufacturer and affiliated companies than between manufacturer (Matsushita) and supplier cooperative association (*kyoei-kai*). If the collaboration is greater with the *kyoei-kai*, the implication is that network organization – management of the supplier pool as an integrated whole rather than a series of independent pairings – counts most for cooperation and sharing.

How, then, does governance in these terms relate to customer-supplier sharing of product and process responsibility as indexed by the Asanuma scale? Our hypothesis is that Matsushita's use of the *kyoei-kai* as an embedded network form explains its propensity to collaborate with suppliers more than Sanyo does for the same type of part. The evidence for that hypothesis is greatest for structure parts, secondarily for PCBs. Structure parts, again, require tailoring to the customer's production and marketing requirements. Sanyo sources such parts from independent suppliers at Level II on the Asanuma scale: The supplier works from blueprints that the manufacturer provides. Matsushita, too, sources structure parts from independent suppliers, but its purchases of this type are preponderantly with *kyoei* companies. Most importantly, Matsushita's procurement of these parts from independent companies, like Sanyo's, is pitched at Asanuma Level II. When Matsushita sources the same parts from *kyoei* members, on the other hand, the supplier's responsibility shifts to Level III: The customer provides only than rough drawings, leaving the detailed designs to the discretion of the supplier.

A parallel pattern for a different part and different mode of network governance is that both Matsushita and Sanyo source PCBs from independent suppliers at Asanuma Level I – the manufacturer monopolizes the design phase, and the supplier merely executes this. Matsushita's sourcing of PCB's from affiliated suppliers, however, occurs at Level III.

Finally, both manufacturers buy electronic parts from a mix of affiliated and independent suppliers. Consistent with other patterns in the table, Matsushita's procurement of electronic parts from affiliated companies – Level VI, the "black box" – is more cooperative and relation-specific than its sourcing from independent suppliers – Level VII, "marketed goods." Indeed, the bulk of Matsushita's outsourced electronic parts come from these two affiliates – Matsushita Denshi Buhin and Matsushita Denshi Kogyo – which provide more than 50 and 80% of the TV division's inputs of cathode-ray tubes and semiconductors, respectively. Matsushita buys the remainder from large independent manufacturers.

As noted above, both Matsushita and Sanyo source all their electronic parts as Level VII marketed goods from a mix of *kyoei*, affiliated, and independent firms. In this case, the part fully determines the nature of the customer-supplier relationship, so our hypotheses as to differences between manufacturers and among governance forms cannot be addressed.

Thus, for the same class of part, Matsushita's purchases from the *kyoei-kai* involve greater supplier responsibility and cooperation than is true of Sanyo's purchases from its independent suppliers. This finding is consistent with the hypothesis that the knowledge-sharing and organizational learning of the *kyoei-kai* have resulted in design and development collaboration between Matsushita and its top suppliers. In Matsushita's case, purchases from affiliated suppliers have similar implications for the nature of the supply transaction-sharing, but we discern no such difference between Sanyo's affiliated and independent suppliers. For Matsushita, *kyoei-kai* and *keiretsu* operate similarly to bind manufacturer and supplier in a collaborative pact such that development tasks are truly shared. In Sanyo's case, there is no *kyoei-kai*, and affiliated companies receive no special treatment. For Sanyo, the division of labor between manufacturer and supplier is fixed, Sanyo controlling all phases of the design process for structure parts and the supplier monopolizing the design and manufacturing of electronic and electro-mechanical parts.

CONCLUSIONS

Stable collaborative interfirm relations are widely seen to be a fruitful alternative to arm's length market contracting and integration under a corporate hierarchy, and considerable recent theoretical and empirical literature addresses their causes and consequences. We study a distinction in organizations' choice of collaborative forms to which a few important studies have given attention, but which on the whole have not received the research scrutiny they deserve. We develop a theoretical argument for the distinctiveness and complementarity of dyadic and network modes of organizing purchase-supply relationships, and we provide some empirical evidence that the distinction is key to how two major Japanese electronics firms differ in the management of their production supply chains.

Our comparison of the procurement practices of the television manufacturing divisions of Matsushita and Sanyo underscore some important differences in how Japanese electronics manufacturers collaborate with, and share responsibility with, their parts suppliers and how governance modes affect those differences. Our principal argument is that through its supplier cooperative association and its coherent *keiretsu* grouping of affiliated companies, Matsushita manages its supplier base as a *network*, not an assemblage of disconnected dyads, and that Matsushita's strategy in this regard accounts for the collaboration and knowledge-sharing in product and process design we find between Matsushita and its primary suppliers as compared with Sanyo. Such collaboration, in turn, has enabled Matsushita to reduce its reliance on highly standardized catalog components by motivating suppliers to make specific investments in parts and assemblies customized to Matsushita's particular needs.

The difference between Matsushita and Sanyo is not, we argue, that the first maintains high-trust relational contracts with its suppliers while the second transacts with them at arm's length. Both Matsushita and Sanyo have stable and supportive relationships with their strategic, elite suppliers. Indeed, Matsushita's pairwise dealings with its suppliers are by reputation, at least, stricter and colder. Sanyo has no *kyoei-kai*, but like Matsushita, it buys parts and subassemblies from an array of subsidiaries and affiliates linked to it by equity ties and personnel placements. Yet, Sanyo's relationships with its suppliers, whether independent or affiliated, are essentially *dyadic*. Sanyo's suppliers are not organized into strategic groupings, nor has Sanyo sought to foster knowledge-sharing and cooperation among the suppliers themselves. The principal horizontal relationship it cultivated among them is competitive rivalry. In contrast, Matsushita, most conspicuously in the *kyoei-kai* but also in its *keiretsu* network of affiliated companies, has fostered active collaboration and responsibility-sharing with its elite domestic supplier pool, although, as part of the same program, it has stoked the flames of competition between that pool and its large and growing offshore supplier base.

These results draw our attention to the need for more research on long-term collaborative interorganizational relationships and for greater theoretical emphasis on network forms. The network perspective, with its stress on the emergent properties of collectivities, is essentially a sociological perspective, contrasting with the individualistic and dyadic perspectives of organizational economics. It thus alerts the researcher to a set of phenomena with important implications for the behavior of firms and the performance of economic systems that economics theories tend to overlook. Both streams of theorizing would, of course, gain from further research on the interplay of network and dyad processes in a variety of interorganizational settings.

Moreover, we need not belabor the value of our research for practitioners. If our perspective on the importance of network structures and processes is correct, the best intentioned and executed strategies of supply chain and other interorganizational management may fall flat, because managers are failing to devote attention to a critical set of causal processes. Managers, as one informant observed (Powell et al., 1996), must look beyond dyadic alliances to how they might identify, organize, and sustain productive relationships at the network level.

We have stressed the benefits to Matsushita from its network approach to supplier relationships with both its affiliated and *kyoei-kai* partners. However, the construction and management of a network come at a price. We noted the heavy investment made by Matsushita's headquarter level purchasing department (the Shizai Center) in the development and administration of the *kyoei-kai*. Furthermore, the management of supply relations within a complex network is more constraining and cumbersome than is the management of a series of independent dyadic customer-supplier ties. Networks are by definition densely coupled systems where interaction effects and other systemic complexities abound. Many of these, such as the learning and responsibility-sharing we have referred to, are desirable from the standpoint of the manufacturer. Others, needless to say, are not. Matsushita's and Sanyo's practice of absorbing a supplier's risks by shifting it between lines of business is fraught with adverse unintended consequences if the skills of the supplier are integral to a nexus of partnerships within the supplier community on which the success of the entire manufacturing operation depends.

Similarly, a manufacturer whose supply relations are essentially dyadic may have to overcome less organizational inertia than one whose purchasing transactions are intertwined in a network form. This is particularly salient in times of economic contraction, when cost reduction is a paramount concern, and reduction of component and materials costs is sought through offshore dispersion of production and procurement. The trend in the Japanese auto industry has been one of increasing standardization and substitutability of parts, so as to reduce development costs and raise economies of scale in purchasing (Ahmadjian & Lincoln, 2001). A casualty of this trend is the withering of traditional *keiretsu-*style supply networks. Advances in technology combined with global diffusion of what were once uniquely Japanese manufacturing methods may enable such developments without the trade-offs in quality that they once implied.

Indeed, as we write in 2002, Sanyo Electric's corporate financial performance has markedly outstripped that of Matsushita and most other large Japanese electronics firms. After an earnings decline of 37% in 1999, Sanyo aggressively cut costs, scrapped uncompetitive lines of business, streamlined its supply chain, and through a series of well-timed and well-chosen acquisitions expanded into several new and profitable lines of business (e.g. rechargeable batteries, digital cameras, and cellular-phone components). Matsushita, by contrast, is regularly criticized for its commitment to low margin businesses and its slowness in jettisoning what some see as a costly and cumbersome organization structure (the decentralized divisional system) and management style (the paternalistic culture descended from the teachings of founder Konosuke Matsushita; Shimotani, 2002).

The economic stagnation of the Japanese economy is a force for change in purchase-supply relations in electronics and other industries. Companies like Matsushita try to weather the hard times while maintaining commitments to a select pool of elite domestic suppliers able to offer customized and sophisticated parts and subsystems. Other manufacturers are more aggressive in letting their domestic suppliers go, abandoning the long-term commitments and relation-specific assets that have been the hallmark of Japanese industrial goods markets and the erstwhile key to Japanese manufacturing success. In the auto industry, Renault-controlled Nissan's radical and, to date, successful overhaul and downsizing of its *keiretsu* supply network is a model of restructuring that other Japanese manufacturers are watching and will likely emulate in growing numbers in years to come. Matsushita's weak earnings performance is driving it to step up cost reductions. Its reliance on offshore suppliers is growing rapidly and its domestic purchases declining. The *kyoei-kai* is in difficulty as a consequence. Member suppliers are leaving, as their business with Matsushita falls off. These developments, in our view, constitute no indictment of the *kyoei* program. Matsushita's investment in upgrading the skill and knowledge of its best suppliers clearly paid off in greater sharing of the burden of innovation with a network of trusted partners and in a greater technological and manufacturing capability for the Matsushita manufacturing enterprise as a whole. Even the best business strategies, however, are undone by circumstances, and the circumstances surrounding Japanese manufacturing have been difficult for some time. Its strengths notwithstanding, the *kyoei* model may have been a better adaptation to the Japanese economy of another day.

NOTES

1. Some of the case study material on Matsushita presented in this chapter previously also appeared in Lincoln, Ahmadjian and Mason (1998).
2. The body of the TV set is composed of "structure parts." Their function is to hold and protect the "active" elements, which are the electro-mechanical and electronics parts.

DIDIER GUILLOT AND JAMES R. LINCOLN

The molds are the metal "casts" in which the plastic parts (mostly the cabinets) are molded.

3. In a personal communication based on his research in the Japanese electronics industry, Tom Roehl suggests that Matsushita's marketing strategy differs from Sanyo's in that Matsushita does *more* frequent product changes and fits products to more specialized market segments.

4. Set manufacturers are the suppliers, which are in charge of the development and/or production of a whole subsystem (combination of different parts) rather than a single part. In the case of a remote control for instance, a part manufacturer would provide only the electric components, or the plastic case, while a set manufacturer would be in charge of the whole product.

REFERENCES

Ahmadjian, C., & Lincoln, J. R. (2001). *Keiretsu*, governance, and learning: Case studies in change from the Japanese automotive industry. *Organization Science, 12*, 683–701.

Asanuma, B. (1984). *Jidosha sangyo ni okeru buhin torihiki no kozo* [The structure of parts transactions in the automotive industry: The mechanisms of adjustment and innovative adaptation]. *Gendai Keizai [Modern Economics], 19* (Summer).

Asanuma, B. (1989). Manufacturer-supplier relationships in Japan and the concept of relation-specific skill. *Journal of the Japanese and International Economies, 3*, 1–30.

Asanuma, B. (1993). Interfirm relationships in the Japanese automobile industry. *Rivista Internazionale di Scienze Economiche e Commerciali, XL*, 12.

Baum, J., Calabrese, T., & Silverman, B. (2000). Don't go it alone: Alliance network composition and startups' performance in Canadian biotechnology. *Strategic Management Journal, 21*, 267–294.

Beer, M., & Spector, B. A. (1981). *Matsushita Electric*. Harvard Business School Case #9–481–146.

Burt, R. (1992). *Structural holes: The social structure of competition*. Cambridge, MA: Harvard University Press.

Career Development Center (2002). *Kigyou gurupu to gyoukai chizu* (Enterprise groups and business world map). Takahashi Shoten.

Dore, R. (1986). *Flexible rigidities*. Stanford, CA: Stanford University Press.

Dyer, J. H., & Nobeoka, K. (2000). Creating and managing a high-performance knowledge-sharing network: The Toyota case. *Strategic Management Journal, 21*, 345–367.

Fruin, M. (1997). *Knowledge works: Managing intellectual capital at Toshiba*. New York: Oxford University Press.

Granovetter, M. (1985). Economic action and social structure: A theory of embeddedness. *American Journal of Sociology, 91*, 481–510.

Hiramoto, A. (1994). *Nihon no terebi sangyo: Kyousou yuui no kouzou* [Framework of the Japanese TV industry competitive advantage]. Kyoto: Minerva Shobou.

Lincoln, J. R. (1990). Japanese organization and organization theory. In: B. M. Staw & L. L. Cummings (Eds), *Research in Organizational Behavior* (Vol. 12, pp. 255–294). Greenwich, CT: JAI Press.

Lincoln, J. R., & Ahmadjian, C. L. (2001). *Shukko* (employee transfers) and tacit knowledge exchange in Japanese supply networks: The electronics industry case. In: I. Nonaka & T. Nishiguchi (Eds), *Knowledge Emergence: Social, Technical, and Evolutionary Dimensions of Knowledge Creation* (pp. 151–198). New York: Oxford University Press.

Lincoln, J. R., Ahmadjian, C. L., & Mason, E. (1998). Organizational learning and purchase-supply relations in Japan: Hitachi, Matsushita, and Toyota compared. *California Management Review, 24,* 241–264.

Lincoln, J. R., Gerlach, M. L., & Takahashi, P. (1992). *Keiretsu* networks in the Japanese economy: A dyad analysis of intercorporate ties. *American Sociological Review, 57,* 561–585.

Nishiguchi, T. (1996). *Strategic industrial sourcing: The Japanese advantage.* Oxford: Oxford University Press.

Nishiguchi, T., & Beaudet, A. (1998). The Toyota Group and the Aisin fire. *Sloan Management Review, 40,* 49–60.

Piore, M. J., & Sabel, C. F. (1984). *The second industrial divide: Possibilities for prosperity.* New York: Basic Books.

Podolny, J., & Page, K. (1998). Network forms of organization. *Annual Review of Sociology, 24,* 57–76.

Powell, W. (1990). Neither market nor hierarchy: Network forms of organization. In: B. M. Staw & L. L. Cummings (Eds), *Research in Organizational Behavior.* Greenwich, CT: JAI Press.

Powell, W., Koput, K. W., & Smithdoerr, L. (1996). Interorganizational collaboration and the locus of learning in biotechnology. *Administrative Science Quarterly, 41,* 116–145.

Reitman, V. (1997) Toyota Motor shows its mettle after fire destroys parts plant. *The Wall Street Journal* (May 8), 1.

Roehl, T. (1989). A comparison of U.S.–Japanese firms' parts-supply systems: What besides nationality matters? In: K. Hayashi (Ed.), *The U.S.–Japanese Economic Relationship: Can it be Improved?* (pp. 127–154). New York: New York University Press.

Sako, M. (1992). *Price, quality, and trust: Inter-firm relations in Britain and Japan.* Cambridge: Cambridge University Press.

Saxenian, A. (1994). *Regional networks: Industrial adaptation in silicon valley and route 128.* Cambridge, MA: Harvard University Press.

Shimotani, M. (1997). *Matsushita Denki 'Kyoei-kai' no rekishi to genzai* [Matsushita Electric's *'Kyoei-kai'*: Past and present]. *Kyoto University Economic Review.*

Shimotani, M. (2002, July 2). *Nihon teki soshiki unei no otehon: Matsushita Denki ga konosuke shistem no genkai* [The Japanese-style organizational management model: The limits of the "Konosuke system" at Matsushita Electric]. *Ekonomisto* (pp. 90–92).

Shioji, H. (1995). *'Itaku'* automotive production: An aspect of the development of full-line and wide-selection production by Toyota in the 1960s. *Kyoto University Economic Review, 65,* 19–42.

Smitka, M. (1991). *Competitive ties: Subcontracting in the Japanese automotive industry.* Columbia University Press.

Stuart, T. E., Hoang, H., & Hybels, R. C. (1999). Interorganizational endorsements and the performance of entrepreneurial ventures. *Administrative Science Quarterly, 44,* 315–349.

Toyo Keizi [Oriental Economist] (various years). *Kigyo keiretsu soran* (Enterprise Keiretsu Survey). Tokyo: Toyo Keizai Ltd.

Uzzi, B. (1996). The sources and consequences of embeddedness for the economic performance of organizations. *American Sociological Review, 61,* 674–698.

Williamson, O. (1985). *The economic institutions of capitalism.* New York: Free Press.

Williamson, O. (1994). Transaction cost economics and organizational theory. In: N. Smelser & R. Swedberg (Eds), *Handbook of Economic Sociology* (pp. 77–107). Princeton, NJ: Princeton University Press.

Williamson, O. (1996). *The mechanisms of governance.* Oxford: Oxford University Press.

Womack, J. P., Jones, D. T., & Roos, D. (1990). *The machine that changed the world.* New York: Rawson Associates.

SAME RULES, DIFFERENT GAMES: VARIATION IN THE OUTCOMES OF "JAPANESE-STYLE" SUPPLY RELATIONSHIPS

Glenn Hoetker

ABSTRACT

Our understanding of Japanese supply relationships comes primarily from studying the automobile industry. This paper identifies three elements of the automobile industry that, although generally assumed to be widespread, are largely absent in the notebook computer industry, leading to a different pattern of supply relationships: a sizable pool of external suppliers; the feasibility of shukko and cross-shareholding to strengthen supply relationships; and the adequacy of these means to manage external supply relationships. This finding debunks the myth of a monolithic model of "Japanese-style" supply relationships and illustrates the importance of idiosyncratic elements of an industry's environment on its supply relationships.

Precisely because Japanese supply chain practice has acquired this standing [worldwide "best practice"], however, it tends to be viewed as all the same. How Japanese companies and industry vary in the supply relations is seriously understudied (Lincoln & Ahmadjian, 2000, p. 1).

Japanese Firms in Transition: Responding to the Globalization Challenge
Advances in International Management, Volume 17, 187–212
Copyright © 2005 by Elsevier Ltd.
All rights of reproduction in any form reserved
ISSN: 0747-7929/doi:10.1016/S0747-7929(04)17008-X

INTRODUCTION

In the 1980s, relations with long-term suppliers were seen as a key Japanese competitive advantage (Dyer, 1996b). As Japan's economy soured, however, these same close buyer-supplier ties were seen as limiting the flexibility of Japanese manufacturers to respond to changing market conditions (Lincoln, 2001). Whether a blessing or a curse, these ties have been studied primarily in one industry – automobiles.[1] Given the importance of this industry and Japan's rapid rise to competitive parity and even superiority, this is not surprising. This concentration has allowed in-depth exploration into the effect of differences in national institutions and management practices. However, it begs the question: How representative of Japanese supply relationships is the automotive industry?

Scholars have increasingly drawn attention to the importance of understanding heterogeneity in supply relationships across Japanese industries (Guillot & Lincoln, 2005; Smitka, 1991). Despite these calls, our understanding of supply relationships outside of the automotive industry remains limited.[2]

Based on observations of the automobile industry, practices such as buyer-supplier shareholding have become part of the commonly held picture of Japanese supply relationships. Given the scarcity of observations in other industries, the widespread presence of such practices has been generally assumed. In this paper, I argue that key elements of "Japanese-style" supply relationships are, in fact, absent in other Japanese industries, resulting in very different patterns of supply relationships across industries. I use the notebook computer industry as one example in which three important elements found in the automobile industry are largely absent: the existence of a sizable pool of external suppliers, the feasibility of *shukko* and manufacturer-supplier shareholding as a means of strengthening supply relationships, and the adequacy of these means to manage the governance and communications difficulties inherent procuring components externally.

In Japan, both the automobile and notebook computer industries prefer long-term suppliers over new suppliers, especially in the presence of uncertainty. In the automobile industry, long-term relationships have permitted manufacturers to engage in extensive outsourcing, providing cost savings, flexibility, and greater innovation than otherwise possible (Dyer, 1996b). However, in the notebook computer industry, Japanese firms engage in very little outsourcing, even to long-term suppliers. They do so even at the cost of not accessing superior technical capabilities available from external suppliers.

This finding has three implications. First, it debunks the myth of a monolithic model of "Japanese-style" supply relationships. Second, it shows that supply relationships are not the inevitable outcome of the larger institutional environment in which they occur. Third, it highlights the need to focus on the role of idiosyncratic elements in an industry's competitive environment that influence the development of supply relationships. Understanding the role of these elements helps us predict under what conditions long-term relationships are most beneficial. Such predictions are especially relevant given efforts in the United States to move from confrontational supply relationships to more Japanese-style collaborative, long-term relationships (Dyer, 1996b; Helper, 1991).

In the next section, I review prior research on Japanese supply relationships, paying special attention to the role played by three elements found in the oft-studied automobile industry: the existence of a sizable pool of external suppliers, the feasibility of *shukko* and manufacturer-supplier shareholding as a means of strengthening supply relationships, and the adequacy of these means to manage the governance and communications difficulties inherent in procuring components externally. I then discuss the notebook computer industry as a contrasting venue for exploring supply relationships. Finally, I present evidence that relationships in the notebook computer industry differ in important ways from the conventional wisdom about supplier relationships in Japan and relate these differences to variation in three elements of each industry's competitive environment.

PRIOR RESEARCH ON JAPANESE SUPPLY RELATIONSHIPS

Prior research has found that a cluster of inter-related traits characterize Japanese supply relationships: concentration of transactions to a small number of suppliers, many of which become long-term partners; support of these relationships by shareholding and the transfer of employees; and heavy reliance on suppliers for the design and development of new components. I examine each of these points in turn and discuss the theoretical explanations put forward for each.

In the automobile industry, it is not unusual for a firm and its main suppliers to have transacted for over 30 years without interruption (Japan Fair Trade Commission [Kosei Torihiki Iinkai], 1993 quoted in Ahmadjian and Lincoln, 2001). Japanese manufacturers rarely change suppliers (Dyer & Ouchi, 1993; Helper, 1991). Dyer and Chu (2000) found the rate at which automotive suppliers won renewal of their contracts averaged 91% across manufacturers, with little variance. In contrast, the re-win rate for suppliers to Korean and U.S. manufacturers averaged 77 and 71%, respectively, with considerable variation across manufacturers.

Some of these relationships are further supported by shareholding. Japanese automakers surveyed by Dyer and Chu (2000) reported holding an average of 11% of their suppliers stock. A broader survey by the Japanese Fair Trade Commission found that each Japanese automaker dealt with an average of 392 suppliers, of which 16.1% were affiliated by shareholding (Dodwell Marketing Consultants, 1995). In some cases, manufacturers held a large portion of a supplier's stock: over 20% in almost a third of affiliated shareholdings. In over 60% of affiliated suppliers, however, the manufacturer held under one-tenth of the supplier's stock. Consistent with this, Gerlach (1992) argues that manufacturers hold stock in suppliers as a symbol of their relationship, rather than to exercise economic control.

Supply relationships are also often accompanied by *shukko*, the exchange of personnel between companies (Asanuma & Kikutani, 1992). One role of *shukko* is to allow the manufacturer to shift surplus employees to suppliers, rather than laying them off. However, it is most important as a means of developing new capabilities and supporting technology transfer. As such, it is often reciprocal. Engineers from the manufacturer may visit a supplier both to learn about a supplier's technology and to teach the supplier new techniques. The supplier may send engineers to the manufacturer in order to better understand the manufacturer's technology (Lincoln & Ahmadjian, 2000).

Supply relationships characterized by long-term affiliation, cross-shareholding and *shukko* are concentrated among a small number of suppliers. Asanuma (1992) found that a typical Toyota plant had only 125 suppliers, compared to 800 for the typical General Motors plant. At the firm level, Toyota had approximately 224 suppliers, compared to over 5500 for General Motors. Japanese manufacturers concentrate their purchases among relatively few suppliers to maximize economies of scale. Through management of long-term supply relationships, they avoid many of the difficulties that would otherwise accompany dependence on a small number of suppliers.[3]

Relying on close relationships, Japanese manufacturers rely heavily on suppliers for the design and development of new components (Asanuma, 1992; Wasti & Liker, 1999). They also outsource the production of many components. Dyer and Ouchi (1993) estimate that Japanese automobile manufacturers make only 27% of their components in-house, while U.S. firms produce 54% in-house. Data from 1987 on all manufacturing industries show that internally produced components are only 31% of total cost of goods sold for Japanese manufacturers, relative to 45% for U.S. firms. Nor is outsourcing limited to simple, standardized components; Japanese manufacturers outsource complex inputs as well (Morris & Imrie, 1992).

The prevalence of outsourcing had led to Japanese firms having lower employee to sales ratios than on average than U.S. firms (Asanuma & Kikutani, 1992; Sako, 1992). The large number of quasi-integrated subcontractors, each serving primarily one manufacturer, means that the average Japanese supplier is also smaller than its U.S. counterpart. Even though the Japanese automotive industry produces one-third of the world's total output, only 19 of the world's top 100 automotive parts suppliers are Japanese (Smitka, 2002).

These practices benefit Japanese manufacturers. Japanese automotive manufacturers obtain a better new product development performance working with external suppliers (Clark & Fujimoto, 1991). Additionally, external suppliers provide higher-quality or lower-cost components than would otherwise be available, even for complex components (Cusumano & Takeishi, 1991; Nishiguchi, 1994).

Theoretical explanations for these practices and the performance advantages they generate focus on their role in improving governance and communication. Manufacturers benefit if their suppliers make relationship-specific investments in physical or human capital (Dyer, 1996a; Parkhe, 1993). Because these investments expose the supplier to potential opportunism, they will only be made when the ensuing governance problem can be solved efficiently (Williamson, 1985).

Long-term relationships, shareholding, and *shukko* all reduce the perceived likelihood of opportunism. Interactions between individuals over a long period of time build trust (Ring & Van de Ven, 1994), which can become institutionalized, thereby increasing inter-organizational trust (Zaheer, McEvily & Perrone, 1998). Consistent with this finding, Sako and Helper (1998) find that Japanese automobile suppliers are more trusting of customers with whom they have transacted for a long time, reducing the supplier's fear of opportunism. By creating more opportunities for managers and engineers from the buyer and supplier to interact over an extended period, *shukko* contributes to building trust. *Shukko* also represents a form of technical assistance from the buyer to the supplier, which Dyer and Chu (2000) and Sako and Helper (1998) found increased a supplier's trust of a customer. Stock ownership can align the economic incentives of a buyer and supplier (Cusumano, 1985; Gerlach, 1992), as well as serving as a public symbol of a relationship, creating conditions for trust to develop (Gerlach, 1987).[4] As a result, Japanese suppliers make greater investments in relationship-specific human capital (Carroll & Hannan, 2000) and physical capital (Asanuma, 1998; Gilson & Roe, 1993) than non-Japanese suppliers.

Even in the absence of opportunism, successful buyer-supplier collaboration depends on timely, accurate communication of technical details. Long-term relationships contribute to this through the development of communication routines (Mitchell & Singh, 1996) and a common language for discussing technical issues (Buckley & Casson, 1976). By giving employees direct exposure to their partner firm, *shukko* also supports the transmission of tacit knowledge (Lincoln & Ahmadjian, 2000; Nonaka & Takeuchi, 1995). The role of stock ownership is more tenuous, but any sense of shared destiny it may create enhances communication in much the same way belonging to the same organization does (Kogut & Zander, 1996).

Informal means of managing potential opportunism are especially valuable when other mechanisms, particularly formal ones such as contracting, are ineffective (Johnson, Levine & Woodruff, 2002). At least three factors make Japan such an environment: low labor mobility, a low level of generalized trust, and scarcity or ineffectiveness of transaction costs engineers, such as attorneys.

Limited Labor Mobility

One effect of so-called "lifetime employment" in Japan is limited employee mobility between companies. This complicates both governance and communication between a buyer and supplier.

When there is labor mobility between firms in an industry, buyers are more likely to know employees at potential suppliers by virtue of contact in earlier positions, which provides a basis for trust. This is less likely to occur in Japan.

The lack of employee movement leads to the development of distinctive technical cultures within companies, each with its own language and problem-solving approaches. This raises the cost of communication between companies, especially in the case of leading-edge technology, which is associated with uncodified, tacit knowledge. In contrast, firms in the United States rely on hiring workers from other companies to break down these barriers (Ettlie, 1985). The general taboo on mid-level hiring removes that option for most Japanese companies.[5]

Shukko is a direct response to this limitation. When it is not possible to hire an employee, firms try to gain the same benefits through the exchange of employees (Lincoln & Ahmadjian, 2000).

Low Generalized Trust

Debate exists as to whether trust is high in Japanese society. Fukuyama (1995) argues that aspects of Japanese culture make Japanese society high in trust. However, Yamagishi and his co-authors (Yamagishi, 1988; Yamagishi, Cook & Watabe, 1998) use surveys and experimental data to argue that trust is very low in Japan when monitoring and sanctioning do not exist. Consistent with Yamagishi's findings, other survey data reveal that general levels of trust are lower in Japan than in the United States (La Porta, Lopez-de-Silanes, Shleifer & Vishny, 1997).

To the degree that trust in Japan depends on monitoring and sanctioning, long-term relationships accompanied by *shukko* and shareholding will be particularly privileged relative to other relationships because they provide the requisite monitoring and sanctioning mechanisms. Besides the obvious impact on governance, communication will also be relatively impeded outside of close relationships. Information in Japan flows freely within groups, but only narrowly outside groups' bonds of trust and familiarity (Lincoln, 2001, p. 131).

Scarce, Ineffective Transaction-Costs Engineers

The idea that Japanese interfirm relationships are a response to an inefficient legal structure goes back at least to 1984 (Cooter & Landa, 1984). An often-cited element of this inefficiency is the lack of lawyers. Japan has only 17,000 licensed attorneys, compared to 900,000 in the United States.[6] Beyond this, there is also a relative lack of other professionals, such as accounting firms and credit-rating agencies (Milhaupt & West, 2000).

Despite assertions, both serious and facetious, that a shortage of attorneys has advantages, it can also be disadvantageous. Attorneys and similar professionals play an important role as "transaction costs engineers," devising efficient mechanisms to deal with market imperfections (Gilson, 1984). Milhaupt and West (2000) show that their absence creates an environment in which organized crime can assume this role and flourish. In the commercial setting, their absence creates at least two difficulties.

First, the ability of firms to perform due diligence and to design legally complex contracts at the beginning of a relationship is curtailed, with lawyers having little involvement in drafting contracts (Smitka, 1994). Second, if a dispute does arise, there are fewer legal resources available with which to pursue litigation. The slow rate at which litigation moves in Japan is a further disincentive to resolve disputes via the legal system (Miyazawa, 1995). Given these disincentives, it is not surprising that the litigation rate in Japan is much lower than in the United States (Hamada, 2000).

A network externality compounds the second difficulty. With limited experience in adjudicating commercial disputes, the courts miss out on the opportunity to develop expertise. Just as "Widely used laws are likely to be well serviced by lawyers and judges" (Milhaupt & West, 2000, p. 95), little used laws are likely to be poorly serviced.[7]

The partial foreclosure of the legal system as an effective way to structure a complex relationship or resolve disputes makes working with an unfamiliar supplier on a complex, uncertain project a daunting task. A trusted long-term supplier or an internal supplier is more attractive.[8]

PROPOSITIONS

The supply relationships described above are premised on the existence of several elements. These include the existence of a sizable pool of external suppliers, the feasibility of employee transfer (*shukko*) and manufacturer-supplier shareholding as a means of strengthening supply relationships, and the adequacy of these means to manage the governance and communications difficulties inherent procuring components externally.

To explore the impact of these elements, I form several propositions reflecting the supply relationships past research would lead us to expect in other Japanese industries. I then test whether they hold in notebook computers, an industry where these elements do not exist to the same degree. The propositions serve as a framework for comparing the notebook computer industry to the conventional wisdom and are not meant as hypotheses to be falsified or confirmed.

Propositions 1a and 1b relate to Japanese manufacturers' use of long-term suppliers. Long-term suppliers offer easier governance and communication than other external suppliers. Unless another supplier offered some offsetting advantage over a long-term supplier, such as lower price or higher quality, long-term suppliers are more attractive.

Proposition 1a. All else being equal, Japanese firms will prefer long-term suppliers to other external suppliers.

By limiting the number of suppliers with which they trade for a given component, Japanese manufacturers can maximize scale economies. Through their management of long-term supply relationships, they avoid many of the difficulties that would otherwise accompany dependence on a small number of suppliers.

Proposition 1b. Japanese suppliers will use fewer suppliers for a component than will non-Japanese firms.

Propositions 2a and 2b concern Japanese manufacturers' ability to avoid vertical integration through superior relationships with long-term external suppliers. Japanese manufacturers rely heavily on external suppliers. They produce a smaller proportion of their inputs internally, whether measured by the number or value of those inputs.

Proposition 2a. Japanese firms will rely less on internal supply than non-Japanese firms.

This difference is amplified under high uncertainty. When a transaction is beset by high uncertainty, contracts with an external supplier will be expensive to write, likely to leave many contingencies unaddressed, and unlikely to be satisfactorily resolved by the court system (Masten, 1984). Absent mechanisms to control opportunism, very-high-uncertainty transactions would not occur outside the firm. However, relying on the benefits of long-term relationships, Japanese manufacturers can carry out complex, uncertain transaction with "quasi-integrated" long-term external suppliers (Cusumano & Takeishi, 1991).

Proposition 2b. Japanese manufacturers' use of long-term external suppliers will be less impacted by high uncertainty than non-Japanese firms.

THE NOTEBOOK COMPUTER INDUSTRY

Manufacturers in the notebook computer industry source a wide array of components. Rather than explore supply relationships broadly, across all components, I examine in depth manufacturer relationships with flat display providers.

I begin by providing background on displays and the interaction that occurs between a notebook computer maker and its display suppliers. Displays are a particularly salient component to study because they are central to the user's overall experience with a notebook computer. They are also among the most expensive components in the computer. Notebook manufacturers therefore take great care in choosing a display supplier.

Competitive pressures compel notebook manufacturers to constantly focus on the next generation of displays, larger and higher resolution than the current generation. For example, when the largest extant notebook display was 12 inches, engineering work was under way for computers with a 13-inch display. The move to a larger display requires at least 9–12 months of engineering effort. Two types of difficulties must be overcome during this period. First, the display itself must be manufactured. Second, the display must be integrated into the new notebook computer.

Manufacturing larger or higher-resolution displays demands new handling equipment and processes. For example, larger displays require applying processes such as vapor deposition or photolithography uniformly over an ever-increasing surface area. Higher-resolution displays require more circuitry on the same-size display, which demands reduced line-widths, tighter tolerances, and more driver chips with more challenging packaging.

The notebook maker and display supplier must communicate continuously during the 9–12 months required to develop a new display and simultaneously design a notebook computer to incorporate that display. The subjective nature of many display specifications drives this communication. For example, it is possible to specify and measure a display's absolute brightness, but designers can determine consumer acceptance of a given brightness only in the context of other parameters, including color matching, brightness uniformity and brightness leakage. As a result, even though the initial specifications from the notebook manufacturer are usually very demanding, the manufacturer and supplier will negotiate compromises during development on a wide spectrum of specifications including driving method, driving voltage, input signal, the dimension of the module, and connector shapes. The changes affect both the display and the design of the computer in which it will ultimately reside.

Because of the time required and the challenges to be overcome, a manufacturer must choose a supplier to develop a new display when the required technology does not yet exist and the parameters of the final product are not known. This means both the selection of a supplier and the development of the new display will be highly uncertain.

There is also an active market for notebooks with displays several generations behind the leading edge. For example, Apple successfully introduced the iBook with a 12.1-inch display in 2001, despite widespread availability of notebooks with displays larger than 15 inches. Lower prices attract some consumers to the smaller display notebooks; their lighter weight and more compact form attract others. Because the technology to build older-generation displays already exists, uncertainty is much lower. However, it is not a spot market because circuitry and dimensions are not standardized. For example, Samsung supplies worldwide but has five different specifications for its 13-inch display. The lack of standardization creates a need for joint engineering effort, even for notebooks using older-generation displays. Once this engineering is accomplished, manufacturers are reluctant to switch suppliers because of the associated cost and delay in re-engineering.

Data

My primary data source for understanding relationships between notebook computer manufacturers and their display suppliers was the COMTRAK database compiled by Stanford Resources, one of the industry's leading consulting firms. For each model produced by a notebook manufacturer, COMTRAK provides the size and resolution of the display, as well as the firm that supplied it. Stanford Resources compiled the information in COMTRAK from interviews with display suppliers and notebook manufacturers from 1992 to 1998. I augmented these data with other data gathered from the trade press and issues of *Laptop Handbook and*

Buyer's Guide. I also interviewed notebook computer and display manufacturers and other industry participants in the United States and Japan.

The result of this effort was a complete inventory of a notebook manufacturer's relationships with each display supplier. This inventory allowed for the identification of notebook models with new displays, those for which the required technology did not exist when the manufacturer chose a display supplier for that model, thereby allowing me to examine supplier relationships under varying levels of uncertainty.

The data include information on 995 different notebook computer models by 22 manufacturers. Six Japanese manufacturers manufactured 310 of the 995 models. There were 116 models for which the manufacturer had to choose a supplier before technology required to produce the new display existed.

An additional advantage of the COMTRAK data was that it allowed me to calculate several measures of a manufacturer's relationship with a supplier at the time the manufacturer was choosing a supplier. I calculated the length of the relationship, that is, the number of years in which the manufacturer had purchased at least one notebook computer display from the supplier. I also measured whether the supplier was a current supplier to the manufacturer when it was chosen or if it had previously supplied that manufacturer when it was chosen (see Table 1).

Manufacturers are more likely to choose a supplier with strong technical capabilities, all else being equal (Hoetker, 2001). To control for this, I followed common practice (Hall, Jaffe & Trajtenberg, 2000) and measured a supplier's technical capability by the number of granted display-related U.S. patents it had applied for in the previous 5 years. This figure is updated annually. I defined

Table 1. Descriptive Statistics and Correlations.

Variable	*M*	S.D.	Min	Max	
Experience with supplier (years)	0.94	1.31	0	5	
Current supplier	0.45	0.50	0	1	
Past supplier, current or not	0.47	0.50	0	1	
Display related patents	446.34	256.04	1	926	
Internal supplier	0.21	0.41	0	1	
	1	2	3	4	5
Experience with supplier (years)	1.00				
Current supplier	0.76	1.00			
Past supplier, current or not	0.77	0.96	1.00		
Display related patents	0.34	0.27	0.27	1.00	
Internal supplier	0.35	0.16	0.14	0.00	1.00

display-related patents as those containing the terms "liquid crystal display" or "LCD" or classified in International Patent Classification section G02F 1/-, G09G 3/-, G09F 9/3-, or G09F 13/-. I selected these patent classifications according to Spencer (1997) and confirmed that they were the classifications common to all patents selected for inclusion in the "Liquid Crystal Display" section of *Industry and Technology Patents Profiles: Electronic Displays and Display Applications*, published by Derwent Information/Thompson Scientific, a leading publisher of patent information. Unreported analyses using display-related patents in the last year and total display-related patents yield the same results as this measure.

FINDINGS

The actual behavior of Japanese notebook computer manufacturers is more complex than that described in Propositions 1 and 2. Consistent with Propositions 1a and 1b, Japanese manufacturers favor a small pool of long-term suppliers over other suppliers. Contrary to Propositions 2a and 2b, however, Japanese firms are more reliant on internal development than are U.S. firms, even at the cost of not accessing external technical capabilities. Uncertainty affected their ability to work with external suppliers as strongly as it affected non-Japanese firms.

Use of Long-Term Suppliers

Consistent with Proposition 1a, Japanese notebook computer manufacturers had longer-term, more continuous relationships with their suppliers than did non-Japanese manufacturers. Table 2 shows that in 54% of procurement decisions, Japanese manufacturers chose a current supplier, compared to 44% for non-Japanese manufacturers.[9] On average, Japanese manufacturers bought from a supplier with whom they had an average of 2.65 years' prior experience, while non-Japanese firms had only 1.16 year of prior experience with the suppliers from whom they chose to buy (Table 3).[10]

Table 2. Number and Percentage of Notebook Models Using Displays from (Non)-Current Suppliers, 1992–1998.[a]

	Non-Current Supplier	Current Supplier
Japanese	124 (46.1%)	145 (53.9%)
Other	392 (57.5%)	290 (45.5%)

[a]p (Japanese use of current supplier > other's use of current supplier) < 0.001.

Table 3. Average Length of Past Relationship With Suppliers, 1992–1998.[a]

Notebook Manufacturer Nationality	Average Length of Past Relationship With Suppliers (S.E.)
Japanese	2.65 (0.13)
Other	1.16 (0.07)

[a]p (Japanese > other) < 0.001.

Consistent with Proposition 1b, Japanese notebook computer manufacturers rely on a small number of long-term display suppliers compared to non-Japanese manufacturers. As shown in Table 4, the average Japanese manufacturer used 2.4 different suppliers over the period 1992–1998, while the average non-Japanese manufacturer used 5.0 different suppliers.[11] This indicates that Japanese firms concentrate on a small group of suppliers but are biased by the fact that Japanese firms were present in the data for fewer years than U.S. firms. Table 5 avoids this bias by presenting the average number of external suppliers used per year. Japanese firms used 2.19 different suppliers per year, while non-Japanese firms use an average of 2.95 manufacturers.[12] Thus, Japanese firms both spread their business less widely each year and switched suppliers less frequently year to year.

In combination, these findings support the conventional wisdom about Japanese manufacturer's relationships with external suppliers. As is the case in

Table 4. Average Number of Suppliers Used by Each Notebook Manufacturer, 1992–1998.[a]

Notebook Manufacturer Nationality Nationality	Average Number of Suppliers (S.E.)
Japanese	2.66 (0.61)
Other	5.00 (0.51)

[a]p (other > Japanese) = 0.006.

Table 5. Average Number of Suppliers Used Per Year by Each Notebook Manufacturer, 1992–1998.[a]

Notebook Manufacturer Nationality	Average Number of Suppliers (S.E.)
Japanese	2.19 (0.24)
Other	2.95 (0.12)

[a]p (other > Japanese) = 0.004.

the automotive industry, Japanese firms prefer to deal with a small number of long-term suppliers.

Interestingly, these results stand in contrast to Chesbrough's (1997) findings for the Japanese notebook computer manufacturer's procurement of 2.5-inch hard disk drives over roughly the same period. Chesbrough found that manufacturers relied on a mix of internal supply, affiliated suppliers, and U.S. suppliers, with whom they had no affiliation. Thirty-six percent of the drives procured by the four firms he studied came from affiliated firms.[13] A potential explanation is that Japanese disk drive manufacturers lagged far behind U.S. competitors in 2.5-inch drives, making U.S. suppliers attractive until Japanese firms increased their quality. I discuss this point in more detail below.

Lincoln and Ahmadjian (2000) have also pointed out that the Japanese electronics sector in general has a history of more arm's length supply relationships and less supplier involvement in product design. It is unclear to what degree this general statement applies to specific components, so it is ambiguous how unusual the findings for displays are within the broad realm of electronic components.[14]

Low Level of Outsourcing

Contrary to Propositions 2a and 2b, Japanese firms rely *more* on internal suppliers than do non-Japanese firms. Of the 310 models for which Japanese firms procured displays, approximately three-quarters (71.29%) used displays from internal suppliers (Table 6). By comparison, only 6% of models from non-Japanese firms used displays from internal suppliers.[15] This contradicts Proposition 2a.

To test Proposition 2b, I focus on the procurement of displays for which the necessary technology did not yet exist, since these were ones for which technical uncertainty was a major concern. If the proposition holds, Japanese manufacturers would be less affected by increasing uncertainty and would be able to continue using external suppliers when non-Japanese firms would have been forced to pursue internal production.

Table 6. Number and Percentage of Displays Procured from External/Internal Sources, 1992–1998.[a]

	External Supplier	Internal Supplier
Japanese	93 (29.2%)	226 (70.8%)
Other	693 (94.3%)	42 (5.7%)

[a]p (Japanese use of internal suppliers > other's use of internal suppliers) < 0.001.

The uncertainty posed by the development of a display depends on the degree of technical advance required to produce the desired display. Display development may be characterized as uncertain in two ways. Certain displays may be subjectively perceived as requiring more technological advances than others. To get at this perception, I employed a 5-point scale to measure "advance beyond existing technology." A researcher in a leading consulting company, an 18-year industry veteran with experience as both a product engineer and product marketing manager, provided this rating for each innovation I observed in my data. As this measure was constructed after the fact, it may be biased by knowledge of which innovations ultimately proved the most difficult. However, the current measure is likely be closely correlated with a priori perceptions of uncertainty unless there were particular innovations that proved surprisingly difficult or simple (which my informants indicated did not occur).

Both Japanese and non-Japanese firms relied on internal supply more for displays above mean uncertainty than for those below mean uncertainty (Table 7). Non-Japanese firms procured 9.1% of their low-uncertainty displays from internal suppliers, a figure that increased to 13.1% for high-uncertainty displays. Japanese firms also increased their internal procurement for high-uncertainty innovations to 69.2%, compared to 50% for low-uncertainty innovations. Uncertainty affected Japanese manufacturers' ability to work with external suppliers as strongly as it affected non-Japanese firms.[16] That is, the strength of the relationship between uncertainty and internal production is the same for Japanese and non-Japanese firms. This contradicts Proposition 2a, which predicted that uncertainty would have a weaker effect on Japanese manufacturers' use of external suppliers.

The second measure of technical uncertainty may be conceptualized as a dichotomous measure of whether suppliers could produce the display by refining existing techniques or if new techniques were necessary. A resolution increase was highly uncertain if it required new process technology or breakthroughs in metallurgy, rather than executing existing materials and processes better. A

Table 7. Impact of Uncertainty on Internal Procurement, 1992–1998 (1).[a]

	Japanese Manufacturer		Other Manufacturer	
	External Supplier	Internal Supplier	External Supplier	Internal Supplier
Low uncertainty	50.0	50.0	90.9	9.1
High uncertainty	30.8	69.2	86.7	13.3

[a] Figures indicate the percentage of displays sourced from each type of supplier. High uncertainty: higher than the mean ranking (2.8) based on an industry ranking of uncertainty on a scale of 1–5 according to the amount of advance beyond the current technical horizon required.

size increase was highly uncertain if it required the assembly of an entirely new fabrication line, as opposed to being possible through improvements in an existing fabrication line. It was clear before development began when the limits of current materials or production lines had been reached. A senior industry participant who worked in the display division of a firm that made both displays and notebooks suggested this measure. For each innovation I observed, he identified whether it required a new process or not.

This measure also reveals that both Japanese and non-Japanese firms relied more on internal supply for highly uncertain innovations. Non-Japanese firms procured 23.1% of high uncertainty innovations internally, compared to just 8.2% of low uncertainty innovations (Table 8). The corresponding figures for Japanese firms are 85.7 and 50%. Again, the strength of the relationship between uncertainty and internal supply does not differ for Japanese and non-Japanese firms.[17]

Detailed examination of individual companies provides additional insight into the drivers of supply relationships. Of the 32 procurement decisions by Hitachi in the data, only one is from an external supplier (Sharp). It was for a display both smaller and of lower resolution than the state of the art. Hitachi was a technical leader during this period, ranking 3rd or 4th in terms of number of display-related patents, which may explain its preference for internal procurement.

Technical strength alone does not explain NEC's behavior, however. NEC ranked between 6th and 10th in number of display-related patents over this period, yet displays for 72 out of 85 models were procured internally. Of the 13 it procured externally, 12 were passive matrix,[18] an older, less technically demanding technology, which NEC had exited. NEC sourced all of its innovative active matrix displays internally.

Toshiba is closer to the conventional image of a Japanese firm: It procured displays for almost half of its models (67 out of 148) from its only external suppliers, Sharp and Sanyo. Despite this general pattern, its behavior when procuring displays for which the necessary technology did not already exist resembled that of Hitachi and NEC. Of 12 such displays, 8 were procured internally.

Table 8. Impact of Uncertainty on Internal Procurement, 1992–1998 (2).

	Japanese Manufacturer		Other Manufacturer	
	External Supplier	Internal Supplier	External Supplier	Internal Supplier
Low uncertainty	50.0	50.0	91.8	8.2
High uncertainty	14.3	85.7	76.9	23.1

Note: Figures indicate the percentage of displays sourced from each type of supplier. High uncertainty: new production process required.

Only 1 of the externally procured displays was active matrix (procured from Sharp). Two passive matrix displays came from Sanyo and one from Sharp.

These findings are largely in keeping with other recent research. Lincoln and Ahmadjian (2000) found a higher level of vertical integration within the electronics industry in general than in the automotive industry. Chesbrough (1997) found that Toshiba depended on internal production for 63% of 2.5-inch disk drives it procured, while Fujitsu and Hitachi sourced approximately half of their 2.5-inch drives internally. The level of internalization I observe in display procurement is more extreme than either of these papers' findings.

Discussion

Long-term supply relationships with a small number of suppliers play an important role for both automobile and notebook computer manufacturers in Japan. While automobile manufacturers are able to use these relationships to delegate design and production of even complex components to external suppliers, a high degree of internal production characterizes the Japanese notebook computer industry. This is true even for companies lagging behind the technical frontier.

These two industries operate within the same economic and institutional environment. Given this, we can conclude that the pattern observed in the automobile industry is not an inevitable outcome of its Japanese institutional environment. Two inter-related differences between the automotive and notebook computer industries can explain the divergence in supply relationships: the distribution of capabilities among suppliers and the speed of technical progress. These differences affect the size of the supplier pool, the availability of shareholding and *shukko* as tools to deepen relationships, and the adequacy of these tools to manage the governance and communications difficulties inherent in procuring components externally.

Relative to most automotive components, the technical expertise required to manufacture flat panel displays is highly concentrated in a relatively few companies. Patenting activity in the United States provides several ways to gauge how widely distributed the required technical knowledge is. At a broad level, 877 companies had at least one patent in U.S. Patent Class 123 (internal combustion engines) between 1992 and 1998, 556 had a patent in Class 188 (Brakes), but many fewer, 327 firms, had a patent in Class 349 (liquid crystal displays). More revealing is the concentration of technical capabilities among industry leaders. The 10 companies with the most patents in brakes combine to make up only 23% of all brake patents, while the top 10 patenting companies in engines generate 38% of all engine patents. In flat panel displays, however, this figure is much higher, 47%.

Furthermore, the high cost of establishing a new fabrication line (up to $1 billion) limits the possibility of new entrants. Together, these factors limit the number of potential display suppliers from which a notebook computer maker can choose.

Another important consideration is that many potential display suppliers are also manufacturers of notebook computers. The nine top patenting companies that manufacture displays also make notebook computers.[19] By comparison, the top 10 engine patenting companies include Bosch, Sanshin, Nippondenso, and Caterpillar, which are not direct competitors for automotive customers. Among brake firms, only two of the top ten patenting firms produce automobiles: General Motors and Nissan. Major independent brake suppliers include Allied Signal, Westinghouse, Tokiko and Eaton.

The concentration of the supply base is accompanied by a much faster rate of technical progress in the notebook computer industry than in the automobile industry. For example, Japanese automobile makers aim at major model changes every 4 years. Transmission designs have a life of approximately 8 years and engines parts a life of 7–10 years (Asanuma, 1992). By comparison, in the 6 years from 1992 to 1998, displays in notebook computers moved from being dominated by 9.5-inch monochrome VGA (640×480 pixels) passive matrix displays to 14-inch color XGA (1024×768 pixels) active matrix displays. Display area increased 299%, and resolution increased 250%. Display makers developed three new generations of fabrication equipment over 6 years to accomplish these advances.

Buyer-supplier communication is difficult under rapid technical progress because the codification of language lags behind the advance of the technical frontier. Japanese automakers use long-term relationships and *shukko* to enable collaboration with external suppliers in similar situations. This approach is less effective when dealing with a supplier that is also a competitor. *Shukko* is unlikely between competitors, given the possibility of information leakage (Lincoln & Ahmadjian, 2000). As a result, firms have fewer opportunities to build a common language and communication routines with suppliers-cum-competitors.

The same factors complicate the governance of supply relationships in the notebook computer industry. Beyond the direct effect of higher uncertainty, Japanese notebook computer makers do not have access to many of the mechanisms used by automobile manufacturers. When working with a direct competitor, firms lose access to shareholding, whether to align incentives or for symbolic purposes. Restraints on *shukko* degrade not only communication, but also the development of trust by limiting interaction between individuals at the buyer and supplier. This is consistent with Chesbrough's (1997) finding that Japanese notebook computer manufacturers purchase from non-affiliated suppliers more when the number of such suppliers increased.

In summary, automakers can draw upon a large pool of potential suppliers, building long-term relationships accompanied by shareholding and/or *shukko* with the most important ones. They are likely to find an appropriate supplier for a given component or innovation among its close suppliers. Even complex and innovative automotive components may have a sufficiently low uncertainty that collaboration with an unfamiliar supplier is manageable. Thus, automobile manufacturers take advantage of long-term relationships but are not limited by them.

Japanese notebook computer makers have a greater challenge and fewer Japanese-style tools to address that problem. There is a smaller pool of display suppliers from which to draw. Many of the best suppliers are also competitors, further limiting the candidates with whom a manufacturer can build strong relationships that would include *shukko* and shareholding. As a result, Japanese notebook computer makers are often unable to find the capabilities necessary for a given component or innovation among their close suppliers. Handicapped in reaching out beyond this set of suppliers, manufacturers are pushed towards internal supply. This is especially likely to be the case for breakthrough technologies and other complex transactions. In essence, each notebook computer manufacturer may be the best potential supplier of those it can easily reach.

CONCLUSION

This research addresses a major gap in our understanding of Japanese supply relationships. Despite calls for attention to the diversity of supply relationships in Japan, our understanding of these relationships still derives overwhelmingly from a single industry, automobiles.

This chapter combines prior theoretical work with a large-scale empirical study to document a pattern of supply relationships very different from the commonly accepted view of Japanese manufacturing and to derive potential explanations for that difference. Doing so provides a more nuanced view of Japanese supply relationships, and also suggests when "Japanese-style" supply relationships – long-term, predominantly relational rather than contractual – are unlikely to succeed.

The environmental constraints governing the Japanese automotive and notebook computer industries are the same: limited labor mobility, low generalized trust when sanctioning is not possible, and a shortage of transaction cost engineers such as lawyers. However, there are also distinct differences between the two industries. Compared to automobile makers, notebook computer manufacturers compete in a faster-moving industry with far fewer players. As a result, the imperatives of the Japanese institutional environment constrain them in ways that do not constrain automobile manufacturers. Consequentially, two very different patterns of supply relationships emerge.

Several insights derive from the findings of this study. The findings reinforce and amplify the call for examining supply relationship in other industries. The findings also make clear that industry specific factors require careful consideration. Based on the display industry, the speed of technical progress and the availability of independent suppliers are likely to be important. Nevertheless, key factors will likely vary across industries.

More generally, the study emphasizes how the impact of economic and social institutions can only be understood in the context of specific industries. At the same time, we can only generalize studies of individual industries if we understand industry-specific practices in the context of macro-level economic and social factors. We cannot assume that the rules by which the companies compete are the same across industries.

The performance of the Japanese automobile industry has encouraged many non-Japanese firm to move towards "Japanese-style" supply relationships, long-term and highly collaborative (Dyer, 1996b; Helper, 1991). This study suggests limits on the usefulness of these relationships. Success will only follow if social, economic, and technical factors allow the development of supporting mechanisms, such as shareholding and the exchange of personnel.

There are also policy implications within Japan. Attempts to "rationalize" Japanese buyer-supplier relationships by deconstructing elements of the old system, such as loosening cross-shareholding ties, may succeed only to the degree that other mechanisms arise to take their place.

Lastly, the study refines our understanding of the boundaries of the firm in the face of technical progress. Keeping pace with rapid change requires firms to invest heavily and to maintain a wider range of competencies than might normally be considered optimal. It also puts the firm at risk of being integrated into a technology that is superseded by technology that draws upon different competencies (Afuah, 2001). As a result, prior work suggests that firms generally avoid vertical integration in the face of rapid technical change (Balakrishnan & Wernerfelt, 1986). However, social, economic and industry-specific factors may make this strategy impracticable. Even if a Japanese notebook manufacturer wanted to exit the display market, there would not be enough suppliers with which they could develop the close relationships necessary to deal with high uncertainty. While it may not be possible to increase the number of suppliers within an industry, factors such as the reliability of formal dispute resolution mechanisms, e.g. the courts, are within the control of policy-makers.

The diversity of supply relationships in Japan provides an opportunity to understand interfirm dynamics under different social, economic and technical conditions. One avenue of research would be to study additional industries. From this perspective, low-technology industries and those in which Japan is not internationally competitive (e.g. textiles) may be as potentially interesting as automobiles, electronics, and biotechnology. Another avenue would be to examine relationships within a single industry in much greater depth. Consider the range of components required to make a notebook computer – hard drives, displays, batteries, hinges, keyboards, and plastic cases. Holding the end product constant would allow a better understanding of supply relationships across these highly diverse components.

NOTES

1. Early work by Asanuma on the electronics industry has not been systematically extended. Smitka (1991) drew attention to the existence of intra- and interdiversity in Japanese supply relationships and provided brief, insightful examples of diverse supply relationships in several industries. In one of the few large-scale empirical studies of supply relationships outside of the automobile industry, Chesbrough (1997) studied hard-drive procurement decisions by notebook computer-makers. His work did not, however, attempt to explain why relationships varied between the computer and automobile industries. Ahmadjian and Lincoln (2000) explored changing supply relationships in the electronics industry. Guillot and Lincoln (2005) examine relationships in the TV industry, while Cusumano (1991) discusses the software industry.

2. Under-appreciation of heterogeneity among Japanese industries and companies is not limited to supply relationships. For example, Pekkanen and Solis (2004) are among the first to explore inter- and intra-industry heterogeneity in attitudes towards trade policy.

3. Despite the attention paid to these close relationships, there is a spectrum of supply relationships, even in the automobile industry. Suppliers range from "quasi-integrated subcontractor" (Carroll & Hannan, 2000), falling between the standard definition of internal and external supplier because of its close ties to a manufacturer, to independent suppliers that sell to multiple manufacturers, even if they have some ties to a manufacturer, e.g. Denso and Toyota (Ahmadjian & Lincoln, 2001)

4. Dyer and Chu (2000) found no relationship between stock ownership and trust in a study of the Japanese automobile supply industry. They speculate that this might reflect a degradation of shareholding's importance over time, shareholding's role as a replacement for trust, or their specific definition of trust. They do not rule out stock holding having a positive impact on cooperative supply relationships.

5. Interestingly, other activities can also contribute to commonality of technical cultures across companies. Examples include interaction with a few large suppliers/customers that are common across an industry, industry associations with their standards committees, professional associations and associated meetings, and use of common specialist service providers, e.g. software or test equipment. Such activities are widespread in Japan and other countries, making it likely that limited employee mobility creates a relative disadvantage for Japanese companies in this dimension. This area is worth future exploration.

6. Milhaupt and West indicate several reasons, including the presence of quasi-attorneys in Japan, that this figure is not as striking as it might seem. Nonetheless, they argue that it remains significant. The issue has recently attracted attention in the popular press also, e.g. Magnier (2001).

7. Ramseyer and Nakazato (1989) use data on litigation after fatal car crashes to argue that the predictability of settlement amounts awarded by Japanese judges is responsible for the low rate of litigation. Because both sides of potential litigation can predict the outcome, devise a private settlement based on that outcome, and avoid the costs and delays of litigation. Whether this reasoning is generally accurate or not (see Hamada, 2000 for a rebuttal of Ramseyer & Nakazato), the complex and idiosyncratic nature of new product development makes it unlikely to apply in that setting.

8. This is not to argue that the courts are an appealing avenue for dispute resolution in high technology, even in the United States. However, multiple cases demonstrate that U.S. high-technology firms can and do use the courts to resolve a variety of conflicts. Examples include Macromedia's patent litigation against Adobe (Macromedia wins $4.9m in Adobe patent suit, 2002), the suit and counter-suit between Tellabs and Riverstone regarding Riverstone's alleged failure to deliver a cable modem termination system of sufficient quality (Weber, 2001), and 3Dfx's suit against Sega and NEC over Sega's cancellation of its contract with 3Dfx, which had agreed to develop a 3-D graphics accelerator chipset for Sega's next-generation home game console (3Dfx sues Sega, NEC over contract, 1997). The amount of formal litigation may understate the difference between the importance of the courts in Japan and the U.S., since the credible threat of litigating may push parties towards private settlement.

9. p (Japanese use of current supplier > non-Japanese use of current supplier) < 0.001.

10. p (Japanese > non-Japanese) < 0.001.

11. p (non-Japanese > Japanese) $= 0.006$.

12. p (non-Japanese > Japanese) $= 0.004$.

13. Note that my results refer to all long-term suppliers, a broader set of suppliers than "affiliated suppliers."

14. Lincoln and Ahmadjian offer the relatively high modularity of electronics components, which enables "off-the-shelf" buying, as a partial explanation of more distant supplier relationships. As discussed above, displays are significantly less modular than this description. This difference may explain my finding of close supply relationships for this specific component.

15. p (Japanese > non-Japanese) < 0.001.

16. Using additive and multiplicative uniform layer models (Goodman & Hout, 1998), it is not possible to reject the null hypotheses that the relationship between uncertainty and internal innovation is the same at conventional levels of significance. The hypothesis that the relationship between uncertainty and use of external suppliers differs for Japanese and non-Japanese firms is rejected at the 0.01 level of significance.

17. Again, both additive and multiplicative uniform layer models (Goodman & Hout, 1998), fail to reject the null hypotheses that the relationship between uncertainty and internal innovation is the same. The hypothesis that the relationship between uncertainty and use of external suppliers differs for Japanese and non-Japanese firms is rejected at the 0.01 level of significance.

18. There are two dominant technologies used in flat panel displays for notebook computers, passive- and active-matrix liquid crystal displays (LCD). Passive-matrix,

although less expensive, has several drawbacks: It relies on ambient lighting, can be difficult to see from an angle, and is subject to "ghosting," the faint afterimage of a rapidly moving cursor. Active-matrix, also known as thin-film transistor liquid crystal display (TFT-LCD), is considerably more complex and expensive. However, it allows the use of a backlight, freeing the user from dependence on ambient lighting. It is also capable of a much faster display and is thus appropriate for full-motion video and other modern multimedia applications. It can also be viewed from a wider angle. Currently, almost all notebook computers use active matrix displays. Passive matrix displays appear only in applications such as PDAs and cell phones.

19. The other top 10 patenting firm, Semiconductor Energy Lab, is not a potential display supplier. It has no manufacturing capabilities and exists purely to generate and license intellectual property.

ACKNOWLEDGMENTS

My understanding of the industry draws upon discussions with numerous industry informants including Dr Steven Depp of IBM; Mark Fihn, Barry Young, and Steve Young of DisplaySearch; David Menteley of Stanford Resources; Takeshi Kawamoto and Takafuji Kakudo at Japan's Ministry of International Trade and Industry (now METI); and several others who wished to remain anonymous. Partial support from the University of Michigan Center for International Business Education and the Asia Technology Information Program is gratefully acknowledged. Comments by Tom Roehl, Mark D. West, Mike Smitka, Saadia Pekkanen, and participants at the Columbia University/George Washington University Japan Economic Seminar and anonymous referees have greatly improved the paper. Any errors are my own.

REFERENCES

3Dfx sues Sega, NEC over contract (1997). *Electronic News, 43*(2184), 8–9.

Afuah, A. (2001). Dynamic boundaries of the firm: Are firms better off being vertically integrated in the face of a technological change? *Academy of Management Journal, 44*(6), 1211–1228.

Ahmadjian, C. L., & Lincoln, J. R. (2001). Keiretsu, governance, and learning: Case studies in change from the Japanese automotive industry. *Organization Science, 12*(6), 683–701.

Asanuma, B. (1992). Japanese manufacturer-supplier relationships in international perspective: The automobile case. In: P. Sheard (Ed.), *International Adjustment and the Japanese Firm* (pp. 99–124). St Leonards, NSW, Australia: Allen & Unwin in association with the Australia-Japan Research Centre, the Australian National University.

Asanuma, B. (1998). Nihon ni okeru meekaa to sapuraiyaa to no kankei [The manufacturer-supplier relationship in Japan]. In: T. Fujimoto, T. Nishiguchi, and H. Ito (Eds), *Supuraiyaa Shisutemu* [Supplier system] (pp. 1–39). Tokyo: Yuhikaku.

Asanuma, B., & Kikutani, T. (1992). Risk absorption in Japanese subcontracting: A microeconometric study of the automobile industry. *Journal of the Japanese and International Economy, 6,* 1–29.

Balakrishnan, S., & Wernerfelt, B. (1986). Technical change, competition and vertical integration. *Strategic Management Journal, 7*(4), 347–359.

Buckley, P., & Casson, M. (1976). *The future of multinational enterprise.* London: Macmillan.

Carroll, G. R., & Hannan, M. T. (2000). *The demography of corporations and industries.* Princeton, NJ: Princeton University Press.

Chesbrough, H. W. (1997). *Dynamic coordination and creative destruction: A comparative analysis of incumbent success and failure in the worldwide hard disk drive industry.* Unpublished doctoral dissertation, University of California, Berkeley.

Clark, K., & Fujimoto, T. (1991). *Product development in the world automobile industry.* Boston: Harvard Business School Press.

Cooter, R., & Landa, J. T. (1984). Personal versus impersonal trade: The size of trading groups and contract law. *International Review of Law and Economics, 15,* 4–22.

Cusumano, M. (1985). *The Japanese automobile industry: Technology and management at Nissan and Toyota.* Cambridge, MA: Harvard University Press.

Cusumano, M. A., & Takeishi, A. (1991). Supplier relations and management: A survey of Japanese, Japanese-transplant, and U.S. auto plants. *Strategic Management Journal, 12,* 563–588.

Dodwell Marketing Consultants (1995). *The structure of the Japanese auto parts industry* (5th ed.). Tokyo: Dodwell Marketing Consultants.

Dyer, J. (1996a). Does governance matter? Keiretsu alliances and asset specificity as sources of Japanese competitive advantage. *Organization Science, 7*(6), 649–666.

Dyer, J. (1996b). How Chrysler created an American keiretsu. *Harvard Business Review, 74*(4), 42–53.

Dyer, J. H., & Chu, W. J. (2000). The determinants of trust in supplier-automaker relationships in the US, Japan, and Korea. *Journal of International Business Studies, 31*(2), 259–285.

Dyer, J. H., & Ouchi, W. G. (1993). Japanese-style partnerships – giving companies a competitive edge. *Sloan Management Review, 35*(1), 51–63.

Ettlie, J. E. (1985). The impact of interorganizational manpower flows on the innovation process. *Management Science, 31,* 1055–1071.

Fukuyama, F. (1995). *Trust.* New York: Free Press.

Gerlach, M. (1987). Business alliances and the strategy of the Japanese firm. *California Management Review, 30*(1), 126–142.

Gerlach, M. (1992). The Japanese corporate network: A blockmodel analysis. *Administrative Science Quarterly, 37*(1), 105–139.

Gilson, R. (1984). Value creation by business lawyers: Legal skills and asset pricing. *Yale Law Journal, 94,* 239–255.

Gilson, R., & Roe, M. (1993). Understanding the Japanese keiretsu: Overlaps between corporate governance and industrial organization. *Yale Law Journal, 102,* 871–884.

Goodman, L. A., & Hout, M. (1998). Statistical methods and graphical displays for analyzing how the association between two qualitative variables differs among countries, among groups, or over time: A modified regression-type approach. *Sociological Methodology, 28,* 175–221.

Guillot, D., & Lincoln, J. (2005). Dyad and network: Models of manufacturer–supplier collaboration in the Japanese TV manufacturing industry. *Advances in International Management, 17,* 159–185.

Hall, B. H., Jaffe, A. B., & Trajtenberg, M. (2000). Market value and patent citations: A first look. National Bureau of Economic Research Working Paper W7441.

Hamada, K. (2000). Explaining the low litigation rate in Japan. In: M. Aoki & G. R. Saxonhouse (Eds), *Finance, Governance, and Competitiveness in Japan* (pp. 179–194). Oxford: Oxford University Press.

Helper, S. (1991). Have things really changed between automakers and their suppliers? *Sloan Management Review, 32*, 15–28.

Hoetker, G. P. (2001). *The impact of relational and technical capabilities on the procurement of technically innovative components in the U.S. and Japan.* Unpublished doctoral dissertation, University of Michigan.

Japan Fair Trade Commission [Kosei Torihiki Iinkai] (1993). *Jidosha buhin torihiki ni kan suru jittai chosa* [A survey of transactions of auto parts]. Tokyo: Kosei Torihiki Iinkai.

Johnson, P., Levine, D. K., & Woodruff, C. (2002). Courts and relational contracts. *Journal of Law and Economic Organization, 18*(1), 221–277.

Kogut, B., & Zander, U. (1996). What do firms do? Coordination, identity, and learning. *Organization Science, 7*(5), 502–518.

La Porta, R., Lopez-de-Silanes, F., Shleifer, A., & Vishny, R. (1997). Trust in large organizations. *American Economic Review Papers and Proceedings, 87*, 333–338.

Lincoln, E. J. (2001). *Arthritic Japan: The slow pace of economic reform.* Washington, DC: Brookings Institution Press.

Lincoln, J. R., & Ahmadjian, C. L. (2000). Shukko (employee transfers) and tacit knowledge exchange in Japanese supply networks: The electronics industry case. University of California, Berkeley: Institute of Industrial Relations Working Paper No. 75.

Macromedia wins $4.9m in Adobe patent suit (2002). *Multimedia Futures, 309*, 3.

Magnier, M. (2001, March 9). No joke: Send more lawyers: Attorneys are few in Japan, and that's a problem. Lawsuits have doubled, but courts don't have enough litigators. *Los Angeles Times*, sec. A, p. 1.

Masten, S. E. (1984). The organization of production: Evidence from the aerospace industry. *Journal of Law and Economics, 27*(2), 403–417.

Milhaupt, C. J., & West, M. D. (2000). The dark side of private ordering: An institutional and empirical analysis of organized crime. *The University of Chicago Law Review, 67*(1), 41–98.

Mitchell, W., & Singh, K. (1996). Precarious collaboration: Business survival after partners shut down or form new partnerships. *Strategic Management Journal, 17*(3), 95–115.

Miyazawa, S. (1995). Chapters 1.3 and 5.1. In: Y. Watanabe (Ed.), *Gendai Shiho* [Japanese judicial system]. Tokyo: Nihon Hyoronsha.

Morris, J., & Imrie, R. (1992). *Transforming buyer-supplier relations: Japanese-style industrial practices in a Western context.* Houndmills, UK: Macmillan.

Nishiguchi, T. (1994). *Strategic industrial sourcing.* New York: Oxford University Press.

Nonaka, I., & Takeuchi, H. (1995). *The knowledge-creating company: How Japanese companies create the dynamics of innovation.* New York: Oxford University Press.

Parkhe, A. (1993). Strategic alliance structuring: A game theoretic and transaction costs examination of interfirm cooperation. *Academy of Management Journal, 36*, 794–829.

Pekkanen, S., & Solis, M. (2004). The winds of change in Japanese trade policy: Textile multinationals and intra-industry clashes over market protection. *Advances in International Management, 17*, 89–111.

Ramseyer, J. M., & Nakazato, M. (1989). The rational litigant: Settlement amounts and verdict rates and Japan. *Journal of Legal Studies, 15*, 262–290.

Ring, P. S., & Van de Ven, A. H. (1994). Developmental processes of cooperative interorganizational relationships. *Academy of Management Review, 19*, 90–118.

Sako, M. (1992). *Prices, quality, and trust: Inter-firm relations in Britain and Japan.* Cambridge: Cambridge University Press.

Sako, M., & Helper, S. (1998). Determinants of trust in supplier relations: Evidence from the automotive industry in Japan and the United States. *Journal of Economic Behavior & Organization, 34*(3), 387–417.

Smitka, M. (1991). *Competitive ties: Subcontracting in the Japanese automotive industry.* New York: Columbia University Press.

Smitka, M. J. (1994). Contracting without contracts: How the Japanese manage organizational transactions. In: S. B. Sitkin & R. J. Bies (Eds), *The Legalistic Organization.* Thousands Oaks, CA: Sage.

Smitka, M. J. (2002). Adjustment in the Japanese automotive industry: A microcosm of Japanese cyclical and structural change? An unpublished Working Paper. It is available at http://home.wlu.edu/~smitkam/autoswithgraphs.pdf.

Spencer, J. W. (1997). *Firms' strategies in the global innovation system: Knowledge sharing in the flat panel display industry.* Unpublished doctoral dissertation, University Of Minnesota.

Wasti, S. N., & Liker, J. K. (1999). Collaborating with suppliers in product development: A U.S. and Japan comparative study. *IEEE Transactions on Engineering Management, 46*(4), 444–461.

Weber, T. (2001). Contract leads to suit, countersuit. *Telephony, 241*(11), 22.

Williamson, O. E. (1985). *The economic institutions of capitalism.* New York: Free Press.

Yamagishi, T. (1988). The provision of a sanctioning system in the United States and Japan. *Social Psychology Quarterly, 51*(3), 265–271.

Yamagishi, T., Cook, K. S., & Watabe, M. (1998). Uncertainty, trust, and commitment formation in the United States and Japan. *American Journal of Sociology, 104*(1), 165–194.

Zaheer, A., McEvily, B., & Perrone, V. (1998). Does trust matter? Exploring the effects of interorganizational and interpersonal trust on performance. *Organization Science, 9*(2), 141–159.

PART III: MNCs ON FOREIGN SOIL

In this section, we examine MNCs operating outside their home country, with three papers focusing on Japanese firms overseas and one on foreign firms operating in Japan. Beechler, Pucik, Stephan, and Campbell tackle a longstanding sore spot in the international management of Japanese corporations: to explain Japanese overseas affiliate performance and Japanese expatriate staffing patterns. Their findings point to the struggle Japanese MNCs face as they strive to make a transition from "multinational" to "transnational." They conclude by noting that the primary challenge for Japanese companies is in growing a cadre of managers possessing transnational skills through providing opportunities for local executives to develop capabilities such that they can fill the role of transnational integrators.

Yoshihara focuses on the performance deficit of Japanese MNCs as their performance in Asia declines, something he anticipated in the 1980s (Bartlett & Yoshihara, 1988). His analysis concludes that the essential elements of "Japanese style international management" – management *by* Japanese *in* Japanese *from* Japanese headquarters *in* Japan was successful in the past, but is now being overtaken by a newer Asian style that has more in common with Western approaches to management.

Beechler, Levy, Taylor, and Boyaçigiller, finding structural responses to globalization inadequate, turn to the development among managers of a global mindset in response to increasing pressures of international competition. After finding that perceptions of top management's global orientation influence employee attitudes, Beechler and her colleagues note that Japanese firms may be able to overcome their management liabilities by leveraging the information sharing orientation of "traditional" Japanese management. That managerial liabilities may hold the seeds of managerial strength constitutes an insight that might also be applied to non-Japanese MNCs.

Firms operating in Japan face their own challenges in response to Japan's decade long recession. Asaba and Yamawaki investigate the performance of Japan-based foreign subsidiaries and find that size and amount of experience are influential in determining foreign subsidiary success in Japan. Their more interesting finding is that foreign subsidiary performance tracked overall industry (i.e. domestic rivals') performance during the 1980s but diverged in the 1990s, either improving or remaining flat as Japanese firms' performance declined, leading to speculation that foreign subsidiaries have become more competitive.

THE TRANSNATIONAL CHALLENGE: PERFORMANCE AND EXPATRIATE PRESENCE IN THE OVERSEAS AFFILIATES OF JAPANESE MNCs

Schon Beechler, Vladimir Pucik, John Stephan and Nigel Campbell

ABSTRACT

Drawing on empirical data from two studies of 119 Japanese affiliates located in the United States and Europe, this chapter focuses on three fundamental questions: (1) What organizational factors influence performance of the overseas affiliates of Japanese MNCs? (2) What impact does expatriate staffing have on the affiliate's performance? (3) What factors influence expatriate staffing patterns in Japanese MNCs? The empirical results lend support to the hypothesis that MNCs characterized by global integration and local responsiveness will outperform less transnational competitors, although there are significant differences between the American and European subsamples on the impact of expatriate presence on affiliate performance. In addition, there is no support for the life-cycle prediction that age or parent company experience influences expatriate staffing levels or for the resource dependence prediction that integration with the parent influences expatriate presence. These results and their implications are discussed.

Japanese Firms in Transition: Responding to the Globalization Challenge
Advances in International Management, Volume 17, 215–242
Copyright © 2005 by Elsevier Ltd.
All rights of reproduction in any form reserved
ISSN: 0747-7929/doi:10.1016/S0747-7929(04)17009-1

INTRODUCTION

Beginning with the pioneering work in international strategy of Bartlett and Ghoshal (1987, 1988, 1989), it has now become accepted wisdom that the winners on today's global economic playing field will be those "transnational" firms which can simultaneously integrate their global operations and respond to local conditions, balancing the complementary and contradictory imperatives of organizational integration and differentiation (Evans & Doz, 1989; Evans, Pucik & Barsoux, 2002; Lawrence & Lorsch, 1967). While the organizational capability to simultaneously balance global integration and local responsiveness is seen as essential to implementing globally competitive strategies, this capability is not easily developed or sustained by multinational corporations (MNCs) (Bartlett & Ghoshal, 1989; Evans, 1993; Evans et al., 2002; Pucik, Tichy & Barnett, 1992).

Although they have made rapid progress during the past decade, most observers agree that Japanese multinational companies have had a particularly difficult time making the transition to transnational status (e.g. DeNero, 1993; Kono & Clegg, 2001; Kopp, 1994, 1999; Rudlin, 2000; Whitehill, 1991; Yoshihara, 1996). These arguments are consistent with a long-held view that Japanese firms have lagged far behind their Western counterparts in their ability to manage international operations (e.g. Campbell & Holden, 1993; Kobayashi, 1985; Tachiki, 1991; Trevor, 1983; Yoshino, 1976), and have experienced relatively low levels of profitability from their investments abroad (Harzing, 1999; MITI, 1994; Pucik, 1999; Wilkins, 1994).

At the same time, there are a number of overseas success stories. Previous studies of Japanese overseas affiliates have attempted to show that these companies are successful mostly because of factors associated with "exporting" Japanese management techniques, such as manufacturing techniques (e.g. Adler, 1993; Cusumano, 1988; Kenney & Florida, 1993; Kenney, Romero, Contreras & Bustos, 1999; Kujawa, 1986; Petersen, Peng & Smith, 1999), quality control (e.g. Ebrahimpour & Cullen, 1993; Sako, 1994), training and development (e.g. Abo, 1994; Kujawa, 1983; Wakabayashi & Graen, 1991) and careful socialization of local employees (e.g. Baliga & Jaeger, 1984; Beechler & Yang, 1994; Brannen & Salk, 1999; Kidd, 1999; Taylor, 1999; Tung, 1982).

As a number of authors have noted, however, while Japanese firms have been adept at exporting systems from the parent company, enabling them to integrate their international operations globally (Johansson & Yip, 1994), they have had a particularly difficult time behaving in a locally responsive way (e.g. Bartlett & Yoshihara, 1988; Fuchini & Fuchini, 1990; Ishida, 1986; Westney, 1993). The source of this difficulty has often been identified as Japanese MNCs' unwillingness or inability to recruit, retain and motivate capable local managers who have the expertise to adapt affiliate operations to the host-country environment (e.g. March, 1992; Paik & Teagarden, 1995; Pucik, 1999; Tachiki, 1991; Yoshihara, 1996).

Indeed, almost since the inception of Japanese MNC overseas ventures, academics, government officials, and citizens from around the world have commented and criticized them for the large number of Japanese expatriates they employ in their overseas affiliates (Yoshino, 1976). The "bamboo ceiling" (Boyacigiller, 1990a), or "rice paper ceiling" (Kopp, 1999) has become synonymous with Japanese investment abroad. However, there is little empirical work examining performance outcomes of these practices (for a notable exception, see Yoshihara, 1996).

In this chapter, we draw on several distinct research streams in the international management literature to address three basic questions: What organizational factors influence performance of the overseas affiliates of Japanese multinational corporations? What impact does Japanese expatriate staffing patterns have on the affiliate's performance. What factors influence expatriate presence? While these three questions have been asked in isolation by previous researchers, this study examines all three questions simultaneously and therefore represents a first step in developing a better understanding of a complex and dynamic phenomenon.

PREVIOUS RESEARCH AND THEORETICAL FRAMEWORK

In this chapter, we draw on two complementary approaches to propose a multilevel model of affiliate performance, linking the organizational control configurations embedded in Bartlett and Ghoshal's work in international competitive strategy (Bartlett & Ghoshal, 1987, 1989, 1992), with organizational demographic factors derived from the international life-cycle theory (Adler & Ghadar, 1989; Dowling & Schuler, 1990; Franko, 1973; Milliman, Von Glinow & Nathan, 1991) and the resource-dependence framework (Aldrich, 1976; Pfeffer, 1992; Pfeffer & Salancik, 1978).

Predictors of Performance

Porter (1986) suggests that industries can be roughly divided into multidomestic industries, in which firms compete against each other locally, uninfluenced by competitive dynamics in other countries, and global industries in which competition in one country influences or is influenced by competition in other parts of the world. Traditionally, much of Japanese manufacturing FDI was concentrated in global industries, such as electronics or automotive, driven primarily by export substitution strategies (Imai, 1993).

Beginning with Bartlett and Ghoshal (1987), a number of authors have suggested that firms competing in global industries which are able to develop the organizational capability to complement global integration with local responsiveness will be most successful (Maljers, 1992; Taylor, 1991b), and this capability has been assessed from several theoretical perspectives (Egelhoff, 1993; Hedlund, 1993; Hennart, 1993). However, it is telling that the leading popular slogan of the transnational era, "Think globally, act locally," actually originated in Japan.

While the dual imperatives of global integration and local responsiveness have been popularized at the corporate level, it is clear that operationally, they are local phenomena. Recent thinking in the strategy literature holds that it is imperative to look at strategies not at the firm level, but at a more micro level of analysis (Govindarajan & Gupta, 1985; Rosenzweig & Singh, 1991). Only a local affiliate can be simultaneously globally integrated and locally responsive (see also Gupta & Govindarajan, 1991; Milliman et al., 1991). While Bartlett and Ghoshal do not argue that all affiliates in an MNC need to be simultaneously globally integrated and locally responsive, we propose that large, well-established affiliates located in major markets, such as those included in this study, do need to be both integrated with their parent company and locally responsive. Thus, we hypothesize that:

H1. For Japanese MNCs operating in global industries, those affiliates that simultaneously exhibit high levels of integration with the rest of the parent firm and high levels of local responsiveness will have higher levels of performance than affiliates with low levels of integration and/or responsiveness.

In addition to global integration and local responsiveness, an affiliate's performance may also be influenced by the presence of expatriates stationed at the affiliate. In this chapter, we build on the work of Boyacigiller (1990a, b) and others (e.g. Kopp, 1999; Taylor, 1991a) to examine both the predictors of and performance outcomes from the staffing policies in Japanese affiliates overseas. Is the assumption, often made but not tested, that the presence of Japanese expatriates enhances global integration but impedes local responsiveness correct? What impact, if any, does the presence of Japanese expatriates have on the performance of the affiliate?

The hypothesized relationship regarding the impact of expatriates on affiliate performance is not straightforward. On the one hand, the international human-resource management literature describes a number of serious problems associated with expatriate-intensive staffing practices, including discontent, low morale, and high turnover among local managers (e.g. Bob & SRI, 1990; Kopp, 1999;

Nakamura, 2000; Pucik et al., 1989; Zeira, 1976). In addition, the use of expatriates may be associated with reduced levels of local responsiveness, leading to lower levels of affiliate and MNC performance (Konomoto, 2000; Pucik, 1999).

At the same time, the international strategy literature postulates that in global industries, high levels of global integration, facilitated by a global network of mobile managers, is critical to MNC success. Too few expatriates can make it difficult for the parent firm to implement its global competitive strategies in an effective manner (Amako, 1991; Evans, Pucik & Barsoux, 2002; Kobrin, 1988; Pucik, 1992).

One way for MNCs to get around this dilemma is to use a truly international cadre of managers to create a global human network across the firm (Evans, 1993; Pucik et al., 1992). However, despite exhortations to the contrary, in most Japanese firms today, it is still primarily Japanese expatriates who make up this international cadre of mobile managers. While the use of expatriates should increase the capability of the organization for global integration through a network of Japanese managers, the use of expatriates to make local decisions and the concomitant constraint on making full use of the talents of local managers may be the "Achilles Heel" of Japanese MNCs (Bartlett & Yoshihara, 1988), negatively influencing their adaptability to local conditions. While there are clearly both benefits and drawbacks to using expatriates to staff local affiliate positions, we believe that the performance effects overall will be negative. Hence, we hypothesize that:

H2. The higher the ratio of expatriates to local nationals in the overseas affiliate, the lower the affiliate's performance.

Affiliate performance can also be influenced by various demographic factors. Drawing on life-cycle theories of internationalization (e.g. Adler & Ghadar, 1989; Dowling & Schuler, 1990; Franko, 1973; Milliman et al., 1991), we start with the premise that MNCs go through a predictable series of stages in their development. According to this school of thought, international experience and expertise are developed over time, and thus, the age and experience of the firm are critical factors that are hypothesized to influence both the management and the performance outcomes in affiliates. Consequently, affiliate age and the MNC's international experience can be thought of as organizational resources that should have a moderating and a positive impact on affiliate performance:

H3a. The older the affiliate, the higher its level of performance.

H3b. The greater the MNC's experience in a host country, the higher the affiliate's level of performance.

Another important factor that may influence affiliate performance is the size of the organization. In general, the greater the size of the organization, the more organizational resources it has and the greater its ability to buffer its core from fluctuations in the external environment (Thompson, 1967). We would therefore predict that:

H4. Organizational size will be positively associated with affiliate performance.

Predictors of Expatriate Presence

If the presence of home-country expatriates influences affiliate performance, as we have argued, what factors influence expatriate presence? Although most writers agree that there have long been expatriate-intensive (ethnocentric) staffing practices in Japanese MNCs (e.g. Boyacigiller, 1990a; Kopp, 1999; Negandhi, 1979; Trevor, 1983; Yoshino, 1976), there is considerable debate as to both the antecedents and the outcomes of these policies.

Following a life-cycle argument (Franko, 1973; Milliman et al., 1991), a number of authors have argued that expatriate-intensive staffing patterns in Japanese MNCs are due to the inexperience of Japanese firms overseas (e.g. Emmott, 1992; Ichimura, 1981). Over time, Japanese companies, as they gain greater levels of experience abroad, will reduce the number of expatriates and "localize" their overseas operations (Beamish & Inkpen, 1998; Ichimura, 1981), just as American and European MNCs have done (Franko, 1973; Kobrin, 1988). Authors writing about MNCs in general have noted that firms have a tendency to use large numbers of expatriates during start-up (e.g. Franko, 1973) and when the MNC is in its early stages of internationalization (Perlmutter, 1969). This is due to the fact that early in their life cycle, MNCs are usually characterized by an ethnocentric culture (Perlmutter & Heenan, 1979), and their preoccupation is with short-term objectives (Adler & Ghadar, 1989; Dowling & Schuler, 1990; Harzing, 1999; Milliman et al., 1991; Taylor et al., 1996).

However, a number of authors, drawing primarily on small sample studies, have found that contrary to American, British, and German MNCs, which gradually moved toward staffing policies that progressively limit expatriates, the Japanese still prefer to use Japanese nationals (Boyacigiller, 1990a; Kopp, 1994, 1999; Oddou, Gregersen, Black & Derr, 2001; Stening & Everett, 1984; Trevor, 1983). At the same time, one recent study has found that over time, Japanese MNCs are reducing their expatriate presence overseas (e.g. Beamish & Inkpen, 1998).

We therefore predict that although Japanese MNCs may have more expatriate-intensive staffing policies than their American or European counterparts, when we look only at comparisons between Japanese firms, we would expect those MNCs with more age and experience in the host country to use fewer expatriates than their younger and less experienced counterparts. We therefore predict that:

H5a. The younger the affiliate, the more expatriates will be used to staff affiliate positions.

H5b. The fewer the number of years of experience of the parent company in the host country, the more expatriates will be used to staff affiliate positions.

Although age and international experience should decrease the reliance on expatriates to staff overseas affiliate positions, there are a number of other factors that may lead MNCs to use a larger number of expatriates in their overseas affiliates. Drawing again on the arguments of Bartlett and Ghoshal (e.g. Bartlett & Ghoshal, 1989), expatriates should increase the capability of the organization to integrate its operations globally since these human resources generally form an international cadre which functions as a critical linking mechanism across interdependent subunits within the MNC (Bartlett & Ghoshal, 1989; Edstrom & Galbraith, 1976; Evans et al., 2002; Pucik et al., 1992).

In addition, expatriates can be used as a mechanism of organizational control (Beechler, 1990; Boyacigiller, 1990b; Brewster, 1991; Edstrom & Galbraith, 1976; Harzing, 1999; Jaeger, 1983; Sohn, 1994). One useful framework to predict the use of control mechanisms by a parent company over its overseas affiliates is the resource-dependence approach (Aldrich, 1979, 1976; Pfeffer, 1992; Salancik & Pfeffer, 1978). This approach is based on the premise that an organization is unable to generate all of the resources necessary to maintain it and is therefore dependent on other actors in its environment. Organizational stakeholders will attempt to initiate control over the actors with whom they have exchanges in order to ensure that the resources necessary to achieve organizational objectives are obtained in an effective and efficient manner (Anthony, 1965; Green & Welsh, 1988).

According to this framework, there are three key factors that determine the dependence of one factor on another (Pfeffer & Salancik, 1978). First is the importance or *criticality* of the resource to the continued operation and survival of the operation (Thompson, 1967). Second is the extent to which an interest group (or individual) has *discretion* over the resource's allocation and use (Pfeffer & Salancik, 1978). Finally, resource dependence is determined by the extent to which alternatives to the resource are available (Pfeffer & Salancik, 1978; Thompson, 1967), that is, its rareness (Barney, 1991).

Because an MNC relies on its overseas affiliate for certain essential resources, it is dependent to varying degrees on the resources controlled by its affiliates. As an MNC's dependence increases, the more control the company will want to exercise over its affiliates (Beechler & Yang, 1994; Gupta & Govindarajan, 1991). Although large affiliates will tend to have more power than small affiliates vis-à-vis their parent organizations because they control a larger pool of resources (Doz & Prahalad, 1981), large affiliates will also be subjected to greater degrees of control by the parent. Staffing key affiliate positions with expatriates may be one way to exercise control over affiliates, especially in Japanese MNCs where socialization of local managers has proven to be difficult (Kopp, 1999; Pucik et al., 1992). We therefore predict that:

H6. The larger an affiliate, the greater its use of expatriates.

In a similar fashion, higher levels of integration between affiliate and parent operations should also lead to the need for higher levels of coordination and control, thus increasing the need for expatriates. We therefore predict that:

H7. The more the operations of an affiliate are integrated with those of the parent, the greater the use of expatriates.

Turning to level of localization and its impact on expatriate staffing, no a priori predictions are made. On the one hand, the more functions are localized, the greater the ability of the firm to attract qualified local managers. If qualified local managers are present, this reduces the pressure on the MNC to staff its affiliate with expatriates. At the same time, however, a greater number of functions present in an affiliate may increase the strategic importance of the affiliate to the parent, increasing the dependence of the parent company on the affiliate and, hence, the need for control. This need for control may, in turn, increase the use of expatriates in the affiliate.

Finally, we expect that in those affiliates that are simultaneously globally integrated and locally differentiated, control demands will be at their highest. These affiliates will have the greatest need for an international cadre of managers to manage the contradictory and complex demands placed on the affiliate. We would similarly expect that those affiliates with low levels of integration and high levels of localization would have the lowest levels of expatriate staffing. We can summarize these predictions in the following hypotheses:

H8a. Affiliates with simultaneously high levels of integration and localization will have the highest levels of expatriate staffing.

H8b. Affiliates with low levels of integration and high levels of localization will have the lowest levels of expatriate staffing.

Methodology

The findings in this chapter are derived from analysis of on data collected from 119 Japanese affiliates in the United States and Europe in two parallel studies of management practices and outcomes in Japanese affiliates overseas. In the U.S. study, the sample was drawn from a non-random stratified sample of 41 affiliates of the 32 largest Japanese-owned firms concentrated in high-tech industries, consumer electronics, automotive manufacturing, and finance and services. With only minor exceptions, all major Japanese investors in the United States were represented in the sample, and all were competing in globally competitive environments.

First, confidential interviews were conducted with two or three members of top management in each company. Then, written questionnaires were given to the managers who were also requested to distribute additional written questionnaires to their peers. Questionnaire responses were received from three to eight local executives in each company.

Sixty-two of the 132 distributed questionnaires were completed for a response rate of 61%. Because there are multiple responses from the U.S. affiliates in the study, the data have been inversely weighted by the number of respondents to counteract the impact of unmeasured company influences on the results reported in this chapter.

While the empirical results reported later in this chapter are based on responses to the written questionnaires, we are able to interpret these results with the knowledge and insights gained in 51 interviews with local executives, Japanese executives stationed at the affiliates, Japanese executives in charge of international operations in the Japanese headquarters, as well as local executives who had been previously employed in Japanese affiliates.

The European study was conducted as a follow-up to the American study to test whether the relationships found in the American data were consistent across host countries. Because of high levels of convergent validity found in the responses of same-affiliate respondents in the American data, in the European study questionnaires were sent only to the top local executive in each affiliate in the sample. Of the 175 questionnaires distributed to the largest affiliates of Japanese firms in Europe, 78 usable responses were received for a response rate of 45%. The final European sample consists of 44 U.K. affiliates, 26 German, 6 French, 3 German, and 3 unidentified European affiliates.

Variables Used in the Study

Descriptive statistics and correlations for all of the variables used in the analyses are presented in Tables 1 and 2.

Table 1. Descriptive Statistics.

Variable Name	Whole Sample			U.S. Subsample			European Subsample		
	M	S.D.	Range	M	S.D.	Range	M	S.D.	Range
Percentage of expatriates in affiliate	0.077	0.096	0–0.6	0.096	0.118	0–0.6	0.067	0.082	0–0.50
Performance (profit level)	2.758	1.036	1–5	2.591	1.077	1–5	2.849	1.009	1–5
Affiliate age***	13.918	8.561	2–39	18.953	9.762	7–39	11.233	6.456	2–31
Parent experience in host***	19.778	10.066	4–46	24.035	10.096	7–40	17.092	9.143	4–46
Affiliate size†	465.694	831.496	5–6000	689.234	1152.078	5–6000	352.433	586.615	14–3500
Average integration**	2.210	0.582	1.08–4	2.022	0.474	1.33–3.42	2.312	0.612	1.083–4
Localized functions	10.202	2.635	0–12	10.366	2.517	0–12	10.115	2.706	0–12
Manufacturing parent*	0.790	0.410	0–1	0.659	0.480	0–1	0.859	0.350	0–1
Manufacturing affiliate**	0.445	0.499	0–1	0.244	0.435	0–1	0.551	0.501	0–1

Note: Significance levels for differences in means between U.S. and European subsamples and correlation coefficients: *ns:* Whole sample = 119; U.S. subsample = 41; European subsample = 78.

† $p < 0.10$.
* $p < 0.05$.
** $p < 0.01$.
*** $p < 0.001$.

Table 2. Correlation Table.

Variable Name	1	2	3	4	5	6	7	8
Percentage of expatriates in affiliate								
Performance (profit level)	−0.013							
Affiliate age	0.114	0.050						
Parent experience in host	0.021	−0.071	0.666***					
Affiliate size	−0.223*	0.117	0.098	0.105				
Average integration	0.017	0.154	0.070	−0.014	−0.075			
Localized functions	−0.169†	0.064	0.003	0.035	0.080	−0.053		
Manufacturing parent	−0.211**	0.158†	0.050	0.178†	0.017	0.145	0.134	
Manufacturing affiliate	−0.280**	−0.166†	−0.426***	−0.269**	0.213*	−0.044	0.118	0.089

Note: Significance levels for differences in means between U.S. and European subsamples and correlation coefficients: *ns:* whole sample: 119; U.S. Subsample = 41; European subsample = 78.

†$p < 0.10$.
*$p < 0.05$.
**$p < 0.01$.
***$p < 0.001$.

Dependent Variables

In order to control for the size of the affiliate, *expatriate presence* was measured by calculating the percentage of expatriates currently stationed in the affiliate relative to all affiliate employees.

Measuring the performance of Japanese affiliates is extremely difficult for two reasons: Japanese accounting laws do not require separate reporting for individual affiliates of Japanese companies, so there are no publicly available figures. Moreover, *affiliate performance* figures are considered to be confidential and proprietary data. Furthermore, even when companies will divulge performance data, financial performance figures at the affiliate level are notoriously unreliable because such inputs as internal transfer prices are manipulated for taxation and other reasons (e.g. Rosenzweig, 1994). Although all measures of performance are biased, we chose to measure performance through self-reported ratings of the affiliate's performance. Previous research has found a strong correlation between objective and subjective performance ratings (Dess & Robinson, 1984; Geringer & Hebert, 1991). As the respondents are top-level executives in the affiliate with knowledge of the affiliate's true performance and because they were guaranteed anonymity, these self-report measures are likely to be more accurate than other financial statistics such as profitability, ROI, etc.

In the questionnaire, we asked a number of questions about various dimensions of affiliate performance, using 5-point Likert-type scales to indicate the level of affiliate performance. In the analyses reported below, we used the respondents' rating of their affiliate's current overall level of profitability vis-à-vis the performance of their top competitor.

Independent and Control Variables

Integration between the affiliate and the parent company was measured by creating an averaged index of integration across the functional areas of operations, procurement, marketing, sales, distribution, business planning, accounting, legal affairs, product development, research and development, and human-resource management. In all cases, respondents were asked to indicate on a 5-point Likert-type scale how integrated each of these functions was between the affiliate and the parent company. Higher values on the index indicate higher levels of integration between the affiliate and the parent company.

Degree of local responsiveness was measured by an additive index of all the major value-chain functions actually performed at the affiliate. We used this measure as a proxy of the affiliate's organizational configuration to represent the extent of the affiliate's interface with the local environment and hence its degree of local responsiveness.

Age of the affiliate was measured in years since the affiliate's founding.

Size was measured by the actual number of employees working in the affiliate.

Parent company's experience in the host country was measured by the number of years since the company first established operations in the host country.

Whether the parent is a manufacturing firm or not and whether the affiliate has manufacturing operations were coded as dummy variables where the variable had a value of 1 if the parent/affiliate was engaged in manufacturing.

RESULTS

Description of Respondents

Most participating companies are among the largest industrial, financial and service firms in Japan. The majority of them are market leaders in their lines of business, with total worldwide sales ranging from $600 million to $45 billion and a global workforce of between 2200 and 163,000 employees, with a mean of 38,400 employees worldwide.

Fifteen percent of respondents hold the top position in their affiliate and an additional 42% of respondents reported to the president or general manager of the affiliate. The remaining respondents hold other executive positions in the affiliate. Respondents have been with their company for an average of 9.18 years, with a range of service of 2–25 years. Nearly all respondents (114 of the 119 respondents) are male.

Subsample Descriptive Statistics

The affiliates included in the sample are, on average, well established in their host country. For the American affiliates, the average age of the affiliates is 19 years old, and parent companies have, on average, 24 years of experience in the United States (Table 1). In the European subsample, the average age of the affiliate is 11 years old, and parent companies have an average of 17 years of experience in the host country (Table 1).

In terms of size, American affiliates have, on average, 689 employees while the European affiliates are smaller, with 352 employees. Sixty six percent of the American affiliates and 86% of the European affiliates have manufacturing parent firms, while 24% of the American affiliates and 55% of the European affiliates themselves have manufacturing operations.

There are some significant differences between the U.S. and European affiliates. Using the difference in means tests between the two subsamples, we found that American affiliates are significantly older ($p < 0.001$) than their European counterparts. Similarly, the parent companies of the U.S. sample have significantly longer experience in the host country (significant at $p < 0.001$). In addition, the average number of employees in the U.S. affiliates is somewhat larger than in the European affiliates (significant at $p < 0.1$).

Integration between the parent company and the affiliate also differs significantly between the two subsamples. European affiliates are, on average, more integrated with their parent companies than U.S. affiliates (mean = 2.31 vs. 2.02; $p < 0.01$). In terms of localization of functions to the affiliate, there is virtually no difference between the American and European subsamples (mean for U.S. = 10.37 vs. Europe = 10.12). In addition, the rank order correlation (Table 2) between integration and localization for the sample as a whole is quite low and negative (-0.0528). However, in the American subsample, the correlation is positive and moderate (0.2560), while in the European subsample, the correlation is negative and moderate (-0.2523).

The U.S. and European subsamples do differ significantly on the extent to which both the affiliate and the parent are engaged in manufacturing activities. At the affiliate level, there is a higher percentage of manufacturers in the European subsample than in the U.S. sample (mean = 0.55 vs. mean = 0.24; $p < 0.01$). At the parent company level, the European subsample also has a higher percentage of firms engaged in manufacturing than the U.S. subsample (mean = 0.86 vs. 0.66; $p < 0.05$).

Multivariate Analyses: Analysis of Performance

In order to test our hypotheses, we performed ordinary least-squares regressions, building our models in a hierarchical fashion. We first entered the variables of affiliate age, parent company experience in the host country, and affiliate size. Then, in a second step, we added the quadratic measure of affiliate size to test for nonlinearity. As discussed below, the addition of the size-squared variable significantly increased the adjusted R^2 statistic in each equation.

Using the profitability of the affiliate vis-à-vis its competitors as the measure of performance, we first performed a regression analysis using the total sample of Japanese affiliates located in the United States and Europe. These results are presented in Table 3. As shown in the table, for the whole sample, profit is a function of affiliate size, level of integration with the parent company, and localization of affiliate functions (adjusted $R^2 = 0.15$; $p < 0.01$).

Size shows a significant quadratic relationship with profitability. In small to medium-sized affiliates, increasing size is associated with decreasing performance ($p < 0.1$). This relationship reverses once affiliate size increases beyond a certain point; size then shows a positive relationship to profitability ($p < 0.1$). While the results are more complex than hypothesized, these results offer partial support for Hypothesis 4, which predicted that size would be positively associated with affiliate performance.

Affiliates with higher levels of integration with the parent also report significantly higher levels of performance than do affiliates with lower levels of

Table 3. Regression Results for Affiliate Profitability.

Independent Variable	Whole Sample		U.S. Subsample		European Subsample	
	Beta	S.E.	Beta	S.E.	Beta	S.E.
Intercept	$1.217^†$	0.6820	$-1.819^†$	0.9267	2.064^*	1.007
Affiliate age	0.001	0.0163	0.0123	0.0201	0.0151	0.0250
Parent experience in host	−0.0078	0.0139	0.0277	0.0185	−0.0284	0.0182
Affiliate size	$-0.0005^†$	0.0031	−0.00025	0.00047	$-0.0012^†$	0.0006
Affiliate size^2	0.000002^{**}	0.0000	1.3×10^{-7}	8.0×10^{-8}	$3.8 \times 10^{-7†}$	2.0×10^{-7}
Expatriate presence	−0.7276	1.103	1.7470	1.4536	$-2.991^†$	1.6285
Average integration	0.5065^{**}	0.1727	1.2869^{***}	0.3096	0.2547	0.2156
Localized functions	$0.0893^†$	0.0479	$0.1184^†$	0.0623	0.1110	0.0689
Manufacturing parent	0.063	0.2598	−0.5570	0.4261	0.1621	0.3576
Manufacturing affiliate	$-0.4226^†$	0.2373	−0.0260	0.4190	$-0.5585^†$	0.3033
R^2/F (df)	$0.15/2.852(9,96)^*$		$0.46/4.395(9,36)^{**}$		$0.13/1.980(9,59)^†$	

$^†p < 0.10.$
$^*p < 0.05.$
$^{**}p < 0.01.$
$^{***}p < 0.001.$

integration ($p < 0.01$). In addition, affiliates with a greater number of localized functions outperform their counterparts with fewer localized functions ($p < 0.1$). Hypothesis 1 is therefore supported.

Hypothesis 2 predicted that affiliate performance would be negatively related to expatriate presence in the affiliate. As shown in Table 3, while the relationship is in the predicted direction, the results are not statistically significant for the sample as a whole. H2 is therefore not supported.

The age of the affiliate, parent company's experience in the host country, the percentage of expatriates in the affiliate, and the control variables for whether the parent company is a manufacturing firm and whether the affiliate has manufacturing operations are all non-significant predictors of affiliate performance. These results do not support Hypothesis 3a or Hypothesis 3b, which predicted that both affiliate age and parent company experience would be associated with higher levels of affiliate performance.

To explore whether these results are consistent across Japanese affiliates in both the United States and Europe, we next performed identical analyses on each subsample separately. These results are also presented in Table 3. As shown in the table, controlling for the presence of manufacturing at the affiliate and the parent, the only significant predictors of affiliate performance in the U.S. sample are integration and localization (adjusted $R^2 = 0.46$; $p < 0.01$). Higher levels of integration between the parent firm and the affiliate are associated with significantly higher levels of affiliate performance ($p < 0.001$), and a larger number of localized functions are associated with significantly higher levels of performance ($p < 0.1$). These results support Hypothesis 1 for the U.S. subsample.

In addition, in the U.S. sample, there is no significant relationship between expatriate presence and affiliate performance. However, contrary to the results for the total sample, size is not a significant predictor of performance for the U.S. subsample, although the direction of the relationship is consistent with that found in the total sample analysis. Thus, for the U.S. subsample, H2 and H6 are not supported.

Turning to the results for the European subsample (Table 3), the size of the affiliate, expatriate presence, and whether the affiliate is engaged in manufacturing significantly predict affiliate performance (adjusted $R^2 = 0.13$; $p < 0.1$). Consistent with the previous analyses, size exhibits a quadratic effect with performance ($p < 0.1$). In small to medium-sized affiliates, increasing size is associated with decreasing performance. This relationship reverses once affiliate size increases beyond a certain point, and then increasing size is associated with increased performance.

While, in the U.S. subsample, there is no significant relationship between expatriate presence and affiliate performance, in the European subsample, an increase in the percentage of expatriates is significantly negatively related to performance ($p < 0.1$). These results support Hypothesis 2. Finally, European affiliates with manufacturing operations have significantly lower levels of performance than affiliates with no manufacturing ($p < 0.1$) and parent company-affiliate integration and localization of functions have no significant influence on affiliate performance, contrary to our prediction in Hypothesis 1.

Interpretation of Performance Results

Examining the results for affiliate performance, the analyses reported above lend support to Bartlett and Ghoshal's assertion that MNCs with both a high level of integration and a high level of local responsiveness will outperform their less transnational competitors. We also tested for an interaction effect between integration and local responsiveness on the level of affiliate performance. However, in neither the sample as a whole nor in the two subsamples was this term significant.

In addition, we examined the data to see whether the relationships between integration and performance and localization and performance were consistent across the range of variable values or whether there are "ideal levels" of integration and/or localization. Examining the scatter plots for each of these variables plotted against performance shows no such "ideal point." The data do indicate that to benefit from a transnational organizational strategy, a certain degree of maturity of the affiliate seems to be required. This may explain why the two configuration variables are so important in the U.S. case (the two variables alone account for 41% of the explained variance in performance) but are not significant in the European sample. This observation fits with the proposition advanced by Rosenzweig (1994) that the critical nature of the American market requires an asymmetric approach to managing affiliates.

Another possible explanation for the low impact of "transnational" variables on performance in the European sample may be due to "over-integration" between the affiliates and the parent companies. On average, Japanese affiliates in Europe are more integrated with their parent firms than are their American counterparts (Table 1). Although we cannot determine causality from these data, high integration may lead to high levels of expatriate presence, which in the European context shows a negative association with performance. In the U.S., however, expatriate presence shows no significant relationship with affiliate performance, although it is worth noting that the coefficient is positive.

The impact of expatriate presence on performance clearly requires further study as the direction of the relationship is opposite for the two subsamples. It is also possible that the critical variable may not be only the expatriate presence per se, but also the role and quality of individual expatriates assigned to the subsidiaries. Based on our interviews with top-level executives in the affiliates, we observed that Japanese expatriates in the U.S. are more frequently found in "shadow" integrating roles, managing a global web of relationships, while their counterparts in Europe are more heavily involved in day-to-day control of affiliate operations.

Some of the divergence between the U.S. and European samples can be attributed to differences in the age of the affiliate and/or experience of the parent company in the host country. However, in our regression models, none of the life-cycle variables are significant predictors of performance. More experience does not lead to higher performance. On the contrary, in the case of European affiliates, the relationship is negative – greater levels of experience are associated with lower levels of affiliate performance.

The differences found between the American and European subsamples also indicate that there does not appear to be a simple linear learning curve which positively enhances the performance of overseas operations. It may be that the organization's ability to learn from the local environment is not merely a function of experience, but of other, unmeasured organizational factors as well.

Turning to the relationship between size and affiliate performance, the nonlinearity of the relationship is striking. There are several explanations for why medium-size affiliates may show the lowest levels of performance. First, their growth may have outpaced the available resource support from the parent company. This could be the case in Europe, which at the time of the study was usually ranked third in priority by Japanese MNCs, after Asia and the United States. Also, we found from company visits that there were several instances where European affiliates were in the process of making a difficult and painful transition from basically an entrepreneurial mode to one of a mature business. Changes in local management, with a correspondingly negative effect on organizational stability, employee morale, and customer relations often accompanied these transitions.

Multivariate Analysis: Expatriate Presence

To further explore the issue of expatriate presence, we conducted an additional set of analyses using the percentage of expatriates to total number of affiliate employees as the dependent variable. These results are shown in Table 4. For the total sample, we find that the level of expatriate staffing is significantly influenced only by size of the affiliate and whether the parent firm is a manufacturer (adjusted $R^2 = 0.17; p < 0.005$).

Hypothesis 7 is partially supported as size exhibits a nonlinear, U-shaped effect on expatriate presence ($p < 0.055$). As size increases from small to medium, the percentage of expatriates declines. However, when size increases past a certain point, expatriate presence increases with size.

Table 4 also indicates that there is no significant relationship between number of localized functions and expatriate presence. Moreover, affiliates of manufacturing parent firms have lower percentages of expatriates in their affiliates than do non-manufacturers ($p < 0.01$). Affiliate age, the presence of manufacturing operations at the affiliate, experience of the parent company in the host country, and integration between the affiliate and the parent company are all non-significant predictors of expatriate presence. Hypotheses 5a, 5b, 6 and 7 are therefore not supported for the total sample.

For the U.S. subsample (Table 4), the results are identical, but the relationships are stronger than those for the entire sample (adjusted $R^2 = 0.26; p < 0.05$).

Table 4. Regression Results for Expatriate Presence in Affiliate.

Independent Variable	Whole Sample		U.S. Subsample		European Subsample	
	Beta	S.E.	Beta	S.E.	Beta	S.E.
Intercept	0.1304^*	0.6410	$0.219^{\dagger}$	0.111	0.0620	0.0862
Affiliate age	0.0010	0.0013	-0.0001	0.0025	0.0030	0.0021
Parent experience in host	0.00002	0.0013	0.0047	0.0023	-0.00015	0.0016
Affiliate size	-0.00008^{**}	0.00003	-0.00012^*	0.00005	-0.00013^*	0.00005
Affiliate size^2	$1.35 \times 10^{-8*}$	1.0×10^{-8}	$1.91 \times 10^{-8\dagger}$	1.0×10^{-8}	$3.18 \times 10^{-8\dagger}$	2.0×10^{-7}
Average integration	0.0152	0.0165	0.0166	0.0394	0.0286	0.0181
Localized functions	-0.0014	0.0046	-0.0044	0.0079	0.0055	0.0059
Manufacturing parent	-0.0643^{**}	0.0238	-0.1207^*	0.0477	0.0042	0.0307
Manufacturing affiliate	-0.0230	0.0227	0.0277	0.0518	-0.00012	0.0261
R^2/F (df)	$0.17/3.457(8,97)^{**}$		$0.26/2.632(8,37)$		$0.14/2.245(8,59)^{\dagger}$	

$^{\dagger} p < 0.10.$
$^* p < 0.05.$
$^{**} p < 0.01.$

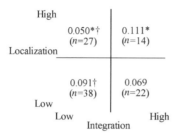

Overall $F=3.57$; interaction=$p<0.03$; *Significant difference, $p<0.05$;
† significant difference, $p<0.10$.

Fig. 1. ANOVA Results of Integration and Localization on Expatriate Staffing.

The parent company's experience in the United States, age of the affiliate, the presence of manufacturing at the affiliate, integration between the parent company and the affiliate, and localization of functions at the affiliate are all non-significant predictors of expatriate presence in the U.S. subsample.

For the European subsample, expatriate presence is significantly predicted only by size of the affiliate (adjusted $R^2 = 0.14$; $p < 0.05$), which again shows a quadratic effect with expatriate presence. All of the other variables are non-significant.

Finally, we also tested for an interaction effect between integration and local responsiveness on the level of expatriate staffing, controlling for all other variables included in the regression equations above. In neither the sample as a whole nor in the two subsamples was this term significant.

In addition, while the regressions are not significant, we did find significant interaction effects when we split the variables into "high" and "low" at either the mean or median point on level of localization and level of integration and performed ANOVAs, controlling for all of the other variables included in the regression equations above. As shown in Fig. 1, we find that after entering the control variables, those affiliates which have simultaneously high levels of localization and high levels of integration have the greatest percentage of expatriates ($r = 0.111$), as predicted in Hypothesis 8a. Also, as predicted in Hypothesis 8b, the lowest percentage of expatriates is found in those affiliates which are low on integration and high on localization ($r = 0.050$).

Interpretation of Expatriate Presence Results

Examining the predictors for expatriate staffing, the results of the analyses provide no support for the life-cycle predictions that the age of the affiliate and parent-company experience in the host country will reduce the affiliate's reliance on expatriates. These results are also contrary to those of Beamish and Inkpen (1998) who found a positive relationship between number of expatriates and date of establishment of Japanese subsidiaries but are consistent with Boyacigiller's (1990a) findings in the U.S. that the age of the affiliate was unrelated to Japanese MNCs' use of expatriates.

At the same time, integration with the parent company does not predict expatriate presence, contrary to our hypothesis based on the resource dependence framework. While we had originally predicted that the need for greater levels of parent company control over integrated affiliates would be reflected in an increase in expatriate presence, the parent companies may be using other forms of control (e.g. bureaucratic rules and procedures, socialization of local employees, direct communications and visits from the parent company, etc.) to manage this interdependence (Evans et al., 2002). Although integration alone does not lead to greater levels of expatriate staffing, the results presented in Table 4 above do support the resource dependence prediction that simultaneously high levels of integration and localization will lead to the highest level of expatriate staffing. Clearly, these relationships deserve further study.

The analyses also show that expatriate presence is influenced by the size of the affiliate for both the U.S. and European affiliates. The results indicate that larger affiliates have the greatest expatriate presence, while medium-sized affiliates have the smallest expatriate presence. While our results do not support traditional life-cycle theory predictions, they do support a modified life-cycle argument where, instead of time in the host country, scope of operations is a critical factor in determining expatriate presence. Expatriates may be sent upon start-up of a new operation and then replaced once the operation is up and running (e.g. Franko, 1973). However, once the operation reaches a certain size, expatriates may again be stationed in the affiliate because of its perceived importance to the parent company, regardless of the age of the affiliate, the parent's experience in the host country, the level of integration between the affiliate and the parent company, or the localization of functions to the affiliate.

DISCUSSION

Given the exploratory nature of the study, a number of observations made here are still tentative and require further study and clarification. While our ability to collect two independent sets of data from two distinct populations of Japanese affiliates allows us to explore a number of previously untested propositions, the complexity of many of the underlying relationships also becomes more obvious. Therefore, additional research is needed to validate and extend the current findings. Two areas in particular should receive close attention.

With respect to several of the organizational-level variables such as global integration and local responsiveness, it may be useful to confirm their predictive power by using alternative, more detailed measures than were available for this study. Finer differentiation by industrial sectors may also be appropriate, as the benefits of transnational strategies are influenced by the sources of competitive advantage and the nature of competition in a particular industry.

In addition, because of the cross-sectional nature of our data, we are unable to determine causality between the variables examined in this study. It may be that size is associated with affiliate performance not because availability of resources improves competitive capabilities, but because successful affiliates simply grow faster than less successful ones. In addition, expatriates may hinder the performance (as in the European sample), or the presence of expatriates may be a reflection of past poor performance of the affiliate. The relationships seem more complex than originally hypothesized for this study and by previous writers. It is likely that the relationship between strategy configuration variables such as global integration and local responsiveness, demographic variables such as the age and size of the affiliate, and the parent company's experience overseas are partially moderated by the presence of expatriates. Unfortunately, we did not collect detailed data on the roles played by expatriates in our sample of affiliates sufficient to adequately explore these relationships further. This could be yet another subject for further investigation.

Our data also seem to indicate that Japanese MNCs currently rely on Japanese expatriates to fulfill the transnational role of global integration. It is possible that Japanese firms are actually under-performing relative to their competitive potential, since it is quite possible that local managers, if properly trained, could perform these roles even more effectively than their Japanese counterparts. Our quantitative data are insufficient to support this proposition, but in numerous interviews with local executives working for Japanese affiliates in the U.S. and Europe, respondents pointed out missed market opportunities caused by both a lack of awareness on the part of Japanese managers that opportunities existed and managers' inability to mobilize the necessary corporate resources to take advantage of these opportunities. Future studies should investigate the roles of managers, local and expatriate, in greater detail than we have been able to do in this study.

CONCLUSION

The results of our research indicate a general support for the proposition regarding the benefits of a transnational strategy as well as highlight some of the organizational dilemmas facing Japanese multinational firms in the "transnational era." First, high integration and high local responsiveness are positively associated with performance of Japanese overseas affiliates. Also, the impact of expatriate presence on performance seems to be linked to their role in implementing transnational, rather than global, strategies (Bartlett & Ghoshal, 1989) – performance is positive when the expatriates are used as "integrators," and negative when they are used as "controllers." Finally, the extent of expatriate presence is primarily driven by a nonlinear U-shaped effect of the size of the affiliate, suggesting that large and complex affiliates have unique "transnational" management needs that are currently served by the Japanese expatriates.

However, if a transnational strategy is the key to success in the current global competitive environment, at least for the companies in our sample, the critical issue facing these firms and probably other Japanese MNCs is how to implement a transnational strategy by quickly developing the appropriate human resource infrastructure to support the simultaneous integration and differentiation of the firm (Evans et al., 2002; Nohria & Ghoshal, 1997; Westney, 1999). As Japanese MNCs continue to expand their operations overseas, they will experience even greater needs for global coordination and integration. Is their current human-resource strategy regarding the staffing of the critical integration roles sustainable?

At this point in their histories, most Japanese MNCs rely on Japanese expatriates to serve as the glue to link their far-flung operations around the world. As Japanese MNCs increase in size and complexity, and as the new transnational imperatives of competition strengthen, this will naturally lead to an increase in the demand for expatriates. This is probably the key reason why, contrary to earlier predictions by a number of authors that expatriates would decrease as Japanese MNCs gained more experience overseas (e.g. Emmott, 1989; Ichimura, 1981), the relative number of Japanese expatriates stationed in overseas affiliates is often stable or actually increasing (Japan Overseas Enterprises Association, 1997; Kono & Clegg, 2001; Pucik, 1999), rather than decreasing, since expatriates are indispensable in their integration role.

The main reason behind this trend is that most local managers probably still do not have the necessary capabilities (language, experience, knowledge of global operations, interpersonal relationships) that would allow them to perform effectively in this capacity; nor do the Japanese firms seem to provide many opportunities for them to develop such capabilities. However, the danger for the Japanese is that there may be a logical limit in terms of supply, cost and local resistance to relying solely on human resource "exports" from Japan.

We do not argue, however, that the answer to the new transnational demands facing Japanese MNCs is in management "localization," as a number of authors critical of Japanese management practices abroad have maintained (e.g. Kopp, 1999; Yoshihara, 1996). For example, it is quite obvious that aggressive localization strategies pushed forward during the 1980s by many U.S. multinationals (perhaps with the very best intentions) created groupings of fragmented "pygmy kingdoms" (in the words of one non-U.S. international executive), rather than well-coordinated global networks of interdependent units.

From our perspective, the primary challenge confronting Japanese MNCs is, therefore, how to increase the supply of managers with transnational skills by providing opportunities for local executives to develop the capabilities that will enable them to perform effectively in the emerging transnational integration role. It is possible, as speculated by Yoshino (1976) at the beginning of Japan's international economic expansion in the 1970s, that because of their culture, language, and internal labor market traditions, the task facing Japanese MNCs may be more difficult than for multinationals from other countries (see also Kono & Clegg, 2001). It may also be true that under the current system of corporate governance in Japan, performance criteria are still secondary to maintaining control and positions for the current management "nomenklatura," so development opportunities for local managers are seen merely as a "citizenship" issue. However, as our study has shown, developing transnational organization capability with a truly global cadre of managers is not just a matter of being a "good local citizen." We believe that this is a business imperative that will influence the very survival of Japanese MNCs in the 21st century.

REFERENCES

Abo, T. (Ed.) (1994). *Hybrid factory: The Japanese production system in the United States.* New York: Oxford University Press.

Adler, P. (1993). The "learning bureaucracy": New United Motor Manufacturing, Inc. *Research in Organizational Behavior, 15,* 111–194.

Aldrich, H. (1976). Resource dependence and inter-organizational relations. *Administration and Society, 7,* 419–454.

Amako, T. (1991). The development of Japanese multinationals as European insiders and European managers' job satisfaction. In: M. Trevor (Ed.), *International Business and the Management of Change: Euro-Asian Perspectives* (pp. 101–120). Aldershot, UK: Avebury Press.

Baliga, B., & Jaeger, A. (1984). Multinational corporations: Control systems and delegation issues. *Journal of International Business Studies, 15,* 25–40.

Barney, J. (1991). Firm resources and sustained competitive advantage. *Journal of Management, 17*(1), 99–120.

Bartlett, C., & Ghoshal, S. (1987). Managing across borders: New organizational responses. *Sloan Management Review, 29,* 43–53.

Bartlett, C., & Ghoshal, S. (1988). Organizing for worldwide effectiveness: The transnational solution. *California Management Review, 31,* 1–21.

Bartlett, C., & Ghoshal, S. (1989). *Managing across borders: The transnational solution.* Boston, MA: Harvard Business School Press.

Bartlett, C., & Yoshihara, H. (1988). New challenges for Japanese multinationals: Is organizational adaptation their Achilles heel? *Human Resource Management, 27*(1), 19–43.

Beamish, P., & Inkpen, A. (1998). Japanese firms and the decline of Japanese expatriates. *Journal of World Business, 33*(1), 35–50.

Beechler, S., & Yang, Z. (1994). The transfer of Japanese-style management to American subsidiaries: Contingencies, constraints, and competencies. *Journal of International Business Studies, 25*(3), 1–25.

Bob, D., & SRI International (1990). *Japanese companies in American communities.* New York: Japan Society.

Boyacigiller, N. (1990a). Staffing in a foreign land: A multi-level study of Japanese multinationals with operations in the United States. Paper presented at the Annual Academy of Management Conference.

Boyacigiller, N. (1990b). The role of expatriates in the management of interdependence, complexity, and risk in multinational corporations. *Journal of International Business Studies, 21*, 357–382.

Brannen, M., & Salk, J. (1999). When Japanese and other nationals create something new: A comparative study of negotiated work culture in German and the United States. In: S. Beechler & A. Bird (Eds), *Japanese Multinationals Abroad: Individual and Organizational Learning* (pp. 33–61). New York: Oxford University Press.

Brewster, C. (1991). *The management of expatriates.* London, UK: Kogan Page.

Cusumano, M. (1988). Manufacturing innovation: Lessons from the Japanese auto industry. *Sloan Management Review, 30*, 29–39.

Dess, G., & Robinson, R. (1984). Measuring organizational performance in the absence of objective measures: The case of the privately-held firm and conglomerate business unit. *Strategic Management Journal, 5*, 265–273.

Dowling, P., & Schuler, R. (1990). *International dimensions of human resource management.* Boston, MA: PWS-Kent.

Ebrahimpour, M., & Cullen, J. B. (1993). Quality management in Japanese and American firms operating in the United States: A comparative study of styles and motivational beliefs. *Management International Review, 33*, 44–58.

Emmott, B. (1989). *The sun also sets: The limits of Japan's economic power.* London: Simon & Schuster.

Evans, P. (1993). Dosing the glue: Applying human resource technology to build global organizations. *Research in Personnel and Human Resource Management* (Suppl. 3), 21–54.

Evans, P., Pucik, V., & Barsoux, J. (2002). *The global challenge: Frameworks for international human resource management.* Boston, MA: McGraw-Hill.

Franko, L. (1973). Who manages multinational enterprises? *Columbia Journal of World Business, 8*, 30–42.

Fuchini, J., & Fuchini, S. (1990). *Working for the Japanese.* New York: Free Press.

Geringer, J., & Hebert, L. (1991). Measuring performance of international joint ventures. *Journal of International Business Studies, 22*, 249–264.

Govindarajan, V. J., & Gupta, A. (1985). Linking control systems to business unit strategy: Impact on performance. *Accounting, Organizations and Society, 10*, 51–66.

Gupta, A., & Govindarajan, V. J. (1991). Knowledge flows and the structure of control within multinational corporations. *Academy of Management Review, 16*, 768–792.

Harzing, A. (1999) *Managing the multinationals: An international study of control mechanisms.* Cheltenham, UK: Edward Elgar.

Ichimura, S. (1981). Japanese firms in Asia. *Japanese Economic Studies, 10*, 31–52.

Ishida, H. (1986). Transferability of Japanese human resource management abroad. *Human Resource Management*, 25(1), 103–120.

Japan Overseas Enterprises Association (1997). *A better way to manage Japanese corporate subsidiaries and administer human resources in the ASEAN region*. Tokyo: JOEA.

Johansson, J., & Yip, G. (1994). Exploiting globalization potential: U.S. and Japanese strategies. *Strategic Management Journal*, 15(8), 579–601.

Kenney, M., & Florida, R. (1993). *Beyond mass production: The Japanese system and its transfer to the United States*. New York: Oxford University Press.

Kenney, M., Romero, J., Contreras, O., & Bustos, M. (1999). Labor-management relations in the Japanese consumer electronics maquiladoras. In: S. Beechler & A. Bird (Eds), *Japanese Multinationals Abroad: Individual and Organizational Learning* (pp. 151–168). New York: Oxford University Press.

Kidd, J. (1999). Working together, but how? The need for intercultural awareness. In: S. Beechler & A. Bird (Eds), *Japanese Multinationals Abroad: Individual and Organizational Learning* (pp. 211–234). New York: Oxford University Press.

Kobayashi, N. (1985). The patterns of management style developing in Japanese multinationals in the 1980s. In: S. Takamiya & K. Thurley (Eds), *Japan's Emerging Multinationals: An International Comparison of Policies and Practices* (pp. 229–264). Tokyo: University of Tokyo Press.

Kobrin, S. (1988). Expatriate reduction and strategic control in American multinational corporations. *Human Resource Management*, 27, 411–432.

Kono, T., & Clegg, S. (2001). *Trends in Japanese management: Continuing strengths, current problems and changing priorities*. New York: Palgrave.

Konomoto, S. (2000). Problems of Japanese companies in East and Southeast Asia. NRI Papers, No. 18, Nomura Research Institute, Ltd.

Kopp, R. (1994). International human resource policies and practices in Japanese, European, and United States multinationals. *Human Resource Management*, 33, 581–599.

Kopp, R. (1999). The rice-paper ceiling in Japanese companies: Why it exists and persists. In: S. Beechler & A. Bird (Eds), *Japanese Multinationals Abroad: Individual and Organizational Learning* (pp. 107–128). New York: Oxford University Press.

Kujawa, D. (1983). Technology strategy and industrial relations: Case studies of Japanese multinationals in the United States. *Journal of International Business Studies*, 14(3), 9–22.

Maljers, F. (1992). Inside Unilever: The evolving transnational company. *Harvard Business Review*, 70(September–October), 46–53.

March, R. (1992). *Working for a Japanese company: Insights into the multicultural workplace*. Tokyo: Kondansha International.

Milliman, J., Von Glinow, M., & Nathan, M. (1991). Organizational life cycles and strategic international human resource management in multinational companies: Implications for congruence theory. *Academy of Management Review*, 16, 318–339.

Nakamura, K. (2000). Localization of management in Japanese-related firms in Indonesia. Bulletin, Vol. 39, No. 7 at http://www.jil.go.jp/bulletin/year/2000.

Negandhi, A. (1979). *Quest for survival and growth: A comparative study of American, European and Japanese multinationals*. New York: Praeger.

Oddou, G., Gregersen, H., Black, J. S., & Derr, C. B. (2001). Building global leaders: Strategy similarities and differences among European, U.S., and Japanese multinationals. In: M. Mendenhall, T. Kuhlmann & G. Stahl (Eds), *Developing Global Business Leaders: Policies, Processes and Innovations* (pp. 99–116). Westport, CT: Quorum Books.

Paik, Y., & Teagarden, M. (1995). Strategic international human resource management approaches in the maquiladora industry: A comparison of Japanese, Korean and U.S. firms. *The International Journal of Human Resource Management, 6*(3), 568–587.

Perlmutter, H. (1969). The tortuous evolution of the multinational corporation. *Columbia Journal of World Business* (January–February), 9–18.

Perlmutter, H., & Heenan, D. (1979). *Multinational organization development.* Reading, MA: Addison-Wesley.

Petersen, M., Peng, T., & Smith, P. (1999). Using expatriate supervisors to promote cross-border management practice transfer: The experience of a Japanese electronics company. In: J. Like, W. Fruin & P. Adler (Eds), *Remade in America: Transplanting and Transforming Japanese Management Systems* (pp. 294–330). New York: Oxford University Press.

Pfeffer, J. (1992). *Managing with power.* Boston, MA: Harvard Business School Press.

Pfeffer, J., & Salancik, G. (1978). *The external control of organizations: A resource dependence perspective.* New York: Harper & Row.

Porter, M. (1986). *Competitive advantage.* New York: Free Press.

Pucik, V. (1999). When performance does not matter: Human resource management in Japanese-owned U.S. affiliates. In: S. Beechler & A. Bird (Eds), *Japanese Multinationals Abroad: Individual and Organizational Learning* (pp. 169–188). New York: Oxford University Press.

Pucik, V., Hanada, M., & Fifield, G. (1989). *Management culture and the effectiveness of local executives in Japanese-owned U.S. corporations.* New York: Egon Zehnder International.

Pucik, V., Tichy, N., & Barnett, C. (Eds) (1992). *Globalizing management: Creating and leading the competitive organization.* New York: Wiley.

Rosenzweig, P. (1994). The new "American challenge": Foreign multinationals in the United States. *California Management Review* (Spring), 107–123.

Rosenzweig, P., & Singh, J. (1991). Organizational environments and the multinational enterprise. *Academy of Management Review, 16,* 340–361.

Sako, M. (1994). Training, productivity, and quality control in Japanese multinational companies. In: M. Aoki & R. Dore (Eds), *The Japanese Firm* (pp. 94–116). Oxford: Clarendon Press.

Sohn, J. (1994). Social knowledge as a control system: A proposition and evidence from the Japanese FDI behavior. *Journal of International Business Studies, 25*(2), 295–324.

Stening, B., & Everett, J. (1984). Japanese managers in Southeast Asia: Amiable superstars of arrogant upstarts? *Asia Pacific Journal of Management, 1,* 171–179.

Tachiki, D. (1991). Japanese management going transnational. *Journal for Quality and Participation, 14,* 96–107.

Taylor, M. (1991a). American managers in Japanese subsidiaries: How cultural differences are affecting the work place. *Human Resource Planning, 14*(1), 43–49.

Taylor, S., Beechler, S., & Napier, N. (1996). Toward an integrative model of strategic international human resource management. *Academy of Management Review, 21*(4), 959–985.

Taylor, W. (1991b). The logic of global business: An interview with ABB Percy Barnevik. *Harvard Business Review, 69,* 90–105.

Thompson, J. (1967). *Organizations in action.* Chicago, IL: McGraw-Hill.

Trevor, M. (1983). *Japan's reluctant multinationals: Japanese management at home and abroad.* New York: St. Martin's Press.

Tung, R. (1982). Selection and training procedures of U.S., European, and Japanese multinationals. *California Management Review, 25*(1), 57–71.

Wakabayashi, M., & Graen, G. (1991). Cross-cultural human resource development: Japanese manufacturing firms in central Japan and central U.S. states. In: M. Trevor (Ed.), *International*

Business and the Management of Change: Euro-Asian Perspectives (pp. 147–169). Aldershot, UK: Avebury Press.

Westney, D. E. (1993). Cross-Pacific internationalization of R&D by U.S. and Japanese firms. *R&D Management, 23*(2), 171–181.

Westney, D. E. (1999). Changing perspectives on the organization of Japanese multinational companies. In: S. Beechler & A. Bird (Eds), *Japanese Multinationals Abroad: Individual and Organizational Learning* (pp. 11–29). New York: Oxford University Press.

Whitehill, A. (1991). *Japanese management: Tradition and transition.* London: Routledge.

Yoshihara, H. (1996). *Immature Japanese multinationals.* Unpublished manuscript, Research Institute for Economics and Business Administration, Kobe University.

Yoshino, M. (1976). *Japan's multinational enterprises.* Cambridge, MA: Harvard University Press.

Zeira, Y. (1976). Management development in ethnocentric multinational corporations. *California Management Review* (Summer), 34–41.

DECLINE OF JAPAN'S PREDOMINANCE IN ASIA

Hideki Yoshihara

ABSTRACT

Until around 1980, Japanese companies occupied a predominant position in Asia. Their Asian operations are managed by Japanese persons and in the Japanese language. This Japanese-style international management is well suited to transfer technology and know-how from Japanese parent companies to their overseas subsidiaries. But, it does not provide opportunities to local managerial and professional employees to display their abilities and initiatives. Japanese companies also have problems in Japan. They invest more in foreign countries than in Japan, which results in the hollowing out at home. Japanese companies are managed by old men and thus lack a strong leadership. Japanese multinationals are facing a challenging task of management innovation both at home and abroad.

PREDOMINANT POSITION OF JAPANESE BUSINESS IN ASIA

Japanese companies have long enjoyed an unchallenged, predominant position in Asia. There were essentially no local Asian companies that were competitive in such industries as iron and steel, shipbuilding, synthetic fibers, chemicals, machine tools, home appliances, electric parts, semiconductors, precision instruments, office machines, automobiles and automotive parts, but there were several local

Japanese Firms in Transition: Responding to the Globalization Challenge
Advances in International Management, Volume 17, 243–260
© 2005 Published by Elsevier Ltd.
ISSN: 0747-7929/doi:10.1016/S0747-7929(04)17010-8

Asian companies that were competitive in the international market in labor-intensive industries. However, in technology industries, Japanese companies enjoyed monopolistic positions in the Asian market.

At the macroeconomic level, Japan is still predominant in Asia at present. Japan's GDP share in Asia has been high from 1980 through to the 1990s: 63% in 1980, and 66% in 1999. During this 20-year period, Japan's market share has fluctuated between 63 and 71%.

The situation is different at the microlevel. In terms of competitiveness and performance of Japanese companies, we see symptoms of a weakening of Japan's Asian predominance. In iron and steel, shipbuilding, and synthetic fiber, the largest companies are no longer Japanese. Other Asian companies now occupy the number one position. There is also severe competition between Japanese and Asian companies in other industries such as electric home appliances, semiconductors, personal computers, mobile phones, and motorcycles. There are now few industries in which Japanese companies have a predominant position; these include automobiles and automotive parts, sophisticated electric parts, manufacturing equipment for semiconductors, industrial robots, engineering plastics, and pharmaceuticals.

Why are Japanese companies losing their competitive position in Asia? Is the Japanese way of management the cause of their decline in dominance in Asia? What kinds of problems are there in Japanese companies both at home and abroad? How are other Asian companies strengthening their competitive position? These questions will be explored in this chapter. The analysis that follows is largely based on my questionnaire-survey data and findings from field research in Japan and Asia.

ASIAN OPERATIONS MANAGED BY JAPANESE, IN JAPANESE, AND FOR JAPANESE

Management by Japanese Persons

Thousands of Japanese companies operate in Asia. Most have Japanese CEOs who are dispatched from the Japanese parent company. According to the author's questionnaire-survey data, 92% of Japanese companies in Singapore and 80% of those in Taiwan have Japanese CEOs (Yoshihara, 1996, p. 21). Japanese companies in other Asian countries have the same percentages.

Localization of management at Asian subsidiaries is a problem which Japanese companies have long tried to solve. I conducted field research in Bangkok, Thailand as far back as 1974 on personnel problems of Japanese companies. At that time, one of my findings was that Japanese companies had more expatriates than American and European firms. In other words, localization of the management of Japanese firms was lagging behind that of Western companies (Yoshihara, 1975). Since that time, Japanese companies have accomplished substantial achievement in the localization at lower- and middle-management levels. Supervisors at factories and sales managers at offices are now mostly local people. Even at the level of functional department heads, the localization has made good progress.

However, localization has not progressed at the CEO level. The percentage ratio of Japanese overseas subsidiaries worldwide that had CEOs of local nationals was 38% in 1972, 47% in 1981, 35% in 1990, and 22% in 1994 (Yoshihara, 1995). Particularly in the case of important large subsidiaries in Asia, the CEO is almost always a Japanese expatriate.

In 1989, I had a chance to make a speech at the Matsushita Electric Industrial managing directors meeting of the subsidiaries in Asia (excluding China) and Oceania. All managers were Japanese. Currently, the company has around 70 subsidiaries in Asia, with less than five headed by a local CEO. The company has nearly 50 subsidiaries in China (including Hong Kong), and all of them have Japanese CEOs. Matsushita Electric Industrial is not exceptional. On the contrary, many Japanese multinationals share low rates of localization of CEOs in their Asian subsidiaries.

In addition to CEOs and other senior managers, there are many Japanese expatriates who are advisory staff. It is not uncommon for these Japanese advisers to take on the role of managers in the treatment of irregular situations or events such as production-line stoppage, quality problems of key parts, or significant customer complaints. Additionally, they often become communication liaisons between the parent company and the foreign subsidiary.

Here, let us pay attention to the localization of the management of Japanese subsidiaries of American and European multinationals, and compare it with the case of Japanese multinationals (Khan & Yoshihara, 1994). Nearly two-thirds (63%) of foreign companies in Japan have local Japanese CEOs. This is in sharp contrast to the case of the foreign subsidiaries of Japanese multinationals. Only 22% of Japanese foreign subsidiaries have CEOs of local nationality. Localization at the level of department head has also progressed more in foreign companies in Japan than in the foreign subsidiaries of Japanese companies.

American and European multinationals have promoted the localization of management further than Japanese multinationals in other countries, too. According to research comparing the localization of American, European, and Japanese multinationals, the percentage of foreign subsidiaries that have CEOs of local nationality is highest in American companies (69%), followed by European firms (52%), and is lowest in Japanese companies (26%) (Kopp, 1994b). Harzing (1999) reported similar findings.

Research comparing the localization of marketing managers in China finds Japanese companies lagging behind Western companies. For instance, Japanese companies average 16 marketing managers, who are Japanese expatriates, to only two Chinese managers, while Western companies have only three managers, who are expatriates, and 13 Chinese managers (Yachi, 1999).

The distinctive characteristic of Japanese-style international management explained above, i.e. the management of foreign subsidiaries by Japanese expatriates, is more evident in non-manufacturing companies than in manufacturing companies. Nearly all of the CEOs of foreign subsidiaries of banks, securities companies, non-life insurance companies, shipping companies, travel companies, and general trading companies are Japanese expatriates. CEOs of local nationality are rare exceptions (Yoshihara, 2001b).

Let us examine more closely the case of general trading companies. Nearly all of the CEOs of overseas offices (presidents of overseas subsidiaries or heads of overseas branches) are Japanese expatriates. Non-Japanese CEOs are exceptions, and they usually work in less important branches in smaller countries and cities. The only exception that the author has been able to identify is that of Itochu. J. W. Chai is the CEO of the U.S. subsidiary and also the CEO of the British subsidiary. He worked in Japan before joining Itochu and has no difficulty with the Japanese language. Mr J. W. Chai retired as the CEO at the American and the British subsidiary companies at the end of June 2002. The succeeding CEOs of both the U.S. and the British subsidiaries are both Japanese expatriates.

The nine major sogo shosha have 1248 overseas branches and subsidiaries (Yoshihara, 2001b). Together, they employ 24,929 in their oversees operations, out of which Japanese expatriates total 4,625. In other words, nearly 20% of the total employees at overseas subsidiaries and branches are Japanese expatriates. More importantly, these Japanese expatiates take the lion's share of top and middle management positions.

In the case of manufacturing multinationals, the number of Japanese expatriates is much smaller than general trading companies. Japanese expatriates account for only 2.3% of the total employees in overseas subsidiaries (Yoshihara, 2001a, p. 205).

An interesting question is: Why are Japanese more evident at non-manufacturing companies than manufacturers? Both non-manufacturers and manufacturers share a similar problem of language (limited English capabilities of Japanese employees), non-internationalization at Japanese parent companies, and transfer of resources from Japanese parent companies to their overseas subsidiaries. One important difference, however, can be seen in the nature of customers. The majority of customers of manufacturing companies are non-Japanese. Consumer goods such as TVs, digital cameras, and automobiles are sold almost inclusively to local buyers. Similarly, the main customers of industrial goods such as machines, semiconductors, electric parts, and automobile parts are local companies. However, in the case of non-manufacturing companies, their main customers are Japanese companies and Japanese individuals. For example, at general trading companies, trading with Japanese companies accounts for around 80% of the total business. The overwhelming majority of travel company customers are Japanese. Given this defining characteristic of the customer base, Japanese people and the Japanese language are naturally better suited to the demands of the market than locals (CEOs and managers of local nationality) and the local language.

Management in Japanese

The second characteristic of Japanese-style international management is management in the Japanese language. Three kinds of languages are used in Japanese multinationals (Yoshihara, 2001a, p. 222). At operation sites in Japan such as factories, sales branches, R&D organizations, and administrative offices, the Japanese language is used. In a similar way, at operation sites of foreign subsidiaries, communication is done in the local language. Either Japanese or English, or both languages are used in international communications. Information exchange between the Japanese staff and the foreign staff is defined as international communication. International communication is typically done between Japanese head offices and foreign subsidiaries. This is also done at Japanese parent companies when Japanese and non-Japanese discuss and exchange information. One also sees international communication at foreign subsidiaries when local managers and Japanese expatriates meet to discuss and make decisions. It is noteworthy that Japanese language plays an important role in the international communication. When Japanese people at the Japanese head office send information to foreign subsidiaries, they often send it in Japanese. For example, when Japanese staff at the Japanese parent company make telephone calls to their subsidiaries in Taiwan and Singapore, they use the Japanese language to communicate with almost all subsidiaries in the two countries: 93% of all subsidiaries in Taiwan and 74% in Singapore. They use English with only 8% of subsidiaries in Singapore. They never use English when they call their Taiwanese subsidiaries. A mixture of Japanese and English in telephone conversations is observed in 18% of Singapore subsidiaries and 7% of Taiwanese subsidiaries (Yoshihara, 2001a, p. 226).

Communication by facsimile follows a similar pattern. When Japanese staff at the parent company send information by fax to subsidiaries in Taiwan and

Singapore, they use Japanese 87 and 57%, respectively. Fax messages in English are sent to only 2% of Taiwanese and 16% of Singaporean subsidiaries.

At foreign subsidiaries, the Japanese language is not frequently used, except in communications among Japanese staff. In communications among local staff, the local language is used, and, communications between the local and Japanese staff are usually done in English.

According to data from my questionnaire survey, at meetings where both Japanese and local personnel attend, English is used at 64% of all subsidiaries in Singapore. Japanese is used at only 3% of the subsidiaries. Some subsidiaries (29%) use both Japanese and English. The situation regarding language use in Taiwanese subsidiaries is quite different. No subsidiaries use English at meetings where both Japanese and Taiwanese attend. Instead, both Japanese and Taiwanese staff use the Japanese language.

Based on my field research, I estimate the language use at Asian subsidiaries of Japanese companies in other Asian countries to be as follows. Singapore is a country where English is a commonly accepted language. By contrast, Taiwan is a country where Japanese is widely used. Other Asian countries fall somewhere between these two extremes. The Philippines, Malaysia, and Hong Kong are more similar to Singapore in that they rely more extensively on English. South Korea is like Taiwan in that many local employees speak Japanese. The remaining countries of Thailand, Indonesia, and China are located between these two groups. As for the case in Thailand, see Sombat (1993).

One characteristic of language usage in the international communications of Japanese companies is that important information is usually exchanged in Japanese. Information exchange regarding routine operations between Japanese parent companies and their foreign subsidiaries tends to be in English. However, when Japanese managers at the parent company talk on the telephone, write letters or send faxes to foreign subsidiaries on rather important business matters such as large-scale investment, introduction of new products, change in marketing strategy, and serious complaints from customers, they usually revert to Japanese. Because their English language ability is often limited, they have difficulty effectively communicating in English about these important matters.

Two points concerning language use in Japanese companies international communication should be stressed. First, Japanese parent companies send information to their foreign subsidiaries more often in Japanese than in English or local language. Second, important information is usually exchanged in the Japanese language between the parent company and its foreign subsidiaries. In light of these two points, Japanese-style international management may well be characterized as management in the Japanese language. Note that the aforementioned two characteristics, management by Japanese personnel and management in the Japanese language, are closely related to one another.

When Japanese expatriates play important roles in foreign subsidiaries, the Japanese language tends to be the de facto common official language. It is natural that Japanese expatriates use Japanese in their international communication. And when Japanese is used, local persons have difficulties in participating in information exchange and decision-making processes. Thus, capable local people are inclined not to want to work at Japanese companies. Consequently, the Japanese head offices conclude that they need to send more Japanese personnel to their subsidiaries to supplement the shortage of staff. As the number of Japanese expatriates increases at foreign offices, the amount of Japanese language used at foreign subsidiaries will increase proportionately. Thus, there a vicious cycle develops between management by Japanese personnel and management in the Japanese language.

Japanese Central Hub Model

The third characteristic of Japanese-style international management is the Japanese central hub model (Yoshihara, Hayashi & Yasumuro, 1988).

Japanese parent companies occupy a place at the center of the multinational corporate system. Foreign subsidiaries are peripheral organizations. Japanese parent companies transfer their resources such as technology, know-how, and brand reputation to their overseas subsidiaries. The transfer is done unilaterally from Japanese parent to its overseas subsidiaries. There is essentially no reverse transfer from foreign subsidiaries back to the parent company.

To transfer technology and know-how, Japanese parent companies dispatch Japanese managers, experts, and engineers to their foreign subsidiaries. There is almost no reverse flow of personnel from the subsidiaries back to the parent companies.

As a consequence, foreign subsidiaries are dependent on Japanese parent companies. They do not stand on their own two feet. Indeed, they cannot survive without a continuous transfer of resources from the parent. The foreign subsidiaries are often likened to Japanese university students who live on the money sent from their parents.

The relationship between Japanese parent companies and their foreign subsidiaries is linear and dyadic. Each foreign subsidiary has a close relationship only with the parent. The relationship between and among overseas subsidiaries is not developed. The central hub model of Japanese multinationals explained earlier is shown in Fig. 1 (Yoshihara et al., 1988, p. 42).

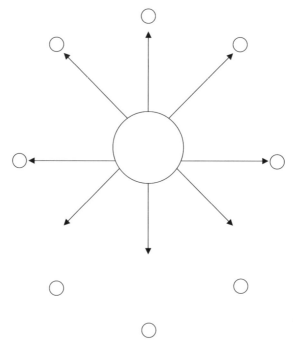

Fig. 1. Japanese Central Hub Model. *Note:* Central Circle: Japanese Parent Companies;
Peripheral Circles: Foreign Subsidiaries; Arrows: Transfer of Resources.

THE BRIGHT AND DARK SIDES OF JAPANESE
COMPANIES IN ASIA

The Successful Japanese Production System

A much vaunted production system has been developed and practiced in Japan. For
many Japanese manufacturers, it is the basis of their international competitiveness.
Research and experience have shown that this production system works not only in
Japan but also in foreign countries, including other Asian countries. Manufacturing
subsidiaries in Asia that have practiced the Japanese production system have
generally performed well.

The Japanese production system is composed of such elements as Kaizen (e.g.
quality control and improvement) campaigns, workers involved in multifunction
positions, information-sharing among workers, participation of workers in

problem-solving, as well as egalitarian treatment of workers and managers. The Japanese style of personnel management is viewed as being a supportive factor in the effectiveness of the Japanese production system. Specific practices of employment security, internal promotion, seniority-based wages and promotion, on-the-job training, and company unions are all closely related with the Japanese production system.

The Japanese production system is attractive to local workers and supervisors at Asian factories of Japanese companies. Their employment is highly secure. They are encouraged to use their minds and participate in problem-solving activities. They appreciate the egalitarian treatment they receive, which is designed to minimize any status differences between workers and managers. Specific practices in this regard include workers and managers wearing the same work uniforms, having the same meals in the same factory canteens, using the same rest rooms, and working according to the same schedule (in terms of starting and ending the working day).

Japanese factories in Asia are a success in the sense that they are doing well with motivated local supervisors and workers executing the Japanese production system. Additionally, an increasing number of local Asian companies have tried to learn and implement the Japanese production system. Indeed, it can be said that the Japanese production system is now widely practiced in Asia and has contributed to production innovation in Asia.

Limits of Japanese-Style International Management

Though Japanese companies in Asia may be attractive to local workers, they are not attractive to capable local managerial, professional and engineering people. There are several reasons. Let us focus on the three characteristics of Japanese-style international management discussed previously.

The first characteristic is the management by Japanese. The position of the CEO and many other important positions are occupied by Japanese expatriates. Promotion opportunities for local persons, especially managerial persons, are limited. It has been demonstrated that in foreign subsidiaries of Japanese companies, there is a glass or "rice paper" ceiling blocking the promotion of local personnel (Kopp, 1994a).

The second characteristic is management in Japanese. Unless local people understand the Japanese language, they have difficulties in participating in the information exchange and decision-making process. Most local personnel do not understand Japanese, nor do Japanese companies encourage learning Japanese.

Consequently, Japanese multinationals that use the Japanese language as the common language find themselves handicapped in recruiting capable, local managerial and professional personnel.

The third characteristic is the Japanese central hub model. At Japanese multinationals, the core personnel are Japanese who work at the Japanese parent companies. They are positioned in the mainstream of information and dominate the decision-making process. However, local personnel are peripheral.

Compared with domestic firms, multinational enterprises are generally in a position to enjoy the advantage of utilizing local resources drawn from many different countries. Among these resources, probably the most important are the local human resources, especially high-level managerial, professional and engineering personnel. Japanese multinationals do not enjoy this advantage because Japanese-style international management discourages local talent from working for them.

CHINESE MANAGEMENT AND FREE-MARKET COMPETITION

Within the Asian region, China is a critical country for Japanese multinationals. China has attracted the largest portion of Japanese manufacturing investment in Asia. Indeed, China is the second largest host country for the Japanese manufacturing investment, lagging only behind the U.S. Second, Chinese companies are swiftly emerging as competitors to Japanese multinationals not only within China but also in other Asian countries and throughout the rest of the world. Third, these Chinese companies are fully taking advantage of their latecomer position. They introduce state-of-the-art technology from Japanese, American, and European companies, and they also apply advanced management systems and know-how. In this regard, American-style management is more popular than Japanese-style management.

Consider the case of Haier. Haier is the largest Chinese manufacturer of electric home appliances. It is ranked ninth worldwide (*Appliance Manufacturer*, February 2001). Our analysis shows that Haier has achieved rapid growth for two reasons. The first reason is its latecomer advantage. Haier adopts technology from German and Japanese companies. It learns foreign technology, digests it, and adapts it to local Chinese market conditions. Haier quickly develops new products on a daily basis.

The second reason for Haier's rapid growth is its management. The characteristic of Haier's management may be most evidently represented in its personnel management of "horse race" without a horse judge (the word "horse race" is used in the company).

At Haier, there is no advance evaluation of employees. Everyone is given an equal opportunity to work in a job. Only after employees finish their work are they evaluated for their results. Thus, at Haier, an employee (horse) is not evaluated as a good horse or a bad horse by personnel managers (horse judge) before the race. Every horse is given a chance to run the race. After the race, the horse is evaluated on the record and given a monetary reward or penalty. This horse race is applied not only to workers but also to managerial personnel.

Human-resource management at Haier has the following characteristics.

(1) individual evaluation (not group evaluation).
(2) instantaneous evaluation (not long-term evaluation).
(3) monetary reward and penalty.
(4) openness about the rules and results of evaluations.
(5) evaluation based on quantitative records.
(6) demotion of a fixed percentage of poorly performing employees.

Let us briefly review these characteristics. Workers and managers are evaluated individually. Teamwork or group activities are not considered in the evaluation. Second, evaluation is done immediately after the job is completed. Workers are evaluated everyday. They learn the results of their evaluation when they finish their jobs each evening. They record their job performance and by that record can know the results of the evaluation (as reflected in their amount of daily wages).

Third, reward and punishment are based on monetary terms. Wages are paid daily on a piece rate. When workers do their jobs properly, they are given better wages, and when they do jobs poorly, they are penalized. Workers who find defects passed on from the person ahead of them on the production line are also given rewards. Fourth, the rules governing evaluation are open to all employees. Employees know how they are evaluated. The results of the evaluation are made public and posted on a notice board on the wall of the shop floor every evening after work. The results (the record of output and amount of daily wages, including rewards and penalties) are listed individually beside the name of each worker.

Fifth, evaluation is made only on the basis of performance. Moreover, the performance record is a quantitative evaluation. There is no room for discretionary or subjective evaluation by supervisors or managers.

Finally, workers and managers with low performance records are automatically demoted. In the case of managers, the lowest 5% of managers are demoted annually. Workers are classified into three categories based on their performance. There are "excellent workers," "good workers," and "trial workers." Trial workers will be fired unless they improve their evaluations.

Human-resource management at Haier is almost the opposite of Japanese-style management. In China, Japanese companies are sometimes viewed as being like state-owned enterprises, while Haier is more capitalistic.

Importantly, Haier is not an exception in China. It enjoys a highly regarded reputation as a model company. Indeed, many Chinese companies are studying and adopting Haier's style management. Particularly among fast-growing Chinese companies, there are many that are more or less like Haier. At the present time, Haier's capitalistic and competitive management appears to fit well with Chinese people. It seems that the physical, psychological, and intellectual energies of Chinese workers are well utilized under this type of Chinese-style capitalist management.

Chinese-style capitalist management may be seen as a reaction to the old management under socialism. Under the old socialistic management, there were no layoffs, and wages were guaranteed and based on age, education, and political factors. Wage increases and promotions were heavily influenced by personal relationships with bosses and connections to political party organizations. No incentives existed for motivating individuals to work harder and compete with one another.

It may be worthwhile mentioning that Haier's style of capitalistic and competitive management is also practiced in Korea, Taiwan, and Singapore. For example, the principle of demotion of a fixed rate (5%) for poorly performing employees and managers is practiced in many Korean companies. During interviews in Taiwan, one Taiwanese employee, commenting on Japanese management, stated, "I am like a civil servant working at some government office."

PROBLEMS IN JAPANESE PARENT COMPANIES

Investment in Asia and Hollowing out in Japan

Japan is no longer necessarily the best site of production for Japanese multinationals anymore. Japan has lost much of its attractiveness for production. For example, wages are higher than elsewhere in Asia. Japanese workers' wages are more than 10 times higher than those of Malaysian and Thai workers and about 30 times higher than those of young Chinese female workers in the Cantonese area. Japanese workers, especially younger workers dislike working at factories. Most Japanese factories in Japan are staffed predominantly by middle-aged females workers. In terms of productivity, these women cannot compete with young Asian female workers who are both dexterous and have good eyesight. The high cost of land is another factor. Similarly, the costs of industrial infrastructure items such as electricity, water, telecommunication, and domestic transportation are among the highest in the world, and there are extensive regulations that take up managerial time and energy. Consequently, increasing numbers of Japanese companies are shifting their domestic production to overseas facilities. Those firms who already have overseas facilities are decreasing or stopping domestic production and increasing foreign production. This shift of production to overseas operations is most evident for matured products. However, even the production of newly developed and technologically sophisticated products is being shifted from domestic factories to foreign facilities, particularly those in Asia. Additionally, the production of some of newly developed products is initiated not in Japanese factories but in overseas plants.

This shift of production from Japan to other Asian countries has led to a hollowing out of Japanese production. The hollowing out of production can be classified into three types as follows (Yoshihara, 2001a, p. 117). The first type is a *relative* decrease in production in Japan. Production in Japan increases, but overseas production increases at a faster rate. This type of hollowing out of production largely started after 1985. The second type is the *absolute* decrease in production in Japan. Japanese companies decrease or stop production at their Japanese factories and shift production to their foreign plants. This type of hollowing out is quite common, as in the production of audiovisual appliances such as TVs and VCRs.

The first two types of hollowing out represent a decrease in domestic production in the quantitative sense. However, the third type is a hollowing out of production in the qualitative sense. Not only is the assembly or fabrication of the final products moved offshore, but the production of parts, devices, and component materials is moved from Japanese factories to overseas plants. Many Japanese multinationals are now in the process of shifting the production of manufacturing equipment, molds, jigs, and software development to overseas factories. In short, core production activities and capabilities are gradually being shifted from Japanese parent companies to foreign subsidiaries. Will Japanese parent companies become empty at the center of their production activities?

The hollowing out of Japanese parent companies is not limited to production. It also extends toward R&D activities. Although the scale is still small, R&D activities have started to shift abroad. Nearly half (47%) of Japanese foreign manufacturing subsidiaries are engaged in some kind of R&D activity. In Asia, subsidiaries conducting R&D activities amount to 37%. Even in China, one-third (32%) of the subsidiaries carry out R&D activities (Yoshihara, Methe & Iwata, 1999).

The home ground of Japanese multinational enterprises is Japan. Their main business activities such as R&D, production, marketing, and administration are still carried out in Japan. Also, Japanese companies continue to develop their resources and capabilities based on their operations in their home ground. Moreover, the resources and capabilities developed in Japanese parent companies constitute a prime source of their international competitiveness. As the hollowing out of Japanese home ground proceeds, Japanese companies will lose their core competitive capabilities.

Changes in the nature of production in Japan are also weakening the competitive edge of the Japanese production system. One of the strengths of the Japanese production system is that it is good at incremental innovation. Many small improvements are continuously being made on the shop floor. These innovations lead to low production costs and low product-rejection rates. At present, incremental innovation is not as important as before. The production situation has changed drastically. Product lines and products themselves are chaning much more rapidly than before. In the case of personal computers, for example, it is usual that the lifespan of a product model lasts for only three months. The duration of production is too short to take advantage of any incremental innovations. Production costs, rejection rates, and the quality of products are basically determined during the product-development stage. There is little room for improvement on these points at the production stage.

Resistance to Change

The negative effect of these developments is exacerbated because Japanese companies are plagued with a resistance to change. The vaunted lifetime employment system is a major factor spurring resistance to change in Japanese companies. No Japanese company has ever publicly declared a policy of lifetime employment. But many companies have pursued the goal of employment security alongside goals of growth and profitability. A drastic reduction of employees in a short period is often avoided, even when such action is necessary to achieve a recovery in profitability and growth. Japanese companies commonly resort to a milder measure of a gradual reduction in employees, first reducing the numbers of temporary employees, then reducing or stopping new employment. Early retirement may be encouraged also for some employees. It takes time to reduce overall employee numbers. Drastic reductions in the number of employees over a short period of time are rare in Japanese companies.

Keiretsu membership is another factor that works against Japanese companies' willingness to change. Keiretsu are stable trade relationships between assembling companies and their suppliers. Similarly, long-lasting, stable trade relationships are developed between manufacturers and marketing companies. These types of relationships are most developed in the automobile industry, but they exist widely in many industries in Japan. Because these are stable trade relationships based on stable transactions over a long period, the system cannot be changed easily. Both assembling companies and suppliers develop specific tangible and intangible assets that are well suited to the specifics of their trade relationship. Suppliers are mostly small and medium-sized companies. Thus, large assembling companies are hesitant in introducing changes in their trade relationship, since they do not want to be held responsible for the bankruptcy of abandoned suppliers. Assembly companies may have to experience real crisis themselves in order to break their traditional keiretsu relationships. Nissan Motor's recovery under Ghosn's leadership provides one such case in point.

Newly emerging Asian competitors in South Korea, Taiwan, and China are not as constrained by similar resistance factors as are Japanese companies. Because they are newcomers, they are in a better position than established Japanese companies to pursue drastic changes in strategy and management.

Management by Internally Promoted Old Men

There is one final consideration. Large Japanese companies hire new university graduates every year. These new hires will stay in the same company for a long time. When they reach about 50 years old, one or two are promoted to the post of directors. Among those promoted to director, one will eventually become president around the age of 60. This pattern of promotion is widely observed among Japanese companies.

Regarding the presidents of Japanese companies, three points are worthy of consideration: (1) it is common practice for presidents to be promoted internally from among existing board members and extremely rare for presidents to be sourced from outside; (2) the existing president of a Japanese company usually selects a successor; and (3) Japanese companies' presidents are usually rather old compared to their European and North American counterparts (generally around 60 years old). Presidents younger than 50 years old are very rare in Japan. The average age of presidents of companies listed on the Tokyo Stock Exchange (3,594 companies) is 59.25. Those presidents who are younger than fifty years old number only 450 (12.52%). Presidents of the large companies, listed on the first section of the Tokyo Stock Exchange, are almost all over 60 (*Nikkei Business*, July 1, 2002, p. 33). Because of these three characteristics, the presidents of Japanese companies generally do not have strong power bases necessary to exercise dynamic leadership.

Internal promotion works against selecting individuals capable of implementing drastic changes in the strategy and management of the firm. Internally promoted presidents are embedded in existing organizations and are accustomed to working within the current situation. They lack novel ideas and an ability to adopt an outsider's view about their companies. In addition, presidents have difficulty in denying the strategy and management of predecessors who appointed them as president. Newly appointed presidents are under pressure to accept the existing practices and avoid the repudiation of prior strategies. What they can do is make gradual and incremental changes. Radical changes in a short period of time are almost impossible. Finally, presidents of Japanese companies may simply be too old physically to work hard and to exercise strong leadership.

Generally speaking, unless companies are in a real crisis, it is difficult to bring about drastic changes in strategy and management. Japanese companies have been in trouble for more than 10 years since the bubble burst in the economy in 1990, and one should ask, "Is the crisis serious enough for Japanese companies to start to make drastic changes in their strategy and management?"

CONCLUDING REMARKS

For the last half century, the international business strategy of Japanese companies has changed drastically, and exports have occupied the central position in their international business strategy for a long time. In 1985, when the Plaza Accord was concluded, this marked a turning point. The Plaza Accord triggered a sharp appreciation in the Japanese yen. Accordingly, the importance of exports declined, and overseas production took central position in Japanese international strategy. Currently, overseas R&D has become the central focus of many firms. Most Japanese multinational enterprises are now trying to operate on a truly global basis. However, the management of their international business changed little. Their global operations are managed by Japanese people, in the Japanese language, from central Japanese hubs.

The combination of global operations and Japanese-style international management has several advantages. It is well suited to respond to Japanese customers and to transfer resources such as technology and know-how from Japanese parent companies to their overseas subsidiaries. As internationalization at Japanese parent companies is not well developed, Japanese-style international management may have fit Japanese multinationals. Indeed, until the latter half of the 1980s, Japanese-style international management might have been considered a contributory factor to the success of the Asian operations of Japanese multinationals.

However, as Asian operations have become more important, and the numbers of Asian competitors such as South Korean, Taiwanese, and Chinese companies have increased, the problematic side of Japanese-style international management has become evident. This style of management does not provide opportunities to local managerial and professional employees to demonstrate their ability and initiative. Under Japanese management, overseas subsidiaries cannot become innovation centers that develop new products, technology, and businesses.

Japanese multinationals are now facing the challenging task of innovation in their international management. Japanese-style international management has continued for a long time. Because of its past success, and because it is based on Japanese management in Japanese parent companies, it will not be easy to change the style of international management.

ACKNOWLEDGMENTS

The author would like to thank the anonymous reviewers, the two commentators at the Colloquium, George Bearnard Graen and Shige Makino, and the Colloquium Special Issue editor, Tom Roehl for comments on earlier drafts.

REFERENCES

Harzing, A. W. (1999). MNE staffing policies for the managing director position in foreign subsidiaries. In: C. Brewster & H. Harris (Eds), *International HRM: Contemporary Issues in Europe* (pp. 67–68). London: Routledge.

Khan, S., & Yoshihara, H. (1994). *Strategy and performance of foreign companies in Japan*, Westport, CT: Quorum Books.

Kopp, R. (1994a). *The rice-paper ceiling: Breaking through Japanese business culture*. Berkeley, CA: Stone Bridge Press.

Kopp, R. (1994b). International human resource policies and practices in Japanese, European, and United States multinationals. *Human Resource Management*, *33*(4), 581–599.

Sombat, N. (1993). *Localization of management of Japanese companies in Thailand, December 1993*. Unpublished Master's Degree Thesis Paper, Graduate Business School of Kobe University.

Yachi, H. (1999). Nihon kigyo no eigyo kanri taisei [Marketing organization of Japanese companies] (Working Paper Series, No. 142). Faculty of Business Administration, Yokohama National University, April 1999.

Yoshihara, H. (1975). *Personnel practices of Japanese companies in Thailand*. Bangkok: Economic Cooperation Center for the Asian and Pacific Region.

Yoshihara, H. (1995). Kokusaika to nihonteki keiei [Internationalization and Japanese management]. In: H. Morikawa & S. Yonekura (Eds), *Kodo Seicho wo Koete* [Beyond High Economic Growth] (pp. 205–240). Tokyo: Iwanami.

Yoshihara, H. (2001a). *Kokusai keiei* [International business], New edition. Tokyo: Yuhikaku.

Yoshihara, H. (2001b). Global operations managed by Japanese and in Japanese. In: M. Berry, M. McDermott & J. H. Taggart (Eds), *Multinationals in a New Era* (pp. 153–165). Basingstoke, UK: Palgrave.

Yoshihara, H. (1996). *Mijuku na kokusai keiei* [Immature international management]. Tokyo: Hakuto.
Yoshihara, H., Hayashi, K., & Yasumuro, K. (1988). *Nihon kigyo no gurobaru keiei* [Global business of Japanese companies]. Tokyo: Toyo Keizai.
Yoshihara, H., Methe, D., & Iwata, S. (1999). Kaigai kenkyukaihatsu no shinten to seika [Overseas R&D and its performance]. *Kokumin Keizai Zassi, 179*(6), 17–31.

DOES IT REALLY MATTER IF JAPANESE MNCs THINK GLOBALLY?

Schon Beechler, Orly Levy, Sully Taylor and Nakiye Boyaçigiller

ABSTRACT

This paper explores the empirical relationships between the global orientation of the top management team, geocentrism of the staffing and promotion system, and boundary spanning structures and processes with the individual outcome variables of employee commitment to, and excitement about, their job and organization in ten units of two highly diversified high-technology Japanese multinational corporations. The results from the study show that employee perceptions of the top management team's global orientation, geocentrism, and boundary spanning structures and processes influence individual attitudes of employees in Japanese MNCs. The implications of these results for further research and managerial practice are discussed.

INTRODUCTION

Globalization has changed the boundaries, competitive landscape, and organizational structure and strategy of firms operating in the world marketplace (Bartlett & Ghoshal, 1989, 1998; Porter, 1986; Prahalad & Hamel, 1994). How multinational firms handle the complex requirements stemming from global competition has become a pressing and persistent issue in the field of international

Japanese Firms in Transition: Responding to the Globalization Challenge
Advances in International Management, Volume 17, 261–288
Copyright © 2005 by Elsevier Ltd.
All rights of reproduction in any form reserved
ISSN: 0747-7929/doi:10.1016/S0747-7929(04)17011-X

and strategic management (Kim & Mauborgne, 1996; Prahalad, 1991). The winners on today's global economic playing field will be those "transnational" firms (Bartlett & Ghoshal, 1989) that can simultaneously integrate their global operations and respond to local conditions, balancing the complementary and contradictory imperatives of organizational integration and differentiation (Lawrence & Lorsch, 1967). While the organizational capability to simultaneously balance global integration and local responsiveness is essential to implementing globally competitive strategies, this capability is not easily developed or sustained.

In the drive toward becoming a transnational corporation, structural responses are inadequate for dealing with these requirements. The common theme across writings by scholars and futurists is that it is only the human organization, with its inherent complexity and flexibility, that will enable firms to successfully meet the new competitive challenges and enable MNCs to succeed (Bartlett & Ghoshal, 1989, 1990; Evans, 1993; Evans, Pucik, & Barsoux, 2002; Pucik, Tichy, & Barnett, 1992).

A key driver of MNC success, then, is the ability of MNCs to develop and manage a human organization to replace the relatively inflexible structural solutions often adopted in the past (Ashkenas, Ulrich, Jick & Kerr, 1995; Bartlett & Ghoshal, 1998; Kanter, 1991). Included in the human organization are a mix of both formal and informal components of the organization that rely on individuals, such as: (1) a global orientation of employees, particularly key managers; (2) boundary spanning structures and processes that cross organizational, functional, geographic, and hierarchical levels, creating the complex information infrastructure needed to implement a global strategy (Bartlett & Ghoshal, 1998); (3) access to information and opportunities (Kobrin, 1994); as well as (4) a clear vision that helps to unite the activities of a diverse set of individuals and organizations into a clear, coherent whole (Ashkenas et al., 1995; Beechler et al., 2000).

Although they made rapid progress during the 1980s and 1990s, most observers agree that Japanese companies have had a particularly difficult time making the transition to transnational status and that Japanese firms continue to lag far behind their Western counterparts in their international management sophistication (e.g. Campbell & Holden, 1993; Kobayashi, 1985; Pucik, 1999; Tachiki, 1991; Trevor, 1983). While Japanese organizations became known for their "human organization," including careful staffing and socialization, participative decision-making processes, and egalitarianism, certain aspects of the human organization continue to be the Achilles heel of Japanese firms operating abroad (Bartlett & Yoshihara, 1988; Kono & Clegg, 2001).

Most Japanese multinational corporations, for example, have struggled with HQ-dominated control systems and decision-making dominated by Japanese nationals, whether they are stationed at HQs or at the local affiliates (Bartlett & Yoshihara, 1988; Harzing, 1999; Kono & Clegg, 2001; Pucik, 1999; Trevor, 1983). Japanese MNCs are also characterized by Japanese-centric staffing policies and practices (e.g. Boyacigiller, 1990; Kono & Clegg, 2001) and the presence of a "rice paper ceiling" (Bartlett & Yoshihara, 1988; Boyacigiller, 1990; Kono & Clegg, 2001; Kopp, 1994, 1999; Pucik, 1999). The results of previous research imply that a core challenge of Japanese MNCs is creating a global orientation in the top management team of the firm, as well as an international staffing policy and boundary-crossing processes and structures that lead to higher levels of inclusiveness in decision-making and open promotion and development opportunities for Japanese and non-Japanese alike.

In order to understand how the human organization is either hindering or helping Japanese MNCs meet their strategic challenges, we examine data from two large Japanese MNCs which are part of a larger study on Organizational Competitiveness in MNCs.[1] In this paper, we examine the relationship between the individual-level outcomes of employee commitment and excitement about working at their firms, and predictors of the global orientation of the top management team, boundary spanning structures and processes, and geocentric human resource management practices.

In the following section, we turn to a discussion of the theoretical background of the specific relationships examined in this paper, before proceeding to a presentation of the results from the Japanese MNCs and their implications for research and practice. It should be noted that in the following section, we draw on a number of theoretical frameworks to develop our hypotheses. This is necessary as we bring together a number of areas that have not generally been studied together in the past.

THEORETICAL BACKGROUND AND HYPOTHESES

Rhetoric in both the academic literature and the popular press has coalesced around the notion that high-performance organizations are characterized first and foremost by their focus on their human assets. In this paper, we focus on three key levers that Japanese multinational corporations can use to maximize their human assets for competitive advantage: a global orientation of the top management team, boundary spanning structures and processes, and a geocentric HR system (see Fig. 1). We postulate that these levers can lead to positive organizational performance outcomes as measured at the individual level. Specifically, we examine the influence of these organizational levers on individuals' *attitudes* of commitment and excitement. We will begin with the lever of global

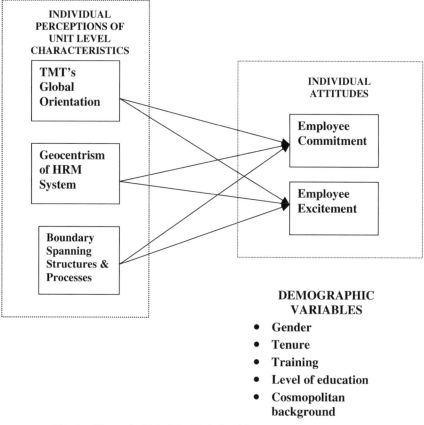

Fig. 1. Theoretical Model of Relationships Between the Variables.

orientation, and examine its potential impact on individual level employee outcomes.

Global Orientation of Top Management

While the concepts of global orientation and global mindset have been accepted into the popular lexicon of both academics and practitioners, there are still no commonly accepted definitions of these constructs (Levy, Beechler, Taylor, & Boyacigiller, 1999). Conceptually, we define global orientation as a characteristic of MNC top management which encompasses an orientation toward the external environment, especially the global marketplace, and the ability to scan the world from a broad perspective and to integrate geographically distant operations as well as diverse trends and opportunities in the global environment (Bartunek, Gordon & Weathersby, 1983; Rhinesmith, 1992). It also encompasses the capability of key decision-makers in the organization to interact with employees and other key stakeholders from many countries and to manage culturally diverse interorganizational relationships with customers, suppliers, and regulators (Goldberg, 1976; Kanter, 1995). As such, it encompasses managers' mindsets, attitudes, skills, and behaviors. Global mindset, however, is more narrowly defined as a cognitive orientation (rather than a behavior or skill) that is characterized by two fundamental underlying dimensions: cosmopolitan orientation and cognitive complexity (Levy et al., 1999).

A global orientation of top management reflects two pervasive managerial challenges in contemporary MNCs: the challenge faced by managers to know about and be responsive to multiple local environments and the challenge to integrate and coordinate across geographically distant and culturally diverse operations and markets (Bartlett & Ghoshal, 1989; Murtha, Lenway & Bagozzi, 1998; Prahalad & Doz, 1987).

In organizations where managers have a global orientation, it is likely that employees will perceive a common mission and set of goals that transcend national and subunit boundaries. Global orientation therefore acts as a common, unifying mechanism at the top of the organization to help focus the attention and efforts of employees around a set of superordinate goals, creating objects of commitment for employees. These objects of commitment can include such things as values, goals, principles, policies, and artifacts of the particular organizational unit (Virtanen, 2000). Therefore, we predict that the presence of a global orientation at the top of the organization will positively influence individual employee feelings of commitment to the organization:

Hypothesis 1A. Employees' perceptions of the global orientation of the top management team will be positively related to employee commitment.

In addition to its positive influence on employee commitment, we predict that global orientation of the top management team will positively impact employee excitement about their jobs and about working for their organization. In this study, we focus on excitement rather than on the more traditional measure of employee satisfaction, following the lead of Prahalad (1998). Prahalad argues that rather than focusing on employee satisfaction, which can translate into complacency, managers should focus on the level of excitement employees feel about their work and their organizations because it is excitement and challenge that drives employees to work hard for the objectives of the firm, to continue to learn and apply their knowledge, and to implement organizational strategy, transforming strategic intent into reality for the organization. Global orientation of the top management team engenders employee excitement by clarifying the goals and global vision of the firm and by expanding employees' vision from the local to the global context and increasing their understanding (and work motivation) of how their activities fit into a broader organizational mission (Hackman & Oldham, 1976). We predict that:

Hypothesis 1B. Employees' perceptions of the global orientation of the top management team will be positively related to employee excitement.

Boundary Spanning Structures and Processes

While a global orientation is important, previous research (e.g. Nohria & Ghoshal, 1997) indicates that a global orientation by itself is insufficient for achieving global success. Boundary spanning structures and processes must exist in order for a global orientation to influence actual decisions made in the MNC. As globalization transforms the external environment, multinational firms can no longer afford rigid traditional organizational boundaries that separate employees, tasks, processes, and places. Rather, they need to establish flexible structures and processes that span boundaries, allow greater fluidity of movement throughout the organization, and support swift, coordinated action. These structures and processes include such mechanisms as global teams, global job responsibilities, and global communication networks. Boundary spanning structures and processes enable multinational firms to cut across functional, geographic, and external boundaries and to move ideas, information, decisions, talent, and resources where they are most needed (Ashkenas et al., 1995).

Boundary spanning structures and processes allow employees to engage with various constituencies both inside (top management, affiliate managers, peers in other functional areas, in other affiliates) and outside the organization (e.g. customers, unions, suppliers). Because organizational commitment is dependent on "the degree to which the individual internalizes or adopts characteristics or perspectives of the organization" (O'Reilly & Chatman, 1986), the heightened interaction across boundaries nurtures this commitment by increasing the individual's perspective of the total organization. Thus, cross-boundary engagement with various organizational entities can lead to greater psychological attachment and higher commitment, leading us to make the following prediction:

Hypothesis 2A. Employees' perceptions of the presence of structures and processes that span geographic boundaries will be positively related to employees' commitment.

Boundary spanning can also positively affect employee excitement. As noted above, Prahalad (1998) argues that in today's complex, competitive environment, having committed workers is not enough. Work and workers demand more. Employees want to be engaged and excited about their work, and the presence of boundary spanning structures and processes provides employees with an enabling context to realize their aspirations. Moreover, as employees come to consider themselves as possessors of human capital essential to organizational performance and innovation, they will seek greater boundary spanning opportunities in order to enhance their learning opportunities. Hence, we predict that:

Hypothesis 2B. Employees' perceptions of boundary spanning will be positively related to employees' feelings of excitement.

Geocentrism

In addition to boundary spanning structures and processes and a global orientation among the top management team, we predict that the perceived opportunities available to employees during their organizational careers will influence their levels of commitment, excitement, and turnover. In this study, we operationalized these perceived opportunities using the framework and measures developed by Kobrin (1994).

Drawing on the seminal work of Perlmutter (1969) and Perlmutter and Heenan (1979), Kobrin (1994) re-introduced the idea of geocentric mindset and its importance in international management in a 1994 study of 68 *Fortune* 500 firms. In this study, Kobrin did not elicit the mindsets of individual respondents, but rather elicited their judgments, attitudes, and expectations about policies and managerial mindsets in their firms. He operationalized this construct with a five-item index of geocentrism. The items comprising the index are aspects of a geocentric managerial mindset reflected in international HR management policy, specifically, the impact of nationality on the selection and careers of managers.

A large part of the Kobrin geocentrism scale focuses on the "perceived" opportunity structure for all nationals within the multinational company. The opportunity for local nationals to advance in MNCs has often been seen as problematic, and indeed, there has been much discussion in the literature on the impact of the "rice paper ceiling" in Japanese firms (cf. Boyacigiller, 1990; Kono & Clegg, 2001; Kopp, 1999).

To the extent that nationality is unimportant in selecting individuals for managerial positions, commitment to the organization may increase, since employees may see increased opportunities for themselves and others like themselves, even if their nationality is different from that of the headquarters country, leading to higher levels of commitment.

As work on commitment by Meyer and Allen (1997) has shown, it is possible to differentiate between continuance commitment where employees remain with an organization because they recognize the costs of leaving and affective commitment, where they will feel more emotionally committed to the organization. In this research, we have focused on measuring affective commitment which is predicted to influence the level of effort an employee will exert toward accomplishing organizational objectives. This leads to the following hypothesis:

Hypothesis 3A. Employees' perceptions of geocentrism will be positively related to employees' commitment.

Similar to the arguments above, the perceived openness of the organization, as implied by the geocentrism scale, will also lead to higher levels of employee excitement.

Hypothesis 3B. Employees' perceptions of geocentrism will be positively related to employees' excitement.

METHODOLOGY

Sample

The sample for this study consists of 521 employees working in 10 organizational units of two highly diversified high-technology multinational firms headquartered in Japan. These two companies are similar in terms of their business lines, size (approximately 150,000 employees worldwide) and degree of internationalization. The sample includes employees working in both the headquarters and eight overseas affiliates located in a total of five countries (Australia, Spain, Philippines, Thailand, USA). To be eligible for participation, overseas affiliates had to have a minimum of 100 employees, and companies were asked to include both relatively successful and relatively unsuccessful units in the sample. Table 1 presents the sample by company and location (By agreement with the participating firms, their identities cannot be disclosed).

Table 1. Number of Employees Participating According to Organizational Unit.

Company	Location	N
Company 1	Japan (HQ)	78
Company 1	USA	63
Company 1	USA	97
Company 1	USA	37
Company 2	Japan (HQ)	54
Company 2	USA	76
Company 2	Philippines	25
Company 2	Thailand	22
Company 2	Australia	42
Company 2	Spain	27
Total		521

In terms of demographic characteristics, 407 (78.1%) of the sample participants were males, 114 were females (21.9%); 42 (8.1%) had high school education, 86 (16.5%) had some college education, 253 (48.6%) had a college degree, 50 (9.6%) had some graduate education, and 90 (17.3%) had a graduate diploma.

Research Methods

Data were collected using a questionnaire survey distributed both in Japan and in overseas affiliates of each of the companies using a random stratified sampling strategy in each unit. The survey included previously validated measures whenever possible, and the original English-language questionnaire was translated into Japanese and Spanish by professional translators and then back-translated and checked for equivalency to the English original. In Japan, Japanese language questionnaires were used. Spanish questionnaires were distributed in Spain. In the U.S., the Philippines, and Thailand, questionnaires were distributed in English, as English is the common language used within the affiliates, and all participants spoke English.

   In addition to gathering questionnaire surveys, members of the research team conducted face-to-face interviews with at least five members of the top management team in each location. These interviews were tape-recorded and transcribed. Interviews lasted between approximately 1 and 2.5 hr. Data from these interviews are used to validate and interpret the quantitative results reported in this paper.

Measures

In the following section, we describe the various measures used in the study. Additionally, individual items for all of the measures are presented in the Appendix.

Dependent Variables

Organizational Commitment

Organizational commitment was measured using the nine-item short form of the Organizational Commitment Questionnaire developed by Mowday, Steers and Porter (1979). Respondents indicated their agreement/disagreement with these items on a 7-point Likert-type scale, where 1 = "strongly disagree" and 7 = "strongly agree." In order to check the psychometric properties, an exploratory factor analysis (principal axis factoring method) was performed. Based on the scree plot, minimum contribution to variance explained (5%), and residuals correlation criteria (Hair, Anderson, Tatham & Black, 1995; Tabachnick & Fidell, 1989), one factor was extracted, which accounted for 55.11% of the overall amount of variance in the items. The minimum loading was 0.48, and the index had an alpha coefficient of 0.91, indicating that this index has an acceptable level of internal consistency.

Employee Excitement

Drawing on Prahalad (1998), we created a four-item index to measure employee excitement. Respondents were presented with statements to which they indicated agreement/disagreement using a 7-point Likert-type scale (1 = "strongly disagree" and 7 = "strongly agree"). The score for this index was a mean composite score, ranging from 1 to 7, with a higher score indicating more excitement. In order to check the psychometric properties, an exploratory factor analysis (principal axis factoring method) was performed. Based on the criteria mentioned above, one factor was extracted, which accounted for 68.73% of the overall amount of variance in the items. The minimum loading was 0.74, and the alpha coefficient of 0.90 indicates that this index has an acceptable level of internal consistency.

Main Independent Variables

Global Orientation of Top Managers

The global orientation index consists of four items based on previous research by Ashkenas et al. (1995). Respondents were asked to respond to four statements about the perceived global orientation of the top management team by indicating agreement/disagreement on a 7-point Likert-type scale (1 = "strongly disagree" and 7 = "strongly agree"). The score of this index was a mean composite score, ranging from 1 to 7, with a higher score indicating that employees perceived their top management to be more globally oriented. In order to check the psychometric properties, an exploratory factor analysis (principal axis factoring method) was performed. One factor was extracted, which accounted for 60.49% of the overall amount of variance in the items, the minimum loading was 0.71, and the alpha coefficient of 0.86 shows that this index has an acceptable level of internal consistency.

Geocentrism
Geocentrism was measured using a scale developed by Kobrin (1994). This measure consisted of five items with which respondents were to indicate agreement/disagreement on a 7-point Likert-type scale, where 1 = "strongly disagree" and 7 = "strongly agree." This measure taps aspects of geocentrism identified by Perlmutter (1969). The score for this index was a mean composite score, ranging from 1 to 7, with higher scores indicating geocentric human resource practices. In order to check the psychometric properties, an exploratory factor analysis (principal axis factoring method) was performed. Based on the criteria mentioned above, one factor was extracted, which accounted for 46.98% of the overall amount of variance in the items. The minimum loading was 0.60, and the alpha coefficient of 0.81 indicates that this index has an acceptable level of internal consistency.

Boundary Spanning Structures, Processes, and Practices
We based our measure on Ashkenas et al. (1995), who developed a conceptualization of boundary spanning that is categorized into human resource practices, organizational structure, and organizational processes and systems. This index includes four statements with which respondents indicated agreement/disagreement using a 7-point Likert-type scale (1 = "strongly disagree" and 7 = "strongly agree"), and emphasizes the organizational structure and processes aspects of boundary spanning. The score for this index was a mean composite score, ranging from 1 to 7, with a higher score indicating a higher level of boundary spanning structures and processes. Exploratory factor analysis (principal axis factoring method) was performed, and one factor was extracted, which accounted for 51.61% of the overall amount of variance in the items. The minimum loading was 0.52, with an alpha coefficient of 0.79, indicating that this index has an acceptable level of internal consistency.

Demographic Variables

We included six demographic variables – gender, tenure with the organization, number of hours of training, level of education, cosmopolitan background, and cultural distance of employees from Japan – factors previously shown to have significant effects on employees' attitudes in organizations. *Gender* was coded 1 for male and −1 for female. *Tenure* was measured in years. *Training* was originally measured in the number of training hours received in the past year. However, due to a large departure from normality (skewness = 7.29, kurtosis = 64.84) a natural logarithm transformation was used on this variable, and a major improvement was achieved (skewness = −0.05, kurtosis = −1.01). *Education* was measured using six categories (some high school, high school, some college, college, some graduate diploma, graduate diploma). The lowest category was eliminated from the analysis due to a lack of respondents. *Cosmopolitan background* was measured using three dichotomous Yes/No questions, and one open-ended question ("How many foreign languages do you speak well?") that were recoded to be dichotomous (none = 0; one or more languages = 1). The score for this index was a sum composite score ranging from 0 to 4, with a higher score indicating a more cosmopolitan background. *Cultural distance* was measured using a procedure originally developed by Kogut and Singh (1988) and subsequently applied by several researchers (Gomez-Mejia & Palich, 1997; present a detailed review of these studies). This measure reflects the cultural distance between various countries on previously established cultural dimensions. We calculated the cultural distance for each employee from Japan using Hofstede's (1980) four cultural attribute scores (i.e. individualism, masculinity, uncertainly avoidance, power distance using the following equation:

$$CDjk = \sum_{i=1}^{4} \left\{ \frac{D - D_I^2}{V} \right\} 4,$$

where $CDjk$ = the cultural distance between Japan and country of origin of an employee; Dij = the score of Japan on cultural dimension I; Dik = the score for employee's country of origin on cultural dimension I; and Vi = the variance of the index for cultural dimension i.[2] This formula corrects for the variance of each cultural dimension and averages across the four dimensions. Each employee received a single score measure reflecting their "distance" from Japan. Obviously, in the case of Japanese employees, this score equals 0.

Data Analysis

The data were gathered through a multistage sampling procedure that can produce correlated observation or dependencies among employees from the same organizational unit. Employees who work in the same unit share a work environment and managers, and can also affect each other through interaction. This means that employees' cognitive, affective, and instrumental behaviors may not be entirely independent. Independence of observations is the strictest assumption in all statistical procedures, and violating it can lead to inaccurate significance tests and biased parameter estimating.

In light of the threat of dependent observations, the data were analyzed using the multilevel analysis technique and hierarchical linear models (HLM4.02) software (Bryk & Raudenbush, 1992). This technique, which is similar to linear regression analysis, lets the researcher control for observation dependency and also to test hypotheses regarding cross-level effects.

Since the purpose of this research was to explore relationships between variables at the individual level of analysis, the multilevel analysis was used only to partial out the correlated observation effect in order to obtain accurate parameters estimates and significance tests. A two-level analysis was performed, with employees as level 1 and units as level 2. The restricted maximum likelihood (REML) method was used to estimate the parameters, and it was preferred over the more frequently used maximum likelihood (ML) methods because it gives more accurate estimators for the random effects in the model, especially when the number of level 2 units is relatively small (less than 30). All level 1 variables were group-centered in order to estimate only their within-group effects, without their influence at level 2.

In order to test the contribution of several variables together to model fit, and because deviance tests are allowed only for random effects when the REML estimation method is used, multivariate wald tests were used. The deviance test was used only when more than five fixed parameters were tested together, which is the maximum number of parameters allowed in multivariate wald tests with the HLM4.02 software.

The analysis included one preliminary analysis and four additional steps:

(1) A preliminary analysis, which was descriptive and included the investigation of the means, standard deviations, distributional forms, and correlations among the variables.
(2) Testing for dependency between observations through the use of an empty multilevel analysis model, and the significance test for the level 2 variances. An insignificant level 2 variance can allow the researcher to abandon multilevel analysis and use ordinary multiple regression instead.
(3) Fitting a basic random intercept model, which includes the relevant demographic variables and testing for moderating effects of level 2 (the unit level) factors on these variables. Significant cross-level interactions will call for the inclusion of random slopes in the model in order to achieve accurate

fixed parameter estimates. This model served as a base model with which to compare the other model.

(4) Adding the main variables to the basic model and testing for moderating effects of level 2 (the unit level) on these variables. Significant cross-level interactions will call for the inclusion of random slopes in the model in order to achieve accurate fixed parameter estimates.

(5) Testing for overall and individual main variables effects.

All the single effect significance tests were one-tailed tests because all the hypotheses regarding the fixed effects assumed a specific direction, and those regarding the random effects (variances) have only one plausible direction, that is a positive one.

In order to achieve deviation parameter estimates for the categorical variables in the model, gender and education were effect-coded, meaning their coefficients represent the specific category effect on the dependent variable. Non-significant demographic variables were kept in the model for theoretical reasons, as control variables.

RESULTS

Descriptive statistics for all of the variables included in the analyses are presented in Table 2. In general, the correlations show support for the predicted relationships in the model. All three independent main variables have significant (all at $p <$ 0.001 level) positive zero-order correlations with the dependent variables, with boundary spanning ($r = 0.53$ with commitment, $r = 0.54$ with excitement) and global orientation (0.51 and 0.50, respectively) exhibiting strong correlations and geocentrism (0.28 and 0.26, respectively) exhibiting only moderate correlations (Cohen, 1988).

Table 2 also shows a sizable amount of variation between the two dependent variables. The coefficient of variation (cv = S.D./M) for both variables exceeds the 20% threshold (29.9% for excitement, 26.6% for commitment). This is true also for the main independent variables (41% for geocentrism, 29.7% for boundary spanning, 27.8% for global orientation). Table 2 also shows a high overlap between the dependent variables ($r = 0.84, p < 0.001$). The only demographic variable that correlates with both dependent variables is gender ($r_{pbis} = 0.12$ with commitment, $r_{pbis} = 0.14$ with excitement, $p < 0.01$ for both), which means that men tend to be more committed to, and excited about, their organizations compared to women.

As mentioned above, all hypotheses were tested using multilevel regression analysis. In order to test Hypotheses 1a, 2a, and 3a regarding the positive main

Table 2. Descriptive Statistics and Pearson Product-Moment Correlations Among Research Variables.[a]

	M	S.D.	1	2	3	4	5	6	7	8	9
Commitment	4.59	1.22	(0.91)[b]								
Excitement	4.72	1.41	0.84***	(0.90)							
Geocentrism	3.46	1.42	0.28***	0.26***	(0.81)						
Global orientation	4.50	1.25	0.51***	0.50***	0.33***	(0.86)					
Boundary spanning	4.18	1.24	0.53***	0.54***	0.33***	0.74***	(0.79)				
Gender[c]	0.78	0.41	0.12**	0.14**	0.03	−0.04	0.03	–			
Cosmopolitan background	0.86	0.89	0.06	0.06	0.14***	0.02	0.11*	−0.01	–		
Tenure	9.29	6.84	0.02	0.02	0.15***	0.04	0.05	0.20***	0	–	
Training	49.08	135.14	0.08	0.07	0.14**	0.13**	0.08	0.01	0.06	−0.14***	–
Cultural distance	7.46	4.78	0.11*	0.04	−0.20***	−0.10*	−0.09*	−0.13**	−0.09	−0.45***	0.09*

[a] Not including the single categorical variable education.
[b] Numbers in parentheses on the diagonal are Cronbach alphas.
[c] The correlations involving gender are point-biserial correlations.

* $p < 0.05$.
** $p < 0.01$.
*** $p < 0.001$.

effects of the independent variables on commitment two models were tested. Model 1 includes only the demographic variables, while Model 2 adds boundary spanning, global orientation, and geocentrism variables to test the main effects. Table 3 below presents the results of these analyses.

A preliminary unconditional model reveals that there is a significant correlation between two employees from the same HQs or affiliate unit (intra-class

Table 3. Multilevel Analysis Results Regressing Commitment on Demographic and Main Variables.

Variable	Model 1: Demographic Variables Only	Model 2: Model 1 + Main Variables
Demographic variables[a]	$\chi^2(9) = 41.49^{***}$	$\chi^2(9) = 31.07^{***}$
Gender	0.146^b (0.065)	0.181^{**} (0.054)
Cosmopolitan background	0.086 (0.058)	0.049 (0.048)
Tenure	0.026^* (0.009)	0.016 (0.008)
Training hours[c]	0.119^{**} (0.030)	0.052 (0.025)
Cultural distance	−0.004 (0.029)	0.019 (0.024)
Education	$\chi^2(4) = 10.56^*$	$\chi^2(4) = 10.28^*$
High school	0.130 (0.158)	0.009 (0.130)
Some college	0.327^* (0.119)	0.259^* (0.097)
College	−0.102 (0.094)	−0.068 (0.077)
Some graduate education	−0.282 (0.144)	−0.254 (0.118)
Graduate diploma[d]	−0.073 (0.119)	0.053 (0.099)
Main variables		$\chi^2(3) = 246.70^{***}$
Geocentrism		0.105^{**} (0.035)
Global orientation		0.237^{***} (0.051)
Boundary spanning		0.305^{***} (0.051)
Constant	4.61^{***} (0.115)	4.61^{***} (0.115)
R^{2e}	0.062	0.368
Source of variance		
Level 2	0.103^{***}	0.111^{***}
Level 1	1.295	0.872
Reliability of level 1 intercept	0.776	0.844

[a] Deviance test using the maximum likelihood estimation method.
[b] $p = 0.052$.
[c] Natural log of training hours.
[d] This contrast was not a part of the model and is shown only for a more complete picture of the education effect.
[e] This is only a proximate pseudo R^2.
[*] $p < 0.05$.
[**] $p < 0.01$.
[***] $p < 0.001$.

correlation = 0.069), which means that 6.9% of the total variance between employees is accounted for by the units. The unit level contribution (variance = 0.102) to the total commitment variability is found to be significant: $\chi^2(9) = 46.62$, $p < 0.001$. These results confirm the importance of the multilevel analysis for the internal validity of this research. The within-unit variance is 1.380, and the reliability for the level 1 intercept is an acceptable level, -0.762.

The next step was fitting a basic model, which contains the relevant demographic variables (Model 1 in Table 3). The results indicate that there are no significant random effects for the demographic variables, which led us to fix all the demographic variable effects. The model with the fixed effects showed a significant contribution of all variables taken together to model fit ($\chi^2(9) = 41.49, p < 0.001$). Three variables had significant effects. The relative changes in training hours ($t = 3.94$, $p < 0.01$) and tenure ($t = 2.87$, $p < 0.05$) have significant positive effects on commitment: a 10% increase in the employee's training hours increases commitment by 0.0119 units, and a unit change in tenure increases it by 0.026 units. Education, $\chi^2(4) = 10.56$, $p < 0.05$, also has a significant effect: Having some college education increases commitment by 0.327 units. Gender has an almost significant effect ($p = 0.052$), meaning that being a man increases an employee's commitment by 0.145 units, and being a women lowers it by the same amount. However, this model accounts for only 6.2% of the total within-unit variance.

In the next model (Model 2 in Table 3) the main variables were added to the base model, Model 1, that included the demographic variables. Testing for possible cross-level interaction effects for the three main variables found non-significant effects. According to these results, the three main variables effects were fixed, and their contribution to model fit were then tested. The results show that the three main variables contribute significantly to model fit, $\chi^2(3) = 246.70$, $p < 0.001$, and that each has a significant positive effect (geocentrism: $t = 3.01, p < 0.01$; global orientation: $t = 4.68, p < 0.001$; boundary spanning: $t = 5.99, p < 0.001$), supporting Hypotheses 1a, 2a, and 3a. As predicted, perceiving the top management team as being more globally oriented and as promoting boundary spanning increases an employee's commitment. Higher perceived geocentrism also increases commitment. Overall, this model accounts for 36.8% of the total within-unit variance, while the main variables account for 30.6% of this variance.

As to the demographic variables, only gender ($t = 3.37$, $p < 0.01$) and education ($\chi^2(4) = 10.28$, $p < 0.05$) have significant effects on commitment above and beyond the main variables, meaning that males are more committed than females (being a male increases an employee's commitment by 0.181 units). Having some college education also increases commitment by 0.259 units.

To sum up the findings regarding employees' commitment to the organization, the results provide strong support for Hypotheses 1a, 2a, and 3a, linking employees' perceptions of global orientation, boundary spanning, and geocentrism with employee commitment. All three variables have significant positive effects on commitment, and there is a sizable contribution of these variables to the explanation of the within-unit variance in the employee's commitment.

In order to test Hypotheses 1b, 2b, and 3b regarding the positive main effects of the independent variables on excitement, two models were tested. Model 1 includes only the demographic variables, while Model 2 adds employees' perceptions of

Table 4. Multilevel Analysis Results Regressing Excitement on Demographic and Main Variables.

Variable	Model 1: Demographic Variables Only	Model 2: Model 1 + Main Variables
Demographic variables[a]	$\chi^2(9) = 31.36^{***}$	$\chi^2(9) = 22.79^{**}$
Gender	0.141 (0.076)	0.177* (0.064)
Cosmopolitan background	0.084 (0.068)	0.046 (0.057)
Tenure	0.021 (0.011)	0.011 (0.009)
Training hours[b]	0.156** (0.035)	0.086* (0.030)
Cultural distance	0.008 (0.034)	0.028 (0.029)
Education	$\chi^2(4) = 2.72$	$\chi^2(4) = 2.73$
High school (edu2)	0.050 (0.185)	−0.083 (0.155)
Some college (edu3)	0.137 (0.139)	0.062 (0.116)
College (edu4)	−0.158 (0.110)	−0.114 (0.092)
Some graduate education (edu5)	−0.003 (0.169)	0.034 (0.141)
Graduate diploma[c] (edu6)	−0.025 (0.139)	0.101 (0.117)
Main variables		$\chi^2(3) = 224.65^{***}$
Geocentrism		0.058 (0.042)
Global orientation		0.278*** (0.060)
Boundary spanning		0.364*** (0.060)
Constant	4.73*** (0.127)	4.73*** (0.125)
R^{2d}	0.043	0.335
Source of variance		
Level 2	0.122***	0.129***
Level 1	1.773	1.231
Reliability of level 1 intercept	0.749	0.817

[a] Deviance test using the maximum likelihood estimation method.
[b] Natural log of training hours.
[c] This contrast was not a part of the model and is shown only for a more complete picture of the education.
[d] This is only a proximate pseudo R^2.
$^*p < 0.05$.
$^{**}p < 0.01$.
$^{***}p < 0.001$.

boundary spanning, global orientation, and geocentrism variables needed to test the main effects. Table 4 presents the results of these analyses.

A preliminary unconditional model reveals that there is a significant correlation between two employees from the same unit (intra-class correlation = 0.061), which means that 6.1% of the total variance between employees is accounted for by the unit. The unit level contribution (variance = 0.121) to the total variability of employee excitement variability is significant, $\chi^2(9) = 45.59, p < 0.001$. These results again confirm the importance of the multilevel analysis for the internal validity of these research findings. The within-unit variance is 1.852, and the reliability for the level 1 intercept is acceptable at -0.74.

The next step was to fit a basic model with the relevant demographic variables (Model 1 in Table 4). No significant random effects were found for any of the demographic variables, which led us to fix all the demographic variables' effects. The model with the fixed effects showed a significant contribution of all variables taken together to model fit, $\chi^2(9) = 31.36, p < 0.001$, but only the relative change in the training hours ($t = 4.40, p < 0.01$) has a significant effect on excitement. A 10% increase in the employee's training hours increases employee excitement by 0.0156 units. However, this model accounts for only 4.3% of the total within unit variance.

In the next model, the main variables were added to Model 1, which already includes the demographic variables. Testing for possible cross-level interaction for the three main variables revealed one almost significant and two significant effects, Geocentrism $\chi^2(9) = 17.84, p = 0.019$, gms $\chi^2(9) = 14.11, p = 0.059$, bs $\chi^2(9) = 20.17, p = 0.009$. The fact that the model did not converge with these three random slopes was a sign of the negligible variances across units, so they were fixed, and the main variables' contribution to model fit were then tested. The results indicate that the main variables have a significant contribution to the model fit, $\chi^2(3) = 224.65, p < 0.001$, but a positive effect, as hypothesized in Hypothesis 1b, 2b, and 3b, was found to be significant only for global orientation ($t = 4.64$, $p < 0.001$) and boundary spanning ($t = 6.03, p < 0.001$), but not for geocentrism ($t = 1.41, p < 0.05$). Perceiving the top management team as being more globally oriented and as promoting boundary spanning increases employees' excitement. This model as a whole accounts for 33.5% of the total within unit variance, while the main variable accounts for 29.2% of this variance.

To sum up the findings concerning the employees' excitement about their jobs, the results support Hypotheses 1b and 2b, showing significant positive effects of global orientation and boundary spanning, along with a sizable contribution of these variables to the explanation of the within-unit variance in an employee's level of excitement about their work. Although the relationship is in the predicted direction, the relationship with geocentrism is not significant, contrary to our prediction.

Turning to the demographic variables, only gender ($t = 2.81$, $p < 0.05$) and training hours ($t = 2.97$, $p < 0.05$) have significant effects on excitement above and beyond the main variables, meaning that being a male increases an employee's excitement by 0.178 units, and being a female lowers it by the same amount. In addition, a 10% increase in the employee's training hours increases their excitement by 0.0089 units.

DISCUSSION

A key challenge facing Japanese MNCs has long been, and continues to be, the staffing of upper management positions with Japanese expatriates. Japanese firms have claimed in the past (Sullivan, 1991) that one of the reasons for their use of large percentages of expatriates to local managers is high turnover among local managers (Kono & Clegg, 2001). It is not possible, they argue, to recruit local employees and steep them in the organization's culture and the Japanese language when they are likely to leave before this significant investment pays off. One implication of the results from this study is that one way to overcome the high levels of dissatisfaction and turnover among employees is in fact to institute a geocentric staffing policy. As the results demonstrate, there is a significant rise in commitment among employees when they perceive that there are greater opportunities for advancement for non-Japanese nationals within the firm. These results are important because committed employees are less likely to leave the organization, and the MNCs will be less likely to lose their valuable investments in human assets. A mistake that many Japanese MNCS make is attributing high levels of turnover as an innate characteristic of non-Japanese, rather than examining the potential contribution that their corporate policies and practices make toward this phenomenon.

A second important result from this study is the finding that employee perceptions of geocentrism do not influence their level of excitement for their job. This indicates that other tools, in addition to staffing policies, need to be implemented in order to engage employees. It is interesting that our research indicates that higher levels of training could be one of those tools. It is possible that as employees feel their own stock of skills and knowledge grow, they become more engaged in their job and their workplace, and motivated in their work. Thus, it is important for Japanese MNCs to consider that they not only gain an increase in human capital from their investments in training, but also may increase the excitement levels of their employees if they invest in training and development for these employees. At the same time, Japanese MNCs must also consider other possible ways to increase the levels of excitement, including looking at such management practices as greater levels of decision-making involvement and empowerment.

Finally, an interesting finding from this study is that male employees in Japanese firms tend to be both more committed and more excited about their jobs than female employees. What we do not know is if men feel more committed because they are given more opportunities and possibility for advancement, relative to women; if men are more excited and engaged because they are entrusted with greater responsibilities and more interesting work tasks; or if Japanese firms are characterized by cultures, systems, or processes that are somehow more comfortable or oriented more toward men than women. This finding is intriguing in light of the literature on the problems Japanese MNCs have had in the U.S. with affirmative action and points to the possibility that Japanese firms have not yet overcome organizational prejudices against women that are still fairly strong in Japanese firms in Japan today (Lamb, 1992).

CONCLUSIONS AND LIMITATIONS

The multilevel regression results provide consistent support for the hypotheses linking global orientation, geocentrism, and boundary spanning with employee commitment and excitement in the two Japanese MNCs in our study. These results suggest that Japanese MNCs that develop an inclusive, fluid, and globally oriented organizational environment, as perceived by their employees, are more likely to engender commitment and excitement among their employees.

Many studies of Japanese transplants overseas have looked at the degree to which Japanese firms transfer their human resource policies and practices to their overseas operations. A question raised by this study, however, is whether it is the policies and practices actually in place or employee perceptions regarding equal access to opportunities, orientation of the top management team, and boundary-spanning mechanisms that drive employee attitudes and behaviors toward their employers. As this study shows, perceptions are important drivers of employee attitudes, and it may be that in a number of Japanese firms, real changes have been made in the policies and practices, but perceptions have lagged behind these changes as a result of communication problems between the Japanese top managers and their employees worldwide.

Past literature on Japanese management practices has emphasized the importance that Japanese management places on the sharing of information with employees (e.g. Cole, 1989). The positive relationship found in this study between boundary-spanning and important employee outcomes such as commitment and excitement indicates that this aspect of "traditional" Japanese management may be an important tool to overcome some of the inherent liabilities in Japanese management overseas, particularly as Japanese firms make the transition from a focus on manufacturing to more knowledge-based work.

Overall, this study highlights some interesting findings and raises a number of questions that deserve further study. At the same time, a number of limitations should be taken into consideration when interpreting the results. First, our sample of Japanese MNCs contains only two firms drawn from the same industry. Second, we relied on surveys to test all of the hypotheses presented in this paper. While we have a large sample of individuals, randomly drawn at each location, there are possible problems with common method bias in this study. Finally, although the number of individuals participating in this study is large, only 10 locations are included in the analyses, limiting our ability to generalize these results to the wider population.

In spite of these limitations, both scholars and practitioners can benefit from this study and its findings. First, we create practical tools to measure those human components of organizations that can help practitioners determine the ways in which they can measure and subsequently increase the global performance of their own firms. Our hope is that this work will be used as a bridge between theory and practice, as has already been exemplified by the active participation of senior executives during the model building phase of our project and by participation in the larger study by MNCs from Asia, Europe, and the Americas. Second, the key role that global orientation plays in creating employee excitement and commitment points to the important role human resources must play in helping to nurture this outlook among top managers of MNCs, and there is increasing attention being given to the various methods MNCs can use to achieve this end (Mendenhall, Kuhlmann & Stahl, 2001). The findings reported should also provide further encouragement for human-resource practitioners seeking to institute global leadership development processes within their firms. Yet, as summarized by Osland and Taylor (2001), it is almost impossible for these initiatives to create a global orientation unless there is long-term, consistent support from top management. Japanese firms have many advantages in the global competitive arena, but if they are unable to exert strong, top leadership to truly "think global," there is little hope that they will really make the transition into the transnational era.

NOTES

1. This chapter contains material that is based upon work supported by the National Science Foundation under Grant No. 0080703. Any opinions, findings, and conclusions or recommendations expressed in this material are those of the authors and do not necessarily

reflect the views of the National Science Foundation. The authors would also like to thank their home institutions, for their support, and colleagues at the Academy of Management and the Academy of International Business, for their earlier comments.

2. There are a few but significant critiques of this method (cf. Kirkman, Lowe & Gibson, 2000). Given that cultural distance is a control variable and not a focal variable in our study, and given the significant cost of measuring cultural values of each employee, we feel justified using this measure as a proxy for cultural distance in this study.

3. Item was reverse-coded for scale calculation.

REFERENCES

Ashkenas, R., Ulrich, D., Jick, T., & Kerr, S. (1995). *The boundaryless organization: Breaking the chains of organizational structure*. San Francisco: Jossey-Bass.

Bartlett, C., & Ghoshal, S. (1989). *Managing across borders*. Cambridge, MA: Harvard Business School Press.

Bartlett, C., & Ghoshal, S. (1990). Matrix management: Not a structure, a frame of mind. *Harvard Business Review* (July–August), 138–145.

Bartlett, C., & Ghoshal, S. (1998). *The transnational solution*. Boston: Irwin.

Bartlett, C., & Yoshihara, H. (1988). New challenges for Japanese multinationals: Is Organizational adaptation their Achilles heel? *Human Resource Management*, *27*, 19–43.

Bartunek, J. M., Gordon, J. R., & Weathersby, R. P. (1983). Developing "complicated" understanding in administrators. *Academy of Management Review*, *8*, 273–284.

Beechler, S., Taylor, S., Boyacigiller, N., & Levy, O. (2000, November). Organizational competitiveness: The roles of organization culture and human resource management in driving MNC success. Paper presented at the Academy of International Business Annual Meeting, Phoenix, AZ.

Boyacigiller, N. A. (1990). Staffing in a foreign land: A multi-level study of Japanese multinationals with operations in the United States. Paper presented at the annual meeting of the Academy of Management, San Francisco, August.

Bryk, A. S., & Raudenbush, S. W. (1992). *Hierarchical linear models: Application and data analysis methods*. Beverly Hills, CA: Sage.

Campbell, N., & Holden, N. (Eds) (1993). *Japanese multinationals: Strategies and management in the global kaisha*. London: Routledge.

Cole, R. E. (1989). *Strategies for learning: Small group activities in American, Japanese and Swedish industry*. Berkeley: University of California Press.

Evans, P. (1993). Dosing the glue: Applying human resource technology to build global organizations. *Research in Personnel and Human Resource Management* (Suppl. 3), 21–54. Greenwich, CT: JAI Press.

Evans, P., Pucik, V., & Barsoux, J. (2002). *The global challenge: Frameworks for international human resource management*. Boston, MA: McGraw-Hill.

Goldberg, A. I. (1976). The relevance of cosmopolitan/local orientations to professional values and behavior. *Sociology of Work and Occupation*, *3*, 331–356.

Gomez-Mejia, L. R., & Palich, L. E. (1997). Cultural diversity and the performance of the multinational firm. *Journal of International Business Studies*, *28*(2), 309–336.

Hackman, R., & Oldham, G. (1976). Motivation through the design of work: Test of a theory. *Organizational Behavior and Human Performance*, *16*, 250–279.

Hair, J. F., Anderson, R. E., Tatham, R. L., & Black, W. C. (1995). *Multivariate data analysis with readings* (4th ed.). New Jersey: Prentice-Hall.

Harzing, A. (1999). *Managing the multinationals: An international study of control mechanisms.* Cheltenham, UK: Edward Elgar.

Hofstede, G. H. (1980). *Culture's consequences: International differences in work-related values.* Beverly Hills, CA: Sage.

Kanter, R. M. (1991). Transcending business boundaries: 12,000 world managers view change. *Harvard Business Review, 69*, 151–164.

Kanter, R. M. (1995). *World class: Thriving locally in the global economy.* New York: Simon & Schuster.

Kim, W. C., & Mauborgne, R. A. (1996). Procedural justice and managers' in-role and extra-role behavior: The case of the multinational. *Management Science, 42*, 499–515.

Kirkman, B. L., Lowe, K. B., & Gibson, C. B. (2000). Twenty years of culture's consequences: A review of the empirical research on Hofstede's cultural value dimensions (Working Paper). Greensboro: University of North Carolina.

Kobayashi, N. (1985). The patterns of management style developing in Japanese multinationals in the 1980s. In: S. Takamiya & K. Thurley (Eds), *Japan's Emerging Multinationals: An International Comparison of Policies and Practices* (pp. 229–264). Tokyo: University of Tokyo Press.

Kobrin, S. J. (1994). Is there a relationship between a geocentric mind-set and multinational strategy? *Journal of International Business Studies, 25*, 493–511.

Kogut, B., & Singh, H. (1988). The effect of national culture on he choice of entry mode. *Journal of International Business Studies, 19*(3), 411–433.

Kono, T., & Clegg, S. (2001). *Trends in Japanese management: Continuing strengths, current problems and changing priorities.* New York: Palgrave.

Kopp, R. (1994). International human resource policies and practices in Japanese, European and United States multinationals. *Human Resource Management, 33*, 581–599.

Kopp, R. (1999). The rice-paper ceiling in Japanese companies: Why it exists and persists. In: S. Beechler & A. Bird (Eds), *Japanese Multinationals Abroad: Individual and Organizational Learning* (pp. 107–128). New York: Oxford University Press.

Lamb, A. (1992). *Women and Japanese management: Discrimination and reform.* London: Routledge.

Lawrence, P. R., & Lorsch, J. W. (1967). Differentiation and integration in complex organizations. *Administrative Science Quarterly, 12*(1), 1–48.

Levy, O., Beechler, S., Taylor, S., & Boyacigiller, N. (1999). What do we talk about when we talk about global mindset? Paper presented at the Annual Meeting of the Academy of Management, Chicago.

Mendenhall, M., Kuhlmann, T., & Stahl, G. (2001). *Developing global business leaders: Policies, processes, and innovations.* Westport, CT: Quorum Press.

Meyer, J. P., & Allen, N. J. (1997). *Commitment in the workplace: Theory, research and application.* Thousand Oaks, CA: Sage.

Mowday, R. T., Steers, R. M., & Porter, L. W. (1979). The measurement of organizational commitment. *Journal of Vocational Behavior, 14*, 224–247.

Murtha, T. P., Lenway, S. A., & Bagozzi, R. P. (1998). Global mind-sets and cognitive shift in a complex multinational corporation. *Strategic Management Journal, 19*, 97–114.

Nohria, N., & Ghoshal, S. (1997). *The differentiated network: Organizing multinational corporations for value creation.* San Francisco: Jossey-Bass.

O'Reilly, C. A., & Chatman, J. A. (1986). Organizational commitment and psychological attachment: The effects of compliance, identification, and internalization on prosocial behavior. *Journal of Applied Psychology, 71*, 492–499.

Osland, J., & Taylor, S. (2001). *Developing global leadership.* Retrieved February 10 from (www.hr.com/Hrcom).

Perlmutter, H. (1969). The tortuous evolution of the multinational corporation. *Columbia Journal of World Business* (January–February), 9–18.

Perlmutter, H., & Heenan, D. A. (1979). *Multinational organization development.* Reading, MA: Addison-Wesley.

Porter, M. (1986). *Competition in global industries.* Boston: Harvard Business School Press.

Prahalad, C. K. (1991). Globalization: The intellectual and managerial challenges. *Human Resource Management, 29*, 27–37.

Prahalad, C. K. (1998). *The role of HRM and global competition.* Presentation at ICEDR Organizational Competitiveness Workshop, University of Michigan Business School Executive Education Center, Ann Arbor, MI.

Prahalad, C. K., & Doz. Y. (1987). *The multinational mission: Balancing local demands and global vision.* New York: Free Press.

Prahalad, C. K., & Hamel, G. (1994). Strategy as a field of study: Why search for a new paradigm? *Strategic Management Journal, 15*, 5–16.

Pucik, V. (1999). When performance does not matter: Human resource management in Japanese-owned U.S. affiliates. In: S. Beechler & A. Bird (Eds), *Japanese Multinationals Abroad: Individual and Organizational Learning* (pp. 169–188). New York: Oxford University Press.

Pucik, V., Tichy, N., & Barnett, C. (Eds) (1992). *Globalizing management: Creating and leading the competitive organization.* New York: Wiley.

Rhinesmith, R. S. (1992). Global mindsets for global managers. *Training and Development, 46*, 63–69.

Sullivan J. J. (1991). *The invasion of the salarymen.* Westport, CT: Praeger.

Tabachnick, B. G., & Fidell, L. S. (1989). *Using multivariate statistics.* New York: Harper & Row.

Tachiki, D. (1991). Japanese management going transnational. *Journal for Quality and Participation, 14*, 96–107.

Trevor, M. (1983). *Japan's reluctant multinationals: Japanese management at home and abroad.* New York: St. Martin's Press.

Virtanen, T. (2000). Commitment and the study of organizational climate and culture. In: N. M. Ashkanasy, C. P. M. Wilderom & M. F. Peterson (Eds), *Handbook of Organizational Culture and Climate* (pp. 339–354). Thousand Oaks, CA: Sage.

APPENDIX A
MEASURES USED IN THE ANALYSES

Organizational Commitment

This scale ranges from 1 to 7, with higher scores indicating higher organizational commitment.

- I am willing to put in a great deal of effort beyond that normally expected to help this organization be successful.
- I talk up this organization to my friends as a great organization to work for.
- I would accept almost any type of job assignment in order to keep working for this organization.
- I find that my values and the organization's values are very similar.
- I am proud to tell others that I am part of this organization.
- This organization really inspires the very best in me in the way of job performance.
- I am extremely glad that I chose this organization to work for over others I was considering at the time I joined.
- I really care about the fate of this organization.
- For me, this is the best of all possible organizations for which to work.

Excitement

This scale ranges from 1 to 7, with higher scores indicating higher levels of excitement.

- While there are good days and bad days, overall, I really look forward to coming to work every day.
- I find working for this organization to be an enjoyable challenge.
- I think that this will be an exciting organization to work for in the future.
- I feel that no matter how long I stay with this organization, I will always have an opportunity to learn new things here.

Global Orientation

This scale ranges from 1 to 7, with higher scores representing higher "global orientation."

- Top managers in our organization have a global outlook.
- Top management has comprehensive awareness and knowledge of changes in the nature of global competition and global markets.
- Top management is currently developing and implementing systems, processes, and structures which will enable our company to successfully meet future changes in the nature of global competition and global markets.
- Top managers in this organization view the global arena not just as a market to exploit but also as an opportunity to learn.

Boundary Spanning

This scale ranges from 1 to 7, with higher scores representing higher "boundary spanning."

- Top management promotes cross-national knowledge sharing and collaboration.
- Top management promotes a vision that transcends functional and geographic agendas.
- Top management promotes collaboration with strategically important customers and suppliers.
- Top management widely shares our company's financial and performance information with all employees in the organization.

Geocentrism

This scale ranges from 1 to 7, with higher scores representing higher "geocentrism."

- A manager who began their career in any country has an equal chance of becoming CEO of this company.
- In the next decade, I expect to see a non-Japanese CEO of this company.
- In the next decade, I expect to see one or more non-Japanese nationals serving as a senior corporate officer on a routine basis.
- In my company, nationality is unimportant in selecting individuals for managerial positions.
- My company believes that it is important that the majority of top corporate officers remain Japanese (R).[3]

Cosmopolitan Background

This scale ranges from 0 to 4, with higher scores representing a more cosmopolitan background.

- Did you receive one year or more of your formal education abroad? Yes/No.
- Have you ever lived abroad, other than for education, for more than one year? Yes/No.
- Do all members of your parent's family have the same nationality as you? Yes/No.
- How many foreign languages do you speak well? _____

CHANGES IN THE DETERMINANTS OF PROFIT: A STUDY OF FOREIGN SUBSIDIARIES IN THE JAPANESE MANUFACTURING INDUSTRIES IN THE 1980s AND 1990s

Shigeru Asaba and Hideki Yamawaki

ABSTRACT

This study examines the determinants of performance of foreign manufacturing subsidiaries in Japan. The study finds that a foreign parent's size, the subsidiary's age, and a complicated distribution system influence a subsidiary's performance. There was little significant change in these determinants over a 20-year period. However, for subsidiaries that survived over the observation period of this study, some determinants changed. We also found that by forming joint ventures with Japanese firms, foreign firms can overcome the obstacle of distribution and circumvent the disadvantage of inexperience. Moreover, the mitigating effects of joint ventures vary, depending on the type of Japanese partner.

Japanese Firms in Transition: Responding to the Globalization Challenge
Advances in International Management, Volume 17, 289–324
Copyright © 2005 by Elsevier Ltd.
All rights of reproduction in any form reserved
ISSN: 0747-7929/doi:10.1016/S0747-7929(04)17012-1

1. INTRODUCTION

Frequent entry and competitive behavior of foreign firms are notable features in the stagnating Japanese economy in recent years. While it has often been pointed out that inward foreign direct investment (FDI) in Japan is significantly low (Yoshitomi, 1996), the increasing presence of foreign firms is one of the most striking characteristics of changing Japan. It is therefore worthwhile to analyze the behavior and performance of foreign firms in Japan in recent periods and draw comparisons with these factors from earlier periods. It is also important to study foreign firms in Japan because the entry of foreign firms can be considered as a driver in boosting the stagnant Japanese economy (White Paper on International Trade, 2000, 2001).

Multinational enterprises enter overseas markets with their distinctive competitive advantages and may take part in different strategic groups than their local competitors (Caves, 1996; Hymer, 1976; Kindleberger, 1969). Consequently, these multinationals may disturb existing competitive forces and bring new foci of competition. Moreover, the entry of foreign firms sometimes intensifies competition. In response to such entry, domestic firms may increase advertising or reduce prices (Cubbin & Domberger, 1988; Williamson, 1986; Yamawaki, 2002).

In Japan as well, anecdotal evidence suggests that successful foreign firms with distinctive competitive advantages have brought increased competition into the domestic market. Well-documented examples include Coca-Cola and Fuji-Xerox (Oketa, 1988). Coca-Cola became the top drink manufacturer with its distinctive products, and Fuji-Xerox, a joint venture between Rank Xerox and Fuji Film, became successful by virtue of its advanced technological capabilities in the copier market. These firms intensively compete with Japanese rivals by employing superior marketing strategies and product development. Foreign firms have brought unique technology, corporate systems and managerial resources into the Japanese market.

However, it is well known that the flow and stock levels of inward foreign direct investment (FDI) in Japan is significantly low (Yoshitomi, 1996). For most of the postwar period, the Japanese government sought to severely restrict inward FDI. Liberalization began in the late 1960s and culminated in the rewriting of the Foreign Exchange Control Law in 1980. The subsequent growth of FDI into Japan was rapid over the course of the late 1980s and early 1990s, but FDI levels in Japan relative to GNP are still quite low (Weinstein, 1996). The ratio of FDI inflow to GNP in Japan is 0.1–0.2%, which is one-tenth that of the U.S., the U.K., and France. The ratio of stock of FDI to GNP shows almost the same trend as the FDI flow ratio (Wakasugi, 1996).

Several scholars have recently studied why FDI in Japan is so low and which business practices in Japan serve as barriers to entry for foreign firms. These studies have proposed several important hypotheses regarding structural impediments for foreign entrants into Japanese markets: corporate groups or *keiretsu* (Lawrence, 1993; Yamawaki, 2004), distribution systems (Ariga & Namikawa, 1991; Ito, 1991), and labor markets (Weinstein, 1996). These impediments may make foreign firms in Japan unprofitable, leading foreigners to be reluctant to enter the Japanese market.

Since the 1990s, however, we have observed more foreign firms enter Japanese markets and play more active roles than before. Toys "R" Us, has brought changes to the distribution system in Japan; it sells toys and other goods at lower prices than its Japanese competitors (Negishi & Tamehiro, 2001). Carrefour, a French discounter, has had a large impact on Japanese retailers, and Wal-Mart, the U.S. giant discounter, revealed its plan to enter the Japanese market. Starbucks Coffee has become a fashionable purchase. In addition, many foreign banks and insurance companies are aggressive in supplying new services and products.

It is sometimes argued that such frequent and influential entries of foreign firms have been induced by Japanese open market policy and deregulation, which started with the Structural Impediments Initiative talks (White Paper on International Trade, 1998). However, the question still remains: Have business practices and the environment in Japan really changed? While we have observed the entry of many foreign firms in the financial and distribution sectors in recent years, has entry also increased substantially in the manufacturing sectors? If the Japanese business environment has changed, has this positively impacted the performance of foreign manufacturers in Japan? It is true that some foreign entrants are more profitable than others. What makes doing business in Japan difficult for foreign firms? Do partnerships with Japanese firms help foreign firms overcome obstacles? What types of Japanese firms should a foreign firm choose as a partner? The purpose of this study is to address these questions.

This study is distinctive from previous studies in the following aspects. Instead of using industry-level data, this study uses subsidiary level data. The sample of foreign manufacturing subsidiaries in Japan is large enough to allow for statistical tests. Instead of examining entry and exit or relative evaluation of performance by subsidiaries' managers, this study analyzes data on subsidiary financial performance. A comparison between the 1980s and 1990s data examines whether there is any change in the determinants of foreign subsidiaries' profits. We also study the effects of different entry modes, joint ventures versus wholly owned subsidiaries, adopted by foreign manufacturers to overcome obstacles, and explore further the effects of the joint ventures with different domestic partners.

The structure of this paper is as follows. Section 2 examines the transition of inward FDI in Japan, reviews the existing studies, and proposes several hypotheses. Section 3 describes the data methodology. Section 4 reports the results of statistical analysis and identifies the determinants of post-entry performance of foreign entrants. Section 5 summarizes the main findings and concludes the paper.

2. INWARD FDI IN JAPAN AND HYPOTHESIS

2.1. The Transition of Inward FDI in Japan

Many researchers have pointed out that the level of inward FDI in Japan is quite low relative to other OECD countries; nevertheless, it appears as though there is frequent entry and a remarkable level of activity of foreign firms in the Japanese markets. Has inward FDI in Japan been low all the time, or has there been any change in the level of investment?

Figure 1 shows the pattern of outward and inward FDI across all industries in Japan. Looking at the transition of FDI in terms of the amount of investment, inward FDI in Japan has always been at a lower level than outward FDI. However, while outward FDI has varied greatly, inward FDI increased slightly in the mid-1980s and has been growing since the mid-1990s. Consequently, the *ratio* between outward and inward FDIs has rapidly decreased from 10.0 in 1983 and 23.6 in 1989 to 3.1 in

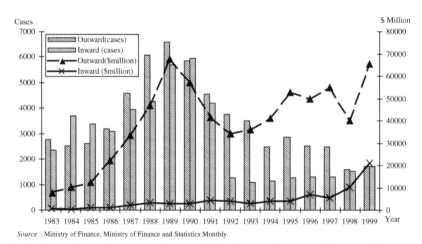

Fig. 1. Transition of Outward and Inward FDI. *Source:* Ministry of Finance, Ministry of Finance and Statistics Monthly.

1999. Moreover, the number of cases of outward and inward FDIs peaked in 1989 and 1990, respectively, and then decreased rapidly. While outward FDI is still sluggish, inward FDI has been gradually increasing since the mid-1990s. Therefore, in terms of the number of cases, inward FDI is nearly comparable to outward FDI.

Comparing manufacturing and non-manufacturing sectors, however, there has been a significant difference in the growth rate of FDI. According to Fig. 2, which shows the transition of inward FDI in terms of the amount of investment, inward FDI in the non-manufacturing sector has grown more than that in the manufacturing sector. The average annual growth rates (1986–1999) of inward FDI in manufacturing and non-manufacturing sectors were 0.24 and 0.29, respectively. Moreover, the cases of inward FDI in the non-manufacturing sector increased from 1516 cases in 1986 to 1701 cases in 1999, while those in the manufacturing sector decreased from 1563 cases in 1986 to only 141 cases in 1999 (Fig. 3).

In summary, inward FDI across all sectors has shown some increase since the mid-1990s, although it should not be considered to be at a high level. Moreover, inward FDI in the manufacturing sector has increased less than that in the non-manufacturing sector. In terms of the number of cases, inward FDI in the manufacturing sector has decreased, while we have seen an increase in non-manufacturing inward FDI during this period. There are several reasons for the variance of inward FDI in Japan. Certainly, the financial performance of foreign firms in Japan might have some influence on the level of inward FDI. The number of cases of inward FDI in the manufacturing sector and the net income-sales ratio

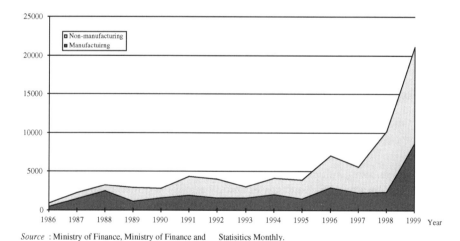

Source : Ministry of Finance, Ministry of Finance and   Statisitics Monthly.

Fig. 2. Transition of Inward FDI (Amount of Investment). *Source:* Ministry of Finance, Ministry of Finance and Statistics Monthly.

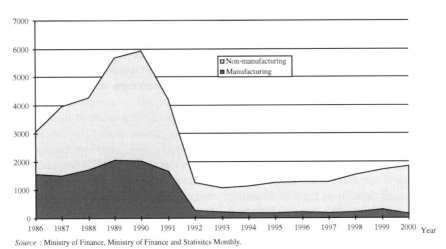

Fig. 3.   Transition of Inward FDI (Cases). *Source:* Ministry of Finance, Ministry of Finance
and Statistics Monthly.

of the foreign manufacturing firms are positively correlated (0.49). This suggests
the value of examining the determinants of foreign firms' financial performance
in Japan.

2.2. Determinants of Profitability of Foreign Firms in Japan

We propose a model to explain the variance of profits among foreign firms in Japan
by using the following three major factors:

$$\text{Profits}_{it} = f(\text{firm-specificfactors}_{it}, \quad \text{structural impediments}_{jt}, \quad \text{entrystrategy}_{it}),$$

where subscript i denotes firm, subscript j denotes industry, and subscript t denotes
time.

2.2.1. Firm-Specific Factors
Foreign firms have disadvantages in doing business in a host country where the
environment is different from that of their home country. Generally, they are less
familiar with the economy, law, politics, and culture of the host country than are
domestic firms. Additionally, the government of a host country sometimes treats
foreign and domestic firms differently by applying special regulations to foreign
firms. Also, foreign firms always face foreign exchange risk.

Hymer (1976) and Kindleberger (1969) argued that foreign firms must have some distinctive competitive advantages in order to compete with domestic firms in a host country in spite of such disadvantages. According to the eclectic theory of Dunning (1988), firms that have ownership advantages, location advantages, and internalization advantages choose FDI instead of export and licensing. If a parent firm possesses superior resources, especially intangible assets, its foreign subsidiary can have a competitive advantage over local firms (Delios & Beamish, 2001; Morck & Yeung, 1992).

Competitive advantages of the firms can be determined by various factors and resources. It is possible to define several relevant resources in a single industry. However, for a cross-sectional study, it is difficult to specify a firm's resources and capabilities in such detail and obtain operation-specific data across industries. Thus, we used firm size as a rough indicator of a firm's capabilities and advantages. In the economic model of Cournot competition, a firm's size in equilibrium reflects its marginal cost.[1] Size is also one of the standard variables used to characterize firms in the literature on business strategy and organization (Porac, Thomas, Wilson, Paton & Kanfer, 1995; Porter, 1979).

Several studies have found that the size of a foreign parent reflects superior managerial resources, which can be transferred from the parent to its subsidiary (Agarwal & Ramaswami, 1992; Kimura, 1989; Makino & Delios, 1996). Thus, we propose the following hypothesis:

Hypothesis 1. Profitability of a foreign subsidiary has a positive relationship with the size of its foreign parent.

To utilize managerial resources transferred from their parent firms and to establish competitive advantages, foreign subsidiaries have to adapt to the social, political, economic, technological, and regulatory environment of the host country. Adaptation is a learning and time-consuming process. Therefore, experience or age of foreign subsidiaries should be an important firm-level factor.

Many existing studies have taken subsidiary age into account. For example, Makino and Delios (1996) found a positive relationship between age and performance of Japanese subsidiaries in Southeast Asian countries. Therefore, we hypothesize as follows:

Hypothesis 2. Profitability of a foreign subsidiary has a positive relationship with its age.

2.2.2. Structural Impediment: Distribution
Several recent studies have proposed hypotheses linking structural impediments to direct investment in Japan. Among structural impediments, some researchers

have argued that the complex and fragmented distribution system is a structural impediment to entry into the Japanese markets (Ariga & Namikawa, 1991; Ito, 1991). The Japanese distribution system is characterized by few large-scale retailers, many small-scale retailers, and many layers of wholesalers. Transactions in such a decentralized distribution system are quite different from a pure market exchange. Manufacturers and retailers often depend heavily on wholesalers for collection of information about market trends and availability of products. For such a system to function properly, there must be communication, cooperation, and long-term relations among firms.

While Japanese manufacturers have a long tradition of keeping close relationships with distributors, new foreign entrants without such experience have to make additional efforts to access the distribution network (Ariga & Namikawa, 1991).[2] They may have to offer more favorable deals for distributors, which squeezes the profit of these foreign manufacturers.

According to a survey conducted by the Ministry of Economy, Trade, and Industry (former MITI) in 1984, difficulties associated with distribution are the second and the third biggest obstacles for foreign firms that conduct business in Japan (Table 1). Distribution was also considered one of the major obstacles in a 1998 survey, supporting a 1996 survey that found that establishing distribution networks is one of the major reasons why foreign firms succeed in Japanese markets. Therefore, in industries with complex distribution systems, the profitability of firms should be low. Thus, we have the following hypothesis:

Hypothesis 3. Foreign firms in industries with complicated distribution system (fragmented distribution) are less profitable.

2.2.3. Entry Mode

Multinational firms enter foreign markets through various modes of entry, such as acquisitions and greenfield investments, with varying degrees of ownership control, ranging from wholly owned subsidiaries to joint ventures. Among these choices, entry by acquisition is relatively rare in Japan. Therefore, the distinction between joint ventures and wholly owned subsidiaries is important in this paper.

Contractor and Lorange (1988) raised seven objectives that joint ventures achieve: (1) risk reduction; (2) economies of scale and/or rationalization; (3) complementary technologies and patents; (4) co-opting or blocking competition; (5) overcoming government-mandated investment or trade barriers; (6) initial international expansion; and (7) vertical quasi-integration. Based on transaction-cost theory, Hennart (1988) argued that joint ventures are a means for parent firms

Table 1. Obstacles and Success Factors of Foreign Firms in Japan.

1984		1996		1998	
Obstacles	Share	Reasons for success	Share	Obstacles	Share
Competition with Japanese firms	19.3	Supplying distinctive goods and services	57.6	High business cost[a]	61.8
Expanding outlets	10.7	Developing products that fit Japanese market	48.9	High tax rate	61.3
Different commercial practice	9.9	Establishing distribution network	27.5	High demand for quality	53.3
Communication with parent firms	9.1	Gathering enough information on demand	25.6	Recruiting	35.5
High corporate tax	8.6	Establishing delivery network	22.7	Complicated distribution channel	33
Recruiting	7.9	Discretion from parent firms	20.4	Anticompetitive commercial practice	27
Regulation and governmental guidance	4.5	Appropriate human resource management	18.1	Communication with parent firms	26.5
Coordination with Japanese partners	4.3	Preparation for after-sale service	15.2	Coordination with Japanese partners	17.3
Gathering Information on demand	2.7	Aggressive facility investment	14.2	Financing	14.8
High income tax	2.2	Aggressive advertising	7.1	Regulation and governmental guidance	12.8
Securing raw materials and parts	1.3	Establishing the network of subcontractors	3.2	Exclusivity of industrial association	10.5
Financing	0.9	Others	3.2	Lack of infrastructure[b]	8.5
Establishing the network of subcontractors	0.7	Multiple responses		Difficulty in receiving governmental favorable actions	7.3
Visa acquisition for foreign workers	0.7			Others	3.8
Personnel management	0.6			Multiple responses	
Nothing	16.6				
Total	100				

[a] Includes the costs of real estate, wage, etc.
[b] Includes school, transportation, communication, etc.

to internalize a failing market with scale or scope economies or with significant management costs. Based on organizational and cognitive theories, Barkema, Bell, and Pennings (1996) and Kogut (1988) proposed that joint ventures are instruments of organizational learning.

According to these studies, it is sometimes economically rational for firms to enter foreign markets by joint ventures. Several existing empirical studies on entry modes found that the choice of international joint ventures is influenced by the size of the partners, by the industrial characteristics, and by the cultural difference between the host and home countries (Caves & Mehra, 1986; Kogut & Singh, 1988).

However, empirical results on the relationship between entry modes and post-entry performance are scarce and at best ambiguous. Using a sample of Japanese firms entering the North American markets, Woodcock, Beamish, and Makino (1994) found that new ventures outperform joint ventures, and joint ventures outperform acquisitions. Nitsch, Beamish, and Makino (1996) found the same result using a sample of Japanese firms entering Western European countries, although their results were statistically insignificant. However, using a sample of foreign firms in Japan, Yoshihara (1994) found that joint ventures outperform wholly owned subsidiaries. While these studies used relative evaluation of financial situations by managers as a performance measure, Hoshino and Takabayashi (1999) used the financial data of foreign firms in Japan to show that joint ventures outperform wholly owned subsidiaries.

Taken as a whole, these studies suggest that wholly owned subsidiaries outperform joint ventures when Japanese firms enter the American and European markets, while joint ventures outperform wholly owned subsidiaries when foreign firms enter the Japanese market. These contrasting results may be due to strict market demands and complicated distribution networks in Japan. Therefore, we propose the following hypothesis:

Hypothesis 4. Joint ventures are more profitable than wholly owned subsidiaries in Japan.

2.3. Changes in the Determinants of Profits

As indicated in Fig. 2, the presence of foreign firms measured by inward FDI in Japan has been increasing since 1990. Figure 3 shows the trend of the number of non-manufacturing FDI cases increasing notably since 1993 after significant drops in the 1990–1992 period. It has often been pointed out that this upward trend in foreign entry is due to deregulation such as the Large Scale Retailer

Law and Foreign Exchange Control Law (White Paper on International Trade, 1998). It is quite plausible that this deregulation promoted entry in the retail and financial sectors, but it is uncertain how much influence this deregulation had in manufacturing industries.

According to Table 1, the main obstacles for foreign firms to operate in Japan are changing over time and different between the two periods. The top three obstacles in the 1980s were competition with Japanese firms and barriers associated with distribution, while those in the 1990s were high business costs, a high tax rate and high demand for quality. In the 1980s, indigenous Japanese firms were formidable competitors for foreign firms, but since the early 1990s, Japanese firms have become so stagnant that competition with them is less of an obstacle for foreign entrants. Moreover, foreign firms might prefer entering the Japanese market without Japanese partners or prefer to form joint ventures with weak and uncompetitive Japanese firms. High business costs and tax rates are still regarded as obstacles, despite the fact that decline in real-estate prices after the bursting of the bubble economy, coupled with a reduction in corporate tax rates, may have mitigated such obstacles (White Paper on International Trade, 2000). JETRO's 1999 survey found that 70% of foreign firms in Japan concluded that the business environment in Japan had improved (JETRO, 2000). Additionally, obstacles associated with distribution channels rank lower in the 1990s survey than in the 1980s survey, although this factor is still one of the main barriers. The causes for this change may lie in the reform of the Large-Scale Retail Law, a de-emphasis in long-term relationships, and an overall weakening of the corporate group structure.

Taking these changes into account, we propose the following sets of hypotheses regarding the impact of firm-specific factors on profitability:

Hypothesis 5. The determinants of foreign subsidiaries' profitability are different between the 1980s and the 1990s.

Hypothesis 5-1. The effect of size of a foreign parent firm on profitability of its foreign subsidiary is different between the 1980s and the 1990s.

Hypothesis 5-2. The influence of age on profitability of a foreign subsidiary is different between the 1980s and the 1990s.

Hypothesis 5-3. The effect on foreign subsidiaries profitability of a complicated distribution system is different between the 1980s and the 1990s.

Hypothesis 5-4. The effect on foreign subsidiaries profitability of forming joint ventures is different between the 1980s and the 1990s.

2.4. *Exploration on Joint-Venture Effects*

While Yoshihara (1994) and Hoshino and Takabayashi (1999) found that joint ventures are a better entry mode than wholly owned subsidiaries, they did not examine why joint ventures outperform wholly owned subsidiaries. Foreign firms entering the Japanese market by joint ventures may be able to utilize the resources and experience of their Japanese partners to compensate for a shortage of ability and experience. That is, foreign subsidiaries can access the complicated distribution network by making use of their Japanese partner's existent distribution channel; in particular, young subsidiaries of small foreign parents can make up for a shortage in experience and resources by collaboration with Japanese partners. Therefore, we suggest the following hypotheses:

Hypothesis 6. The relationship between profitability of a foreign subsidiary and the size of its foreign parent firm is weaker for joint ventures with Japanese partners than for wholly owned subsidiaries.

Hypothesis 7. The relationship between profitability and age of a foreign subsidiary is weaker for joint ventures with Japanese partners than for wholly owned subsidiaries.

Hypothesis 8. The complicated distribution network of Japan is a weaker impediment for joint ventures with Japanese partners than for wholly owned subsidiaries.

The extent to which joint ventures outperform wholly owned subsidiaries may depend on the types of Japanese partners chosen. This is primarily because individual Japanese partners have different capabilities, resources, and mechanisms, which enable joint ventures to outperform wholly owned subsidiaries.

It is not unusual for foreign firms to form joint ventures with trading companies. Williamson and Yamawaki (1991) suggested positive and negative effects of forming joint ventures with trading companies. Trading companies may help foreign firms distribute their products in the Japanese markets. By taking advantage of their business network and experience, trading companies make up for the foreign partner's shortage of experience. At the same time, trading companies are apt to dominate the relationship, and foreign partners may learn little about the Japanese market through such a partnership. Therefore, we do not hold any expectation as to whether or not a joint venture with a trading company has a more mitigating effect than that with a non-trading company partner.

When the Japanese joint venture partner is in the same industry as the foreign firm, then the Japanese company might bring useful capabilities and assets to the relationship, including procurement of scarce inputs, production facilities, technological capabilities, marketing skills, distribution channels, and so forth. In addition, in a single industry partnership, the two firms may find other synergies. Therefore, we anticipate that in a joint venture with a Japanese firm in the same industry as the foreign parent firm, there is a greater mitigating effect on other variables than when the Japanese firm is in a different industry.

As we have argued above, the size of the foreign parent is hypothesized to have a positive effect on the performance of its subsidiary because the size of a foreign parent reflects superior managerial resources. Continuing in this same vein, we can also suppose that a large Japanese joint venture partner has superior managerial resources. Therefore, we expect that a joint venture with a large Japanese firm has a more compensating effect than that with a small partner.

Some foreign firms set up joint ventures with Japanese *keiretsu* members. Lawrence (1993) has argued that the prevalence of *keiretsu* is likely to constitute impediments to FDI in Japan. Market entry may be hindered by collusive practices, by difficulties of acquiring *keiretsu*-related firms because of cross-shareholdings, or by the inherent cost of capital advantages enjoyed by *keiretsu* members. If so, foreign firms may be able to overcome such disadvantages by forming joint ventures with *keiretsu* members.

3. DATA AND METHODOLOGY

3.1. Data

The sample for this study was constructed from the survey data at the individual subsidiary level compiled by Toyo Keizai and Dun and Bradstreet and published in *Gaishikei Kigyo Soran (Foreign Affiliated Companies in Japan: A Comprehensive Directory)*. They surveyed 3321 foreign affiliated companies, which are classified into two groups: 1357 primary companies with detailed data and 1964 companies with less detailed data (in the 1999 version). In principle, companies are listed as primary if capital is more than 50 million yen and foreigner's control more than 49% of the company's equity.

The sample of foreign subsidiaries in the analysis below was generated in the following way. Among the primary companies in *Gaishikei Kigyo Soran* in 1999, we selected manufacturing subsidiaries that reported their sales and net income for each year from 1994 to 1997. Among 831 manufacturing subsidiaries listed in the

1999 *Gaishikei Kigyo Soran*, 145 subsidiaries report net profit and sales data for the 4-year period. From these, we excluded several subsidiaries because the data on foreign parent's sales were not available. We also excluded some subsidiaries that were partial equity acquisition of existing Japanese firms, or subsidiaries of foreign subsidiaries in Japan. Consequently, excluding these 48 subsidiaries from the 145 observations, we were left with a final sample of 97 subsidiaries. The subsidiaries that report their performance every year might be relatively aged and larger. Therefore, the analysis in this paper might only represent determinants of profitability for aged and larger subsidiaries, which may differ from younger, smaller subsidiaries.

To see if there was any change during the 20-year period, we collected comparable data from the early 1980s and performed statistical tests on data for the two observation periods. We collected the data on the foreign manufacturers in Japan that reported their sales and net income for each year from 1982 to 1984 from the 1996 *Gaishikei Kigyo Soran*. Applying the same criteria to this 1980s sample, we extracted a sample of 150 subsidiaries.

As shown in Table 2, among 97 subsidiaries in the 1990s sample, 65 subsidiaries (67.0%) have U.S. parents, nine subsidiaries (9.3%) have German parents, and eight subsidiaries (8.2%) have U.K. parents. When subsidiaries are grouped by industrial classification, 34 subsidiaries (35.1%) are in the chemical industry, 19 subsidiaries (19.6%) are in industrial machinery, and 19 subsidiaries (19.6%) are in the electric equipment industry.

Among 150 subsidiaries in the 1980s sample, 108 subsidiaries (72%) have U.S. parents, 14 subsidiaries (9.3%) have German parents, and 8 subsidiaries (5.3%) have U.K. parents. Forty-four subsidiaries (29.3%) are in the chemical industry, 34 subsidiaries (22.7%) are industrial machinery, and 29 subsidiaries (19.3%) are in the electric equipment industry.

Roughly speaking, there is little difference in the distribution of foreign subsidiaries among nationality and among industrial classification between the 1980s and the 1990s samples. Forty-two subsidiaries are included in both the 1980s and the 1990s samples. As these 42 subsidiaries survived and reported financial results for more than 10 years, they are considered relatively stable and successful foreign subsidiaries.

3.2. Performance Measure

For a financial performance measure of foreign subsidiaries, most studies to date have used a subjective assessment by managers in the firm, such as "great success," "success," "neutral," "failure," and "complete failure" (Delios &

Table 2. Foreign Subsidiaries in the Sample.

	1990s		1980s	
	Number of Subsidiaries	Percentage	Number of Subsidiaries	Percentage
Nationality of foreign parents				
U.S.	65	67.0	108	72.0
Germany	9	9.3	14	9.3
U.K.	8	8.2	8	5.3
Switzerland	6	6.2	4	2.7
Canada	2	2.1	2	1.3
France	3	3.1	3	2.0
The Netherlands	2	2.1	4	2.7
Sweden	2	2.1	4	2.7
Belgium	0	0.0	1	0.7
Australia	0	0.0	1	0.7
Denmark	0	0.0	1	0.7
Total	97	100.0	150	100.0
Industrial classification of subsidiaries				
Food products	2	2.1	5	3.3
Apparel and other textile	1	1.0	3	2.0
Pulp and paper	1	1.0	2	1.3
Printing and publishing	1	1.0	0	0.0
Chemical	34	35.1	44	29.3
Petroleum and coal products	3	3.1	3	2.0
Rubber	1	1.0	0	0.0
Stone, clay, and glass	3	3.1	7	4.7
Nonferrous metal products	3	3.1	3	2.0
Metal products	1	1.0	7	4.7
Indsutrial machinery	19	19.6	34	22.7
Electric equipment	19	19.6	29	19.3
Transportation equipment	6	6.2	4	2.7
Precision equipment	3	3.1	1	0.7
Other manufacturing	0	0.0	8	5.3
Total	97	100.0	150	100.0

Beamish, 2001; Makino & Delios, 1996; Woodcock et al., 1994; Yoshihara, 1994). However, assessment by managers may lack objectivity. An exception to these studies is Hoshino and Takabayashi (1999), who used recurring profit-sales ratios as a measure of performance. However, their performance measure was based on a single year of data and was thus susceptible to a time-lag effect. In this study, we adopt a several-year average (1982–1984 for the 1980s observations and 1994–1997 for the 1990s observations) of net income-sales ratio (PROFIT) as a performance indicator extracted from *Gaishikei Kigyo Soran*, which reports sales and net income for many foreign affiliated companies.

This performance measure may also have some drawbacks. Scherer and Ross (1990) suggest that economic profit ratio, defined as supra-normal profit (= sales revenue – non-capital costs – depreciation – capital costs) divided by sales revenue, is theoretically relevant as a measure of excess profits. Although some previous research has estimated this ratio by using accounting data, reliable data to estimate non-capital costs and capital costs in our sample of foreign subsidiaries in Japan were unavailable and thus prevented construction of an excess profit rate measure. An alternative measure to the excess profit rate is return on investment. ROI, however, also has potential drawbacks because equity and asset data of foreign investment in subsidiaries are only reported at the book value. Profit rates measured by using assets and equity at book value may diverge significantly from a measure of economic profit rate (e.g. Odagiri & Yamawaki, 1990).

Another potential source of bias in the profit rate lies in the use of transfer pricing by the multinational corporation. The multinational parent could maximize its global profit by manipulating its subsidiaries' accounting profits to take advantage of differences in national tax systems. One way to correct for this is to use a gross income-sales ratio instead of net income-sales ratio to estimate pre-tax earnings. However, our data set does not allow us to construct the gross income-sales ratio because *Toyo Keizai* only reports subsidiaries' after tax income figures. We expect that gross and net ratios are highly correlated and that any bias in using the net ratio would be insignificant (Sakakibara & Yamawaki, 2000).

3.3. Independent Variables

We constructed four major independent variables to test our hypotheses. First, we constructed LOGFPSIZE in order to test Hypothesis 1, which stated that the size of a foreign parent reflects its competitive advantages and has a positive relationship with profitability of its subsidiary in Japan. LOGFPSIZE is the log of foreign parent's sales reported in *Gaishikei Kigyo Soran*. The coefficient of this variable is expected to have a positive. Second, to examine Hypothesis 2, which described the relationship between profitability and age of subsidiaries, we constructed LOGAGE, the log of the number of months from the establishment of each subsidiary to the end of 1997. This variable is expected to have a positive coefficient.[3]

Third, Hypothesis 3 stated that complicated distribution in Japan is a structural impediment. Manufacturers sell their products directly to consumers and to other manufacturers or sell them through distributors. Selling the products to wholesalers means that the distribution is multi-layered. Thus, we adopted the share of manufacturers' sales to wholesalers as a measure of the degree of complexity of the distribution network in each industry to which the subsidiary belongs. The log of the share of the sales to wholesalers (LOGWS) is expected to have a negative coefficient. These data were obtained from *Report on the Basic Survey of Commercial and Manufacturing Structure* and *Activity*, Vol. 1 in 1988 by the Small and Medium Enterprise Agency and Research and Statistics Department, Minister's Secretariat, Ministry of International Trade and Industry.

Finally, to test Hypothesis 4, which stated that joint ventures outperform wholly owned subsidiaries, we constructed a dummy variable, JV. JV is equal to one if the subsidiary is a joint venture with a Japanese company and 0 otherwise. The coefficient of JV is expected to have a positive sign.

In addition to these independent variables, we constructed a 4-year average of net income-sales ratios for each industry (INDPFT). We calculated the average net income-sales ratio for domestic firms in the same industry and at the same level of capital stock as the subsidiary in each year to control for industry and size effects. Since foreign subsidiaries in a favorable industry should show a high performance, we expect that INDPFT has a positive coefficient. We also included three country dummies in the regression models. The three countries were chosen based on their importance as major source countries of the foreign multinationals in Japan. USD, GRD, and UKD are equal to 1 if the parent of the subsidiary is a U.S. firm, German firm, and U.K. firm, respectively, and 0 otherwise.

For the 1980s sample, we constructed the same independent and control variables as before, LOGWS, LOGFPSIZE, LOGAGE, JV, USD, UKD, GRD, and INDPFT. LOGAGE is the log of the number of months from the establishment of each subsidiary to the end of 1984. LOGFPSIZE and LOGWS are defined in the same way as before. The data for LOGWS were obtained from *Report on the Basic Survey of Manufacturing Structure and Activity*, Vol. 7 in 1987 by Small and Medium Enterprise Agency and Research and Statistics Department, Minister's Secretariat, Ministry of International Trade and Industry. INDPFT is a 3-year average of net income-sales ratios for each industry for the 1980s sample. The data for INDPFT were collected from the Ministry of Finance's *Annual Report of Corporate Statistics*.

We ran a regression analysis for each sample as well as for a combined sample, and performed *F* tests to see if there was any difference in the structure of the regressions between the two time periods. Moreover, for the models, which show a significant difference between the two periods, we ran a regression including the interaction between D90 and the independent variables. D90 is a dummy variable, which is equal to 1 for the 1990s observations, and 0 otherwise. The mean, standard deviation, and a correlation matrix of these variables are described in Table 3.

3.4. Interactions

Hypotheses 6, 7 and 8 described the relationship between entry modes and the influences of firm factors and a structural impediment on subsidiaries' profitability. To test these hypotheses, we included the interaction terms of JV with other independent variables in the regression models and tested for coefficient significance. If the coefficients of the interaction terms were significantly different from 0, then corporate structure would influence the magnitude of effect on financial performance of the other variables.

Hypothesis 6 stated that forming joint ventures compensates for the poor capability or the small size of foreign parents. If Hypothesis 6 holds, the coefficient of LOGFPSIZE for joint ventures should be different from that of wholly owned subsidiaries. Therefore, the coefficient of the interaction term of JV and LOGFPSIZE is expected to have a negative sign, the opposite of LOGFPSIZE expected to be positive.

Hypothesis 7 stated that forming joint ventures compensates for the shortage of subsidiary' experience. If Hypothesis 7 holds, the coefficient of the interaction term of JV and LOGAGE is expected to have a negative sign, the opposite of LOGAGE, expected to have a positive sign. Hypothesis 8 stated that forming joint ventures with domestic firms mitigates difficulty in accessing the complicated distribution network in Japan. If Hypothesis 8 holds, the interaction term of JV and LOGWS is expected to have a positive coefficient since LOGWS is expected to have a negative coefficient.

Moreover, we explored the effects of different kinds of Japanese joint-venture partners. To see if forming joint ventures with different kinds of Japanese firms has different effects on the financial performance of joint ventures, we examined the sample of joint ventures (73 observations) in more detail. We set four dummy variables of Japanese JV partners. SHOSHA is equal to 1 if the Japanese partner is one of the six major trading companies, and 0 otherwise. SAMEIND is equal to 1 if the Japanese partner is a firm in the same industry as the foreign parent, and 0 otherwise. LARGE is equal to 1 if the amount of the Japanese parent's sales is more than 100 billion yen, and 0 otherwise. Finally, KEIRETSU is equal to 1 if the subsidiary is a joint venture with a Japanese company that belongs to the presidents' club of the leading six financial groups in the periods examined, Mitsui, Mitsubishi, Sumitomo, Fuyo, Sanwa, and DKB. Then, we included the interaction

Table 3. Mean, Standard Deviation, and Correlation Matrix.

	PROFIT	LOGFPSIZE	LOGAGE	LOGWS	JV	INDPFT	USD	UKD	GRD
PROFIT	1								
LOGFPSIZE	-0.0354	1							
LOGAGE	0.0856	0.41652	1						
LOGWS	-0.0017	0.40864	0.27711	1					
JV	-0.0956	0.038849	-0.0002098	0.0026907	1				
INDPFT	-0.0511	0.07581	0.015697	0.11705	-0.11919	1			
USD	0.1109	0.015028	0.05616	-0.19299	0.061317	-0.089888	1		
UKD	0.0312	0.061256	0.037232	0.114	-0.051053	-0.028223	-0.4024	1	
GRD	-0.0514	-0.021472	-0.12844	0.052077	0.076308	0.05114	-0.48994	-0.084332	1
M	0.0318	9.8106	5.4162	3.1246	0.7692	0.0185	0.7004	0.0648	0.0931
S.D.	0.0480	3.6934	0.6902	0.7986	0.4222	0.0128	0.4590	0.2466	0.2912

terms of each partner dummy with other independent variables in the regression models and tested for coefficient significance.

4. RESULTS

4.1. Firm Factors and a Structural Impediment

The results of the regression analysis for the full sample are shown in Table 4, and those for the matched sample are shown in Table 5. For each sample, we ran the regression for the observations in all the industries, in high-growth industries, and in low-growth industries.

One of our firm-specific variables is LOGFPSIZE, the measurement of foreign parent's sales. The sign of the coefficients for this variable differed between samples and time periods. For the full sample reported in Table 4, LOGFPSIZE has an insignificant coefficient in any of the equations tested. When the sample is split according to a high- and low-growth industry dichotomy, the coefficient for LOGFPSIZE is likely to show an expected positive sign in the high-growth industry, and a negative sign in the low-growth industry. Turning to the matched sample in Table 5, LOGFPSIZE has a significant positive coefficient in the high-growth industry in the 1990s (Eq. (5)). However, in low-growth industry in the 1990s (Eq. (6)), its coefficient is insignificant.

These results indicate that among the relatively old and stable foreign subsidiaries represented by firms in the matched sample, those with larger foreign parents, especially in high-growth industries, show higher profits. Thus, Hypothesis 1 is supported for the observations in high-growth industries in the matched sample.

The variable that measures a subsidiary's age, LOGAGE, reflects its experience. It has a positive coefficient as expected in Eqs (1)–(3). The coefficient is significant at the 5% level in Eqs (1) and (2) but insignificant in Eq. (3). Therefore, a foreign subsidiary's age has a positive association with financial performance. However, this variable has a negative coefficient in Eqs (4)–(6), and significant at the 5% level in Eq. (6). These results indicate that the relatively old subsidiaries in low-growth industries are more likely to show lower profits than the younger subsidiaries. Therefore, Hypothesis 2 is supported only for the observations of the matched sample (except for those in low-growth industries).

The coefficient of the structural impediment variable, LOGWS, is not significant for the full sample. For the matched sample, however, it is positive and significant at the 10% level in the high-growth industry in Eq. (5), while it is negative and significant at the 1% level in the low-growth industry in Eq. (6). Therefore,

Table 4. Determinants of Foreign Subsidiary's Financial Performance (Full Sample).

	All Industries			High-Growth Industries			Low-Growth Industries		
	Equation (1) (1990s)	Equation (1') (1980s)	Equation (1'') (1990s + 1980s)	Equation (2) (1990s)	Equation (2') (1980s)	Equation (2'') (1990s + 1980s)	Equation (3) (1990s)	Equation (3') (1980s)	Equation (3'') (1990s + 1980s)
Const	−1.26E-01 (−2.02)*	−5.00E-03 (−0.13)	−8.20E-03 (−0.30)	−0.23 (−3.03)***	−0.06 (−1.06)	−0.05 (−1.60)	3.25E-02 (0.27)	4.42E-02 (0.76)	3.97E-02 (0.92)
LOGFPSIZE	1.01E-03 (0.45)	−1.23E-03 (−0.53)	−1.24E-03 (−1.28)	1.49E-03 (0.59)	3.47E-04 (0.10)	−1.01E-03 (−0.73)	−2.17E-03 (−0.43)	−4.83E-04 (−0.14)	−2.32E-05 (−0.02)
LOGAGE	2.05E-02 (2.25)**	3.91E-03 (0.63)	7.73E-03 (1.57)	2.68E-02 (2.39)**	1.46E-02 (1.63)	1.95E-02 (2.92)***	7.75E-03 (0.50)	−5.32E-03 (−0.58)	−2.33E-03 (−0.32)
LOGWS	3.41E-03 (0.37)	2.76E-03 (0.52)	2.02E-03 (0.47)	2.00E-02 (1.61)	−1.31E-03 (−0.09)	−6.57E-03 (−1.01)	−7.87E-03 (−0.52)	3.99E-03 (0.50)	3.11E-03 (0.48)
JV	−2.32E-03 (−0.23)	−1.57E-02 (−1.51)	−1.24E-02 (−1.70)*	−9.99E-03 (−0.79)	−5.40E-03 (−0.36)	−7.37E-03 (−0.80)	3.78E-03 (0.19)	−2.80E-02 (−1.90)*	−2.17E-02 (−1.92)*
USD	2.33E-02 (1.89)*	1.53E-02 (1.19)	2.03E-02 (2.24)**	3.28E-02 (1.97)*	1.51E-02 (0.84)	2.16E-02 (1.77)*	1.24E-02 (0.63)	1.22E-02 (0.68)	1.13E-02 (0.84)
UKD	2.65E-02 (1.45)	7.10E-03 (0.33)	2.07E-02 (1.43)	2.03E-02 (0.97)	1.78E-02 (0.58)	2.15E-02 (1.25)	6.39E-02 (1.30)	−1.02E-02 (−0.33)	1.10E-02 (0.45)
GRD	1.56E-02 (0.90)	1.72E-03 (0.09)	1.22E-02 (0.94)	4.17E-02 (1.74)*	2.99E-02 (0.82)	3.32E-02 (1.69)*	−1.32E-02 (−0.50)	−9.61E-03 (−0.39)	−9.03E-03 (−0.49)
INDPFT	−0.37 (−1.59)	1.14 (1.74)*	−0.17 (−0.71)	−0.49 (−1.82)*	0.86 (0.93)	−0.29 (−1.13)	0.15 (0.28)	1.33 (1.29)	0.39 (0.76)
R^2	0.14	0.06	0.05	0.32	0.12	0.15	0.12	0.09	0.06
Adj. R^2	0.07	9.33E-03	0.01	0.2	−4.00E-02	0.08	−0.08	6.00E-03	−0.1
Number of observations	97	150	247	53	53	106	44	97	141
F value		1.21[a]			1.21[b]			0.59[c]	
Critical value (5%)		1.88			1.99			1.88	

Note: Numbers in parentheses are t-statistics.

*The level of significance for a two-tailed test is: 10%.

**The level of significance for a two-tailed test is: 5%.

***The level of significance for a two-tailed test is: 1%.

[a]The degree of freedom of the F value is $(9, 229)$ and that of the critical F value is $(9, \infty)$.

[b]The degree of freedom of the F value is $(9, 88)$ and that of the critical F value is $(9, 90)$.

[c]The degree of freedom of the F value is $(9,123)$ and that of the critical F value is $(9, \infty)$.

Table 5. Determinants of Foreign Subsidiary's Financial Performance (Matched Sample).

	All Industries			High-Growth Industries			Low-Growth Industries		
	Equation (4) (1990s)	Equation (4') (1980s)	Equation (4") (1990s + 1980s)	Equation (5) (1990s)	Equation (5') (1980s)	Equation (5") (1990s + 1980s)	Equation (6) (1990s)	Equation (6') (1980s)	Equation (6") (1990s + 1980s)
Const	4.43E-02 (0.41)	-1.85E-02 (-0.36)	1.56E-02 (0.44)	-6.68E-02 (-0.87)	-2.92E-02 (-0.26)	5.92E-03 (0.14)	0.66 (2.93)**	-2.47E-02 (-0.38)	2.65E-02 (0.39)
LOGFPSIZE	5.28E-03 (1.83)*	-1.94E-03 (-0.74)	1.07E-03 (0.90)	7.04E-03 (3.53)***	-6.00E-03 (-1.24)	-8.14E-04 (-0.42)	-2.51E-03 (-0.47)	8.00E-04 (0.26)	2.65E-03 (1.50)
LOGAGE	-1.27E-02 (-0.90)	5.90E-03 (0.77)	7.45E-04 (0.12)	-1.22E-02 (-1.12)	1.48E-02 (1.07)	6.44E-03 (0.74)	-6.17E-02 (-2.22)**	2.91E-03 (0.29)	-4.60E-03 (-0.41)
LOGWS	-6.10E-03 (-0.53)	1.23E-03 (0.18)	-3.75E-03 (-0.74)	1.71E-02 (2.08)*	-5.41E-03 (-0.19)	-6.51E-03 (-0.80)	-6.63E-02 (-3.35)***	8.03E-03 (1.30)	3.07E-04 (0.05)
JV	4.77E-03 (0.41)	-2.05E-02 (-1.66)	-4.73E-03 (-0.57)	-1.28E-03 (-0.16)	-1.46E-02 (-0.63)	-3.54E-03 (-0.31)	2.73E-02 (1.26)	-1.49E-02 (-1.20)	-1.40E-02 (-1.16)
USD	-7.51E-03 (-0.51)	3.70E-03 (0.23)	-5.15E-03 (-0.48)						
UKD	2.54E-02 (1.17)	-3.30E-02 (-0.93)	1.37E-02 (0.77)						
GRD	-2.12E-02 (-0.86)	-2.48E-03 (-0.10)	-1.46E-02 (-0.85)						
INDPFT	0.77 (1.87)*	2.05 (2.60)**	0.99 (2.90)***	0.58 (1.88)*	2.99 (1.63)	1.17 (2.62)**	-0.10 (-0.15)	0.58 (0.65)	0.58 (1.16)
R^2	0.27	0.27	0.15	0.62	0.46	0.24	0.49	0.2	0.11
Adj. R^2	0.09	9.00E-02	0.06	0.51	0.16	0.12	0.31	7.56E-03	-1.87E-03
Number of observations	42	42	84	22	15	37	20	27	47
F value		1.22[a]			6.47[b]			3.13[c]	
Critical value (5%)		2.02			2.49			2.37	

Note: Numbers in parentheses are t-statistics.

*The level of significance for a two-tailed test is: 10%.

**The level of significance for a two-tailed test is: 5%.

***The level of significance for a two-tailed test is: 1%.

[a]The degree of freedom of the F value is (9, 66) and that of the critical F value is (9, 70).

[b]The degree of freedom of the F value and the crtical F value is (6, 25).

[c]The degree of freedom of the F value and the critial F value is (6, 35).

for relatively old and stable subsidiaries in high-growth industries, performance rises as the share of subsidiaries' sales to wholesalers increases, while for low-growth industries, the performance falls as the share of subsidiaries' sales to wholesaler's increases. In other words, a complicated distribution system is a structural impediment for relatively old subsidiaries in low-growth industries. Thus, Hypothesis 3 is supported only for firms in low-growth industries of the matched sample.

The variable of entry mode, JV, has an insignificant coefficient in all six equations, and its sign is mixed. The coefficient of JV in Eqs (1) and (2) is not the intercept of the regression line for the observations of joint venture, but the difference of the intercepts between joint venture and wholly owned subsidiary observations. The intercept of the regression line for joint venture observations was -0.14 $(= -0.13 - 7.46E\text{-}03)$, which is also negative. Therefore, Hypothesis 4 is not supported.

Regarding country variables, the coefficient of the U.S. dummy is positive for the full sample and is significant at the 10% level in Eqs (1) and (2) but negative for the matched sample. The coefficient of UKD is positive but insignificant in all four equations. GRD has a positive coefficient in Eqs (1) and (2), and it is significant at the 10% level in Eq. (2). However, it is insignificant and negative in Eqs (3) and (4). The industry average net income-sales ratio has an unexpected negative coefficient in Eqs (1), (2), and (6), and is significant at the 10% level in Eq. (2). However, it is positive in Eqs (3)–(5) and significant at the 10% level in Eqs (4) and (5).

4.2. Comparison Between the Two Time Periods

To see if there is any change in determinants of foreign firm's financial performance for the past 20 years, we also ran the regressions for the 1980s observations and combined observations of the 1980s and 1990s. In Tables 4 and 5, equations denoted by a single prime, e.g. n' (n: 1–6) are for the 1980s sample, and equations denoted by a double prime n'' are for the combined sample. Using these results, we performed F tests.

According to the F values and the critical F values at the bottom of Table 4, the null hypothesis that the structure of the model is different between the 1980s and the 1990s is not rejected for the full sample. In the matched sample in Table 5, the results suggest that the null hypothesis is not rejected for the observations in all the industries. However, when the sample is split into high- and low-growth industries, it is rejected for each subsample (high- and low-growth industries). Therefore, for the sample as a whole, there is no statistical evidence for any significant difference between the two time periods. For the matched sample, however, there is a significant difference between the 1980s and 1990s. In other words, as far as relatively old and stable foreign subsidiaries in Japan are concerned, the determinants of financial performance have changed since the 1980s, and Hypothesis 5 is supported.

Since the F tests above found some significant difference in model structure between the 1980s and the 1990s in the matched sample, we ran regressions, which included the interaction terms of D90 with the independent variables. The results of the regressions are shown in Table 6. Equations (7) and (7′) are for the observations in high-growth industries, while Eqs (8) and (8′) are for the observations in low-growth industries.

In Eq. (7′), D90 × LOGFPSIZE has a significant coefficient. This result indicates that the coefficient of LOGFPSIZE is significantly different between the 1980s sample and the 1990s sample. The coefficient (−0.006) is negative for the 1980s sample, while it is positive (0.004 = 0.01–0.006) for the 1990s sample. Therefore, as far as the observation in high-growth industries of the matched sample is concerned, Hypothesis 5-1, which stated that the effect that the size of a foreign parent firm had on profitability of its overseas subsidiary was different between the 1980s and the 1990s, is supported.

In Eq. (7′), D90 × INDPFT also has a significant coefficient. This result suggests that the effect that industry average profit had on profitability of the firm's overseas subsidiary was different between the 1980s and the 1990s. Based on the analysis, this was a significant source of difference in the determinants of foreign subsidiaries' profit in Japan between the two periods.

In Eq. (8′), the interaction terms of D90 and LOGAGE, LOGWS, and JV have a significant coefficient. This result indicates that the coefficients of LOGAGE, LOGWS, and JV were significantly different between the 1980s sample and the 1990s sample. The coefficient of LOGAGE is positive for the 1980s sample, while it is negative for the 1990s sample. The coefficient of LOGWS is positive for the former sample, while it is negative for the latter sample. The coefficient of JV is negative for the 1980s sample, while it is positive for the 1990s sample. Therefore, as far as the observations in low-growth industries of the matched sample are concerned, Hypothesis 5-2, Hypothesis 5-3, and Hypothesis 5-4, which stated, respectively, that the effect of the age of a foreign parent firm, the complicated distribution system, and the joint venture structure with Japanese firms on profitability of the subsidiary were different between the 1980s and the 1990s, are supported.

Moreover, D90 is positive and significant at the 1% level. Therefore, the intercept of the regression line for the 1990s sample is higher than that for the 1980s sample.

Table 6. Comparison of the Determinants Between the Two Time Periods
(Matched Sample).

	High-Growth Industries		Low-Growth Industries	
	Equation (7) (1990s + 1980s)	Equation (7′) (1990s + 1980s)	Equation (8) (1990s + 1980s)	Equation (8′) (1990s + 1980s)
Consdt	−3.39E–02	−2.92E–02	4.41E–02	−0.02
	(−0.58)	(−0.38)	(0.59)	(−0.33)
D90	−2.65E–02	−3.76E–02	1.17E–02	0.68
	(−0.98)	(−0.26)	(0.58)	(3.30)***
LOGFPSIZE	9.41E–04	−6.00E–03	1.22E–03	8.00E–04
	(0.36)	(−1.79)*	(0.40)	(0.23)
D90 × LOGFPSIZE		0.01		−3.31E–03
		(2.80)***		(−0.57)
LOGAGE	9.55E–03	1.48E–02	−5.59E–03	2.91E–03
	(1.03)	(1.55)	(−0.49)	(0.25)
D90 × LOGAGE		−0.03		−6.46E–02
		(−1.34)		(−2.43)**
LOGWS	7.48E–04	−5.41E–03	−5.81E–04	8.03E–03
	(0.07)	(−0.28)	(−0.08)	(1.14)
D90 × LOGWS		0.02		−0.07
		(0.96)		(−4.03)***
JV	−4.50E–03	−1.46E–02	−1.35E–02	−1.49E–02
	(−0.39)	(−0.92)	(−1.11)	(−1.05)
D90 × JV		0.01		0.04
		(0.65)		(1.80)*
INDPFT	1.03	2.99	0.59	0.58
	(2.19)**	(2.37)**	(1.17)	(0.57)
D90 × INDPFT		−2.41		−0.68
		(−1.77)*		(−0.59)
R^2	0.26	0.54	0.11	0.42
Adj R^2	0.12	0.34	−0.02	0.24
No. of Obs	37	37	47	47

Note: Numbers in parentheses are *t*-statistics.
The degree of freedom of the F value and the critical F value is (6, 25).
*The level of significance for a two-tailed test is: 10%.
**The level of significance for a two-tailed test is: 5%.
***The level of significance for a two-tailed test is: 1%.

4.3. JV Effects

The results of the interaction terms of JV with other variables for the 1990s observations of the full sample are reported in Eq. (9) in Table 7. First, the

Table 7. Effects of JV and Different Partners (1990s Observations in the Full Sample).

	Equation (9)	Equation (10)	Equation (11)	Equation (12)	Equation (13)	Equation (14)	Equation (15)	Equation (16)	Equation (17)
Const	-7.46E-03	-0.14	-0.15	-0.12	0.19	-0.15	0.03	-0.15	-0.12
	(-0.06)	$(-2.17)^{**}$	$(-2.38)^{**}$	$(-1.67)^{*}$	(1.14)	$(-2.22)^{**}$	(0.22)	$(-2.19)^{**}$	(-1.38)
LOGFPSIZE	-1.34E-02	2.29E-03	2.41E-03	2.42E-03	0.01	2.21E-03	-4.21E-03	2.30E-03	1.68E-03
	$(-1.88)^{*}$	(1.04)	(1.12)	(1.11)	(1.36)	(1.00)	(-1.11)	(1.04)	(0.67)
JV × LOGFPSIZE	1.55E-02								
	$(2.06)^{**}$								
SHOSHA × LOGFPSIZE			0.23						
			(1.50)						
SAMEIND × LOGFPSIZE					-4.22E-03				
					(-0.90)				
LARGE × LOGFPSIZE							0.01		
							$(2.11)^{**}$		
KEIRETSU × LOGFPSIZE									3.27E-03
									(0.60)
LOGAGE	5.29E-02	0.02	0.02	0.01	-0.02	0.02	-9.75E-04	0.02	0.02
	$(2.67)^{***}$	$(1.68)^{*}$	$(1.78)^{*}$	(1.25)	(-0.85)	$(1.68)^{*}$	(-0.04)	$(1.74)^{*}$	(1.09)
JV × LOGAGE	-3.77E-02								
	$(-1.70)^{*}$								
SHOSHA × LOGAGE			1.26						
			$(1.74)^{*}$						
AMEIND × LOGAGE					0.04				
					(1.43)				
LARGE × LOGAGE							0.02		
							(0.82)		
KEIRETSU × LOGAGE									7.87E-04
									(0.04)

	(1)	(2)	(3)	(4)	(5)	(6)	(7)	(8)	(9)
LOGWS	−2.89E−02 (−1.69)*	0.01 (1.08)	0.01 (1.26)	0.01 (1.25)	−0.02 (−1.03)	0.01 (1.03)	0.01 (0.74)	0.01 (1.02)	0.01 (0.52)
JV × LOGWS	3.97E−02 (2.08)**								
SHOSHA × LOGWS			−2.12 (−1.89)*						
SAMEIND × LOGWS					0.04 (1.77)*				
LARGE × LOGWS							−2.13E−03 (−0.10)		
KEIRETSU × LOGWS									0.01 (0.47)
JV	−0.13 (−0.99)								
SHOSHA		0.01 (0.30)							
SAMEIND			−2.63 (−1.19)	−0.01 (−1.28)	−0.37 (−2.07)**				
LARGE						0.01 (0.69)	−0.24 (−1.68)*		
KEIRETSU								6.91E−04 (0.07)	−0.09 (−0.60)
USD	1.88E−02 (1.54)	0.01 (0.97)	0.01 (0.97)	0.01 (0.86)	0.01 (1.03)	0.01 (0.95)	0.01 (0.79)	0.01 (0.93)	0.01 (0.91)
UKD	2.90E−02 (1.61)	0.03 (1.36)	0.03 (1.35)	0.03 (1.30)	0.02 (1.18)	0.03 (1.41)	0.03 (1.63)	0.03 (1.34)	0.03 (1.21)
GRD	1.17E−02 (0.68)	−0.01 (−0.38)	−0.01 (−0.36)	−0.01 (−0.52)	−0.01 (−0.59)	−0.01 (−0.36)	−0.01 (−0.31)	−0.01 (−0.42)	−0.01 (−0.49)
INDPFT	−0.18 (−0.77)	−0.10 (−0.35)	−0.24 (−0.65)	−0.12 (−0.44)	−0.17 (−0.66)	−0.08 (−0.31)	−0.06 (−0.22)	−0.07 (−0.26)	−0.05 (−0.17)
R^2	0.21	0.15	0.23	0.17	0.29	0.15	0.22	0.14	0.15
Adj. R^2	0.11	0.04	0.09	0.06	0.16	0.04	0.08	0.04	−9.43E−04
Number of observations	97	73	73	73	73	73	73	73	73

Note: Numbers in parentheses are *t*-statistics.

*The level of significance for a two-tailed test is: 10%.

**The level of significance for a two-tailed test is: 5%.

***The level of significance for a two-tailed test is: 1%.

coefficient of the interaction term between JV and LOGFPSIZE is positive and significant at the 5% level. The result shows that the impact of foreign parent's size on the performance of joint ventures is significantly different from that on the performance of wholly owned subsidiaries, although the sign of the coefficient is opposite to our expectation.[4] The size of a foreign parent has a positive impact on performance of joint ventures. Therefore, Hypothesis 6 is not supported. This unexpected result may suggest that foreign firms that form joint ventures with a Japanese firm have advantages associated with economies of scale. Therefore, the coefficient of LOGFPSIZE for joint venture observations is positive and significantly different from that for non-JV observations.

Second, the interaction term between JV and LOGAGE has a negative coefficient as expected. The coefficient is significant at the 10% level. This indicates that the influence of a subsidiary's age on the performance of joint ventures is significantly different from that on the performance of wholly owned subsidiaries. Wholly owned subsidiaries with long experience tend to show a high profitability, while the age effect is much less for joint ventures. Since the result indicates that forming joint ventures with Japanese firms weakens the relationship between age and performance of foreign firms, Hypothesis 7 is supported.

Third, the interaction term of JV with LOGWS has a positive coefficient, as expected. The coefficient is significant at the 5% level. This indicates that the influence of complicated distribution on the performance of joint ventures is significantly different from that on the performance of wholly owned subsidiaries. As we pointed out above, the influence is negative for wholly owned subsidiaries, while it is positive for joint ventures.[5] Since the result indicates that forming joint ventures with Japanese firms mitigates the impediment of the complicated distribution network in Japan, Hypothesis 8 is supported.

We further explored the effects of different kinds of joint venture partners for 73 subsidiaries forming joint ventures with Japanese partners. The results are also reported in Table 7. In Eqs (10) and (11) including SHOSHA and its interactions with other independent variables, SHOSHA × LOGAGE has a significantly positive coefficient, and SHOSHA × LOGWS has a significantly negative coefficient. This means that the effects of age and distribution are not mitigated by forming a joint venture with a trading company, which is significantly different from the mitigating effect on age and distribution of non-*shosha* joint ventures. According to the prior analysis, the positive effect of subsidiary's age on the performance of joint ventures is much less than that on the performance of wholly owned subsidiaries. In other words, forming a joint venture mitigates age effects. However, the significantly positive coefficient of SHOSHA × LOGAGE in Eq. (11) suggests that forming a joint venture with a trading company does not mitigate the positive effect of age. Similarly, the significantly negative coefficient of SHOSHA × LOGWS suggests that forming a joint venture with a trading company does not mitigate the obstacle of complex distribution.

In Eqs (12) and (13), including SAMEIND and its interactions with other independent variables, SAMEIND × LOGWS is the only significant interaction term. Its positive coefficient suggests that foreign firms can overcome the obstacle of complex distribution by forming a joint venture with a Japanese firm in the same industry as the foreign parent. Since LOGWS in Eq. (13) is negative, the mitigating effect of joint ventures on the obstacle of distribution found in the prior analysis is almost solely a result of joint ventures with firms in the same industry as the foreign parent.

In Eqs (14) and (15), including LARGE and its interactions with other independent variables, LARGE × LOGPFSIZE is the only significant interaction term. In the prior analysis, the size of the foreign parent has a positive impact on the joint venture's performance, while the positive coefficient of LARGE × LOGPFSIZE in Eq. (15) suggests that for the joint ventures with large Japanese firms, the size of the foreign parent has a positive impact on the joint venture's financial performance. This might suggest that large foreign and Japanese partners find synergies.

In Eqs (16) and (17), including KEIRETSU and its interactions with other independent variables, there is no significant interaction term. This suggests that joint ventures with a *keiretsu* member have no significantly different impact on performance than joint ventures with non-*keiretsu* firms.

To understand the different effects of entry modes and joint-venture partners on foreign subsidiaries' performance, Figs 4A and 4B show simplified regression lines. To compare the slope of paired sets of regression lines, each line is drawn as if it has the same intercept, although the intercepts are in fact different.

Figure 4A describes the relation between LOGWS and PROFIT. For WOS (wholly owned subsidiaries), the relation is negative, as shown in Eq. (9) of Table 7. However, forming a joint venture with a Japanese firm has a mitigating effect on the obstacle of complex distribution, since JV × LOGWS has a significantly positive coefficient, as shown in Eq. (9) of Table 7. In other words, the JV (joint venture) corporate structure mitigates the effects of structural impediments of distribution.

Forming a SAMEIND (a joint venture with a Japanese firm in the same industry as the foreign parent) mitigates the obstacle of complex distribution more than JV, since SAMEIND × LOGWS has a significantly positive coefficient in Eq. (13) of Table 7. Therefore, SAMEIND has a mitigating effect on structural impediment of distribution.

However, SHOSHA × LOGWS has a significantly negative coefficient, and the coefficient of LOGWS for joint ventures with a trading company is negative

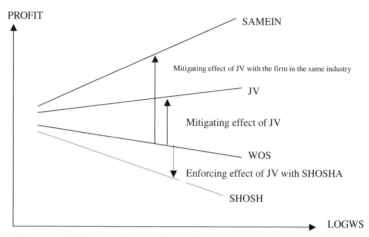

Fig. 4A. Mitigating Effects of Joint Ventures on Structural Impediments.

$(-2.11 = 0.01 - 2.12)$. Therefore, forming a joint venture with a trading company has an enforcing effect rather than mitigating effect.

Figure 4B describes the relation between LOGAGE and PROFIT. For WOS, the relation is positive, as shown in Eq. (9) of Table 7. However, JV × LOGAGE has a significantly negative coefficient, as shown in Eq. (9) of Table 7. Therefore, forming a joint venture can mitigate the positive effect of a subsidiary's age, but

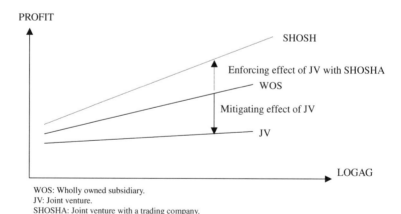

WOS: Wholly owned subsidiary.
JV: Joint venture.
SHOSHA: Joint venture with a trading company.
SAMEIN: Joint venture with a Japanese firm in the same industry as a foreign parent.

Fig. 4B. Mitigating Effects of Joint Ventures on Age.

SHOSHA × LOGAGE has a significantly positive coefficient. This suggests that forming a joint venture with a trading company has an enforcing effect rather than a mitigating effect.

5. DISCUSSION AND CONCLUSION

This study has examined the determinants of financial performance of foreign subsidiaries in Japanese manufacturing industries by using subsidiary-level data. Several important findings emerged from the analysis.

First, the recent financial performance of subsidiaries in Japan is determined by both firm factors and structural impediments. However, effects vary across samples. The main results from testing the hypotheses are summarized in Table 8.

The size of foreign parents has a positive association with profits of subsidiaries in high-growth industries in the matched sample but has a negative impact on profits of wholly owned subsidiaries in the full sample (Eq. (9)). This result suggests that it is likely that large foreign parents have deep pockets from which subsidiaries can draw resources in order to compete in growing industries. Additionally, subsidiaries in the matched sample were those that had been in business in Japan for a relatively long period and were well established in their respective markets. They were more likely to have adapted to a corporate structure that facilitates communication between headquarters and local operations. It is also likely that their parents consider the Japanese market to be strategically important.

The age of foreign subsidiaries has a positive relationship with subsidiary's profits in the full sample, suggesting that subsidiaries with more experience doing business in Japan are more profitable than inexperienced subsidiaries. However, in low-growth industries in the matched sample, relatively older subsidiaries exhibited a lower performance than relatively younger subsidiaries.

Complicated distribution systems in Japan are a structural impediment for wholly owned subsidiaries (Eq. (9)). In other words, wholly owned subsidiaries that sell into markets with complex distribution systems are generally less profitable. For both wholly owned subsidiaries and joint ventures, complicated distribution has a negative impact on profits in low-growth industries for firms represented by the matched sample. It appears as though the inefficiency of the complex distribution system is more significant when industry growth is low. Conversely, complicated distribution has a positive impact on profits of subsidiaries in high-growth industries of the matched sample. This suggests that the inefficiency associated with complicated distribution in Japan is mitigated in high-growth industries, and that complex distribution in these industries works well for both domestic firms and foreign subsidiaries with some experience.

Table 8. Summary of the Results.

Hypotheses	Variable/Statistics	Expectation	Full Sample			Matched Sample			Matched Sample		Whole Sample
			All	High Growth	Low Growth	All	High Growth	Low Growth	High Growth	Low Growth	1990s
			Equation (1)	Equation (2)	Equation (3)	Equation (4)	Equation (5)	Equation (6)	Equation (7′)	Equation (8′)	Equation (9)
H1 (foreign parent's size)	LOFPSIZE	+	Insig[a]	Insig	Insig	+	+	Insig			− (WOS)[b]
H2 (subsidiary's age)	LOGAGE	+	+	+	Insig	Insig	Insig	−			+ (WOS)
H3 (complicated distribution)	LOGWS	−	Insig	Insig	Insig	Insig	+	−			− (WOS)
H4 (JV)	JV	+	Insig	Insig	Insig	Insig	Insig	Insig			
H5 (change)	F value	> critical F value	Insig	Insig	Insig	Insig	Sig	Sig			
H5-1 (change in size)	D90 × LOGFPSIZE								Sig	Insig	
H5-2 (change in age)	D90 × LOGAGE								Insig	Sig	
H5-3 (change in distribution)	D90 × LOGWS								Insig	Sig	
H5-4 (change in JV)	D90 × JV								Insig	Sig	
H6 (JV effect on size)	JV × LOGFPSIZE	−									Sig (+)[c]
H7 (JV effect on age)	JV × LOGAGE	−									Sig (−)
H8 (JV effect on distribution)	JV × LOGWS	+									Sig (+)

[a] Insig and sig mean insignificant and significant, respectively.
[b] The results of H1–H4 in Equation (9) are for wholly owned subsidiaries (WOS).
[c] The sign of interaction is in parentheses.

Second, we found modest significant statistical evidence showing that the structure underlying the model of determinants of financial performance of foreign subsidiaries in Japan was different between the 1980s and the 1990s. For observations in low-growth industries, the impact of subsidiaries' age, complicated distribution, and joint venture was different between the 1980s and the 1990s. In low-growth industries, complicated distribution has a negative impact and is an important structural impediment. In high-growth industries, the size of foreign parents has a positive impact.

Moreover, though industry average profits and foreign subsidiaries' profits were positively correlated in the 1980s, they were weakly or even negatively correlated in the 1990s. That is, in the 1980s, foreign subsidiaries' profits followed industry trends and were thus influenced by industry characteristics, while in the 1990s, the performance of foreign subsidiaries diverged from that of their Japanese rivals. Indeed, the foreign firms performed better even where domestic firms showed a poor performance in the same industry. This finding suggests that it is Japanese firms that changed, rather than foreign subsidiaries. Indeed, foreign subsidiaries' competitiveness may have increased due to the relative decline in competitiveness of Japanese firms, not necessarily due to an absolute increase in competitiveness of foreign subsidiaries.

Third, the effects of structural impediments and firm factors on the performance of wholly owned subsidiaries differed from those influencing the performance of joint ventures. Complicated distribution and the foreign parent's size have a positive effect on the performance of joint ventures. The age of joint ventures has a positive impact on their performance, but much less than the impact of age on the performance of wholly owned subsidiaries. The results of distribution and age suggest that forming joint ventures with Japanese firms mitigates the negative impact of complicated distribution systems and the positive impact of subsidiary's age.

Finally, different effects of joint ventures are shown to depend on the kinds of Japanese partners. Partnership with Japanese firms in the same industry mitigates the obstacle of complex distribution. Forming joint ventures with large Japanese firms can strengthen the positive effect of the size of foreign parents. However, joint ventures with trading companies do not mitigate the positive effect of age and the negative effect of distribution. The effects of joint ventures with a *keiretsu* member are not significantly different from those of joint venture with non-*keiretsu* firms. In sum, forming a joint venture has differing compensating and mitigating effects depending on the type of partner.

Recently, inward FDI in Japan has been increasing, and more foreign firms are expected to enter Japanese markets in the future. However, the current trend of increasing inward FDI is mainly observed in non-manufacturing sectors. There are less often increases in manufacturing sectors. There are also minor changes in the determinants of profits for foreign manufacturing subsidiaries. The results of this study do not show a consistent pattern of firm-specific factors having more impact and structural impediments having less impact. Rather, the results suggest that foreign subsidiaries succeeded in recent years not necessarily because they increased competitiveness but because Japanese firms lost competitiveness. To succeed in Japan, forming a joint venture is still one of the more effective ways of overcoming difficulties in doing business in Japan. Moreover, when forming joint ventures, foreign firms should carefully select suitable Japanese partners depending on the types of roles they expect the joint venture to play.

NOTES

1. Regarding the Cournot model; see, for example, Scherer and Ross (1990, pp. 227–229). The model uses firm's market share as its size and indicates that marginal cost declines with increase in market share. This relationship holds only in homogeneous goods markets, but even in differentiated goods markets, firm size may be a good proxy for capabilities and advantages, assuming that advertising and R&D expenditures are dependent on it.

2. Ito (1991) correctly argued that the Japanese distribution system is a barrier to new entrants, both foreign and domestic.

3. One might argue that a positive relation between profitability and age of subsidiaries has nothing to do with experience of subsidiaries. Instead, new entrants have to make initial investment and show low profits, while older subsidiaries have depreciated their initial investments and show higher profits. However, new entrants with strong products can be successful without heavy initial investment, while old subsidiaries have to invest to maintain their positions. Moreover, in our sample, the minimum value and the average of subsidiaries' age was more than 7 years and 29 years, respectively. Therefore, there is no new entrant in our sample.

4. In this specification of the analysis, the coefficient of an independent variable for joint venture observations is the sum of the coefficients of the independent variable and its interaction terms. In the case of LOGFPSIZE, the coefficient of the variable for joint venture observations is 0.21E-02 ($=-1.34$E-02 $+ 1.55$R-02).

5. The coefficient of LOGWS for joint venture observations is 1.08E-02 ($=-2.89$E-02 $+ 3.97$E-02).

REFERENCES

Agarwal, S., & Ramaswami, S. N. (1992). Choice of foreign market entry mode: Impact of ownership, location and internationalization factors. *Journal of International Business Studies, 23*, 1–27.

Ariga, K., & Namikawa, H. (1991). Ryutsu hiyo to sannyu shoheki [Distribution costs and barriers to entry]. In: Y. Miwa & K. Nishimura (Eds), *Nihon no Ryutsu [Distribution in Japan]* (pp. 159–188). Tokyo: University of Tokyo Press.

Barkema, H. G., Bell, J. H., & Pennings, J. M. (1996). Foreign entry, cultural barriers, and learning. *Strategic Management Journal, 17*, 151–166.

Caves, R. E. (1996). *Multinational enterprise and economic analysis* (2nd ed.). Cambridge: Cambridge University Press.

Caves, R. E., & Mehra, S. K. (1986). Entry of foreign multinationals into U.S. manufacturing industries. In: M. E. Porter (Ed.), *Competition in Global Industries* (pp. 449–481). Boston, MA: Harvard Business School Press.

Contractor, F. J., & Lorange, P. (1988). Why should firms cooperate? The strategy and economics basis for cooperative ventures. In: F. J. Contractor & P. Lorange (Eds), *Cooperative Strategies in International Business* (pp. 3–30). Lexington, MA: Lexington Books.

Cubbin, J., & Domberger, S. (1988). Advertising and post-entry oligopoly behavior. *Journal of Industrial Economics, 37*, 123–140.

Delios, A., & Beamish, P. W. (2001). Survival and profitability: The roles of experience and intangible assets in foreign subsidiary performance. *Academy of Management Journal, 44*, 1028–1038.

Dunning, J. H. (1988). The eclectic paradigm of international production: A restatement and some possible extensions. *Journal of International Business Studies, 19*, 1–31.

Hennart, J. F. (1988). A transaction costs theory of equity joint ventures. *Strategic Management Journal, 9*, 361–374.

Hoshino, Y., & Takabayashi, S. (1999). Zainichi gaishi-kei kigyo no shinshutsu keitai to gyoseki (Entry modes and performance of foreign subsidiaries in Japan). *Soshiki Kagaku [Organizational Science], 32*, 65–75.

Hymer, S. H. (1976). *The international operations of national firms: A study of direct foreign investment.* Cambridge: MIT Press.

Ito, M. (1991). The Japanese distribution system and access to the Japanese market. In: P. Krugman (Ed.), *Trade with Japan: Has the Door Opened Wider?* (pp. 175–189). Chicago: University of Chicago Press.

JETRO (2000). *JETRO white paper on foreign direct investment.* Tokyo: JETRO.

Kimura, Y. (1989). Firm-specific strategic advantages and foreign direct investment behavior of firms: The case of Japanese semiconductor firms. *Journal of International Business Studies, 20*, 296–314.

Kindleberger, C. P. (1969). *American business abroad: Six lectures on direct investment.* New Haven, CT: Yale University Press.

Kogut, B. (1988). Joint ventures: Theoretical and empirical perspectives. *Strategic Management Journal, 9*, 319–332.

Kogut, B., & Singh, H. (1988). The effect of national culture on the choice of entry mode. *Journal of International Business Studies, 19*, 411–432.

Lawrence, R. (1993). Japan's low levels of inward investment: The role of inhibitions of acquisitions. In: K. A. Froot (Ed.), *Foreign Direct Investment* (pp. 85–111). Chicago: University of Chicago Press.

Makino, S., & Delios, A. (1996). Local knowledge transfer and performance: Implications for alliance in Asia. *Journal of International Business Studies, 27*, 905–927.

Morck, R., & Yeung, B. (1992). Internalization: An event study test. *Journal of International Economics, 15*, 555–567.

Negishi, S., & Tamehiro, Y. (2001). *Global retailer [Global retailer].* Tokyo: Toyo Keizai Shinpo-sha.

Nitsch, D., Beamish, P., & Makino, S. (1996). Entry mode and performance of Japanese FDI in Western Europe. *Management International Review, 36*, 27–43.

Odagiri, H., & Yamawaki, H. (1990). The persistence of profits: International comparison. In: D. C. Mueller (Ed.), *The Dynamics of Company Profits: An International Comparison* (pp. 129–146). Cambridge: Cambridge University Press.

Oketa, A. (1988). *Gaishi kigyo in Japan [Foreign firms in Japan]*. Tokyo: Dobunkan.

Porac, J. F., Thomas, H., Wilson, F., Paton, D., & Kanfer, A. (1995). Rivalry and the industry model of Scottish knitwear producers. *Administrative Science Quarterly, 40*, 203–227.

Porter, M. E. (1979). The structure within industries and companies' performance. *Review of Economics and Statistics, 61*, 214–227.

Sakakibara, M., & Yamawaki, H. (2000). What determines the profitability of foreign direct investment? A subsidiary-level analysis of Japanese multinationals. *Academy of Management Proceedings, Best papers*, IM: J1–J6.

Scherer, F. M., & Ross, D. (1990). *Industrial market structure and economic performance* (3rd ed.). Boston: Houghton Mifflin.

Wakasugi, R. (1996). Why foreign firms' entry has been low in Japan: An empirical examination. In: M. Yoshitomi & E. M. Graham (Eds), *Foreign Direct Investment in Japan* (pp. 111–135). Cheltenham, UK: Edward Elgar.

Weinstein, D. (1996). Structural impediments to investment in Japan: What have we learned over the last 450 years? In: M. Yoshitomi & E. M. Graham (Eds), *Foreign Direct Investment in Japan* (pp. 136–172). Cheltenham, UK: Edward Elgar.

Williamson, P. J. (1986). Multinational enterprise behavior and domestic industry adjustment under import threat. *Review of Economics and Statistics, 68*, 359–368.

Williamson, P. J., & Yamawaki, H. (1991). Distribution: Japan's hidden advantage. *Business Strategy Review, 2*, 85–105.

Woodcock, C. P., Beamish, P. W., & Makino, S. (1994). Ownership-based entry mode strategies and international performance. *Journal of International Business Studies, 25*, 253–273.

Yamawaki, H. (2002). Price reactions to new competition: A study of U.S. luxury car market, 1986–1997. *International Journal of Industrial Organization, 20*, 19–39.

Yamawaki, H. (2004). Who survives in Japan? An empirical analysis of European and U.S. multinational firms in Japanese manufacturing industries. *Journal of Industry, Competition, and Trade, 4*, 135–153.

Yoshihara, H. (1994). *Gaishi-kei kigyo [Foreign subsidiaries]*. Tokyo: Dobunkan.

Yoshitomi, M. (1996). Introduction. In: M. Yoshitomi & E. M. Graham (Eds), *Foreign Direct Investment in Japan* (pp. xiii–xvi). Cheltenham, UK: Edward Elgar.

SET UP A CONTINUATION ORDER TODAY!

Did you know you can set up a continuation order on all JAI series and have each new volume sent directly to you upon publication. For details on how to set up a continuation order contact your nearest regional sales office listed below.

To view related Business, Management and Accounting series, please visit

www.ElsevierBusinessandManagement.com

30% DISCOUNT FOR AUTHORS ON ALL BOOKS!

A 30% discount is available to Elsevier book and journal contributors ON ALL BOOKS plus standalone CD-ROMS except multi-volume reference works.

To claim your discount, full payment is required with your order, which must be sent directly to the publisher at the nearest regional sales office listed below.

ELSEVIER REGIONAL SALES OFFICES

For customers in the Americas:

Customer Service Department
11830 Westline Industrial Drive
St. Louis, MO 63146
USA
For US customers:
Tel: +1 800 545 2522
Fax: +1 800 535 9935
For customers outside the US:
Tel: +1 800 460 3110
Fax: +1 314 453 7095
Email: usbkinfo@elsevier.com

For customers in the Far East:

Elsevier
Customer Support Department
3 Killiney Road, #08-01/09
Winsland House I,
Singapore 239519
Tel: +(65) 63490200
Fax: + (65) 67331817/67331276
Email: asiainfo@elsevier.com.sg

For customers in Europe, Middle East and Africa:

Elsevier
Customer Services Department
Linacre House, Jordan Hill
Oxford OX2 8DP
United Kingdom
Tel: +44 (0) 1865 474140
Fax: +44 (0) 1865 474141
Email: amstbkinfo@elsevier.com

For customers in Australasia:

Elsevier
Customer Service Department
30-52 Smidmore Street
Marrickville, New South Wales 2204
Australia
Tel: +61 (02) 9517 8999
Fax: +61 (02) 9517 2249
Email: service@elsevier.com.au